SOCIAL ORDER AND
POLITICAL CHANGE

Social Order and Political Change

CONSTITUTIONAL GOVERNMENTS AMONG THE CHEROKEE, THE CHOCTAW, THE CHICKASAW, AND THE CREEK

DUANE CHAMPAGNE

Stanford University Press, Stanford, California

Stanford University Press
Stanford, California
© 1992 by the Board of Trustees of the
Leland Stanford Junior University
Printed in the United States of America

CIP data appear at the end of the book

ACKNOWLEDGMENTS

Numerous people helped in the writing and intellectual preparation of the manuscript. While not all will agree with what I have written, the book is influenced directly or indirectly by the advice of S. N. Eisenstadt, Stephen Cornell, Theda Skocpol, and Jeffrey C. Alexander. The search for empirical material took me across the country, and in particular I thank the library staff and Mr. Elder at the University of Texas, Austin, and the Houghton Library staff at Harvard University for their assistance in securing several old manuscripts. The preparation, proofing, and copy editing of the text owes much to the hard work of Liana Champagne, Jan Berenstein, and Shirley R. Taylor. Finally, I gratefully acknowledge research and writing assistance from the National Science Foundation Grant #SES 8503914, the Ford Foundation, and the American Indian Studies Center at UCLA.

D.C.

CONTENTS

SOCIAL ORDER AND
POLITICAL CHANGE

1 INTRODUCTION

THE FORMATION OF A stable democratic constitutional government is a rare event in world history, and one such government cannot easily serve as a model for another nation. As Tocqueville noted in his analysis of American democracy, each nation has to modify the model to conform to its own institutional and cultural order, and it follows that some institutional orders may not be compatible with democratic culture and laws and would have difficulty adopting and maintaining democratic constitutional governments.[1] What are the conditions under which democratic governments can be formed, and under what conditions can they become stable or institutionalized?

An opportunity to study variation in the process of democratic institution building in a controlled, comparative historical context presents itself in the situation of four American Indian societies—the Cherokee, Choctaw, Chickasaw, and Creek—which in various ways and at different rates formed constitutional governments during the nineteenth century. The Cherokee formed a constitutional government in 1827, while under intense pressure from the United States to remove westward across the Mississippi River. Under similar geopolitical pressure, the Creek and Chickasaw were not willing to adopt constitutional governments, and a Choctaw attempt to form a centralized government in 1830 failed owing to regional opposition. These nations formed constitutional governments thirty to forty years later than the Cherokee, under greater coercion than had the Cherokee, and also under different geopolitical conditions (after removal west of the Mississippi River and faced with less intensive threats to land and national sovereignty)—the Chickasaw in 1856, the Choctaw in 1860, and the Creek in 1867.

A primary goal of this study is to explain the differences among the four southeastern societies in the rate of formation of the constitutional governments and their stability—in sociological terms, the degree of institutionalization of the constitutional governments. The location of the four nations in the American southeast gives us a control for conditions of American and colonial political and cultural hegemony and for the sequence of world-system market incorporation. The historical situation of similar geopolitical and market incorporation simplifies the analytical task, since it allows a primary focus on the effects of group relations and institutional order as determinants of the variation in political institution building.

An Institutional Approach to the Study of Political Change

Before we proceed to the historical studies, it will be helpful to define the concepts of institutional change and normative institutionalization and to review some theories of political change and institutionalization. I do not propose to engage in an extended metatheoretical discussion of the pros and cons of materialist versus normative determinants of social action.[2] True, this is a matter central to sociological theory, but the question ultimately must be decided on the basis of which set of assumptions best explains human action in its broadest contexts. The present study compares political change in four non-Western societies. Each society has a cultural-normative order that differs not only from the cultural-normative order of Western societies but also from those of the other three societies. If we are to assume instrumentally rationalistic social action on the part of the members of all four societies, then we must explain social change patterns in materialistic terms, since cultural-normative arguments will not explain the variation in paths of institutional political change. In my view, the materialist argument is too restrictive. Therefore, I shall assume that an integrated normative and materialist argument will better explain social change in the four southeastern societies than reliance on a primarily materialist view of social action.

Historical social action cannot, of course, be explained by patterns and norms of culture in any broad sense. Societies have specific cultural and normative codes, and it is necessary to understand these codes in order to use them in an explanation of social action within a set of universal categories. Toward the end of formulating a generalizable comparative analysis of cultural-normative order, some principal arguments can be extracted from the paradigm of sociological functionalism. Thus, assuming that the functionalist arguments have empirical referents, and assuming that the empirical referents of concepts like societal differentiation, social and political solidarity, world view, institutional and economic tradition-alism, and political culture and values can all have independent effects on the processes of political change and institutionalization, I shall analyze the four nations in specific terms of those categories.[3]

All else being equal, functionalist theory predicts that societies with more complex levels of societal differentiation, greater levels of social and political solidarity, rationalistic world views, and democratic political cul-tures will have a greater capacity for institutionalizing change and forming democratic governments. But to have valid explanatory value, function-alist arguments must hold within contingent historical contexts and must survive against rival materialist arguments. In particular, the theory of differentiation needs to be extracted from its broad evolutionary contexts and applied to more local and historically contingent settings, in much the same way that class arguments have been applied to a variety of historical situations and explanatory contexts. Furthermore, the evolutionary theory of differentiation suffers from the general problem of stage theories of social change, in that the theory does not pay enough attention to the his-torical causes and social movements that create transitions from one level or form of societal differentiation to another. It takes too little account of variation among relations of differentiated institutions and of the way in which different institutional configurations constrain or influence social action in specific historical contexts.[4]

The historical situation of the four southeastern societies allows us to consider the more materialist arguments of class conflict, geopolitics, and world–economic system incorporation in conjunction with the analysis of the kinds of cultural-normative arguments I have sketched above. Within a historical narrative of events, the logic of empirical history should supplant the logic of functionalism, for it allows us to weigh the rival arguments against one another in concrete historical contexts and in so doing evalu-ate the relative contribution of each to explaining the variations in political change.[5] I am not proposing to determine the value of the rival theoretical arguments and paradigms; rather, I want to determine the most powerful combination of explanatory arguments, both materialist and normative, that can account for the variation in political change among the south-eastern nations. Such a theoretically informed and empirically derived set of arguments will provide a basis for building more powerful explanatory arguments and suggest hypotheses for further study in other cases and historical contexts.

According to Max Weber, historical sociologists do not seek to explain contingent historical events but rather attempt to determine the pattern of events. Nevertheless, a problem for the historical sociologist is how to preserve the particularism of the case and yet at the same time develop and elaborate general theories and concepts. One way to avoid the seamless web of historical contingency is to study the rise, fall, and stability of institutions. Using institutions, rather than people or events, as the focus of analysis allows one to sort out events, groups, and conditions as they relate to changes in the political institutional order, that is, to the interests and cultural-normative codes that define and uphold a specific pattern of organization, commitment, and mutual expectations among actors within a society.

Tempting though it is to treat institutions, such as states or bureaucracies, as "real," it is obvious that institutions are real only to the extent that group consensus and/or holders of power will sustain the rules and goals of a particular institution and reward conformity and punish non-conformity.[6] The rules of a constitutional government, for example, are explicitly written into the constitutional document itself, but the document has little meaning if the rules of governmental organization are not supported by a general cultural-normative consensus of the major social and political groups within the society. We may say that societies that have a broad consensus over the rules of political order are institutionalized normatively, and that societies in which there is little consensus over the basic rules of the political order are unstable normatively. In the latter case, in societies like South Africa, to name a clear example, the government will have difficulty securing the commitment and participation of those members who are dissatisfied with the rules of political inclusion.[7] Such a state can maintain itself in power for long periods of time, but only if it can control the means of force against its opponents. In other words, longevity alone does not imply normative institutionalization, and the use of coercion to suppress dissent over the rules of political organization among significant social or political groups is inversely related to normative institutionalization.

This is not to say that a society with a normatively institutionalized political order is necessarily free of political and economic conflict. Such a political order merely creates a set of rules under which most members of the society agree, more or less, to conduct legitimate competition. People may still break or bend the rules in their self-interest, but they are liable to some form of punishment if they are caught. A normatively institutionalized polity attempts to routinize and regulate competition and conflict, but it does not reduce society to some idealistic equilibrium. The rules of the legitimate political order are themselves open to negotiation, and constitutional governments often have explicit mechanisms by which the rules or laws of the constitution can be changed.

Political change is often defined in relation to class conflict and revolution, but significant political change must involve change in the central rules and organization of the political institutional order. In Marx's scenario of class revolution, the working class is envisioned as struggling not merely to assume the positions of the capitalist class but also to inaugurate a new economic, social, and political order in which economic exploitation, private property, and the state would be abolished. The formation of this new socialist order was more significant than the mere struggle for economic resources or political power. Not all class revolts, as we know, conform to Marx's vision of the construction of alternative social and political orders. In China, Russia, and France, as Theda Skocpol has shown, the rebellious peasants were mainly interested in acquiring land for farming and in freeing themselves from the economic exploitation of the landholders. The leaders and articulators of alternative social and political orders came from other social groups—in the Chinese case, from the Communists—not from the peasant classes themselves.[8] Another example is seen in the cyclical interpretation of Chinese history, in which a recurring sequence of peasant revolutions against imperial dynasties installed new emperors and leaders, who over the centuries concentrated landed wealth and increased exploitation of the peasants, leading eventually to another peasant revolution and the formation of a new imperial dynasty. Dynasties that failed to extract sufficient resources from the peasantry for national defense succumbed instead to foreign invasion.[9] Thus class revolutions or revolts may not necessarily lead to social revolutions, if the revolutionaries, associated classes, or leaders do not construct and institutionalize significantly different models of social and political order.

What is critical in social and political change is the proposal and construction of alternative models of institutional order. Barrington Moore argues that the formation of the early American state was not an example of significant political change because it was not associated with any significant change or revolution in class relations.[10] This argument associates significant political and social change exclusively with changes in class relations. Yet we have seen that not all class revolutions lead to new social and political orders; what is central is the construction and institutionalization of new rules of social and political order, and these can be made without major alterations in class relations. The new institutional form created by the American constitutional government in 1787–89 is the major case in point. As the American case shows, significant change in political order can be achieved by means of lesser degrees of conflict and more incremental forms of negotiation of the rules of political order. What matters is not class revolution or political conflict per se, but rather the nature of the conditions under which the rules of political order are reconstructed and become stable, and whether the new institutions are sustained by consensus or by coercion.[11]

Defining a Differentiated Constitutional Government

The "state" has been variously defined. Weber and others argue that a major characteristic of a state is the concentration of legitimate force in the government.[12] This is a useful definition, but it does not help us to distinguish between types of states. According to this definition, the absolutist states of Europe, the Aztec empire, and the American government all constitute states, but obviously these states vary a great deal in organizational structure, relations between state and society, and political culture and normative order. For comparative purposes this definition must be supplemented by a definition of the state that can distinguish differences in stability and organization. A second tradition following Weber emphasizes the state as a bureaucratic organization. But this definition, centering on the role of the bureaucracy or executive, pays scant attention to the role of political parties and interest groups, judicial and legislative institutions and relations, and the cultural and normative order of the society at large. The bureaucracy is only one institutional sphere within the polity; it gives only one view of political relations.

A third view, Marx and Engels's argument that a primary purpose of the state is the protection of private property and the promotion of material accumulation, has had more attention in the literature on the southeastern governments.[13] Defining the state as a class-dominated organization with a primary goal of fostering economic accumulation does not, however, help to explain the variations in the rate of state formation and the stability of the states or the differences in the organization of the four southeastern governments. Neither class structure nor the material interests of classes or other groups, to my mind, truly define the organization of the state. Marx and Engels's argument that the state, or cultural and normative order of societies, is ultimately reducible to the interests and orientations of the dominant economic class must be considered a hypothesis that requires verification within specific historical settings. The relations between state and class, or state and society in general, are here considered analytically independent: conceptually, relations between a state and society can be so variable that they must be sorted out by data in each historical instance. The state may be potentially differentiated from society and economic class order, but as is well known from many societies in world history, leading economic classes have often consistently dominated the political institutions of their societies. Therefore the empirical relations between the state and the groups that constitute the social order have to be looked upon as a major factor in determining the political relations of any society.

Nevertheless, a more comprehensive analysis of political order can be obtained if the analysis of political relations includes an analysis of relations between polity and culture, analysis of organizational relations within the polity, and analysis of political culture and the relations between the polity and the institutions of social and political solidarity. For comparative purposes, one can define the state, or more generally the polity, in terms of the relations of internal institutional specialization or differentiation within the polity, and in terms of relations between the polity and the other major spheres of society—culture, social solidarity, and economy. In other words, the polity can be broadly defined by both internal and external differentiation.[14]

External differentiation of the polity refers to the relation between political institutions and religion, culture, kinship, economy, and institutions of social and political solidarity. These relations may vary considerably from society to society, and can significantly affect political action and the possibilities of further secularization or differentiation of the polity. Relations between polity and culture can be determined by the power of political decision making by priests or religious specialists, by adherence to nonsecular world views by the dominant political actors or groups, or by the religious or mythical ordination of the rules and structure of the political order. A polity in which political action and rules of political order are determined by religious or cultural groups or cultural prerogatives is said to be nondifferentiated from cultural or religious order. A polity in which religious and cultural prerogatives are considered secondary to political prerogatives is said to be secular or differentiated from cultural order. A polity that is differentiated from economy indirectly regulates economic organization and relations with positive law; a society in which polity is not differentiated from economy has a dictatorial or command economy, in which the polity organizes and dictates economic action. In cases where economy is embedded in local group or kinship relations, the economy is segmented or nondifferentiated from the polity, depending on the relation between polity and kinship. Societies in which the norms of social order are the same as or similar to the rules that govern the polity have nondifferentiated relations between polity and the institutions of normative integration. If the polity has rules of organization and procedures distinct from the rules that govern social relations, then the polity shows normative differentiation from society.

Ideally, political action within a differentiated polity is based primarily on political interests and contingencies; considerations of the prerogatives of other major societal institutions—religion, culture, kinship, economy, and social solidarity—are of secondary consideration. A completely differentiated polity is an ideal type, and in practice institutional prerogatives and interests intrude and influence political decision making. It is the analyst's task to understand the relations between polity and society in any given society, and only after social scientists have investigated the societal differentiation of a wide range of historical and contemporary cases will it be possible to form a more accurate classification and understanding of the variation in social and cultural order among human societies. Although little work has yet been completed on the multidimensional classification of societal orders, such empirical investigation and classification is most likely a precondition to any general theory of social change.

The codes of internal political differentiation are concerned with the relations among legislative, executive, and judicial powers, the formation of political parties, the rules and procedures of the polity, the centralization of legitimate force, the rules of individual and group rights and prerogatives, the rules of bureaucratic organization and administration, and perhaps others. The polity is not internally differentiated when there is little separation of powers, no bureaucracy, and no political parties, when the rules of social decision making are the same as those used to make political decisions, and when there is little centralization of legitimate coercive authority. The rules of political solidarity focus on loyalties and political commitments. Societies in which primary political loyalties, identities, and/or commitments are given to kin groups, localities, or regions or to religious institutions are said to be less politically solidary than societies in which primary political loyalties, identities, and/or commitments are given directly to the national political government.

By defining the polity or state as a configuration of political solidarity, and as a collectivity subject to internal and external differentiation, it is possible to compare over time the four southeastern societies according to their particular form of differentiation, social and political solidarity, and other dimensions of cultural normative order. This brings us to a more precise definition of significant political change: it is change in the centralization of legitimate force in the polity, change in the level of political solidarity, and/or change in the configuration of internal and external differentiation of the polity.

Various permutations of differentiation are possible even with the limited number of relations identified. Contrary to orthodox functionalist approaches, I do not assume that there is an evolutionary trend toward more differentiated political or social organization. A significant number of people or major groups in some societies may be strongly resistant to adopting differentiated political forms and may prefer to participate in less differentiated forms of political organization. If the four southeastern nations eventually adopt more differentiated polities, specific historical causes must be cited.

A great deal of earlier differentiation theory was written under the rubric of systems theory, and bore an abstract and ahistorical character. Ultimately, differentiation must be seen as an aspect of the organization of a cultural-normative order. Differentiation is a norm, code, or rule that defines the boundaries between societal institutions. In highly differentiated societies these rules are written in the form of constitutions or bylaws, but in less differentiated societies the rules are more diffuse and are carried about by the people of the society as part of the general normative order. The concept of differentiation need not be imposed on the organization of a society by the social scientist. Rather, rules of differentiation are understood by the participating actors and can be derived by observing, by reading historical documents and political treatises, or by participating in social interaction or interviewing informants who know the rules and are willing to explicate them. Even though the actors within a society may not understand the social scientist's purpose in distinguishing the specific aspects of normative order that characterize differentiated institutions, the social scientist's goal is to study social change or comparative social structures with the aid of the concept of societal differentiation—which is, of course, a purpose that does not usually motivate social actors to participate in and understand their own institutional order.

Because the theory of differentiation, though it is an appropriate means of conceptualizing variation in political organization, says little about the historical causes of differentiation of the polity, group interests, the content of culture, or the process of institutionalization, any study of institutional change requires a historical narrative that examines culture and normative codes and major group formation and interests. According to revisions of earlier, more abstract versions of functionalist theory, groups that introduce innovations in institutional order may face potential obstacles in terms of cultural fundamentalism, resistance from groups that wish to maintain a less differentiated institutional order, the material and/or cultural interests of competing groups, the absence of political support and commitments to the new innovations, and the absence of sufficient material resources.[15] Therefore, an analysis of institutional change should focus on how groups introduce innovations and gain the material, cultural, political, and economic support necessary to institutionalize a proposed change in the social or political order. Lacking sufficient support, the institutional entrepreneurs may fail to make any significant change in the institutional order; or, if an innovating group has sufficient control over the means of force, it may use coercion to force compliance with its proposed changes.

Method

This study employs a quasi-experimental design that gives approximate
controls for several important analytical factors. The location of the four
societies in the southeastern United States allows us to approximate controls for geopolitical environment, market or world-system relations, class
structures, and material culture. All four societies are studied over the
same historical period, and all were incorporated into similar sequences
of markets—initially the fur trade, and after 1817 the southern plantation
economy.[16] All four societies were subject to similar hegemonic domination,[17] policies, and threats to land and national autonomy from the United
States. In all four nations class structures emerged, with a small group of
market-oriented plantation owners and merchants and a majority of families engaged in small-scale subsistence farming. The controlled conditions
for the southeastern societies allow us to eliminate geopolitical context,
world-system context, and class structure as sufficient explanations for
the variation in the rate of formation and the stability of the constitutional
governments of the southeastern societies.

   This is not to say that world-system context, class structure, and geopolitical context are not important for understanding political change in
the four southeastern societies. Quite the contrary: without any or all of
the latter conditions, there might not have been any constitutional governments formed by the southeastern societies in the nineteenth century.
Rather, the controls imply that geopolitical context, class structure, and
world-system context must be supplemented by cultural-normative arguments in order to explain the variations in the rate of formation and in
the stability of the constitutional governments of the four southeastern
societies. The focus of the analysis must be on comparisons of the levels
of differentiation of the polity, cultural rationalization, political decentralization, political solidarity, and social and political norms of decision
making. And it is by controlling for the geopolitical and world-system
contexts and the rise of class structures that we are able to concentrate
on the socio-cultural conditions that supplement the controlled conditions
and help to account for the differences in political institution building and
stability.

   We shall find similarities among the four southeastern societies in terms
of material culture, cultural rationalization, political decentralization, and
social and political norms of decision making, and also variations in social
and political solidarity and internal political differentiation. The design of
the study is meant to control for several major variables, some of which
may be necessary conditions for explaining the formation and institu-

tionalization of states, but none of which can be considered sufficient to explain the differences in the rate of development and institutionalization of the state governments in the nineteenth century. Yet, although the design and controlled variables are helpful for understanding the context and conditions that explain the processes of political change, a mechanistic application of the design would not in itself explain the process of political differentiation and constitution building. In the end, the comparative analysis must rely on historical narratives of interacting groups and sequences of historical events. The various rival arguments must find verification within the sequence of historical events that account for the variations in political change among the four nations. Arguments that have little independent effect on the historical events that account for the formation and stability of the constitutional governments can be eliminated as a causal argument or relegated to the status of necessary but not sufficient conditions in much the same way that multivariate or experimental designs eliminate and control variables.[18]

Because the quasi-experimental design allows the four southeastern cases to be studied over the same historical period, by incorporation into the same sequence of world–economic system relations, and within the same geopolitical contexts, the four cases cannot be considered independently from one another. All four nations were historically interactive before Western contact, and their leaders were aware of developments in the other nations in the postcontact period. Nonindependence creates a potential bias toward uniformity of response, since after the Cherokee adopted changes in political integration and political differentiation between 1810 and 1827, the other three southeastern nations had a local model for making similar institutional innovations. The possibility of diffusion of institutional innovations and the similarity of geopolitical and world-system environments biases the cases against the proposed argument of differential institutional responses to similar conditions of contact with Western societies. Since the nonindependence of the cases works against the argument of diversity in institutional change, the issue of nonindependence does not present a logical defect in the design of the comparisons.

Data from both secondary and primary sources were gathered for the study. The conceptualization of world views, differentiation, solidarity, and other aspects of cultural-normative order are not discussed systematically in the secondary sources, which implicitly upheld conceptualizations of social and political order fundamentally different from those proposed here. For example, the conceptualization of normative institutionalization and of the processes and conditions of formation of a differentiated constitutional government could not be relied on. New variables therefore had to be constructed and large amounts of primary data were consulted.

In order to interpret political action more accurately and in more depth, the points of view of actors must be investigated and their interpretations of important events incorporated into the narrative. This study does not aim, however, at writing an ideographic history of the four societies, and the emphasis on historical narrative in no way implies an intention to write ethnohistory or history "from the point of view" of the Cherokee, Choctaw, Chickasaw, and Creek. Rather, the primary intention is to investigate systematically a set of normative and materialist conditions and variables that can explain how, and for how long, and under what kind of coercion, the four southeastern nations formed differentiated constitutional governments. If this can be accomplished, we shall have developed a theory that can be applied to other variations in political change and political order in other societies and historical contexts. This, of course, is the goal of all theory-building in social science.

2 A COMPARISON OF EARLY SOCIAL AND POLITICAL ORGANIZATION

MANY OBSERVERS OF southeastern cultures have agreed that they were similar in cultural views, shared Crow-type kinship systems, and had similar material culture and economic organization.[1] There were important cultural, structural, and economic similarities among the southeastern nations, but there were also significant differences in differentiation of polity from society and in social-cultural integration. The four major southeastern nations had similar cultural and value orientations; they had local and decentralized political loyalties, democratic political cultures, and little internal political differentiation; and they had horticultural and hunting subsistence economies and nonacquisitive economic orientations. But these similarities, though they serve as controls, do not provide an explanation for differences in the rate of formation and stability of differentiated constitutional governments or variation in use of coercion. The four nations differ in the degree of political secularization, in social-cultural integration, and in differentiation of polity and kinship organization, and these differences may provide an explanation for the variation in the rate of state formation and stability during the nineteenth century.

The following comparisons are not an attempt to portray a complete ethnographic description of each of the early southeastern nations; rather, they are meant to locate similarities and identify differences in societal organization that may provide hypotheses for understanding the variation in political change during the eighteenth and nineteenth centuries.[2]

The Cherokee were located in what is now eastern Tennessee and the western Carolinas, having arrived perhaps during the 1400's and 1500's. The Cherokee had about 25,000 people in the early 1800's. The early

Choctaw were located primarily in the present state of Mississippi and in parts of western Alabama. They perhaps had one of the largest populations in North America at the time of early Western contact in the 1700's and numbered about 30,000 in the early 1800's. The Chickasaw, related to the Choctaw and the smallest of the four major southeastern nations, lived in what is presently northern Mississippi and western Tennessee. Their population was probably hardly ever much over 5,000 during the 1700's and 1800's. Both the Choctaw and the Chickasaw spoke a dialect of the Muskogee language, and the languages of the two nations were intelligible to each other. Such a close linguistic association suggests a kindred relationship, and this seems to be borne out by the migration myths of the two nations. The Creek, also Muskogean speakers, lived in what is now central Georgia and eastern Alabama. They numbered about 20,000 in the early nineteenth century.

Controlled Conditions

CULTURAL DIFFERENTIATION AND RELIGIOUS RATIONALIZATION

Internal cultural differentiation refers to the degree of interpenetration of views of causality, ceremony, morality, and religion. Members of societies with low levels of internal cultural differentiation carry animistic world views and believe in the efficacy of magic, charms, and ceremonies for achieving this-worldly ends. Highly rationalized cultures are characterized by scientific or secular views of causality, the separation of artistic performance or ritual from causality, and non-moral interpretation of causal sequences of this-worldly events. Referring to cultural differentiation in tribal societies, Max Weber remarked that the members of tribal societies live in a magical garden, and in a general sense this characterization fits the cultural views of the southeastern societies. The southeastern societies in the early 1700's exhibited internally nondifferentiated cultural world views; they believed that ceremony and ritual could effect causal events, and they had a moral-religious interpretation of causality in social and natural events.[3]

Besides internal cultural rationalization, a second dimension of world view is the degree of this-worldly and otherworldly tension and the cultural-normative solution to the tension. According to the work of Weber and Eisenstadt, the greater the tension between the this-worldly and otherworldly realms, the greater the need to develop more consistent and elaborate religious doctrines to reconcile the tension within a coherent religious world view. Cultures and religions vary according to the interrela-

EARLY SOCIAL AND POLITICAL ORGANIZATION

tion of this-worldly and otherworldly tension, and the cultural-normative solution provides insight into the values and motivations pertaining to life in this world and culturally grounded attitudes toward change and continuity of the institutional order.

For example, both Christianity and Hinduism exhibit extreme tension between this-world and the otherworld, but their solutions to the tension differ greatly and have repercussions for understanding traditionalistic motivations toward preservation or change within this-worldly institutional order. In Hinduism, the solution to the religious tension resides in a mystical union within the next or sacred world: this-world is transient; the other, sacred, world is the "real" world. This-worldly social action must adhere to the dharma, or caste duties, in order to make certain that multiple reincarnations will result in ever higher rebirths in the caste order, which ultimately will result in union with the godhead and escape from the wheel of rebirth. The Hindu solution to the tension between this-world and the otherworld directs social action toward otherworldly ends and goals and is based on a belief that this-worldly institutions are immutably ordained within the religious-cosmic order, and that this-worldly institutions cannot be changed without otherworldly repercussions, such as the loss of caste or the return to a lower-order, nonhuman form in the next rebirth.

Christianity also emphasizes otherworldliness, but some sects have a more activistic orientation toward this-worldly institutional change. As Weber pointed out, Calvinists believed that men lived in this-world but were not of it. In Christian and Calvinist doctrine, men were directed to transform the earth according to the divine will of God, as instruments of God's will. Economic, social, and political conditions of this-world were not divinely ordained as immutable parts of the cosmic order, and since this-world was an evil and sinful place, it was man's duty to transform it and make it more perfect in God's image. Thus Christian doctrines, or more specifically those of some Protestant sects, provide a world view and religious doctrine that allow secular orientations toward the this-worldly institutional order, and, expressly within the Protestant traditions, a sense of negotiability and the possibility of reordering this-worldly institutions.

The argument of religious rationality and the study of the doctrines of salvation developed by Weber help identify traditionalistic cultures where institutional change is avoided and resisted while identifying the features of cultures where negotiation and institutional change may be more acceptable within the existing cultural framework. According to Weber, Eisenstadt, and others, societies in which there is little tension between this-worldly and otherworldly realms will tend toward beliefs in the immutability of the institutional order as part of the cosmic-religious order,

and adherents to such world views will regard institutional change as un-
desirable and dangerous transgressions of the religiously ordained order
of nature.[4] Societies with religions that embody little this-worldly and
otherworldly tension will tend to have traditionalistic orientations toward
institutional change. As will be seen, the four southeastern societies share
a world view that has little this-worldly and otherworldly tension, and
therefore it can be expected that the well-socialized members of the southeastern nations will uphold traditionalistic orientations toward institutional change. In the southeastern world views, the absence of strong this-
worldly and otherworldly tensions, combined with a strong this-worldly
orientation and the view that transgressing sacred law and norms were
the cause of this-worldly misfortunes and evil, accentuated traditionalistic
orientations toward change in the existing institutional order.

CHEROKEE WORLD VIEW

The nondifferentiation of causality and ritual is illustrated by the Cherokee belief in the efficacy of spirits, ceremonies, rituals, omens, and incantations as agents of this-worldly events and fortunes. The Cherokee
believed that wizards and witches, by using ritual incantations, could cause
illness or death in victims whom the witches did not like or whom the
witches were paid by third parties to harm. Often it was necessary to
hire a doctor or "witch shooter" to protect oneself from the attacks of a
witch or to recover from the illness that was caused by the activities of a
malevolent witch.[5]

Cherokee theodicy or doctrine for the justification of evil or misfortune in the world further illustrates the nondifferentiation of causality,
morality, ritual, and religion in the Cherokee world view. Among the
Cherokee, as in the other southeastern societies, the Great Spirit was considered a benevolent gift and lawgiver. Major calamities such as plague,
famine, defeat in war, or community disruption were caused not by the
will of the Great Spirit but by the failure of the people to adhere to ritual,
sacred law, or moral order. Misfortune, drought, disease, or other calamities were caused by the displeasure of the Great Spirit or other spiritual
beings, who visited misfortune upon the people as punishment for their
moral, religious, or ritual transgressions. For the Cherokee, there was no
ethical or otherworldly atonement for the sins of this-world. Rather, it
was necessary to restore the goodwill of the Great Spirit by means of ritual
ceremonies aimed at removing the pollution that resulted from not following the laws of the Great Spirit. For example, those who ate from the
harvest before the first fruits had been offered in thanks to the Great Spirit
in the Green Corn ceremony were considered polluted transgressors; they

were whipped, their houses and property were destroyed, and they were driven out of the town, for they were regarded as having broken both the laws of the town and the sacred law given by the Great Spirit.[6] It was believed that neglecting the rituals and duties required by the spirit world caused droughts, crop failures, deaths, disease, and losses in war, and that individual transgressions placed the entire community in jeopardy.

In terms of religious rationalization, the Cherokee had little concept of this-worldly and otherworldly tension; most orientations were this-worldly, and major emphasis was placed on ritual purity and avoidance of pollution. Each year at the annual Green Corn ceremony, all transgressions of the preceding year were forgiven and the entire community was ritually purified. There was no concept of man as an instrument to carry out the will or divine plan of the Great Spirit, and there was little inner-worldly tension. The Cherokee vision of an afterlife was divided into a pleasant place and a bad place. The pleasant place consisted of a large forest with plenty of game, fruits, and flowers sweet to the smell. Access to the happy immortality of the pleasant afterworld was gained by this-worldly exemplification of the Cherokee virtues of wisdom, hospitality, and bravery. The bad afterworld was a mirror image of the pleasant afterworld. The spirits of people who were banished to the bad afterworld were relegated to an existence of hunger, hostility, and darkness, and were within hearing distance of the happiness and rejoicing of the pleasant afterworld. Another Cherokee version of the afterlife states that the souls of the departed traveled west to a similar but better world. All Cherokee went to the pleasant afterworld, except victims of murder, whose spirits temporarily dwelled in this-world and caused misfortune for their delinquent clansmen until they avenged the victim's death.[7]

The requirements for obtaining the pleasant afterworld focused on prescriptive moral injunctions. To obtain the pleasant afterworld, one had to adhere to religious and moral law and exemplify the virtues of wisdom and bravery. There was little emphasis placed on obtaining the pleasant afterworld, and even the emphasis on ritual purity was believed to lead to this-worldly ends. The moral injunctions against certain behaviors inhibited people from straying too far from the prevailing religious and moral order. Thus, whatever tension did exist in the Cherokee religious views tended to legitimate the prevailing moral, religious, and institutional order.

CHOCTAW WORLD VIEW

The Choctaw world view fused together causality, morality, religion, and ceremony. The Choctaw had several grades of medicine men or men with knowledge about supernatural things and the secrets of the universe.

There were prophets, doctors, and rainmakers. These men were highly respected for having gained access to the signs and will of the Great Spirit and other supernatural beings, and for having gained limited control over the laws of nature. The prophets, in particular, were believed to have the power to foretell the future; they had special ritual wisdom and knowledge to heal people when they were sick, to provide spiritual protections during war, and to ward off evil spirits. Prophets and conjurors interpreted dreams, explained signs, prophesied future events, and conjured cures for the sick. During times of drought, rainmakers were called upon and paid to bring rain; in times when there was too much water, fair weather makers were called upon to bring sunshine.[8]

Choctaw religious views showed little tension or anxiety over salvation, and the Choctaw emphasized this-worldly orientations. In the Choctaw view of the afterlife, it was said that the souls of people traveled to a land where there was always plenty of good weather, food, dancing, and games. According to one version, the afterworld was very similar to this-world, and men went there to perform deeds and acts similar to those in this-world. Access to the afterworld was not directly contingent on moral behavior or rank in this-world. Almost everyone went to the good hunting ground: "No spiritual qualification, no purification of the heart, no amendment of the life, was necessary." The transition to the other world was considered a matter of course—not a reward for obedience, but simply the order of nature.[9]

In some versions of the Choctaw afterlife, transgressions that prevented access to the good hunting ground included murder, lying that led to murder, divorce of a pregnant wife, and gossiping. Those who committed such transgressions were assigned to an unhappy place full of want and need, but within hearing distance of the pleasures and festivities enjoyed by those in the good hunting ground. Other versions state that upholding Choctaw moral virtues of truthfulness, honesty, and purity assured access to the good afterlife. Actions that were perceived as contributing to the well-being of society and to the strengthening of the nation were commended by the community and helped assure a place of tranquillity in the next world. Nevertheless, the Choctaw viewed access to the afterlife as contingent not on lifelong moral conduct but rather on avoidance of a few proscriptive laws. As in Cherokee society, each year the community was purified by participation in the Green Corn ceremony. Since all debts and difficulties were supposed to be settled before the cleansing ceremony, most transgressions of personal conduct were purified by the annual absolution.[10]

Most Choctaw life and ritual were aimed at attaining this-worldly rewards. The rewards of the afterlife were considered virtually assured and required little concerted effort. Aside from observing the sacred laws, moral codes, and rituals, there was little that people could do to manipulate the spirits or influence the favor of the Great Spirit. Adherence to the existing moral and institutional order was the means by which to enjoy both this-worldly and otherworldly bounty. The laws, ceremonies, and institutions themselves were gifts of the Great Spirit, and therefore if the people followed the proscriptive commandments and laws of the Great Spirit, they were bound to have good fortune in this-world and a place in the good hunting ground after they died.[11] The absence of this-worldly and otherworldly tensions, and the this-worldly orientation of the Choctaw fostered traditionalistic views toward upholding the existing institutional order.

CHICKASAW WORLD VIEW

The Chickasaw world view was similar to those of the other major southeastern societies in the sense that causality, morality, religion, and ceremony were tightly interrelated or nondifferentiated. Daily life among the Chickasaw was one of observance of sacred law and recognition of the effects of spirits on everyday social action. Natural events were interpreted as manifestations of the will of the Great Spirit, who, along with other good spirits or witches, also ordained events and occurrences. But seers and medicine men not only could foretell droughts, make rain, cure diseases, and exorcise witchcraft and evil spirits; they also could control thunder and lightning.[12] The Chickasaw believed that the rituals and ceremonies of the prophets and doctors were effective in enlisting the aid of the spirits that were the cause of events in both spirit and natural worlds.

The Chickasaw view of theodicy and the afterlife largely served to legitimate participation in and adherence to the Chickasaw normative and institutional order. The Chickasaw world view was strongly oriented toward this-world. Most rituals were oriented toward avoiding this-worldly evils and ensuring this-worldly health, prosperity, and victory in war. The emphasis on ritual purity by strict adherence to the sacred and divine law was intended to keep the good favor of the Great Spirit and associated lesser spirits.[13]

The Chickasaw afterworld was described as a place where there was plenty of game, grass, and water and where there were no storms. In this version there is no mention of any moral requirements for gaining access to the afterworld: a brave warrior expected to gain the happy afterworld with all pomp and military honor. A warrior who lost his scalp in battle, however, could not go to the good hunting ground but had to be reborn on earth so that he could live a courageous life that ended with an honorable death. Industrious and active warriors assured themselves a place in the pleasant afterlife, and so did all others who did not kill, steal, or lie; only murderers, thieves, and liars went to an afterworld of poverty and misery.[14] There were no doctrines of individual salvation, and access to a pleasant afterlife could be obtained by avoidance of a few proscriptive laws.

The Chickasaw world view emphasized conservative attitudes toward change in the existing institutional order, since change threatened to bring this-worldly retribution. Consequently, it can be expected that most culturally socialized Chickasaw will show little enthusiasm for or interest in normative or institutional change. Change in the institutional order of Chickasaw society most likely will stem not from the symbols and inner tensions within the Chickasaw cultural sphere but from sources external to Chickasaw society.

CREEK WORLD VIEW

Like those of the other major southeastern nations, the Creek world view combined causality, ceremony, religion, and morality in a common framework of belief. The Creek believed that from time immemorial they had had a covenant relation with the Great Spirit and that by accepting the Green Corn ritual and following the Great Spirit's sacred laws, they would have divine protection in war and against all this-worldly misfortunes. The Creek Green Corn ceremony was partly a ritual of thanksgiving, in which the people of a village gathered and danced and sang songs of thanks to the Great Spirit for sparing them from death and misfortune during the preceding year. If famine, deaths, or defeats in battle had occurred, the songs of thanksgiving were intermingled with lamentations and mourning, but because the Great Spirit was always a benevolent gift giver, the misfortunes were blamed on the moral and religious transgressions of the people, not on divine punishment, and along with the ritual purification the people asked for pardons and forgiveness lest more this-worldly misfortune await them in the coming year. Breaking the rules by eating the harvest corn before the purification rites was thought to bring on sickness.[15]

Although the Creek world view evinced little differentiation between causality, religion, morality, and ceremony, and also evinced a this-worldly orientation, Creek culture exhibited little tension between this-world and the afterworld. The Creek had a dual view of an afterworld. Those who were good hunters and providers and/or active warriors and did all the good they could went to a pleasant afterlife with plenty of food, women, fair weather, feasting, and dancing, while those who had murdered, robbed, stolen another man's wife, or made fun of the Great Spirit were consigned to an unpleasant afterworld of darkness, hunger, and no women. By some accounts, a warrior who was scalped was sent to the unpleasant afterlife until his death was avenged, after which he went immediately to the place of the pleasant afterlife. Other sources indicate that all Creek went to the pleasant afterlife. Instead of invoking otherworldly retribution for transgressing the religious moral order, the spirits would simply not assist the immoral person in this-world.[16] The emphasis in Creek culture was not on sin or guilt, but rather on ritual purity. Each year at the Green Corn ceremony, the entire village community was ritually purified, and all transgressions, except perhaps murder, were forgiven. There was no great tension or anxiety over achieving access to the next world; in Creek society tension persisted over maintaining ritual purity and upholding the sacred laws, which were considered a precondition to obtaining favorable this-worldly fortunes.

The Creek theodicy and myths directly legitimated participation in and adherence to the sacred laws and institutions of Creek society. In fact, in Creek society, acts that broke the sacred laws or norms of moral order directly threatened the welfare of the entire village community. Thus the Creek world view engendered traditionalistic orientations against significant change in the sacred institutional order.

VALUES

The primary value orientations of all four southeastern societies derived from the southeastern cosmological view of order in the universe. According to that view, the universe was divided into three levels: an upper world, a lower world, and a middle world. The upper world was the vault of the sky and heavens, where the spirits lived. It was symbolized by the color white, which stood for peace, order, purity, well-being, and harmony. The beings of the upper world had supernatural abilities and were not constrained by the physical laws affecting human beings. The lower world, below the crust of the earth, was symbolized by the color red. The lower world was symbolic of change, disorder, struggle, strife, danger, war, and fertility. The beings of the underworld were ghosts, monsters, witches, cannibals, and other threatening creatures. Between these two great forces of the universe, the red and white, human beings lived in the middle level, on earth. They had the protection of the spirits of the upper world, but the spirits of the underworld crept into the world of men through rivers, lakes, and caves and caused trouble and harm.

The doctors and priests were called to elicit aid from the spirits of the upper world against the malevolent spirits of the underworld. By means of rituals, the priests attempted to manipulate the opposing cosmic forces and sometimes play them against one another. If the opposing cosmic forces were in balance, the human world was in balance, but disturbances of the cosmic-moral order and a disruption of balance between the contending cosmic forces could bring on sickness, famine, or other misfortunes.[17]

In Cherokee society, the principle of opposing cosmological forces was reflected in the ideal of harmony in social relationships and with the spirits and forces of the spirit world. Disharmony in the social world or with the spirit world was certain to bring misfortune or trouble. Harmony and order were contingent on keeping the sacred laws and rules of society, which included strict rules against disturbing the harmony and balance of cosmic forces. Those who broke the law disturbed the balance of forces and harmony with the environment and thereby incurred this-worldly retribution.

The principle of revenge was part of the order and operation of the universe. Whenever persons of one group harmed those of another group, the injured persons had the right to seek revenge, and harmony and balance were not restored until those in the injured group were satisfied. The same notion applied to nature: if man abused or mistreated nature, it would strike back. Special ritual precautions were necessary when hunting and killing animals, for the spirits of the animals would be reincarnated in different life forms after death, and if ritual protections were not observed, the spirit of the dead animal sought to inflict sickness or death on the hunter. Overkilling of animals, too, led the animals to take revenge by causing illness among men. A hunter was expected to make a small sacrifice to the chief of the animals after a kill, to show that the animal was killed of necessity for the subsistence of men.[18]

The central values of harmony and order in Cherokee society applied in all spheres of this-world: town political relations, interpersonal relations, and national tribal affairs. Maintaining harmonious interpersonal relations involved avoiding giving offense, as well as showing generosity and goodwill by giving time and material goods. There was a sense of justice and balance in interpersonal relations, and anyone who upset the perceived balance warranted restitution from the victim. Since the sense of balance was restored by revenge or retaliation, upsetting the harmony of interpersonal relations could be costly to one's person and family.[19] If men were the cause of disorder, they would suffer the consequences of retaliation from other men, from nature, or from the spirits. Thus, harmonious relations with other Cherokee, with nature, and with the spirit world were the surest means of ensuring this-worldly well-being and avoiding dangerous retaliation, according to the cosmic principles of justice and order.

The Choctaw notion of a universe divided into dualistic forces was in most ways similar to that of the Cherokee and, like the Cherokee, the Choctaw tried to maintain harmonious relations with the two cosmic forces and to use their relations with the upper world to balance the ill effects that might be caused by the spirits of the underworld. Doctors, prophets, conjurors, and witches had rituals and sacred knowledge that allowed them to communicate with the spirits and invoke the aid of the good spirits in times of distress, which were assumed to be caused by the spirits of the underworld. The Choctaw believed that the spirits of the upper world were benevolent and would provide for and protect them if they observed proper ritual precautions and laws, and therefore they tried to maintain a balanced and harmonious relation with their cosmic and natural environment. Like the Cherokee, they believed that the spirits within nature would retaliate for any unnecessary disturbances caused by men, hence killing animals when there was no need for the food or skins invoked retaliation, to the extent that hunters who killed without need lost their skill and luck in the hunt. The Choctaw elders taught that men must be humble and not consider themselves masters of the natural world.[20] Choctaw world view and values did not condone the active transformation, manipulation, or subjugation of nature for the benefit of man. Rather, the forces of nature were considered much more powerful than the powers of human beings, and interference with the contending and powerful spirit forces of nature would bring on severe retaliation and punishment.

The Chickasaw called the helpful spirits who inhabited the upper regions of the vault of the sky "the holy people," or the relations of the Great Spirit. The "accursed people" or "accursed beings" lived in the west and had power over evil or bad people, whereas the holy spirits aided the good and moral people. The Chickasaw also believed in the red and white cosmic symbolism, white being a symbol of the goodness of the upper world and red a symbol of the lower. The world of men stood between the struggle of the opposite forces of the spirit world, and men attempted to maintain the sacred law in order to keep the favor of the holy spirits and avoid the influence of the accursed beings. Like the other southeastern nations, the Chickasaw held the view that nature and/or the spirit world would retaliate if, by immoral behavior or carelessness, men upset the natural order. By keeping the sacred law, men conformed to the natural order of the universe; by transgressing against the law, men acted against the natural/sacred order, and the spirits that ruled the universe moved to restore the balance and recoup any costs they might have suffered by the acts of men. Virtue, honesty, courage, harmony, and balance, in social relations as in all things, were highly prized values in the Chickasaw sense of cosmic order and justice.[21]

The Creek shared the dualistic world view of the other major south-

eastern nations. As in the other southeastern nations, each year at the
Green Corn ceremony the Creek ritually purified their families and villages and restored the order that had been disturbed by the breaking of the
sacred laws during the preceding year. In this way the Creek reestablished
harmony with the cosmic order. Disturbing the sacred laws and order of
cosmic forces caused ritual pollution that resulted in this-worldly retribution such as death, illness, or defeat in war. For this reason, much of Creek
ritual and social action was informed by the need to keep ritual harmony
with the forces in the cosmic order. Harmony and avoidance of direct,
face-to-face political conflict were strongly valued in Creek society.[22]

Southeastern values of order and harmony in interpersonal relations,
in relations with nature, and in relations with the supernatural contrast
sharply with secular Western values that emphasize the exploitation or
transformation of nature for the benefit of man. Southeastern values were
not oriented toward transforming or controlling nature for the development of material well-being. Rather, emphasis was placed on conformity
to ritual and sacred laws, which ensured harmony and favor with the
spirit and the natural worlds, and thereby provided protection against
this-worldly misfortune and ensured prosperity, health, and success in
war. An active or transformative orientation toward nature was not considered wise within the framework of the southeastern world view. Thus
southeastern values were predisposed against the instrumental economic
orientations that characterize modern Western societies and the European
societies with whom the southeastern nations came into contact in the
1700's. Southeastern values and orientations toward nature predisposed
well-socialized southeasterners against readily adopting the more instru-
mentalist orientations of the Europeans.

POLITICAL SOLIDARITY

Functionalist theory suggests that in a consensually organized nation-
state the formation of national political allegiances is a precondition to
the institutionalization of a stable and differentiated polity. In the southeast, none of the four societies constituted politically unified nations in
the sense that the general population upheld national loyalties and obligations over local or kinship loyalties. All four societies had institutions
of social, symbolic, and political integration in the sense that the societal
members shared common values, norms, and traditions of societal origin.
Nevertheless, the traditions of the southeast did not legitimate national-
level political commitments that superseded allegiances to regions, local
villages, and kinship groups. The primary political loyalties and commitments were given not to the national councils but to local village or kinship

groupings. According to functionalist theory, if the southeastern nations are to forge stable and differentiated national polities they will need to adopt centralized conceptions of political allegiance and national political unity. Otherwise, the southeastern nations will experience difficulties in forming and maintaining differentiated national governments.

Cherokee political relations were decentralized and locally oriented; the fundamental political unit which received primary political loyalty was the village. These numbered about sixty, and they were sovereign, autonomous political units that retained the power to make war or peace and to engage in diplomacy. Larger coalitions of villages were formed according to the exigencies of defense or war and for pressing political issues that required more than a local village response. Beyond the village, there was little regular political coordination of Cherokee political affairs, although the Cherokee polity was more than a loose confederation of towns.

Although in the early 1700's there was no regular national political mechanism in Cherokee society, there was an integration according to the norms of kinship obligations and a common symbolic or ceremonial order. The towns had a symbolic and regional order. There were five regional coalitions of towns: overhill towns, valley towns, lower towns, middle towns, and out towns. Though the towns and regional councils might cooperate under pressing crisis conditions, they had political autonomy and made war and peace independently, often in competition and with disregard for the actions of the other regions.[23] The major geographical divisions did not form a unified defensive or offensive military alliance. If one region was engaged in war, the other regions were not required to provide aid.

Alexander Cuming observed in 1730 that the Cherokee nation was governed by seven mother towns. Each of the seven mother towns chose a town chief, who was regarded as the regional leader of the affiliated daughter towns. The regional mother towns were Tannassie among the overhill towns, Ustanali, Estatoe, and Keowee among the lower towns, Telliquo and Noyohee among the valley towns, and Keetoowah among the middle and out towns.[24] The mother towns commanded the respect and deference of the daughter towns, although the daughter towns were free to make independent decisions on most issues, and the mother towns did not wield authoritative or coercive power to force compliance with their views or decisions. But the regional mother towns could still be influential politically and could command the adherence of their subordinate towns.

The Cherokee national council met irregularly; it convened primarily to manage crisis situations of national concern. Regional and national councils were formed by an aggregation of village chiefs and their assistants, the town head warriors and their assistants, and beloved men and town priests, who were sent as a delegation to represent the views of the village community. (The beloved men were retired and respected old men who had contributed years of service to their village community.) Unanimous agreement was required for binding decisions in the national council. The seven mother towns and the five geographical divisions gave the Cherokee polity a certain structure and hierarchy, but because of the political autonomy of the regions and villages, the polity had no strong sense of cooperation or collective capacity for coordinated national political action. Most political action was local and regional.

In Choctaw society, which had an overlapping kinship and political organization, social and political solidarity were synonymous. The primary political units in Choctaw society were local family iksa (lineages based on common matrilineal descent) or groups of kindred family iksa that formed local villages. The local villages were often associated with larger central villages, forming a chiefdom or intermediate-level iksa. There were six major iksa, consisting of several of the chiefdoms or intermediate-level iksa, and these in turn formed two phratries. Local villages retained considerable political autonomy, and leaders of higher-ranked iksa had little authority over local matters. Decisions in the local, regional, and national councils were binding only if all the villages agreed. Dissenting villages were not obligated to participate in the implementation of any decision they had not approved; they merely withdrew and did not participate. Political authority was thus decentralized, and each locality acted with considerable independence.[25]

The Choctaw polity was characterized by predominantly local and regional political allegiances to segmentary kinship units. Political solidarity in Choctaw society was predominantly local and particularistic; regional and national solidarity depended on gaining consensus among the numerous local leaders. If a sustained level of national political solidarity is a precondition to the formation of a differentiated constitutional government, then the Choctaw, with their local and kinship-oriented political orientations, should experience difficulties. In order to form a centralized and differentiated society, the Choctaw will need to institutionalize a differentiation of locality and kinship from political organization, and at the same time build political commitments to national government that supersede local, regional, and kinship loyalties.

The Chickasaw polity was similarly decentralized, with local villages and kinship iksas managing most routine issues; issues that could not be handled by the local captain or council of elders were brought before the national council or the principal chief. There were four districts in the Chickasaw nation, all led by large villages. In 1708 there were seven major villages (the number varied up to eleven) and one mother town or capital village. The chiefs of the villages were subordinate to the chief of the mother town, but the principal chief had only nominal authority, and the local villages managed most of their own affairs. The local towns and iksas were largely self-governing and were united mainly for purposes of mutual defense and common interests. In times of war the Chickasaw palisaded and gathered their villages close together for mutual defense; in times of peace the people scattered over the countryside and lived in small settlements.[26] During the 1700's, despite the potential for local, segmentary, and kin-based political cleavages, the Chickasaw showed remarkable military unity, and their culturally legitimated and kin-based national religious, military, and civil offices which they used to mobilize political and military unity in times of crisis or external military threat, were altogether far more centralized than those of the other major southeastern societies.

The Creek confederacy was divided into two geographical regions, called by the English upper towns and lower towns. After 1715, the lower towns were located on the Chattahoochee River in present western Georgia; "lower towns" meant that they were closer to the English settlements than the upper town Creek villages, which were located on the Coosa and Tallapoosa rivers in the present state of Alabama. Politically and institutionally, the upper and lower towns were independent of one another: they carried on war and diplomacy independently, and the involvement in war of one district did not obligate the other district to join in the hostilities.[27]

Both the upper and lower towns were divided into symbolically ordered red and white towns. The two districts were institutionally and symbolically complete and could carry out the required division of labor in the government between red and white towns at the regional level. The national or confederate council was formed by the gathering of representatives from villages. The red towns ruled in times of war and performed legislative and judicial activities during times of peace; the white towns acted as executive during times of peace. The groups of white and red towns did not, however, form a political unit; political allegiances between the white and red towns were superseded by regional and local loyalties, and leading towns in one region could not rally towns together from the other region merely by appealing to their symbolic or color relations. The ties of political solidarity between the two regions were weak: indeed, at times during the colonial period the upper towns informed the colonists that the two districts were two separate nations.

Every village in the Creek confederacy had a ceremonial square that was considered a sovereign political unit. Villages or tribal towns enjoyed religiously legitimated particularistic identifications and autonomy. Most villages had special sacred objects that symbolized a particularistic covenant relation between the village and the Great Spirit. The confederate council did not challenge or interfere with local decision making unless it was unanimously agreed to by all the village delegations in the council.[28] Primary political, social, and cultural identifications and loyalties belonged not to the confederate council or even to regional and subregional leading villages, but to the village and ceremonial square of the clan of one's mother. Beyond the village level, Creek political solidarity was thus situational and decentralized and showed little potential for concerted collective action.[29] It is said that the Creek towns rarely came to a unanimous agreement on a particular issue, such as declaring war, and even within a particular village there was rarely unanimous agreement in support of a declaration of war. Those who favored the action to take up war did so; those who were for peace simply did not participate. Given such local and particularistic political loyalties, functionalist theory suggests that before the Creek can institutionalize a differentiated constitutional government they must create collective symbols of national political identity and centralized political loyalties and commitments beyond the local villages or towns.

POLITICAL CULTURE

All four southeastern nations exhibited a similar form of democratic political culture. The early southeastern "republics" differed from contemporary democracies in the degree of internal and external political differentiation, but there was an emphasis on egalitarianism, accountability of leadership, and negotiated political decision making. Because the political cultures of the southeastern nations were similar, political culture is not a variable that can help explain the differences in the formation of democratic and differentiated polities. Nevertheless, the presence of democratic political norms within the southeastern nations appears to be a favorable condition for the formation and continuity of a democratic form of government.

Cherokee norms of political participation were egalitarian, and decision making depended on negotiation and consensus both in the national council and in the local village councils. Discussion continued until a consensus was obtained, or, if none was possible, the decision was postponed. There was no concept of majority rule. Since harmony and avoidance of conflict were highly valued, negotiation continued until some decision was made, but a dissenting village could withdraw from the council and not be bound by the decisions of the others. The town chiefs did not have authority to force a decision onto a dissenting minority. In practice, it was difficult for all villages to agree on any given question heard before the national council, and so there were few nationally binding laws. Perhaps the clearest early law was the prohibition, on pain of death, for any Cherokee to sell land without the consent of the national council.[30]

But even though every Cherokee had the right to have his voice heard in the local and national councils of the nation, not every man's voice weighed the same. Men were ranked socially and politically in Cherokee society according to community reputation and recognition. Political influence was based on charisma and ability, and men who won war titles for acts of bravery or leadership were accorded more weight in council than men of lesser achievements. Town chiefs and councilmen, however, held no special authority and relied on persuasion to gain the support of the community. The old and influential men might give a talk and influence the younger men for a time, "but everyone is his own master": "The very lowest of them thinks himself as great and as high as the rest, and everyone has to be courted for their friendship, with some kind of feeling, and made much of."[31] The town chief and national leaders had to gain the confidence and consent of the people in order to implement decisions. Leaders who acted contrary to the prevailing sentiment of the people were deposed from office for negligence of duty, and they lost influence and the ability to lead the people. To a large extent, the actions of the local town chiefs reflected the will of the town council and people.

In the absence of coercive institutions of political control, community sanctions and the threat of spiritual retribution for breaking sacred law were the primary mechanisms for enforcing social control. Cherokees did not assert public claims to power or openly use power for personal or political ends; doing so was explicitly rebuked in practice by community consensus as well as in mythology. Egalitarianism, accountability, avoidance of direct conflict in political decision making, noncoercive authority relations, and harmonious social and political relations were central themes in Cherokee political culture.[32]

Much the same spirit applied in Choctaw political culture. Leaders were accountable to the people, and decisions were made by consensus and negotiation among the leaders. Ideally, the people were the sovereign power among the Choctaw, and leaders whose conduct or leadership displeased the people were subject to removal from office.[33] Those who were found to be inefficient or incompetent could be impeached by the people directly. Choctaw political norms emphasized individual, social, and political autonomy: "They do not usually do what is requested of them, except when they want to; it may be said that this is an ill-disciplined government."[34] To assume a stance of forceful political leadership, even in times of war, could lead to repudiation by the general population, and even respected national leaders had to use persuasion and argument to convince others to accept a position on any particular issue. War leaders during military expeditions had to legitimate their command by appeals to greater knowledge and experience, because ordering men about without their consent put them in peril of desertion, possibly even attack from their own men. The principal chief and other leaders were never seen as having absolute or despotic powers. Authority was local, segmentary, and decentralized. As one early observer noted, "All the villages are so many little republics in which each does as he likes." [35]

Like the other major southeastern nations, the Chickasaw already had a consensual political order in the 1700's. Chickasaw political culture emphasized negotiated decision making, consensus formation, egalitarianism, and noncoercive authority. The primary means of social control were the Chickasaw normative and sacred laws. Community opinion informed the actions of the leadership and the decisions of the national council, which was indeed less a lawmaking body than a body for making national policy on specific pressing issues of national concern. No leader could uphold a position consistently when the weight of community opinion was against him, and the principal chief had little autonomous or coercive power; his decisions could be overruled by the decisions of the council. Decisions by the national council were binding only if all the villages and iksa agreed. Dissenting groups were not bound by the decision of the majority.

Decisions made by local town councils were obeyed only with the agreement and assent of the members of the town, and the discussions in the council are reported to have been egalitarian and peaceful: "Their voices to a man have due weight in every public affair, as it concerns their welfare alike." [36] Men were influential because of reputation and merit alone; in other respects all were considered equal.

Creek political culture, too, was relatively democratic and emphasized consensus decision making, egalitarianism, decentralized noncoercive authority relations, and accountability of leadership. Political decision making in the national and village councils was based on negotiation and discussion until a unanimously acceptable position could be agreed upon. The political ethic emphasized that social harmony should prevail among the villages and that conflict should be minimized in the village and national councils. Village chiefs and influential national figures did not have coercive powers; they ruled by means of personal charisma, reputation, age, persuasion, and eloquence in council. Chiefs and leaders whose actions and opinions did not conform to the general consensus and laws of the nation could be ignored by the people or deposed from office by agreement in the national council or the village council. [37] The nonhierarchical leadership, decision making by consensus and negotiation, noncoercive powers of leadership, and the accountability of leadership are elements of political culture that embody democratic principles that may have facilitated adoption of constitutional democratic forms of government among the Creek.

INTERNAL POLITICAL DIFFERENTIATION

None of the four major southeastern nations showed any great degree of internal political differentiation. Though details of laws and customs varied, the rules in general were those of negotiation and consensus formation. The Cherokee had no national executive office or bureaucracy, and most decisions were made by a legislative framework of national, regional, and village councils, which had no specialized rules and procedures. The towns had civil and priestly courts to weigh infractions against town law and also to handle cases of sacrilege. The town government had the right to levy fines for infractions of town laws, and for some crimes a convicted townsman could be executed. The national council tried cases of treason. Although the Cherokee national council hardly could be called a state because it had the power to try and execute people for treason, nevertheless there existed in Cherokee political relations the precedent for village and national councils to enforce limited use of legitimate force.[38]

A large body of Cherokee judicial powers, however, was outside the jurisdiction of the political councils at any level and lay instead in the domain of the laws and norms regulating clan relations, chiefly involving cases of personal injury or property damage. The primary law here was the law of blood. If a person was killed by a member of another clan, even by accident, the victim's clan was obligated to restore the balance by claiming a life of a member of the other clan. The murderer was obligated to surrender voluntarily to the vengeance of the victimized clan; if the murderer did not come forward but showed his indifference to his clan ties and affiliations, he was excommunicated from the clan, and therefore from the nation. If the victim was a person of significantly greater respectability than the murderer, then the avenging clan had the right to bypass revenge on the murderer and select for revenge a man of higher rank among the murderer's clan. If the clansmen of the victim were dilatory in avenging his death, it was believed that the spirit of the victim would cause harm and misfortune among his own living clansmen in order to prod them into timely fulfillment of their duty to avenge his death.[39]

In cases of accidental death the murderer had the right to place himself under the protection of a priest in one of four "white" towns or towns of refuge. In general, crimes short of murder, including even the most trifling private infractions, were settled by negotiation. If a matter involved town clan segments, the town leaders might intervene in clan judicial proceedings in order to quell a dispute that threatened to disrupt local social relations.[40] There was, however, no government mechanism for intervening in disputes between members of clans from different towns or with members of other nations; such negotiations were left to the clan elders.

In Choctaw society, there was, again, little formal separation of powers. Most political business was conducted by the village, regional, or national councils. There was a nominal principal chief, and there were chiefs of the various major and local iksas, but these leaders had little autonomous power or authority. The ultimate decision making power was vested in the consensus of the national council of local headmen. According to the oral history, the national council had the right to examine the actions of the members of the nation and to mete out justice according to the crime.[41] Thus there is some indication that the national council, if in agreement, could use force to uphold its laws and to punish for treason.

At the same time, however, even though the national council had limited jurisdiction over some offenses against the nation, most judicial action, including all cases of murder, was conducted by the iksas or major kinship groups. Cases of murder or other private infractions were decided first by local headmen from the two Choctaw phratries; if a case could not be decided, it was moved to the jurisdiction of higher-ranked iksa, where the two highest ranked major iksa had the final decision.[42] As in Cherokee society, the rules of blood revenge applied in cases of murder. When a murder was committed by a person from another nation, the kinsmen of the victim were obligated to take revenge against the foreign nation—perhaps, if the family was influential, joined by other families and iksas. In cases of murder, or even of accidental death, within the nation, the guilty person had to surrender his life. Death was the only honorable way in which the murderer could atone for the death of his victim directly to the victim's spirit. If the murderer fled, a member of his family was forced to pay with his or her life to settle accounts. The law was designed to restore balance between the two iksas, and it also served as a deterrent against murder and injury to members of other iksas.[43]

The Choctaw polity showed little internal differentiation. The national council assumed limited legislative and executive powers; and most judicial matters were embedded in kinship relations. Though there were mythical tales of legitimate use of force by the national council, the enforcement of civil injuries was relegated to the norms governing kinship relations and the law of retaliation. There were no political parties, and the rules of political decision making required consensus. Most routine political issues were managed by councils of local iksa elders. There is little indication that the national council was invested with coercive powers even in cases of treason. Community norms and sanctions regulated the punishment for petty crimes and transgressions. Villages had the right to enforce fines against persons who did not contribute their labor to the preparing and planting of the common village field.

Personal injury issues were managed by the law of blood revenge between iksas. If these were minor personal injury and property cases, a local council of kin elders decided the issue, but in cases of murder, the offended iksa was allowed to avenge a death with a man considered of equal value from the iksa of the murderer. The older brother of the victim was obligated to avenge his younger kinsman's death, otherwise the spirit of the unavenged relative would linger nearby until released to travel to the next world by the avenging of his death.[44] Most murderers conformed to the community demand for voluntary surrender, but if a murderer fled, a near relative was executed in his place. If the escaped murderer returned, he was forever stigmatized and ostracized as a coward.

In Creek society, although there was a division of labor between the symbolically ordered red towns and white towns over leadership in executive, legislative, and judicial functions, this allocation of duties did not constitute a significant internal differentiation of political functions, since the division of labor within the polity was not differentiated from the cultural symbolic order or from the major social units, the tribal towns. The symbolically ordered division of labor defined segmented duties between red and white villages, but did not specify institutionally specialized functions within the polity itself. The confederate council performed executive, legislative, and some judicial functions, including the right to try and execute treasonous offenders. Such executions were carried out by the leading red towns, for no blood could be spilled in the white towns, which were sanctuaries for anyone who killed by accident. For lesser crimes the accused might be severely beaten. This tradition indicates that the Creek were willing to delegate limited use of coercive authority to the national and village governments. The acts of punishment for violators of public law required agreement by the national council.

The clans managed most judicial relations that involved personal injury and property, and the deliberations of the clans were independent of the town and national councils. In cases of murder, the clansmen of the victim were obligated to seek revenge against the offending clan in order to placate the spirit of the victim, who could not journey to the spirit world until his death was avenged. The village government punished those who broke ceremonial or village rules. In the event that two local clan segments could not settle a dispute by the usual methods of negotiation by clan elders, the village government intervened in order to preserve harmony in the town. When clans from two different towns could not come to an agreement, matters were settled by the confederate council.[45] In sum, the

Creek polity exhibited little internal differentiation, there was little separation of powers, and judicial functions were embedded in the councils
and in kinship groups.

ECONOMIC CULTURE AND ORGANIZATION

Before there was any significant contact with Europeans, the southeastern societies had horticultural and hunting subsistence economies.
Although there was trade with other tribes, especially in products for
ceremonial purposes, most production was destined for local consumption. Among the Cherokee and Creek, and among the Chickasaw and
Choctaw in times of war, village governments organized the planting of
a common field, with each clan or iksa having an assigned area and each
lineage having a plot within the field. In addition, family households kept
private gardens for raising food for their own consumption. Each spring
the beloved men of the town council designated the day of the communal clearing and planting of the common field, in which all able-bodied
persons in the village were expected to help. The staple crops were corn,
beans, and squash. After spring planting, the females of each household
cultivated and harvested the family plots in common. At harvest time,
every family contributed a share of its produce to a common village crib,
which was drawn on by the village leaders to aid the needy and to support ceremonial and town government activities. Men supplemented the
vegetable diet by hunting deer, turkey, raccoon, bear, and other edible animals and by fishing. Wild herbs and berries were gathered for food and
medicinal purposes.[46]

None of the southeastern nations had acquisitive attitudes toward the
accumulation of wealth. Before the introduction of the slave trade and fur
trade by the Europeans, members of these nations lived in a subsistence
or need economy: production was gauged largely to satisfy subsistence
requirements, and little surplus was created for trade. In and of itself,
wealth had little meaning in terms of social and political relations. More
important was the redistribution of wealth as a means of securing the
obligations and respect of friends and kinsmen. Personal valor, wisdom,
and generosity were more highly regarded as virtues than the hoarding
of material wealth. Indeed, the southeasterners were openly disdainful of
personal wealth and accumulation and scorned those who were stingy and
greedy. Until at least the 1770's, it was the custom to destroy most personal property, usually consisting of horses, arms, and ornaments, when
a person died, or to bury it with him so that he could enjoy it in the
next life. The burial of personal property, though done partly for religious
reasons, prevented disputes over inheritance, and it tended to inhibit the
accumulation of material wealth.

Following the religiously legitimated norms and values that de-emphasized accumulation of personal wealth, men worked to satisfy the material needs of a normatively defined subsistence way of life.[47] Given this tradition, one can expect that if the southeasterners participated actively in markets in the post-European contact period, they would very likely have to adopt new orientations toward specialized economic roles and toward the accumulation of wealth and the production of surplus value.

Variable Comparative Conditions

DIFFERENTIATION OF POLITY AND CULTURE

The four southeastern nations share a similar migration myth in which the people are guided by a pole that gives the instructions of the Great Spirit, but the myths vary in the emphasis on polity and priesthood. In the Cherokee oral tradition, first recorded in the 1820's, the dominant priesthood was overthrown in a rebellion that occurred in some long-ago time. This story of rebellion describes early Cherokee society as composed of three groups of people: the headmen or civil leaders of the towns, the Proud or priesthood, and the common people. The Proud claimed to be teachers of divine knowledge that was granted to them by their predecessors at the time of creation.[48]

By the early 1700's, the Cherokee had differentiated political and religious roles. The priests no longer organized and dominated national political affairs as they had done in mythology and in the oral history but were instead clearly placed in the role of intermediaries and interpreters of communications from the spirit world—often consulted by the Cherokee leaders for their wisdom in spiritual matters, and always respected. When a priest was consulted on an important question, his findings were considered to be the will of the spirits, and men could not change the fate of the issue in question. Political action was therefore informed by relatively nonsecular and nondifferentiated cultural orientations, and decision making on important issues involved an appeal to the priests to use ritual means to seek out the will of the spirits.[49]

The Choctaw oral tradition also gives an account of the overthrow of an oppressive and powerful theocratic priesthood, which in the Choctaw case is succeeded by the council of minkos (principal chiefs) and iksas as the leading political authority in the nation, but it suggests a differentiation of political and cultural spheres in Choctaw society. The Choctaw usually did not consult their prophets and seers on important political decisions, as did the Cherokee until at least the 1760's. This oral account, however, collected by Gideon Lincecum in the 1820's, may well have been a tale told by warriors and civil chiefs that legitimated the exclusion of the priests from political influence and decision making. Nevertheless, the French records of the eighteenth century also do not indicate that priests or shamans played an overt role in either local or national Choctaw government.[50]

Even in the mythical tradition, the Chickasaw differentiated the role of principal chief from the roles of prophets and medicine men. The Chickasaw migration, according to oral traditions, was led by priests who mediated relations between the spirits and the people. One oral fragment tells of three leaders: a prophet who communicated with the spirits above, a medicine man, and a civil chief.[51] There appears to be no tradition of an overthrow of an oppressive priesthood, as in the Cherokee and Choctaw oral histories, and this absence of an overthrow or separation of religious leadership from national political affairs may suggest that the Chickasaw polity and society retained more theocratic elements than did the Cherokee and Choctaw societies.

We know that during the historical period in Chickasaw society, the roles of the two Hopaye or phratry holy men were differentiated from the role of principal chief or minko. Nevertheless, Chickasaw religion interpenetrated Chickasaw political organization and social institutions. The Chickasaw believed that the Great Spirit was the head of their national government and directed the government through his communications with the prophets. The chief and the priests addressed the people as the "holy people" and constantly implored them to keep strictly to the sacred law in order to ensure continued good fortune and the blessings of the Great Spirit. The national council usually met at the time of the annual Green Corn ceremony, but political business, undertaken between ceremonial activities, was less important than the ceremonies.

The Chickasaw believed that the priests and prophets were in direct communication with the Great Spirit and holy beings who had power over the course of nature and over human issues and affairs, and it was therefore necessary for the national and village councils to consult them on all political and, especially, military matters, and the national council never made decisions of significance without the counsel and approval of the high priests.[52] If the priests foretold ill consequences for a particular decision, the national or village council heeded their advice and changed their plans or decisions accordingly. In all aspects of decision making in the Chickasaw polity, the Chickasaw cultural world view, which legitimated the influential role of priests or prophets in important decisions of national concern, thus prevailed.

The Creek migration tradition is similar to the Chickasaw in not telling of a revolution against an oppressive and politically dominant theocracy.[53] The Creek polity was tightly interpenetrated and ordered by Creek culture in three primary ways: by the cultural particularism of the towns, by the role of priests in political decision making in the towns, and by the political ordering of the Creek towns into red and white towns, symbolic of the struggle between the dualistic forces of the cosmic order. Both major geographical political divisions, the lower and upper towns, had leading red and white towns, and the confederate council gathered at one of the four leading towns. The red and white towns had a long history of antagonistic relations, and the two groups were ceremonially and socially distant from each other. Much of Creek political history can be understood as a struggle for leadership between men from leading red and white towns.[54]

The 80–90 towns, organized as local segmentary tribal groups, were the basic political and cultural unit in Creek society. Certain towns had a ceremonial square, which represented a particularistic covenant relation with the Great Spirit: it was he who gave the town its special laws, rituals, and holy utensils and vessels. Smaller towns often allied to a mother town with a ceremonial square and identified with its people. The towns or villages respected the special customs and beliefs of the others and did not interfere with the sacred rituals of the others. It was thought that the town was obligated to perform its special sacred rituals and maintain its sacred objects in order to keep the protection and good will of the spirit beings. Consequently, the Creek towns were religiously legitimated and culturally particularistic social and political groupings.[55] The towns had considerable cultural and political autonomy; each town had the right to make its own internal decisions and could send a delegation to the national council, which was composed of delegations from all the villages that cared to attend.

Although within the Creek village there was a differentiation of roles among ceremonial leaders, civil leaders, and war leaders, the acts of the Creek village and national polity were considered religious acts. "Every act of the Muskogee government, or of the officers thereof, was considered a religious act. Councils were always convened with religious ceremonies."[56] Creek national and village councils were always held in a sacred town ceremonial square. It was believed that the council deliberations were guided and directly observed by the Great Spirit. The town chief was considered the direct representative of the Great Spirit. He presided over the town council and was obligated to administer the sacred laws, norms, and ceremonies that were given to the town by the Great Spirit. The town priest acted as intermediary between the town and the spirit world, and since his ability to read and interpret the messages and signs of the Great Spirit and other spirit beings was highly regarded as necessary for undertaking any significant task, he could have great influence over town affairs.[57]

The Creek polity was the most strongly structured and interpenetrated by culture and symbolic order of the southeastern nations. Town autonomy was directly legitimated by particularistic covenant relations with the Great Spirit, and the Creek polity was symbolically ordered into red and white towns. The Creek should experience more difficulties in accepting political secularization and further differentiation of the polity than the other southeastern nations, where symbolic order and culture did not directly determine the political units and organization of the polity.

SOCIAL SOLIDARITY

Of the four southeastern nations, the Cherokee had the most socially integrated national clan system, which also was differentiated from national political organization. Although the Choctaw and the Chickasaw had national phratry systems, the iksa identifications were local and regional, and kinship organization was not differentiated from political institutions. The Creek clan system also emphasized local and regional identities, but clans, though symbolically integrated at the local level, were not strongly integrated at the national level. None of the southeastern societies, though members shared common beliefs, myths, norms, and identities, formed political nationalities in which national commitments and obligations took precedence over local and/or kinship prerogatives.

In Cherokee society, the community consisted of shared norms, shared cultural orientations, symbols, ceremonies, and kinship organization. There were seven clans, represented in most of the villages in the nation. The clans were matrilineal and exogamous, and membership was determined by birth. Certain clan obligations prevailed: clansmen were obliged to protect and provide hospitality to one another, so that a traveler in an unfamiliar part of the nation had only to ask for a house of his clan in order to be given food, shelter, protection, and hospitality as a member of the family.[58]

The seven Cherokee clans played a central role in Cherokee creation mythology and in accounts of the ancient ceremonies of the prehistorical theocratic society. The ancient rendition of Cherokee ceremonial and kinship organization shows a close relation between the organization of the seven clans and the Cherokee ceremonial activities. Together the seven clans composed the Cherokee nation, and they were the basic ceremonial units in the organization of the national festivals that symbolized and reenacted the unity of the nation. The seven priestly councillors in association with the theocratic head priest determined the day that the annual purification feast would begin—usually late in the year, sometime during the months of September through November. In preparation for the ceremony the head priest's assistant appointed seven councillors, one from each of the seven clans, who were responsible for administering the ceremony. Seven women, one from each clan, also were appointed to direct preparation of food for the feast, and seven cleaners were assigned to clean the village council house and public buildings. In a similar way during the annual national Cementation ceremony, seven councillors, one from each clan, and their wives fasted seven days. On the third day of the First Green Corn ceremony, seven clan councillors called on their clansmen to pray. When the Cherokee nation met to celebrate the Feast of the Green Fruits, seven men and seven women, a man and a woman from each of the seven clans, were appointed to manage the festival. During the ceremonies, the clans remained segregated in their assigned seats and duties. Anyone who mingled with other clans was severely reproached.[59] In the Cherokee creation myth, the seven clans were led by seven sons of the Great Spirit, who in turn appointed chiefs to each of the seven clans, but the clan chiefs were subordinate to the priests and high priest. During the historical period, the clans continued to play an integral role in the organization of ceremonies and community events within Cherokee society.[60] Because they represented the entire nation, the regular inclusion of the seven clans in the organization of the ceremonies gave the clans a symbolic unity, and created cultural legitimation of a religious or ceremonial national identity.

In the ancient theocratic Cherokee society, the religious side of Cherokee life was given precedence over the civil side. The oral history accounts give a picture of ancient Cherokee society organized along religious and ceremonial lines. In some versions, the high priest managed both civil and religious leadership of the nation, but other versions mention the role of a civil leadership in the villages and even a national chief, subordinate to the high priest and relegated to civil affairs, who were considered less important than management of the ceremonies and relations with the Great Spirit. The Cherokee were organized anciently by a series of towns, with one central ceremonial town where the national officers resided and where the seven national clans gathered for the national ceremonies. Every town of considerable size had a head priest with seven councillors as assistants. The priests managed local ceremonies in coordination with the high priest and leadership of the principal ceremonial town. The town chiefs or kings—as the English called them—handled only local civil matters; occasionally they were included in the national council, composed of priests and priestly councillors, but only to the extent that the civil authorities were thought necessary to the discussion of national affairs.[61] The traditional accounts of prehistorical Cherokee society subordinate the roles of military and civil leaders to a highly structured ceremonial society under the direction of priestly leaders.

It is likely that a majority of Cherokee in the eighteenth century also considered the religious sphere more important than the civil sphere. The cultural and kinship unity of Cherokee society did not necessarily translate into political unity but was a relatively autonomous form of social and cultural integration, which in the minds of many Cherokee had precedence over the political sphere. As will be seen later, a major distinguishing characteristic of Cherokee society is the national kinship and ceremonial unity in conjunction with the relative autonomy of the polity from kinship-ceremonial organization. In theoretical terms, political relations in Cherokee society were differentiated from the institutions of social and cultural unity. The combination of national unity based on kinship and ceremonial organization and the differentiation of institutions of social-cultural integration from political organization gave the Cherokee the most extensively solidary and differentiated social and political institutions of the four major southeastern nations.

According to several sources, the ancient Choctaw societal community was composed of matrilineal family kinship groups called iksa, that is, a group that claimed common matrilineal descent, however remote. The evidence on Choctaw sociopolitical organization suggests that the Choctaw were grouped anciently into at least six major geographically specific iksa and the six iksa were grouped into two phratries, the Inhulata and the lesser phratry, the Immoklusha (in some versions called Kishapa Okla—"The Divided People").

Within each phratry, each iksa had its own territory, and social and political membership was defined by identification with an iksa. The six major iksa were subdivided into smaller iksa or family iksa, and so the social organization within the major iksa also was segmentary, because each subunit was a relatively autonomous economic, cultural, and political group. Each family iksa had its leader, its own local territory, and its own local ceremonies. The phratries and iksa were interrelated by ties of marriage and the obligations and reciprocities that were involved in the marriage arrangements, but social, political, and cultural identification remained tied to the iksa and phratry of birth.[62] Because the Choctaw iksas and phratries designated particularistic and local kinship, geographical, dialectical, and political identifications, the form of social integration was more segmentary than in the Cherokee case, where the seven ceremonially integrated clans were located in each region and within each major village in the nation. Thus, given the local and regional segmentary character of their social organization, the Choctaw can be expected to experience more difficulties in forming sustained national unification than the more socially and symbolically unified Cherokee.

The Chickasaw were organized into two phratries called Imosaktca and Intcukwalipa. The Imosaktca phratry was higher in rank. Each phratry was composed of matrilineal exogamous iksa that were ranked, with the kin group of the principal chief ranked highest; it was possible to marry within the same phratry but not within the same iksa. The iksas were composed of groups of related families that claimed a common mythical origin and descent from a special animal protector, such as a raccoon, panther, or skunk. At various times in history there seem to have been between seven and fifteen iksas among the Chickasaw. The principal chief, head warriors, leading second chiefs, and head priests or Hopaye were selected from hierarchically ranked iksas. Consequently, kinship, political organization, and organization of the religious institutions were not differentiated.

Cultural integration was more extensive in Chickasaw society than in Choctaw society, where the Green Corn ceremony was performed by local villages and iksa and the national ceremonies occurred only in the mythical tradition and oral history. The emphasis on national ceremonial integration among the Chickasaw surpassed even that of the Cherokee, who during the historical period did not gather the entire nation for the performance of the annual Green Corn ceremony.

In Chickasaw society, villages gathered for a national Green Corn ceremony if they were close enough together; if they were not, several Green Corn ceremonies at different locations were performed. The tradition of a national Green Corn ceremony that was linked to the national phratry-iksa system provided Chickasaw society with a culturally integrated ceremonial and kinship system. At the national gatherings the people formed according to iksa and performed their duties according to a division of labor based on phratry and iksa rank.[63] In Cherokee society, although the seven clans were integrated symbolically in the Green Corn ceremony, the ceremonies were performed by the villages. The Creek Busk or Green Corn ceremony was more disciplined and religiously organized than the Chickasaw Green Corn ceremony: "They do not keep the busks as the Ochesees [lower town Creek] but only make a great general dance, when they eat the first green corn."[64] Nevertheless, although Chickasaw society evinced a relatively strong sense of national cultural-kinship integration, the institutions of national integration were embedded within a nondifferentiated institutional framework of cultural, political, and kinship relations.

The Creek did not have a national level kinship system like the Cherokee seven clans or the two phratries of the Chickasaw and Choctaw. The most important social, political, and cultural unit in Creek society was the tulwa or tribal town, and the kinship system was specific to each town.

Within each village the matrilineal clans were divided into red clans and white clans, which reflect the symbolism of the dualistic and antagonistic cosmic forces common to the southeastern cultures. The towns also were divided into red and white towns, and ideally the white clans led in the white towns and the red clans led in the red towns. Each village had both red and white clans, but the two divisions were not necessarily considered kindred groups. The red and white town phratries did not regulate marriage, and the two town phratries were not exogamous, although the red and white clan affiliations were important in ceremonial and political relations.

Unlike the Cherokee kinship system, where seven clans were represented in each village of the nation, there were about fifty Creek clans that were spread regionally throughout the nation. Some clans were represented only in one village; other clans were found only in a few villages. There were four principal red clans and four principal white clans, but even they were not represented in each town in the nation. There were at least nine collections of clans that formed exogamous subphratries, but not all the clans were included in the subphratries. Towns that shared kinship groups or had members that were intermarried were often friends or allies, and kinship ties made up a network of informal intervillage relations. Outside the village context, kinship groups were primarily important in regulating judicial relations between clans. Clan and town affiliation determined social and political membership. Children belonged to the clan and town of the mother. Membership within a clan was a precondition to participation in the political and ceremonial life of the village.[65]

Creek ceremonial relations also were specific to each village. Though the Green Corn ceremony was a symbol of confederate integration, the towns shared a Busk or Green Corn ceremony only with other towns that were of the same symbolic color, but the two symbolic divisions were not explicitly units of ceremonial integration—that is, the whole collection of red or white towns did not share a Green Corn ceremony. Thus the institutions of ceremonial and social integration in Creek society were local and particularistic to specific towns and allied towns.[66] There were no regular ceremonies or institutions of national or even regional integration; the Green Corn ceremony was performed primarily by local village communities. Consequently, Creek kinship relations and the ceremonial relations were local and particularistic and did not provide an institutional framework for national political integration.

DIFFERENTIATION OF POLITY AND KINSHIP

In terms of differentiation of polity from kinship, the Cherokee and Creek had the most differentiated national polities; the Choctaw and Chickasaw national polities were not differentiated from kinship organization and prerogatives. In Cherokee society, villages were the primary political units, and though local clan segments were important in the town councils, Cherokee clans were not corporate political groupings and the national council was not organized by clan affiliation or prerogatives. The national council was composed of village delegations that represented the views and interests of their local town councils, not the views of the seven clans or local clan segments. Consequently, the national council was differentiated from the clan system, and clan prerogatives and organization were not the basis of political decision making or of the principles of organization of the national government. The town council was responsible for the collective welfare of the village, and the village government had precedence over the individual clan segments within the village community. Local clan segments did not participate in political relations outside the village or in the regional or national councils. There was no clan government; the clans did not have official recognition within the national or regional councils of village headmen. Clan chiefs did not speak for the nation or for their individual clans in the political councils outside the local villages. Village leaders were expected to act for the local village community as a whole and not in the interests of any particular clan.[67] Consequently, the Cherokee national polity was differentiated from kinship organization.

In sociology this kind of dual activity is called role differentiation. Everyone plays a variety of roles in life—student, husband, citizen, son, Boy Scout master, and so on. These roles and their associated expectations are invoked in specific situational contexts. The roles that people play and the contexts under which they become operable differ from society to society and over time. My argument, for the Cherokee and later for the Creek, but not for the Choctaw and Chickasaw, is that the roles of clansman and political leader were differentiated. Every member of Cherokee society belonged to a clan, and these clan associations involved certain rights and obligations. The leaders who were sent by the village council to the national council were representatives of their village, a collective political role, and were not representing their local clan segments; yet they remained clansmen, and if one of their kinsmen was murdered they were obligated to seek revenge. But that activity was separate from their political role in the national council, which did not extend control over blood revenge until the early 1800's. Role conflict could occur if in a certain situation a Cherokee chief was called on to choose between his political duties and clan obligations: for example, the obligations of Cherokee blood revenge usually took precedence over political loyalties and duties. So it was not a contradiction when, for instance, in the early 1800's Turtle-at-Home was a member of the national clan council and at the same time a prominent political figure among the Cherokee upper towns. I argue that the chiefs went to the national council and assumed their roles as village leaders, but their roles as clan leaders were held in abeyance during this time. Each society has its particular roles and has norms about the situations when roles are invoked.

The point of whether local Choctaw political organization was based on corporate villages or local iksa or kinship groups may seem obscure, but it is of major interest for determining the value of Choctaw institutions in the theory of differentiation. French colonial sources observed that the national council was composed of village chiefs, but since they did not explicate the relationship of the local and major iksa to village leadership, we cannot tell whether the men from the villages who composed the national council were representing villages or local iksas.[68] Descriptions of the Choctaw moiety and kinship relations are, indeed, unclear, lacking in critical detail, and sometimes contradictory. Some sources, for example, mention exogamous moieties, others do not. Probably we do not have enough information to describe the entire Choctaw kinship structure and its internal relations with any accuracy, but despite the ambiguities, the data are detailed enough to establish a reasonable argument for the nondifferentiation of Choctaw kinship and political organization.

An oral history and evidence from the early 1800's suggest that iksa relations and identification superseded village membership. The oral history portrays the national council as composed of the headmen from each of the family iksas within the nation. After the diaspora from the ancient central city of Nanih Waiya, the various Choctaw iksa formed villages at dispersed locations. Usually an iksa was composed of several villages, while local family iksa formed settlements.[69] Iksa identification was more significant socially and politically than village identification, and the national council continued to be composed of the headmen of the various iksa. The oral history portrays a Choctaw polity that was not differentiated from kinship organization.

Reports from the early 1800's also indicate that the villages were subordinate to the iksa identification. By the early 1800's the Choctaw were grouped into three major districts, which were further subdivided into many smaller local iksa, and each of the subdivisions had a headman, "who was elected by the people of his 'clan.' "[70] In each local settlement or village, a man was elected headman or "captain" by his neighbors, and his appointment was confirmed by the district council composed of the district minko, the headmen, and all the men of the district.[71] Lincecum's observations on Choctaw society in the 1820's also suggest that the Choctaw districts were composed of numerous local iksa.[72] More evidence can be seen in Bushnell's study of the Bayou Lacomb Choctaw, where local villages were considered to be exogamous and the eldest male was the leader of the local group.[73] The latter evidence suggests that villages or local settlements were composed of one family iksa or of several kindred family iksas, and that the local settlements and villages were subunits of larger iksa. Therefore, it seems plausible to conclude that kinship identity permeated the local organization of iksa and villages.

Consequently, the Choctaw polity was not differentiated from local kinship organization. Local headmen, who composed the councils of regional iksa and the national council, were representatives of the family iksas that formed villages or local communities. Regional and major iksa also had headmen, and they formed the higher ranks of political leadership over the leaders from the local iksa or villages.

It has already been seen that culture, normative order, and polity were nondifferentiated in Chickasaw society; kinship and polity were also nondifferentiated. The Chickasaw national council was composed of iksa and village chiefs.[74] The village chiefs were hereditary within the tiger, turkey, and eagle iksas; the heads of the tiger, muclese, and raccoon iksas, together with the village chiefs, formed the national civil or peace council. National officers like the principal chief and the head warrior were hereditary within iksa and phratry. The principal chief was always selected from the minko iksa within the symbolically superordinate Imosaktca phratry, also called the panther or tiger phratry. The second chiefs were selected from the raccoon iksa in the opposite phratry. The iksa chiefs held their status and rank according to the rank of their iksa. Local iksa elders decided on a leader who represented the iksa in the national council at Pontotoc, the central village. Some national military offices were hereditary within iksa, and war parties also were organized by iksa. The iksas sat in the council square according to phratry and iksa rank.[75] Political membership and access to national political office and rank were determined by iksa affiliation.

In Chickasaw society, iksa and phratry prerogatives controlled the appointments to leading political, military and religious offices and also determined the organization and composition of the national council. The latter was, therefore, little more than an extension of the existing iksa-phratry organization of the society, and thus there was little differentiation in Chickasaw society among polity, society, and culture.

In Creek society, kinship, symbolic order, and rank were significant in the selection of officers within the village governments, and the organization of the village council was based on clan organization and leadership.[76] Within the village, the clans were divided into red and white clans, and each had ceremonial and political functions to perform. Officers in the civil hierarchy generally were selected from the white clans, and officers of the military hierarchies were selected from the red clans. Each clan or village clan segment regulated its own internal affairs under the leadership of a clan elder, who also represented his clan in the village council. In the town square, during ceremonial exercises and during political councils, each clan occupied a separate space, and the clan elders sat in honored positions.

In the national council, in contrast to the village councils, kinship and clan affiliations did not define political relations. Clans did not have recognition as political units beyond the village; clans did not meet to present issues within the national council, nor were they recognized within the national council. The national or confederate council was composed of village delegations that represented their village as a corporate unit; the town leaders did not represent their local clans, and they were obligated to present the views of the local town council.[77] The differentiation of kinship from polity in extra-village political relations indicates that there will most likely be less resistance from well-socialized actors in Creek society to change in the political order at the national level than at the village level, where political, symbolic, and kinship relations were nondifferentiated.

PROSPECTS FOR FURTHER DIFFERENTIATION OF THE SOUTHEASTERN POLITIES

The four major southeastern societies exhibit many similarities in economic and cultural organization. Within the framework of the rise of differentiated constitutional governments in the nineteenth century, the similarities in southeastern societal organization can be considered controlled variables. All four nations exhibited similar nondifferentiated cultural orientations with little tension between the mundane and spiritual worlds, and all four cultures evinced a this-worldly orientation. Furthermore, the southeastern theodicy strongly supported the laws and institutional framework of the southeastern societies with direct religious legitimation and divine threats of this-worldly retribution for breaking the sacred laws. Southeastern values emphasized ritual harmony with and order in the natural, social, and sacred worlds; ritual disharmony or pollution invited retaliation and this-worldly injury to individuals and communities. The cultural traditions inculcated conservative orientations toward the existing institutional and normative order, and it might be expected that during the historical period the southeasterners would resist change in their social and political institutions. According to theory, the conservatism and orthodoxy of the southeastern world view will tend to inhibit the formation of groups that will challenge the existing institutional order and also to inhibit the success of proposed institutional differentiation of the existing political order. If more differentiated or rational cultural orientations are a prerequisite to formation and institutionalization of a differentiated constitutional government, then some groups, if not the majority of the members of the southeastern societies, will necessarily have to adopt more differentiated cultural orientations and persuade the others of the need for change in the cultural and political order. Since the cultural orientations were orthodox for all four societies, traditionalistic cultural orientations cannot explain the variation in the rate of formation or stability of more differentiated polities in the nineteenth century.

All four southeastern societies were politically decentralized; political allegiances and loyalties were owed to local villages, regions, or kinship groups, and national loyalties were secondary. If the institutionalization of a differentiated constitutional government requires the formation of national loyalties that have precedence over local and kinship loyalties, then each of the four southeastern nations will have to forge new symbols of national commitment and national loyalties.

All four southeastern nations had democratic political cultures that emphasized political egalitarianism, negotiated and consensus decision making, noncoercive political leadership, and accountability of political leadership. Assuming that democratic culture is necessary to support democratic political institutions, the southeasterners will need to ensure that their preexisting democratic political norms are allowed to continue to inform political organization and action. If the southeasterners are to institutionalize a differentiated constitutional government, they may have to ensure that their political cultures, which may be specific to a nondifferentiated polity, will be compatible with the institutions of a more internally and externally differentiated form of political democracy.

Since none of the four nations had much internal political differentiation, they can form constitutional governments only by centralizing judicial functions in the national government and institutionalizing the separation of executive, legislative, and judicial powers in the national polity. Adopting specialized procedures for political decision making and judiciary functions will further accentuate the differentiation of polity from society, as well as the internal differentiation of the polity. Finally, the formation of political parties that are relatively independent of local kinship and village allegiances will lead to further internal differentiation of the polity. Since all four of the southeastern nations in the early 1700's showed little internal political differentiation, in this respect none had an advantage for adopting a more differentiated polity.

In terms of the last controlled condition, economic organization and economic culture, the similarities persist. All four nations were primarily hunting and horticultural societies, in which trade was minor. They were nonacquisitive, oriented primarily toward subsistence production for local consumption, and were ill suited to active participation in markets or specialization in the economic division of labor. If a market economy is a precondition to the formation of a differentiated polity, then the economic orientations of at least some southeasterners necessarily will have to change toward active private material accumulation and profit making so that market relations will be supported and demands placed on the polity for regulation of market and contract relations.

The four cases vary significantly in terms of differentiation of polity from culture, differentiation of polity from kinship, and social solidarity. The Choctaw had the most secular national and local polity, the Cherokee and Chickasaw priests were influential in decisions of political consequence, and the Creek polity was the most strongly interpenetrated and organized by the cultural sphere. Creek towns had independent and religiously particularistic identities; the political division of labor was symbolically ordered, and priests had an indirect influence in political decision making. Of all the major southeastern nations, the Creek had the least differentiated configuration of relations between polity and culture, and they should experience the greatest difficulties in attempting to secularize and change the polity. For the Cherokee and the Chickasaw, further secularization of the polity will require the exclusion of priests from their roles as spiritual intermediaries, and a lessening of belief in the efficacy of the priests to influence the course of political events because of their sacred knowledge. The Creek political order, with the religious particularism of the villages and the symbolic ordering of the red and white towns, was far more interpenetrated and defined by cultural norms than were the Cherokee, Choctaw and Chickasaw societies, and consequently the Creek should be the least amenable to political change.

The Cherokee exhibited the most extensive institutions of national solidarity in combination with the differentiation of polity and kinship relations. Their kinship system, though nationally extensive and ceremonially integrated, did not have a direct role in the organization of the national council. The Chickasaw kinship system was ceremonially integrated but segmentary and local, and their institutions of social solidarity were not differentiated from the organization of the polity or national council. The Choctaw and Creek social organizations were similarly local and particularistic, but Choctaw political relations were embedded in regional and local kinship units, whereas the Creek national political offices were differentiated from kinship prerogatives because the Creek kinship system was organized in local and regional segments. Consequently, though the Choctaw had the most secular polity, the Cherokee had the most extensive and cohesive social integration and a polity that was the most differentiated from the institutions of social integration. The more socially cohesive and differentiated Cherokee society should be more institutionally predisposed toward further change and adaptation than the less socially integrated and less differentiated Choctaw, Chickasaw, and Creek polities.

The theory of social integration and differentiation cannot, however, explain the subsequent changes in the southeastern polities without taking into consideration the sequence of events and conditions that led to the formation of differentiated constitutional polities. Such an analysis must include the narratives of the group conflicts, interests, conditions, and movements that resulted in the national centralization and differentiation of judicial and kinship relations, the further differentiation of polity from society, the further secularization of the southeastern polities, the centralization of legitimate force in the polity, and the separation of judicial, legislative, and executive powers. The southeasterners had lived for centuries under their old polities, and there was no evolutionary reason why they had to follow a path of centralization and further political differentiation. That they did so in the nineteenth century was the result of specific historical conditions and events following the colonization of their territory by Europeans.

3 GEOPOLITICS, WORLD-SYSTEM INCORPORATION, AND POLITICAL SECULARIZATION IN THE EIGHTEENTH CENTURY

DURING THE EIGHTEENTH century the southeastern societies were gradually incorporated into the world-economic system and were subjected to intense geopolitical competition and a series of wars that resulted from European colonial struggles for control of territory and trade in North America. Incorporation into the expanding fur trade and competitive geopolitical relations placed demands on the southeastern nations to centralize regulation of trade relations and to form a coherent national strategy of geopolitical survival. Under such pressure, however, they showed little institutionalization of increased political differentiation or increased political solidarity. During the early 1750's the Cherokee centralized diplomatic and trade relations, but the disruptions caused by the American Revolutionary War created internal political conflicts that led to a return to regional and local political allegiances. In the late 1780's a small group of Creek leaders tried but failed against stiff opposition to set up a constitutional government, with no significant differentiation of the Creek polity. The Creek confederacy strengthened its strategic trade and military position by adopting more villages and nations into the confederacy, but since each village or group of villages was adopted within the existing institutional framework, there was no further differentiation or increased political solidarity or centralization. The Chickasaw who evinced relative political and military unity during the period of intense war between 1731 and 1760, split into two political groups during the American Revolution, one favoring alliance with the United States and the other favoring alliance with the Spanish colony in the Floridas. Their political conflicts were, however, contained within the traditional kinship-political structure. Choctaw political organization tended toward decentralization and regionalization, and after 1751 the Choctaw were divided into three politically autonomous regions, which had only tenuous national commitments and cooperation. The most significant change in political differentiation among the southeastern nations during the eighteenth century was the increased secularization of the Cherokee, Choctaw, and Chickasaw polities. The Creek polity and societal institutions remained nonsecular.

The history of the four southeastern nations can be traced through a sequence of similar geopolitical contexts, both hegemonic and competitive. In the southeast, competitive geopolitical relations arose around 1699, after the French established the Louisiana Colony, and continued until the defeat of the French in late 1759 in the French and Indian War and the final treaty agreements in 1763. During the period 1699–1763, the British and French, and to a lesser extent the Spanish in Florida and West Florida, contended for control over trade, military, and diplomatic relations with the major southeastern nations. In accordance with the terms of the Treaty of Paris (1763), which ended the Seven Years War, the British eliminated the French and Spanish from contention for trade and territory in the southeast. The outbreak of the American Revolutionary War put an end to the British hegemony and reopened another period of competitive relations as British and Americans contended for trade and strategic influence in the southeastern interior. The Spanish recaptured Florida and West Florida from the British, and after the war the Americans and Spanish vied for trade and political alliances among the major southeastern nations. The period 1777–95 saw the return of competitive geopolitical relations.

The Creek and Choctaw traded earliest with the Spanish in Florida, but within fifteen years after the establishment of Charles Town in 1670, the English started trading deep in the interior. During the late 1680's and 1690's, to alleviate labor shortages in the colony, the English assisted the Cherokee, the Creek, and the Chickasaw in conducting slave raids, often against the Choctaw, by supplying them with muskets and ammunition and offering bounties. After the French settled in Louisiana Colony in 1699 and established New Orleans (1718), they began supplying the Choctaw with weapons for their defense, an act that won them the enduring support of several major Choctaw iksa such as Kunsha, Chickasawhay, and the Six Towns. The volume of the Indian slave trade reached its peak at the time of the Yamasee War (1715–17). Indian slaves proved difficult to keep in captivity in their native country, and the English, more and more bent on expanding the fur trade, began sending Indian slaves to the Caribbean Islands and importing black slaves. But the slave trade had impressed upon the indigenous nations the need for reliable supplies of guns and ammunition: without such weapons, they could muster little defense in war and only weak resistance against slave raids.

The fur trade proved to be the primary economic relationship between the Indians and European colonists in the southeast throughout most of the eighteenth century. Deerskins, which the Indian women tanned and made into leather for export to Europe, were the primary item of trade, and the eastern indigenous nations were from early contact amenable to trading skins as well as furs and slaves for European manufactured goods such as guns, lead, powder, textiles, hatchets, hoes, needles, paint, glass beads, and axes.[1] It is reported that the Cherokee at first showed little interest in European goods other than guns and ammunition, but by 1690 most Cherokee villages were incorporated into the Charles Town trade.

European manufactured goods quickly replaced indigenously produced tools and implements that formerly had been made from stone, bone, clay, and flint. European metal goods, especially, were quickly found to be more efficient than the old stone and bone tools. With metal knives and hatchets for clearing fields, tasks that formerly took ten men now could be done more quickly by one man. The substitution of European manufactured goods for tools and implements led to the decline in the use of indigenous techniques of manufacture and increased the incentive to specialize by hunting furs and skins for trade. Thus the fur trade, far from introducing new skills or production techniques, created less self-sufficient and more economically specialized consumers of European products. The southeastern nations quickly lost the capability to reproduce the material basis of their own society and became dependent on exchange to satisfy their new material requirements.[2]

The widespread organization of the southeastern fur trade included import-export centers, intermediary trade posts, and periodic exchanges in the villages of the southeastern nations. The port cities of New Orleans, Charles Town, and to a lesser extent Pensacola were the major import-export entrepôts. Merchants in the port cities would import goods on credit from European manufacturers and extend goods on credit to traders and smaller merchants, who then either supplied traders with goods on credit or commissioned traders to transport goods to the villages in the interior. The traders with the help of hired men took the goods into the interior and bartered them for furs in local semiannual exchanges. The usual practice was to extend credit to the Indian hunters in the form of guns, ammunition, and supplies, during the fall before the coming winter and spring hunt, in return for which the hunters later repaid the trader in skins, and used any surplus to trade for supplies for their families.

It often happened, however, that a hunter would not return with enough skins to repay his debts, and so he would fall into a chronic debt relation with the trader. Often, too, traders used abusive means to try and collect their debts. The potentially hostile relations between traders and debtor hunters that developed were a source of conflict that periodically caused murders of traders by their hunter debtors, and sometimes led to full-scale war. The Yamassee War of 1715–17, for example, was precipitated by the actions of traders who tried to enslave members of the families of debtors as payment for debts. Throughout this period colonial officials attempted to regulate the fur trade in an effort to prevent war and the alienation of the hunters from the trade, and also to prevent the Indian nations from seeking trade and political alliances with a rival European trade partner.[3] European manufacturers were motivated to provide strong political support for fur trade interests in North America because the major share of the profits from the trade accrued to the export-import merchants and the European manufacturers.[4] The fur trade was the basis of many early North American fortunes, and profits from the trade also contributed to capital formation in Europe during the eighteenth century.

Incorporation in the fur trade markedly changed the material conditions of the southeastern nations. Not only did the indigenous nations lose their economic self-sufficiency, but after 1700, the hunters and their wives, who cured the skins, became increasingly specialized as laborers in the fur trade networks. Whereas Indians had formerly hunted mainly for food, taking only what they needed, now they hunted from fall to early spring not only for subsistence but to provide skins for the trade, spending considerably more time hunting than they had before contact with European colonists.[5] Nevertheless, although the fur trade commercialized and modified the economic division of labor, it did not introduce new class formations but only led to increased specialization within the preexisting division of labor; it did not introduce new production techniques or significantly new social relations of production. During most of the eighteenth century, only a few southeastern Indians became traders, and those who did traded largely as a substitute for hunting. The fur trade did not change southeastern economic orientations of subsistence or need. The southeastern hunters did not seek to maximize profits or material wealth in the market, nor did they share in the understandings or agreements that the Europeans had concerning the operation of the market mechanisms or the fluctuation of prices. The hunters preferred a standard set of exchanges of skins for goods and complained bitterly when the exchange rates of skins to goods were adjusted according to market demand and price.

The hunters did not fit well into the capitalist world of the merchants and traders. They hunted to obtain a set quantity of required goods and had no desire to maximize profits, so whenever the hunters' subsistence requirements were met, they ceased to trade skins. If the exchange rate of manufactured goods to skins was lowered, the Indians traded fewer skins, since a smaller quantity satisfied their material requirements. Lowering

the relative price for manufactured goods did not lead to more productivity in furs traded and more demand for manufactured goods but instead
led to less productivity and flat demand. The traders could force more
productivity from the hunters only by raising the relative exchange rate of
skins to manufactured goods, since more skins were required to satisfy the
basic subsistence needs for manufactured goods. The only real stimulus to
increased hunting was the increasing dependency on European goods.[6]

Profit making among Indians did not appear until after the American Revolution, in the 1780's and 1790's, when small groups of market-
oriented southeasterners, mostly families of traders who had intermarried
with Indian women, began to emulate the ways of the colonists. In the
matrilineal societies of the southeast, where children belonged to the kin
group of the mother, children of traders had immediate social and political
membership. Some traders strategically married into the lineages of local
chiefs in order to enhance their trade possibilities, and their children often
stood in line for positions of authority and political leadership. In many
cases the traders took little interest in their mixed-blood offspring and
the children grew up with Indian cultural orientations, but some traders
sought education for their children and taught them the trade business.
Many of the children of the traders adopted the profit motives of the trade
and a few received an education in the colonial settlements. Furthermore,
after the American Revolution many traders and disgruntled Tories retired
to the interior nations and started plantations with the use of black slave
labor. Thus by the last two decades of the eighteenth century small groups
of profit-oriented merchant-traders and plantation owners were emerging in the major southeastern nations.[7] The large majority of southeastern
Indians, however, still retained their traditional nonacquisitive subsistence
economic orientations.

Competitive Geopolitical Conditions, 1699–1763

The establishment of European colonies and the fur trade in North
America created new requirements for economic and political survival
among the indigenous eastern North American societies. Early European
rivalries for access and control over trade relations with the indigenous
nations soon developed into competition for control over the territory of
eastern North America. In the southeast, after the establishment of Louisiana Colony in 1699, a period of intense colonial competition arose when
the French attempted to implement a strategic plan to build a chain of forts
along the Mississippi River in order to gain control of the Mississippi Valley and thereby contain the English colonies at the eastern seaboard. The

French plan was carried out by forming political and economic alliances with the indigenous nations along the Mississippi River. The English, who could get cheaper, better quality goods from England than the French could from France, countered the French plan by sending traders to lure the indigenous nations away from alliance with the French by offering lower priced, better quality, and more abundant trade goods. Their superior trade position gave them a distinct advantage over the French in winning the economic and political allegiances of the indigenous nations. By treaty, between 1716 and 1730 the French bought English goods at Albany, but after this ceased, the French trade position steadily weakened. By the beginning of the French and Indian War, the English traders had driven the French trade from the Louisiana area.

Although during times of impending war both European powers extensively distributed gifts to attract Indian allies, the French, especially during the period 1700–1763, had to make annual distributions of gifts to loyal chiefs and warriors; during those years the Choctaw allies of the French were more mercenaries than traders.[8] The weak French trade enabled the Choctaw to obtain necessary guns through mercenary action primarily against the Chickasaw after 1730. It was, of course, cheaper for both French and English to hire Indian mercenaries than to bring armies from Europe. For the Indians, the gifts gained in diplomatic bargaining were an alternate source of manufactured goods that they ordinarily would have obtained by hunting and trading skins.

Thus, during the period of competition between the rival European colonial powers, the smaller, weaker indigenous nations were relegated to the role of politically, economically, and technologically dependent allies of one or the other European power. They were as nations focused on preserving political autonomy, and maintaining trade and defense against European powers and hostile indigenous nations. But even with this focus, there was no uniform centralization or differentiation of their polities. The responses of the four southeastern nations to the trade and geopolitical competition took place within their preexisting institutional frameworks without any significant differentiation or integration of the polity. The Cherokee adopted the most dramatic response, with political centralization around the central town of Chota in the early 1750's. The Creek response was effected through a strategy of neutrality, balance of power, and confederacy building in order to bolster strategic strength. The Choctaw were racked by civil war, regionalism, and internal political conflict. The Chickasaw, too, endured nearly constant warfare between 1730 and 1760 as a strategic English ally on the Mississippi River, but there was little significant change in Chickasaw political institutions.

CHEROKEE POLITICAL CENTRALIZATION

By 1715, trade relations between Carolina and the Cherokee were brisk and profitable. The Carolina officials, however, were hard pressed to work out satisfactory political and trade relations with the decentralized and shifting coalitions of Cherokee leaders and in vain sought to impose a central leader. Keowee, one of the seven Cherokee regional mother towns located in the lower towns, was considered influential, but in 1716 Carolina appointed as principal Cherokee chief the head priest of the village of Tugaloo, which was the holiest town in the Cherokee nation and the place where the Cherokee received the sacred fire from the Great Spirit; the head priest of Tugaloo was considered by the Cherokee the most influential man in the nation. After the death of that head priest in 1720, Carolina officials urged the Cherokee to select a principal chief, but the Cherokee declined and continued the traditional practice of making major decisions by consensus among the headmen of the sixty-odd towns.[9]

Between 1725 and 1752 Carolina recognized several different warriors as "emperor" of the Cherokee, but these men had only nominal political authority and recognition among the Cherokee themselves. In 1725 Carolina named as Cherokee principal chief the head warrior of the overhill village of Tennessee, who exercised little influence beyond the overhill villages. In 1730 Moytoy, the head warrior of Great Tellico, the central village of the valley towns, claimed the title of Cherokee emperor; Carolina did not recognize him until 1738, but after that, Chota, the mother town of the overhill towns, entered into competition with Tellico for national leadership.[10] In 1741 Moytoy was killed in a campaign against the Choctaw, and the English appointed Moytoy's young son, Ammonscossittie, as the new principal chief and the Raven of Hiwassee as regent. From then on until 1752 the English recognized a coalition of the two major villages from the valley towns, Hiwassee and Tellico, as the leadership of the nation. The overhill towns still continued to challenge the leadership of the valley towns, however, and between 1745 and 1748 Chota was engaged in negotiations with the French, hoping to force Carolina to recognize Chota's claim to national leadership. But lacking protection from marauding French allies, to whom they had allowed free access, the overhill towns were compelled to continue their alliance with the French.

The Cherokee gave the Hiwassee-Tellico coalition little recognition within their centralized political framework: the Hiwassee-Tellico leadership was an intermediary in trade and diplomatic negotiations with the English, and as such was no more than an English-imposed convenience. Cherokee political institutions still remained essentially local and decentralized. Between 1747 and 1751 the Cherokee were engaged in a prolonged war with the Creek that caused a severe shortage of trade goods and weapons. Because of the fighting, many Cherokee were unable to hunt and therefore were unable to pay their outstanding debts to the Carolina traders. The traders, under pressure from their merchant creditors, resorted to abusive measures to regain their investments. To exacerbate matters, the Carolina traders were supplying weapons and supplies to both the Creek and the Cherokee in the war. In the spring of 1751, three Cherokee villages plundered the goods of their resident traders, and, in a separate incident, a Carolina trader was killed by a Cherokee in a skirmish with the Creek. The Carolina traders fled the Cherokee country, and Carolina officials demanded payment for the plundered goods and for the death of the trader. In June 1751, Carolina imposed a trade embargo on the Cherokee villages, which left the villages critically short of military supplies needed to carry on the war with the Creek and with other adversaries.

During the embargo Chota tried to exploit anti-English sentiment among the lower Cherokee towns. Discontented villages from the lower towns were invited to resettle in the overhill region, and when it appeared that Chota could not reestablish trade relations with Carolina, the overhill towns sought alternative trade relations with Virginia, the Ohio traders, and the French.[11] In November 1751, the Raven of Hiwassee managed to get the trade embargo lifted and Carolina continued to recognize the warrior leadership of Tellico-Hiwassee. But because the Carolina traders were reluctant to return to the Cherokee country, the Cherokee remained desperately short of trade and military supplies.

In the spring of 1752, the Cherokee lower towns, under Tellico-Hiwassee leadership, were defeated and overrun by the Creek, and most of the people in the lower town villages migrated to the middle and overhill regions. The head chief of Chota, Old Hop, and the head warrior of the overhill towns thereupon proclaimed to Carolina that Chota was the "mother town" of the Cherokee nation and the legitimate political center. Most Cherokee villages now deferred to Chota's authority.[12] When Carolina officials continued to support the warrior leaders of Tellico and Hiwassee, Chota mustered warriors to fight in the English interest against the Choctaw; Chota leaders also cut their trade and political ties with the French and drove the French-allied northern warriors from the overhill towns. In the face of this opposition from rival Chota, Emperor Ammonscossittie of Tellico and Ostenaco, the head warrior of Hiwassee, began losing their influence and standing. The emperor had not managed to restore good trade relations with the English, and in late 1752 a general suspicion among the Cherokee that he had unlawfully ceded land to Virginia finally finished his political career. After February 1753, Cherokee national leadership was transferred from the head warriors of the valley towns to the head chief of Chota.

Chota consolidated control over national leadership in the spring of 1753. Ostenaco of Hiwassee began to participate in the Chota council, and the valley towns recognized Chota's leadership. The Cherokee villages delegated to Chota the power to negotiate trade and diplomatic relations for the entire nation, and after Chota made a trade agreement with Carolina, Old Hop, the aged and crippled head chief of Chota, was declared Cherokee emperor. Ammonscossittie and regional village centers were prohibited from engaging in diplomatic relations with foreign powers.[13]

With the centralization of management of foreign affairs in the hands of Chota, the head chief of Chota became the principal chief of the nation, and the second chief of Chota became the second chief of the nation. The head warrior of Chota was elevated to head warrior of the nation; the position of second head warrior of the nation was granted to Ostenaco of Hiwassee in order to incorporate the warrior leadership of Hiwassee and the valley towns into the new national government. The authority of the principal chief was dependent on the consensus and support of the Cherokee national council, which was composed of headmen from all the villages in the nation. Previously, the national council had met only under pressing circumstances, but under Chota's guidance the council met more regularly, and eventually annual meetings were held at Chota, where the national council gathered between the events of the annual Green Corn ceremony.

The Cherokee also delegated limited coercive powers to the new national government. Since a Carolina trade embargo exposed the Cherokee to military defeat and economic marginalization, the Cherokee responded by strengthening internal control over the actions of individuals and villages in the fur trade. After the trade embargo was lifted in 1751, the Cherokee national council held villages and individuals responsible for any actions that might threaten to disrupt trade relations with Carolina. Carolina held the Cherokee collectively responsible for the acts of a few villages, and the Cherokee strengthened internal coercive controls in order to prevent disruption of trade relations. Individual Cherokee were subject to prosecution and possible execution for the plundering or murder of traders.

With the delegation of limited coercive powers to the national government, the Cherokee polity took on a major characteristic of a state. The Cherokee national polity, however, did not adopt any new changes in internal or external differentiation. Regions and villages still retained control over local internal affairs. Priests still were consulted on issues of importance in national affairs, and the national council was composed of village headmen who decided national legislative, executive, and judicial issues by consensus; blood revenge and personal infractions remained in the hands of the clans, not the national or village governments.[14] In fact, the Chota leadership was unable to extend its control over blood revenge. After a border incident with Virginia frontiersmen that resulted in several Cherokee casualties, Chota could not prevent the relatives of the slain warriors from seeking revenge and attacking frontier settlements. Such retaliatory action ignited the Cherokee-English war of 1759–60.

Before 1760, the changes in the Cherokee polity involved limited centralization of coercive powers and no significant differentiation of the polity, and until Chota became the national center, the British-appointed national leaders did not have institutionalized support from the Cherokee villages. The centralization that took place was, however, largely a modification of the preexisting institutional order and a reinterpretation of the old symbolic order of the hierarchy of Cherokee mother towns.[15] The Cherokee villages delegated limited coercive authority and management of trade and diplomatic relations to the leadership of the symbolically centralized village of Chota, but the political centralization that occurred at Chota did not involve further differentiation of the polity.

CHOCTAW POLITICAL REGIONALIZATION

Within a few years after the establishment of Louisiana Colony in 1699, Choctaw villages allied with the French or the English. Kunsha and Chickasawhay in the late 1680's and 1690's had borne the brunt of the English slave raids; Chickasawhay was reduced from ten villages to one. The French supplied the two embattled Choctaw iksas with guns to defend themselves, and in return both Chickasawhay and Kunsha became ardent French allies, resistant to English trade overtures. By 1700, English traders had posts at Couechitto, the capital village, and Cushtushas, the central village of the western villages. The English allied villages attacked Chickasawhay and Kunsha, and the French moved to support their allies. The early pro-English coalition collapsed when its leader, Conshak Emiko, was killed by his brother and warriors from the iksas of Kunsha and Chickasawhay.

Until 1730 there were few independent trade goods among the Choctaw. The French distributed goods to faithful Choctaw leaders, favoring the recognized chiefs, who redistributed goods along kinship lines. Many men who did not have any official title thus had limited access to goods because of the weak French trade and the controlled distribution of goods engineered by the French colonial authorities. The French did attempt to centralize Choctaw political relations by offering the title of Choctaw principal chief, Mingo Chitto, to Chicaha Oulacta of Couechitto, on the assumption that he would distribute the annual French gifts to the rest of the chiefs. But the Choctaw looked upon the Mingo Chitto as merely one chief among many, and local and regional leaders commanded more deference than the Mingo Chitto. The Mingo Chitto and successors had little authority, and there was little political centralization around the principal chief during the 1700's.

Between 1730 and 1760, a primary means for the Choctaw to gain goods from the French was selling their services as mercenaries in the French wars against English allies, mainly against the Natchez and then against the Chickasaw. The French paid bounties for Natchez and Chickasaw scalps and provided guns and supplies for several major military campaigns against Chickasaw villages. In six years, between 1727 and 1732, the French destroyed the Natchez nation as punishment for refusing to pay taxes to the French. After some of the Natchez retreated to the protection of the Chickasaw, who refused to surrender them to the French, the French used the Choctaw against the Chickasaw, who not only were allies of the English but also occupied a strategic location along the Mississippi River. Between 1730 and 1760 the Choctaw and Chickasaw were in a nearly constant state of war.

Starting in the late 1720's, English traders began to make inroads into the Choctaw trade. The leading central iksa, led by Couechitto, preferred the cheaper, more abundant, and better quality English goods to the more expensive French goods.[16] Other villages, including Custusha, the major regional village of the western villages, objected to the presence of the English traders; briefly, when the French in 1731–32 were short of goods, many villages started to turn to the English trade, but this enthusiasm flagged after a Choctaw delegation led by Red Shoes, the head warrior of Couechitto, failed to negotiate an acceptable trade agreement with the English at Charles Town in 1734. A coalition of eastern villages led by Red Shoes worked out an agreement with English traders, two years later, but after the leaders of the western villages, including Alibamon Mingo, a prominent leader of Kunsha, decided to remain allied to the French as long as the French supplied enough goods, and after another failure with the English at Charles Town, Red Shoes and the pro-English villages returned to an alliance with the French.[17] The Choctaw delegation with Red Shoes was mainly dissatisfied with the gift system of the English, and many villages deserted the coalition. Red Shoes had to restore himself to alliance with the French by helping lead the Choctaw in a major campaign against the Chickasaw in 1739.

The alliance with the French was an uneasy one, however. The French-appointed chiefs had little authority, and local political allegiances took precedence over regional or national loyalties. Between 1744 and 1748, the War of Austrian Succession, or King George's War as it was called in North America, disrupted the ability of the French to import trade goods, and the Choctaw became increasingly dissatisfied with the French trade. In 1744 Red Shoes of Couechitto again sought English trade, and in 1745 Alibamon Mingo of Kunsha, who generally favored French trade, also looked to secure English trade relations. By 1746, with the French unable to supply the Choctaw with trade, all but two villages had sought trade and political alliance with the English. But the return of French trade at the end of King George's War in 1748, together with unreliable English trade, led about half of the Choctaw villages to renew trade and political alliance with the French.[18] Meanwhile, civil war erupted in 1747, when the pro-English Red Shoes had three French traders killed for attempting to seduce his wife. The French authorities demanded retaliation, and in the summer of 1747 Red Shoes was assassinated. During the civil war, the English-allied villages were chronically undersupplied with weapons and ammunition, and they were defeated by the end of 1750.

Three major iksa formed the nucleus of victorious French allies in the Choctaw civil war—Six Towns, Chickasawhay, and Kunsha. The three iksa formed the major portion of the Okla Hannali district, one of three geopolitical districts that emerged during the war. The remnant of the central iksa of Taboka, formerly led by Couechitto, formed a second district in the northeastern part of the nation.[19] The northeastern district claimed the traditional right of having its district chief considered the nominal principal chief of the nation. The northwest district, Okla Falaya, was formed by a remnant of the ancient Immoklusha iksa and the Okla Falaya iksa. All three districts were politically autonomous and mutually hostile. Each had a chief, and the three chiefs were accorded equal rank, although only the principal chief could call a national council composed of the three district chiefs and local iksa leaders. Choctaw national political relations remained decentralized and locally particularistic.

The shifting alliances among the Choctaw villages and local iksa continued through the French and Indian War. After the Choctaw civil war the French trade rates were high and the French demand for skins was limited. By 1752, about twenty villages again were friendly to the English. Between 1754 and 1756 the Choctaw were divided between villages that wished to carry on trade with the English and other villages that wished to attack the Chickasaw villages in the French interest. With the outbreak of the war, a British blockade prevented the French from supplying their allies adequately with trade, and by the spring of 1757 the English-allied villages were actively seeking English trade. The Okla Hannali district

and most of the western villages favored the French, while the northeastern villages and a few western villages allied with the English. The two
opposing Choctaw coalitions engaged in open military conflict during the
war, although after the British blockade took effect and cut off the flow
of French trade goods, the entire Choctaw nation was forced to seek an
alliance with the British.[20]

During the period of competitive geopolitical and trade relations between 1699 and 1760, the Choctaw displayed political decentralization
and internal political cleavages, and occasionally engaged in civil war. The
major change in Choctaw political organization was the formation of three
regional political districts, based on the old iksas, each with a head chief
and council. But the three political districts, though they were a more in-
clusive form of national political organization than the ancient collection
of iksas, did not represent a major change in national political unity or
organization. Choctaw political identities and loyalties still were regional
and locally particularistic. Thus, the Choctaw polity in the competitive
colonial period remained embedded in kinship or local iksa relations and
did not institutionalize any significant political differentiation.

CHICKASAW STRATEGIC SURVIVAL

As early as 1673 the Chickasaw had acquired weapons of European,
probably Spanish, manufacture, and by the 1690's they were engaged in
trade with the eastern English colonies. The French, too, recognized the
Chickasaw as one of the most powerful indigenous nations in the region,
and between 1699 and 1730 the Chickasaw were subject to both British
and French attentions for political alliance and trade.[21] The Chickasaws'
location near the Mississippi River made them vital to French interests as
one link in a chain of indigenous nations whose support the French needed
in order to gain control of and maintain access to the Mississippi Valley.
The British colonies attempted to disrupt the French plan by establishing
trade and political alliances with both the Choctaw and the Chickasaw.

The rebellion of the Natchez against the French, and the destruction of
the Natchez nation by the French and their allies the Choctaw, brought
the Chickasaw into protracted warfare with the French and the Choctaw
after a group of Natchez fled to Chickasaw territory for protection. For 30
years, starting in 1730, the Chickasaw traded with and were supplied with
weapons by the British, while the French supplied weapons and goods
to the Choctaw to be used against the Chickasaw. To protect themselves
against raids on isolated villages, the Chickasaw fortified their villages at
a single defensive location, and they were successful against their joint
Choctaw-French enemies in four major campaigns—1736, 1739, 1752,
and 1753.[22]

The Chickasaw were at times hard pressed and often divided about how to respond to the steady military pressures of their enemies. Between 1737 and 1743 one group of Chickasaw, including many Natchez, migrated to the protection of their Creek allies, to a location near the English trade entrepôt at Abihka, the leading white town among the upper town Creek. There the Chickasaw and Natchez formed the Breed town or Naucee town, which was incorporated into the Creek confederacy. One group of Chickasaw, led by a coalition from the Land Tortoise iksa, which had political and kinship ties to the second principal war chief of the nation, favored making peace and alliance with the French and Choctaw in order to relieve the constant military pressures, but in general throughout the period of intense warfare that lasted until 1760, the Chickasaw maintained trade and political alliances with the English.[23]

The Chickasaw suffered significant casualties in the wars and skirmishes; at one period, in the early 1740's, there were only several hundred warriors left. During the early 1750's the Chickasaw were under constant siege by the Choctaw and/or French. Between 1753 and 1756 the attacks were so strong that the Chickasaw could not hunt safely, and, having no skins to trade, could not get weapons and supplies from the English traders. In 1754 the Chickasaw were so discouraged that plans were made to dissolve the nation: three villages would settle among the upper town Creek, and the other four villages would settle among the overhill Cherokee towns. The Chickasaw remained in their home territory, however, though by 1758 they were reduced to a handful of men, and were wholly dependent on English gifts for their defense.[24] Relief came only after the French were defeated in the French and Indian War at the end of 1759. The establishment of British political and trade hegemony during the 1760's brought an end to the conflicts with the Choctaw and the French.

There was little change in Chickasaw political institutions during the competitive period. The Chickasaw villages did show a stronger sense of military unity during the competitive period 1699–1760 than did the other southeastern nations, but the Chickasaw, like the other southeastern nations, had some internal political differences in strategy over whether to make peace with the French or to remain allied with the English. Yet the Chickasaw national unity cannot be attributed solely to external military pressures; rather the unity may have come from their national religious ceremonies, national chiefs, and national military leaders, which were an essential part of the Chickasaw phratry and iksa structure. One can say that, although the Chickasaw showed a capacity for national unity under intense military pressure, there is little evidence of change in the internal or external differentiation of the Chickasaw polity, which remained embedded in local kinship groups. The Chickasaw defensive military unification was achieved within the preexisting institutional order.

CREEK CONFEDERACY BUILDING

The early Creek response to trade and European colonization was to formulate a strategy of confederacy building and balance of power among the contending Spanish, French, and English colonial powers. This confederacy building expanded the confederacy but it did not alter the nondifferentiated features of the Creek national polity, nor did it lead to increased centralization of coercive power. Villages or groups of tribal towns were incorporated into the confederacy and assumed a town color—red or white. The confederacy did not interfere with internal village government, and often the new tribal groups had different languages, customs, ceremonies, and ethnic ties from those of the Muskogee nation, the central nation of the Creek confederacy. The incorporated tribes, while keeping their customs and local governmental structures, usually adopted Creek village government forms and ranks and participated in the national government according to Creek political culture and institutions. The process of confederacy building merely added more segmentary units, or tribal towns, to an already culturally ordered segmentary structure.[25] The competitive colonial period intensified conflict between the leading Creek villages, but this conflict took place within the preexisting institutional framework and therefore was routine. There were no civil wars, as there were among the Choctaw, and much of the conflict and competition was engaged by the leaders of the central red and white towns, falling within the boundaries of political conflict and segmentary autonomy within the preexisting political order.

During the 1600's and 1700's the Creek confederate council met irregularly, or not at all if there was no pressing need. Often not all the towns were present at the meetings. The members of the Creek confederacy agreed not to make war on one another. After 1700, however, the confederacy gravitated toward a defensive diplomatic alliance, although the towns that composed the confederacy remained locally independent and the union did not obligate towns or regions to come to the defense of Creek towns that were under attack.

According to the oral tradition, when the Muskogee migrated into the Georgia region, they encountered the Apalachicola, a people who spoke the Hitchiti language. After conquering the Apalachicola, the Muskogee incorporated them into their confederacy. The villages of the Apalachicola or Hitchiti towns became white towns and were assigned leadership among the Creek lower towns during times of peace. The villages of Sawokla, Okmulgee, Oconee, and Apalachicola were the central white towns of the lower town Creek and were closely associated with the Cussetah, the major Muskogee white town. Cussetah and the Hitchiti white towns competed for political leadership with Coweta, the major red town among the lower town Creek. Other towns or groups of tribal towns that joined the Creek were Tuckabatchee, Pakane, Okchai, the Alabama towns, Natchez, Shawnee, Tuskegee, and the Koasati towns. Pakane, Okchai, some of the Alabama towns, Tuskegee, and Koasati towns became white towns; Tuckabatchee and perhaps some of the Alabama towns became red towns. The Natchez were closely associated with Abihka, a major white town, and the Shawnee were associated with Coosa, another major white town, so most likely the Shawnee and Natchez participated in the Creek confederacy as white towns.[26] Many of the towns, including the Hitchiti, Yuchi, and Shawnee villages, spoke different languages and had different customs from those of the Muskogee towns, but within the scope of the confederacy each incorporated town was allowed to maintain its own local customs, and some groups like the Yuchis and Shawnee retained considerably different cultural traditions from those of the other towns.

The confederacy after 1700 was composed of a variety of ethnic and cultural groups. These groups retained considerable autonomy but were incorporated into the confederacy, and they adopted Creek symbolic political order and Creek town government. The confederacy was not a political nationality, however, political commitments to Creek national government did not take precedence over village and kinship commitments and allegiances. Nevertheless, the Creek confederacy was culturally and normatively integrated by shared culture and shared understandings of proper political relations and political order. The symbolic division between red and white towns defined political relations and functions, and specific leading red and white towns claimed political leadership.

A major turning point in Creek confederacy building came in the aftermath of the Yamasee War in 1715. The Creek and their allies were defeated in the war, and the lower town Creek retreated from central Georgia westward to the Chattahoochee River. There several other nations joined the Creek. After the Yamasee War, the Creek, led by Coweta, attempted to implement a strategy of confederacy building and also attempted to play the role of neutral middlemen in a balance of power strategy between the contending European colonies.[27]

If the oral tradition is correct in recounting the traditional political supremacy of the white towns, in times of peace, then already in the early contact period the Creek polity showed a corruption or disaggregation of the old relations and duties of the Creek towns. The major lower white towns, Cussetah and Apalachicola, were active in the 1670–1760 period, but they were eclipsed in the colonial records by the activity of Coweta, the major red town among the lower towns. Apalachicola, the leading village of the Hitchiti white towns, had alliances with the Spanish, and at times the lower Creek were divided into competing alliances with the English and the Spanish. For example, in 1742 the English demanded the head of the chief of Apalachicola because of the Spanish influence among the Apalachicola villages. The strong anti-English sentiment persisted among the Apalachicola into the late 1750's, although at the same time Cussetah, the major white town, and Coweta favored harmonious relations with the English. The English accentuated the leadership role of Coweta by recognizing the headman of Coweta as emperor (a title of English creation) of the Creek. The title did not give Coweta coercive powers over the other Creek villages, however, and in fact the leaders of Coweta resigned the title in 1763; it was simply an attempt by the English to cement Creek trade and political alliance and to centralize negotiations with one leader in order to make relations with the numerous decentralized Creek villages somewhat easier.[28]

Among the upper towns, the white towns were politically predominant throughout the 1700–1763 period of competitive geopolitical relations. From at least 1700, and probably earlier, until 1746 the leading village was Abihka, an ancient principal white town and close associate to Coosa, another ancient white town; in 1708, Oakfuskie, a white town, was the leading village among the Tallapoosas, the most eastern group of upper Creek towns. These three white towns led the Creeks in the peace treaty negotiations of 1717 with the English after the Yamasee War, and during the 1730's the council of the upper Creek towns met at Abihka. Although Abihka attempted to assert its leadership and authority in order to prevent losses of land to the English (1733–35), the Abihkas in the years 1718–38 generally preferred trade and alliance with the English; some of the other upper towns, like the Alabama towns near the French Fort Toulouse, often favored alliance with the French. But while Abihka led the upper town Creek, between 1700 and 1746, it was successful in maintaining neutrality and a trade alliance with the English, and the town itself was in the 1740's a trade entrepôt for English goods that were carried to the Choctaw and Chickasaw.

Abihka's dominance ended after 1746, when the Gun Merchant, who was chief of the white town of Okchai, emerged as leader of the Creek upper towns; for the next ten years Okchai was unchallenged as the central upper Creek town. In 1754, on the eve of the French and Indian War, Abihka remained loyal to the English; the leadership of Okchai was split over allying with the French—as favored by Mortar, the head war chief of Okchai and brother-in-law to the Gun Merchant—or with the English, as favored by those of the upper town Creek chiefs who wished not to take any side at all. In August 1756, the Wolf of the village of Muccolossus, one of those who urged neutrality, was heralded as the new chief of the upper towns in place of the Gun Merchant of Okchai. The Wolf of Muccolossus attempted to steer a path of neutrality and open trade with the English, but the Alabamas and Mortar of Okchai turned to an alliance with the French. Mortar was strongly fundamentalist in his opposition to European influence over the Creek and was generally anti-English. After the defeat of the French in the French and Indian War, Mortar of Okchai claimed leadership of the upper Creek towns and evinced a strong anti-British sentiment. Okchai led the upper Creek towns, but did so in conjunction with Oakfuskie and Little Talisee, both white towns led by prominent men.[29] The leadership of the upper towns follows the traditional ideal: the white towns were predominant politically, while the red towns remained in the background.

During the period of geopolitical competition, 1700–1763, the Creek did not institutionalize any major changes in political differentiation or in increased national political solidarity. The strategy of confederacy building involved the symbolic and loose political incorporation of foreign tribal towns, a procedure that conformed to the already segmentary institutional organization of the Creek confederacy, and though there were struggles for leadership, these struggles did not modify organizational principles: internal political relations and conflict among the Creek followed the traditional pattern of antagonism between red and white towns, and the white towns remained politically dominant in the upper towns. The rise of Coweta, the major red town in the lower towns, violated the rank order between red and white town political leadership, but though Coweta's assumption of leadership broke with the past, it did not involve a change in the differentiation of the Creek polity; it was simply a variation on an ancient political pattern.

British Hegemony

The defeat of the French in the French and Indian War at Quebec in late 1759 opened the way for the extension of British military influence over eastern North America. At the conclusion of the Seven Years War in Europe the British were granted control over Canada and the territory east of the Mississippi River, and during the fourteen years between 1763 and 1777 England was the primary colonial power with which the eastern indigenous nations negotiated trade and diplomatic relations. Under the conditions of colonial competition, the English had vied with the French and the Spanish for political alliance and trade with the indigenous nations, and in the competitive situation the indigenous nations had held a relatively favorable strategic bargaining position. With the French and Spanish effectively out of the colonial picture, the indigenous nations lost their bargaining position, which had been an effective means of gaining political and economic concessions from the Europeans. Moreover, British political and trade domination over eastern North America posed a direct threat to the political autonomy of the indigenous nations, in the form of military occupation of their territory, the imposition of British laws and administrative control, and the encouragement of western expansion by settlers and land speculators.

Between 1760 and 1763, the indigenous nations, alarmed at what lay in store under British trade and political hegemony, made some attempts to organize a military confederacy against the British. The southern nations, led by Mortar of the Creek, considered an alliance against the British, but the Cherokee, who had been defeated by the English in 1760–61, were reluctant to take up arms again, and war broke out between the upper town Creek and the formerly French-allied Choctaw. In the north, the rebellion of an anti-British confederation led by Pontiac was quelled in 1763, and thereafter the northern nations did not oppose the British with open military force.

Many of the fears of the indigenous nations were realized during the period of British hegemony. The British occupied the old French forts in the interior, regulated the trade in powder and lead, and curtailed the distribution of gifts that had been necessary to gain alliances during com- petitive times. Now the British insisted that the Indians gain all their trade goods by hunting and trapping, under an exchange rate that varied accord- ing to supply and demand on the market. Land encroachments by colonial settlers and land speculators became a constant source of contention and a major threat to the political autonomy of the indigenous nations, primarily the Creek and Cherokee but to some extent also of the more isolated Chickasaw and Choctaw. British manufacturers with fur trade interests in North America were powerful enough to influence imperial policy and caused the issuance of an order in 1763 that restricted settlements east of the Allegheny Mountains. This policy was supposed to protect the in- digenous nations from settler encroachments, thereby preventing a costly outbreak of war with the Indians, but it also, of course, protected the labor supplies of the traders and merchants who depended on the Indian hunters and trappers.

The policy of constraining settler expansion was a failure. Settlers streamed into the trans-Appalachian territories, and after 1765 relations between the colonists and the Indian nations deteriorated steadily as settlers encroached on hunting territory, destroyed game, and threatened the basis of the fur trade economy.[30] The increasingly rebellious colonies were willing to sacrifice the fur trade in favor of settler and agrarian ex- pansion. In 1774 the British attempted to implement a policy of direct administration of the Indian nations, but the outbreak of the American Revolutionary War and the associated return of competitive political conditions prevented the plan from making significant inroads.

The brief period of British hegemony put the southeastern nations under the trade relations of a single colonial power. The British demanded that the Indian hunters pay their own way in the fur trade and that the nations be collectively responsible for property and personal injury to traders and British citizens. In particular, the British put pressure on the Indian nations to punish murderers of traders. This pressure induced the Indian nations to try and extend national governmental control over the previously autonomous clan administration of cases of murder, but despite British efforts and coercion, the southeastern nations did not permanently abandon the clan and kinship administration of cases of murder, and there were only sporadic and coercive attempts to control blood revenge in order to satisfy the British demands. The Cherokee made the most concerted attempt to gain national control of the blood revenge mechanism as applied to British citizens, but the attempt was disrupted by the outbreak of the American Revolution and did not become institutionalized. The most significant long-term change among the southeastern nations was the increased secularization of Cherokee, Choctaw, and Chickasaw social and political institutions; the Creek, on the other hand, remained strongly attached to their nonsecular social and political institutions. In general, the British did not carry out plans to "civilize" or change the institutional order of the Indian nations. Rather, British policy sought to preserve the Indians as a cheap source of labor for the fur trade industry.

Throughout the period of British hegemony, the Cherokee were pressured by colonial land encroachments and a decline in colonial interest in the fur trade. The ceding of land to the colonists by Cherokee chiefs exacerbated internal political cleavages among the Cherokee. The national leadership favored land cessions as a means of paying off trade debts and avoiding military confrontation with the colonies, for they were convinced that a challenge to British colonial power would lead to military defeat, disruption, and the possible destruction of the whole Cherokee nation. When warriors of several villages opposed the cession of hunting land, the Cherokee leaders moved to exert stronger internal control so as to prevent unauthorized acts that might disrupt peaceful relations with the colonies. In 1759 the Cherokee became involved in a brief war with the British after the relatives of several men slain on the Virginia frontier defied the national Cherokee government at Chota and attacked settlers to get blood revenge. The Cherokee were defeated and many of their villages were destroyed. The Cherokee national council then imposed sanctions against violators of treaty agreements with the colonists. To restrain the warriors and curb the autonomy of blood revenge, the national council brought the warriors into the national decision-making process and invested the national Head Warrior with priestly powers, that is, the Head Warrior assumed judicial powers formerly held by priests, and he could use religiously sanctioned coercive power to restrain and punish violators of the treaties with the British. After the 1760's, the role of the priests in Cherokee society was reduced to nonpolitical and local activities such as conjuring, doctoring, and leading ceremonies. The Cherokee national government usurped the symbols of religious legitimation in order to promote sociopolitical integration and to legitimate internal coercive control and punishment of treaty violators, whose acts threatened the safety of the collective Cherokee nation by provoking retaliation from the increasingly powerful British colonial governments.[31]

Chota formalized and consolidated its leadership during the period of British hegemony. Nevertheless, despite the centralization of coercive powers over treaty violators and the secularization associated with the exclusion of the priests and conjurors from political decision making, the Cherokee national polity remained largely a confederacy of symbolically ranked towns. Chota managed trade and diplomatic relations, but the Cherokee regions and villages retained much of their traditional autonomy, and the national council continued to require unanimous agreement among the village headmen for binding decisions.[32]

The imposition of British hegemony put a temporary curb on internal political warfare among the Choctaw. The three independent Choctaw geopolitical districts—Ahepat Okla, Okla Falaya, and Okla Hannali—which had emerged during the French and Indian War were still antagonistic toward one another, the northeastern district being pro-English and the formerly French-allied western and southern districts being only reluctantly reconciled to the new geopolitical situation. Ancient iksa with head villages and daughter towns tended to decentralize as formerly dependent towns asserted greater independence, which was recognized by the British. (A major exception was the southern Six Towns iksa, which remained well integrated into the nineteenth century.) The trend toward local village autonomy continued through the 1760's and 1770's. Choctaw political leadership became more fragmented and competitive; the civil chiefs lost authority, and the distinction between war chiefs and hereditary chiefs became blurred.[33]

After 1763, the British insisted that the Choctaw hunt for their trade goods and not depend on the British to supply their needs in diplomatic exchanges, as they had done during the earlier period. Nevertheless the Choctaw principal chief continued to ask the British for goods, since the distribution of goods had long been the primary means by which the Choctaw leaders extended influence over the warriors. Moreover, by the 1770's, game was becoming increasingly scarce in Choctaw country, and the Choctaw were compelled to begin hunting more extensively west of the Mississippi River in order to supply their subsistence and trade requirements.[34]

As in the Cherokee case, there are reports of the increasing secularization of Choctaw social and political institutions in the 1770's. The Choctaw were adhering less and less to strict religious and moral prescription, even to the performance of the Green Corn ceremony, which was the annual means of atonement and purification.[35] Although many traditional norms and rituals continued to be practiced by local groups and individuals, national religious ceremonies declined. There was, however, no significant differentiation of the national polity from kinship and local political organization, and the Choctaw continued to adhere to local and regional political loyalties over national political loyalties and commitments. Except for the increased secularization of the national polity and the national political leadership, the Choctaw polity remained decentralized and nondifferentiated.

For the Chickasaw, the period of British hegemony brought relief at last from the incessant military onslaughts of the French and their Indian allies; but the British hegemony also brought an end, as it did for the other southeastern nations, to diplomatic gifts and mercenary employment. During the 1760's and 1770's, the Chickasaw were divided into two major political coalitions, both based on kinship-affiliated groupings. As before, the Land Tortoise iksa was the main opposition to the pro-English iksas and leaders. Although kinship and political organization remained nondifferentiated, the selection of the principal chief became more rationalized, because the principal chief was no longer hereditary in the Tiger or Panther iksa, and the largest iksa now held the highest command.[36]

Chickasaw social institutions were also shedding their strict religious prescriptive orientations. The English trader James Adair observed that by the 1760's the strength of the early Chickasaw sacred law had subsided, but the people were still materially supporting the livelihood of a group of old beloved men or religious specialists, who argued that they deserved to be supported by the labor of others because their services prevented the young from violating the sacred customs and bringing misfortune to the community. According to Adair, religious fasts and purifications were becoming shorter, and social dances longer. The practice of sacrificing the first deer of the hunting season to the deity was kept by only a few who adhered strongly to the old religious prescriptions. But the Chickasaw still continued in the 1770's the tradition of celebrating a national

Green Corn festival in a sacred village square whenever the entire nation could be gathered. Adair attributed the corruption and disintegration of the Chickasaw's early strict religious and normative order to the influence of the traders, who had lived among the southeastern nations since the early 1700's.[37]

The Creek, on the other hand, adhered strongly to their old religion and institutions and in general exhibited a much stronger adherence to cultural and institutional orthodoxy than did the other southeastern nations. With the establishment of British hegemony in 1763, Coweta, the leading red town of the lower Creek towns, resigned the British-recognized title of Creek emperor, and from then until 1777, the white towns of Cussetah, Okmulgee, and Apalachicola asserted leadership over the lower towns. Coweta, the central red town, remained important, but it played a secondary role to the leadership of the white towns. In the upper towns, the white town, Okchai, was the leading town until 1766, led by the pro-English Gun Merchant and his brother-in-law, the anti-English Mortar or Head Warrior of Okchai, and it remained an important town until the middle 1770's, despite the British having appointed Emisteseguo of Little Talisee as leader of the upper town Creek. Little Talisee was a white town and a daughter town of Coosa, the ancient central white town, and the British had hoped that by appointing Emisteseguo they could undermine the influence of Mortar of Okchai. A war with the Choctaw over hunting territory along the Tombigbee River diverted the attention of Mortar and other anti-British Creek of the upper towns from 1765 to 1774. Mortar of Okchai complained that game was declining and that the Creek needed cheaper prices for the trade.[38] Mortar of Okchai led the Creek into the Choctaw hunting grounds on the Tombigbee River, whereupon the southern Choctaw district made war on the Creek in order to protect their increasingly scarce hunting resources. Meanwhile, the upper Creek towns were meeting at Emisteseguo's village at Little Talisee; other prominent upper towns and leaders were Handsome Fellow of Oakfuskie and Duvall's landlord of Paccantalhassee, both white towns. Tuckabatchee, the main red town of the upper Creek towns, remained in the background.

The British, for their part, began to act as if the loose confederacy of villages formed a well integrated collective Creek nationality. In particular, British officials held the entire nation responsible for the murder of British citizens and for the loss of property of British traders and threatened to withdraw trade if the Creek did not cooperate. In 1766 the Creek, under Emisteseguo as British-appointed leader, suspended blood revenge against the British, and Emisteseguo assumed responsibility for the execution of Creek murderers of British citizens. Creek law in the 1760's, however, forbade the execution of a murderer without the permission of the clan of the murderer; if a man was executed without the consent of his clan, the executioners themselves would be subject to blood retaliation. Therefore, the Creek could centralize coercive power in the national government with respect to murderers of British citizens only to the extent that the clans agreed to give up their blood revenge prerogatives.

With these constraints in force, it was unlikely that the attempt to centralize limited internal control over blood revenge would lead to permanent change in the Creek polity. Though Emisteseguo had enough influence in the upper Creek towns to enforce the execution of murderers of British citizens, he had very little influence in the lower Creek towns, certainly not enough to control blood revenge. In 1773, while the upper Creek towns were engaged in war with the Choctaw and in need of British trade goods, the lower Creek towns refused to execute a member of the tiger clan who had killed a British trader. The upper Creek towns threatened Coweta with war if the execution did not take place, thereby precipitating a trade embargo by the British. After Coweta, a town with many tiger clansmen, refused to execute the murderer, Cussetah carried out the execution, though that alienated Coweta and swung its political orientation strongly against the British. The start of the American Revolutionary War and the end of British hegemony, however, effectively concluded this phase of suspending clan blood revenge in deference to British pressures, and the prerogatives of blood revenge returned to their former status.[39]

Thus, despite a few temporary deviations, there were no major institutionalized changes in the Creek polity during the period of British hegemony. Even the reported secularization of the polity among the Cherokee, the Choctaw, and the Chickasaw was absent among the Creek. More than the other major southeastern nations, the Creek showed continuity and adherence to prescriptive norms and religious values. The Creek national council and village councils continued to convene and transact business in the sacred square of one of the prominent towns, where, according to Creek belief, the watchful eye of the Great Spirit could guide the decisions of the prophets and seers and, in turn, of the town chiefs.[40]

Thus the period 1763–77 was one of reassertion of leadership by the white towns among the Creek—that is to say, a reassertion of the traditional leadership roles between the red and white towns. There were many political cleavages and there was considerable competition for political leadership, especially from the anti-British Mortar of Okchai and, after 1773, from disaffected Coweta, but the competition for leadership took place within the segmentary political order of the Creek polity. No leader proposed an alternative political structure or rallied resources and support

for establishing a new form of government. The Creek merely reestablished their traditional institutional framework as a response to British
political and trade hegemony.

Competitive Geopolitical Conditions, 1777–95

With the outbreak of the American Revolution, competitive geopolitical
conditions returned to eastern North America. Military conflict resumed
with Lord Dunmore's War in 1774, which was followed by the American
Revolutionary War and a period of intermittent border wars between 1783
and 1795. During those years many of the eastern indigenous nations were
caught up in almost constant warfare. Even after the Revolutionary War
was ended, the new American republic was embroiled in strategic competition with the English and Spanish colonies, while the indigenous nations
tried to preserve territorial and political autonomy within the context of
American and European trade and strategic rivalries. Between 1782, when
the Spanish recaptured the Floridas from the English, and 1794, the Spanish tried to control access to the Mississippi Valley as a way of cutting off
American commerce and slowing down American expansion west of the
Alleghenies. Part of the Spanish strategy was to gather the major southeastern nations into a military alliance that would block American territorial
expansion, and to that end the Spanish supplied the southeastern nations
with weapons and goods in order to support their resistance to American
settler encroachments. The Spanish also built forts in the southeast and
made overtures to western settler communities in Kentucky and Tennessee
in order to lure the settlers away from American political ties.[41]

The new American confederation, with meager financial resources and
little strength, could neither curb settler encroachments onto Indian territory nor field consistent military or diplomatic campaigns against the
Spanish colony in Florida or the English in Canada or their Indian allies.[42]
By 1787 the American confederation was drifting into a general border
war with the Indian nations, and it was also faced with possible defections
of frontier settlements in Kentucky and Vermont for alliances with the
Europeans. But in 1789 the new American constitution centralized more
power in the federal government, which made it possible to carry out
more unified strategic, trade, and military policies with the Indian nations
and to compete more effectively with the Spanish and English colonies in
trade, diplomatic, and military matters.

The end of the competitive period came in 1795, when both Spain
and England began to withdraw military support from their Indian allies.
Between 1790 and 1794 the United States mustered three major military
campaigns in the old northwest territory. After defeat in the first two

campaigns, an American army claimed victory against a confederation of western Indian nations at the Battle of Fallen Timbers in 1794. The English declined to give direct military aid to their Indian allies during the battle, and in late 1794 the English agreed to Jay's Treaty, which stipulated that the English withdraw from the forts they occupied in the northwest. Without English military and material support, the Indian nations of the old northwest were forced to treat with the United States and make political and territorial concessions. The southern nations also were forced to curtail overt military opposition to American expansion when the Spanish withdrew material support.[43] War with Napoleon in Europe consumed Spanish resources and attention. The withdrawal of the English and the Spanish from trade and strategic competition in eastern North America left the Indian nations without the European allies they needed to carry on active opposition to the American expansion.

During the period of intermittent warfare between 1777 and 1795, the major trend in political organization among the major southeastern nations was the gradual increase in political secularization among the Cherokee, the Choctaw, and the Chickasaw; the Creek still remained resistant to political secularization. But the return of competitive geopolitical relations after 1775, rather than leading to increased political centralization among the southeastern nations, led, on the contrary, to increased internal political conflict as decentralized and segmentary units allied themselves with competing powers. Only in the Creek case did a leader in the years after the American Revolutionary War propose an alternative to the preexisting political order, and this proposed change did not lead to the institutionalization of a more differentiated or centralized Creek polity. The southeastern polities remained decentralized, and there were no significant trends toward political integration or differentiation.

Among the Cherokee, Chota had centralized leadership over trade and diplomatic relations and asserted limited control over blood revenge in the period before the American Revolutionary War. It had restrained Cherokee warriors from attacking settlers who located on Cherokee hunting territory. Cherokee political unity and Chota's political authority were shattered in April 1776, when a dissident coalition of Cherokee towns and warriors decided to attack American settlements. Though the Chota leadership urged neutrality in the impending American rebellion, a group of war chiefs saw the conflict as an opportunity to drive back encroaching colonists from Cherokee territory.[44] In retaliation for the Cherokee attack, the four surrounding colonies destroyed the lower and middle Cherokee towns. In the spring of 1777, the lower, middle, and overhill towns, reasserting their right to make treaties, independently made peace with the colonists. Chota never regained its central leadership role in Cherokee society. Though it was recognized as the head village of the nation until 1788, its effective influence was confined to the overhill towns.

Most Cherokee villages favored neutrality during the American Revolutionary War, but a minority coalition of warrior leaders and villages, the Chickamaugas, preferred to ally with the British. Five villages at first—the five lower towns—and eventually eleven villages in all withdrew from the Cherokee national council and, supported by both English and Spanish supplies, became English allies and engaged in intermittent warfare with American settlers throughout the war period and up until 1795. Tories and English traders joined the Chickamauga raids against the American settlements in present-day Kentucky and Tennessee. Many of the Tories intermarried among the Chickamauga and their offspring were to play important roles in Cherokee political relations during the early 1800's.

The Chickamauga towns waged war independently against the American settlers; the Cherokee national council took no responsibility for Chickamauga actions and ceased to recognize the Chickamauga as part of the Cherokee nation. The annual national festivals at Chota lapsed, and by the middle 1780's the local villages performed the Green Corn ceremonies without national coordination from Chota. The Cherokee national council met only in crisis situations, and its power was limited to specific decisions that required unanimous agreement from the participating villages. It had no control over blood revenge, in part because relatives of warriors slain in the border skirmishes often joined the hostilities merely as a way of satisfying revenge obligations and for no other reason. This failure to control the autonomy of blood revenge was an essential aspect of the weakening of internal political influence and national unity that had been maintained by the Cherokee national council.[45]

Chota did what it could to try and keep the Chickamauga villages from raiding American settlers, and it persuaded most Cherokee villages to maintain neutrality, but its influence came to an end when the principal chief, Corn Tassel, and several other national leaders were assassinated by American frontiersmen in 1788. This event precipitated the abandonment of Chota and the overhill towns for safer terrain in present-day northwestern Georgia. Many relatives of the leading Cherokee lineages joined the Chickamaugas and sought revenge against the Americans.

After 1788, the Cherokee national council was reestablished at Ustanali, one of the seven mother towns from the pre-1750's lower towns region. The national council elected Little Turkey principal chief. Little Turkey was not a member of the Chota leadership, and after 1788 the Cherokee no longer elected the principal chief from Chota or expected the national council to meet at Chota; thereafter the selection process for Cherokee national leadership became more rationalized and less embedded in ascriptive ties to Chota. Hanging Maw, from the valley towns, contested the leadership of Little Turkey, although Hanging Maw exerted little influence outside of the valley towns. Between 1788 and 1792 most Cherokee villages attempted to maintain neutrality in the border warfare, and Little Turkey denied the Chickamauga participation in the national council as long as they were carrying on hostilities. But in 1792, Little Turkey, swayed by early victories by the northwest Indians against the Americans and assurances of reliable supplies of Spanish weapons and trade goods, abandoned his neutrality and joined the Chickamaugas. All three major Cherokee political groups were united in the spring of 1793, when a Cherokee peace delegation was attacked by Americans and nine leaders were killed. The entire nation rallied behind the Chickamaugas in 1793–94 until after the defeat of the northern confederacy at the Battle of Fallen Timbers and the withdrawal of Spanish material support. The Cherokee were forced to reconcile themselves to peace with the Americans. After the death of Hanging Maw in 1795, Little Turkey was the undisputed leader and principal chief. He tried to reunite the three major Cherokee political divisions, although regional political cleavages continued to persist into the next century.[46]

During the period 1777–95, Cherokee political institutions became more secularized and rationalized, but at the same time decentralized and fragmented. Chota's experiment in centralizing limited control over blood revenge failed during the period of intermittent border warfare, and the practice of administering blood revenge was reclaimed by the clans. The local villages also took over administration of the Green Corn ceremony, and the priests and conjurors were relegated to local concerns and were excluded from the national polity. Furthermore, Chota, the symbolic mother town of the nation, lost its position as the focus of national leadership; with the principal chief no longer required to be the headman of Chota and the national council not required to meet at Chota, the selection of national leadership and the organization of the Cherokee polity became disembedded from ascriptive affiliation with the symbolic national center at Chota. What was left was a coalition of villages, the unanimous consent of which was necessary for binding decisions.[47]

The immediate Choctaw response to the introduction of competitive political conditions after the start of the American Revolutionary War was the reemergence of antagonistic political cleavages that resulted from alliances by the autonomous Choctaw political districts with rival European powers. The Okla Hannali district sided with the Spanish against the English, while the other Choctaw districts favored the English. The Choctaw districts teamed with their respective European allies and fought against one another during the American Revolution.[48] After the Spanish victory in the Floridas, the Choctaw established trade and diplomatic relations with the Spanish colony. From 1783 to 1795 the Choctaw were subject to American and Spanish competition for trade and diplomatic influence in the southeastern sector of North America.

After the American Revolutionary War, the Choctaw reestablished a loose confederation of three political districts. The Choctaw national polity, which by 1777 already had a tradition of excluding priests and conjurors from national decision making and political leadership, remained secular throughout the competitive period. The three political districts of the Choctaw nation became institutionalized during the competitive period. Though the Choctaw had a nominal principal chief, the polity remained decentralized, divided into three districts and further subdivided into local and family iksa. Each of the three districts had a head chief and a district council that was largely independent of the other two district councils. The councils of the three districts met irregularly in the national council; decision making in the national council required unanimous agreement. The members of the district and national councils were local iksa leaders and thus kinship and political relations remained nondifferentiated. The three districts did not delegate power to the national council but instead managed their own district and local affairs independently.[49] The three districts exhibited little national unity and, except for the secularization of the polity, there was little internal or external differentiation or centralization of the Choctaw polity.

Similarly, during the same period, there was no significant centralization or internal political differentiation in the Chickasaw polity. The trend toward secularization that was reported in the 1760's and 1770's continued, and by the first years of the nineteenth century the Chickasaw national council no longer was required to meet in a sacred village square or to engage in preliminary religious ceremonies before convening the national council to deliberate on important national issues.[50]

During the American Revolutionary War, conflict between the old English-allied and French-allied groups among the Chickasaw intensified, with the latter in 1784 turning to the Spanish after the defeat of the English in the Floridas. However, the intensified Chickasaw political conflict of the 1777–95 period did not lead to the disintegration of Chickasaw political institutions. The Chickasaw continued to maintain the institutions of a principal chief and first and second war chiefs, who were selected from specific iksa. The old kin-based political coalitions controlled national political offices; the hereditary principal chief and the second war chief generally favored the Spanish in the geopolitical competition for domination and trade in the lower Mississippi Valley, while the Piomingo, or first war chief, and the old English-allied coalition favored an alliance with the

Americans after the American Revolutionary War. The Piomingo also had the support of the Tory traders among the Chickasaw and their anglicized children who formed the American party.[51]

In the struggle between Spain and the United States for control of the lower Mississippi Valley, the Chickasaw sought to take advantage of both sides, but the competition broke the Chickasaw into antagonistic kin-based political coalitions. In 1784 Mingo Homa, the Chickasaw principal chief, who favored an alliance with the Spanish, died. His successor, his nephew, Toski Etoka, and the second war chief, Wolf's Friend, continued this alliance with the Spanish, and in the early 1780's the Spanish party was in the majority, though the smaller American party, too, was getting some support from its ally. In 1791 Piomingo and the American party assisted the American militia against the confederated nations of the northwest. But in 1792 the Chickamauga leader, Dragging Canoe, convinced Toski Etoka to join the confederated Indian nations that were in open conflict with the United States. The United States responded by increasing its aid to the Chickasaw, hoping to win them away from the Spanish. As that aid continued to increase and Spanish trade became unreliable, the Spanish party declined in numbers and influence. In 1793, Piomingo was successful in convincing the Chickasaw national council to reject confederation with the Indian nations that were engaged in hostilities with the Americans and to make war on the Creek, who had been attacking the American frontier. This ploy came to an end, however, when the major trading house in the southeast, Panton, Leslie and Company, ceased all trade with either side while they were at war. In 1794 the principal chief, Toski Etoka, died and was succeeded by his nephew and kinsman, Chinibee. Chinibee, who served as principal chief until 1820, remained loyal to Wolf's Friend and favored an alliance with the Spanish, as had his uncle, the former principal chief. But after 1795 the Spanish were very unreliable as trade and military allies, and members of the Spanish party were forced to reconcile themselves to peace with the Americans.[52]

The cleavages in the Chickasaw polity during the 1777–95 period were, of course, no more than continuations of kinship and political cleavages that had formed during the earlier period of French and English competition. Given the decentralized and kinship particularistic loyalties of the Chickasaw polity, competition between and autonomous actions by rival kinship groups were within the bounds of Chickasaw political organization. Furthermore, the records indicate that religious leaders did not play a significant role in Chickasaw political leadership; the primary actors in the major political conflicts and cleavages were war and civil leaders. The Chickasaw polity thus became more secularized, though it was still nondifferentiated from kinship organization.

The war period 1775–95 did not result in any permanent centralization, unification, or differentiation of the Creek national polity; on the contrary, it exacerbated internal competition among the towns of the confederacy. As war broke out, the leading Creek lower towns, Coweta and Cussetah, decided to pursue the old strategy of balance of power: they would accept aid from both the Americans and the English but not take sides with either. Some of the proto-Seminole villages among the lower towns favored the English, as did also Emisteseguo of Little Talisee, who kept most of the upper town Creek in the English camp. For a time, the three major white towns, Oakfuskie, Talisee, and Cussetah, favored neutrality or alliance with the Americans, but the American sympathies lapsed when the Americans, after 1780, were unable to supply the Creeks with necessary trade and war materials. Coweta, the major red town of the lower towns, favored neutrality early in the war, but in 1776 the tiger clan could not get satisfaction for a murder of a clansman at the hands of an American, and the clan turned the town against the Americans. The tiger clan was also represented in Tuckabatchee, the Alabama towns, Okchai, Cussetah, the Hitchitis towns, and Yuchi town. Coweta also feared that the Americans would continue to encroach on Creek lands and that American trade would turn out to be unreliable. The rest of the lower towns favored neutrality in 1776, especially after the defeat of the Cherokee in the same year.

The pro-English and neutral Creek coalitions nearly came to civil war over their different strategic alliances. Oakfuskie insisted on the death of leading English agents and of Emisteseguo, the influential pro-English leader of the upper towns. In return, English officials urged the assassination of Eneah Micco of Cussetah and Opothle Micco of Talisee, the leaders of the pro-American and neutral villages. In late 1778, Emisteseguo abdicated leadership of the upper towns in favor of William McGillivary, who was the son of a trader among the Coosa villages. McGillivary was at this time probably only eighteen years old, but he had been educated and trained in business at Charles Town and already had some influence among the Creek. Emisteseguo probably chose him because of his ability to speak English and negotiate with the English and the Americans. Nonetheless, the choice of one so young was certainly an anomaly in a polity that highly respected age, experience, and wisdom. The immediate reason for Emisteseguo's abdication was assassination threats from the neutral and American-allied towns, which were trying to pressure the English-allied Creek towns to break their English ties. McGillivary was a member of the wind clan, which was large and symbolically prominent among the Creek towns. Emisteseguo told McGillivary that his wind clan affiliation would protect him and the English agents from assassination, whereas he himself, as a member of a low-ranked stinkard clan, had no such protection. Emisteseguo's reasoning may have been correct; at any rate, McGillivary appears not to have been troubled with threats of assassination during his political career. Since McGillivary was in 1778 a member of Little Talisee, a white town and the same town whence Emisteseguo had led the upper Creek towns since the middle 1760's, his selection continued the white town leadership of the upper towns, just as the American party was led by the major white towns of Cussetah, Oakfuskie, and Talisee. At times, when the fortunes of war and trade access changed, some major villages like Coweta, Tuckabatchee, Atasi, and Oakfuskie experienced internal divisions over whether to ally with the English or with the Americans or to remain neutral.[53]

Between 1779 and early 1780 the neutral party disintegrated owing to an absence of reliable American trade and because the neutral villages could not prevent the English-allied Creek from attacking the American frontier. The formerly neutral towns turned to the English for the remainder of the war, although they proved reluctant allies. Most lower town Creek, except Coweta, did not aid the English in their losing fight to retain control of the Floridas against Spanish invasion.

The Spanish defeat of the English at Pensacola in May 1781 brought a major change in Creek geopolitical relations. The Creek were soon desperate for trade, threatened by American land encroachments and hegemony and looking for ways to strengthen the confederacy. Some Creek lower towns, thereafter called Seminoles, withdrew from the confederacy altogether. In 1782 Georgia officials demanded large land cessions between the Oconee and Okmulgee rivers. Coweta refused to cede any land, although pro-American sympathizers at Coweta, Talisee, and Cussetah attempted to gain peace with the Americans.[54]

British sources state that William McGillivary was elected principal chief and Head Warrior of the confederacy in response to the new geopolitical conditions. McGillivary attempted to shunt off American territorial threats by strengthening and centralizing the Creek confederacy, and between 1782 and 1790 the Creek under McGillivary tried to use their alliance with the Spanish to counterbalance the territorial and political threats of the Americans. But the divisions among the Creek after the American Revolutionary War made agreement impossible. Talisee and Cussetah, the two major white towns and leaders of the formerly neutral and American towns, who mistrusted McGillivary because of his youth and, in their eyes, lack of a legitimate right to leadership, directly opposed McGillivary's plan to centralize and regularize the Creek confederacy by elevating the town warrior chiefs to leadership positions over the town civil chiefs.

In the 1780's McGillivary resided in the ancient holy white village of

Hickory Town, where he set up a large plantation, bought and exploited slave labor, and lived in the style of a southern planter.[55] McGillivary was one of a small group of market-oriented Creek who inherited property and commercial knowledge and values from fathers who were English traders and at the same time inherited social and political membership in Creek society through the clan affiliations of their mothers. During the 1780's and 1790's the market-oriented Creek had little political influence. What influence they had, as in McGillivary's case, was derived from their standing within the old political order and was not based on wealth or their emergent class position.

In 1783, 1785, and 1786 the towns led by Cussetah and Talisee, acting on their own, signed treaties that ceded substantial portions of land to the United States. The treaties were not recognized by the majority of towns led by McGillivary, however, and at the time of the convening of the last treaty at Shoulderbone, in late 1786, Eneah Micco of Cussetah and Opothle Micco of Talisee were detained in jail and threatened by a mob of angry Georgians. The two Creeks were ultimately released, but thenceforth, Opothle Micco of Talisee turned actively against an alliance with the Americans. He pursued a career of fundamentalist opposition to American influence and to adoption of American economic and political innovations among the Creek.

In 1790 McGillivary, accompanied by representatives of 26 Creek chiefs, signed a treaty with George Washington in New York. The major towns represented in the treaty were Oakfuskie, Talisee, Cussetah, Tuckabatchee, Coweta, and Mikusuki. Less than half of the Creek villages were represented in the New York treaty, and many of the lower towns later rejected the terms of the treaty and McGillivary's right to make a treaty that concerned land that they occupied. McGillivary was not able to unify the local and particularistic Creek villages behind his centralization plan; nor could he gain national support for the 1790 treaty.[56]

McGillivary had high hopes of creating a Creek government modeled after the new American government, but even his modest attempt to place the warrior leaders in political authority over the town miccos did not represent an innovation in further differentiation of the Creek polity. It was merely a variation on the old political order. McGillivary could not centralize coercive political power; the national council continued to maintain ultimate national political authority, and decisions in the national council required a negotiated consensus among the town leaders. McGillivary's power lay in his ability to control trade through his association with the leading southeastern trading house, Panton, Leslie and Company, and his ability to control the distribution of diplomatic presents. He also attempted to use coercion to bolster his political leadership by means of a body of personal retainers, and he tried to exploit his membership in the symbolically central and numerically large wind clan. But all his innovations met with strong resistance and they did not become institutionalized in Creek society.[57] For the last five years of his life he worked to unify the Creek political order, but without success.

McGillivary died from natural causes in early 1793. At the time of his death the leading Creek towns were Oakfuskie, a white town, and the red town of Tuckabatchee, which was led in the confederate council by Mad Dog, a confidant of McGillivary. The old Creek political order was soon reestablished; the miccos returned to their ancient positions of civil political authority, and the war leaders returned to their advisory roles. The Creek confederacy continued as a loose alliance of autonomous villages with irregular meetings of the confederate council and no permanent capitol. The strongly anti-American Opothle Micco of Talisee claimed the right to succeed McGillivary as leader of the confederacy, but the Americans instead recognized Mad Dog of Tuckabatchee; in doing so they acknowledged the leadership of a red town over the traditional white town leadership in the upper towns region.[58]

Despite American demands for cessions of territory and the threat of American political hegemony, the Creek did not permanently adopt McGillivary's proposed political centralization and reordering of relations between war leaders and miccos. The Creek polity returned to adherence to the traditional rules of the national political order. Furthermore, the Creek national council continued to meet in the sacred squares of the leading towns, which indicates that the Creek polity had not experienced the same level of political secularization as had the Cherokee, Chickasaw, and Choctaw. In consequence, the Creek polity remained largely without centralization of coercive powers, and clans continued to exact blood revenge. The Creek polity showed little internal or external differentiation during the 1777–95 period. Though the Creek confederate council was traditionally differentiated from formal kinship organization, the Creek polity remained symbolically ordered by white and red towns and by the particularistic religious identity of each of the tribal towns. The most significant change in the polity was the rise to leadership of the red town of Tuckabatchee in 1793, but this change did not constitute an increased centralization or differentiation of the Creek polity.

Summary

Despite incorporation into the world-system by way of the fur trade and intense competitive geopolitical relations, the four major southeastern societies during the eighteenth century showed little increased differentiation or political centralization, except for the secularization of the Cherokee, Choctaw, and Chickasaw polities. Adair argued that the decline in the old religious and normative order was due to contact with and influence of traders. That the political secularization process accelerates during the 1770's to 1790's might seem to indicate that the Tories and English traders who lived among the southeastern nations had a significant influence on the rationalization of political decision making among the Cherokee, the Choctaw, and the Chickasaw. Certainly the need to manage increasingly complex and competitive trade and diplomatic relations influenced the process of political rationalization, but none of these explanations helps us to understand the absence of the secularization in the Creek polity; after all the Creek, too, were subject to trader influences and trade and diplomatic relations. Moreover, an explanation for the strong Creek orthodoxy cannot lie with the nondifferentiated cultural world views, since the other major southeastern nations had comparable internally nondifferentiated world views. But there was one major difference between Creek society and the other three southeastern nations—the form of nondifferentiation of polity and culture. Creek society, with its symbolic determination of political order between red and white towns and religiously particularistic town identity and sociopolitical membership, retained the least secularized polity.

Most southeastern Indians retained nondifferentiated world views and nonaccumulative economic orientations and values. In the southeastern polities that became more secularized, the priests, conjurors, and doctors, who were excluded from formal political decision making, were relegated to local and nonpolitical duties; they continued to perform their rituals, but only for local and private purposes. All four polities remained segmentary and decentralized and continued to exhibit egalitarian political cultures. None of the four southeastern societies formed unified political nationalities in the sense that commitments to national institutions took precedence over loyalties to local, regional, or kinship groups.

One partial explanation for the absence of more differentiation or centralization in the polities of the southeastern nations lies in the fact that incorporation into the fur trade did not lead to the formation of new class structures or the adoption of acquisitive market orientations. The fur trade led to further specialization in hunting and skin-curing activities, but these skills were not new techniques. The Indians traded for limited quantities of manufactured goods that they needed, but they did not hunt to accumulate wealth. Economic action still continued to exhibit the characteristics of a need or subsistence economy. Even the few Indians who became traders retained a subsistence economic orientation and merely substituted the work of the trade for that of the hunt. They did not constitute a trader class. Only after the American Revolutionary War, when many Tories and English traders took residence among the southeastern nations, did a group of market-oriented or acquisitive persons appear among the southeastern nations. And not all the traders and Tory families continued to pursue market orientations and skills, acquisitiveness, and property. It is clear that the small nascent merchant and planter class that emerged in the 1780's did not arise merely from the availability of the fur trade market opportunities: these opportunities existed before the 1780's without creating a new class. The new group only emerged as the outgrowth of European acquisitive values, values that were not indigenous to the southeastern cultures, which were transmitted through the trader and Tory families. Nevertheless, the trader families did not have significant political influence before 1795, and, except for McGillivary, who failed to restructure and centralize political relations permanently among the Creek, the trader families did not actively try to restructure the southern Indian polities.

Despite the presence of intense competitive and hegemonic geopolitical relations during the course of the eighteenth century, there was no permanent political centralization among the southeastern nations. Throughout the century the European colonies attempted to convince the southeastern nations to adopt more centralized leadership and decision making because the Europeans found it difficult to manage relations with a large group of autonomous local leaders. But aside from their policy of appointing principal chiefs, the Europeans did not attempt to restructure the polities or economies of the southeastern nations. The colonial officials and trading interests viewed the Indians primarily as a source of cheap and specialized labor and had little interest in changing their economic or political conditions.

All four southeastern nations adopted principal chiefs during the eighteenth century, but their leadership was generally nominal and they were not associated with the centralization of legitimate coercive powers. The absence of permanent or institutionalized political national unity among the southeastern nations indicates that geopolitical competition is not a sufficient condition to foster a collective or institutional response of national political integration. In fact, during the competitive period, the southeastern nations were generally rent by internal cleavages as autonomous villages and regions allied with opposing European colonial powers.

The events of the eighteenth century left the Cherokee the most differentiated and socially integrated nation in the southeast. The Cherokee polity over the course of the eighteenth century became relatively secular; at the same time, the Cherokee polity remained differentiated from kinship organization and remained socially integrated through the seven national clans, although after the 1780's most ceremonial activities were carried on at the village level and were no longer part of the organization of the national polity. The Cherokee experimented with limited political centralization in the 1750's and 1760's and adopted a principal chief. During the 1780's and 1790's the office of principal chief became separated from its original ascriptive ties to the headman of Chota. Nevertheless, although the Cherokee polity was now relatively secular and differentiated from kinship, Cherokee political loyalties were given primarily to villages and regional coalitions.

In comparison, although the Choctaw and Chickasaw polities also became more secular, their political organizations remained embedded in kinship organization. Like the Cherokee, the Chickasaw and Choctaw did not institutionalize significant changes in internal differentiation of the national polity or institutionalize a national political solidarity or unity. The Creek national polity, traditionally differentiated from kinship organization, remained nondifferentiated from cultural and symbolic order. As in the other southeastern nations, there was little change in internal political differentiation and little increased national political solidarity in the Creek polity.

Consequently, after the eighteenth century, the Cherokee polity, with its differentiation of polity from kinship and culture, was the most differentiated and exhibited the most social solidarity, and therefore was the society best positioned for further acceptance of change in the polity. Nevertheless, the Cherokee still would have to accept major institutional changes in internal differentiation of the polity, centralize legitimate use of coercive power, and forge a national political unity before institutionalizing a differentiated constitutional government. The Choctaw and Chickasaw, like the Cherokee, needed to form a political nationality, centralize legitimate use of coercive power, and adopt major changes in internal political differentiation. In addition, the Choctaw and Chickasaw needed to differentiate the national polity from local kinship organization before it would be possible to say they had institutionalized a differentiated constitutional government. The Creek had yet to create institutions of national political unity and would have to accept major changes in internal differentiation of the polity, centralize legitimate use of coercive power, and differentiate the national polity from the symbolic and religious order before they would be able to institutionalize a differentiated constitutional polity.

4 LIMITED POLITICAL CENTRALIZATION AND THE CONSOLIDATION OF U.S. HEGEMONY

DURING THE PERIOD from 1795 to 1817, the Cherokee, who had the most socially solidary and differentiated polity of the four southeastern nations, made the most extensive changes in national political unification, political centralization, and internal political differentiation. The Choctaw and the Chickasaw, who had less solidary and nondifferentiated kinship and political institutions, accepted only limited political centralization, which was demanded of them by U.S. officials as a means of fulfilling treaty obligations. The Creek, with local and particularistic forms of social identity and a culturally defined political order, were divided over issues of change. Between 1812 and 1814 the Creek were engaged in a civil war, the Red Stick War, which was fought primarily over the issue of accepting or rejecting American-inspired political and economic innovations in Creek society. With the aid of American troops, the fundamentalist Creek were defeated, and within a few years after the war they accepted abolishment of blood revenge and limited centralization of political authority. Although the differences in sociopolitical order suggest several hypotheses for explaining the variation in political change in the southeastern societies, any such arguments need to be verified from a narrative of historical conditions and events.

Early U.S. Hegemony

Between 1795 and the conclusion of the War of 1812, the new American government worked toward consolidating political control over the eastern portion of the present United States. After the British withdrew military and diplomatic support from the Indian nations in the old northwest in 1795, British agents kept their ties and influence with the northwestern nations with annual distributions of gifts. British traders, with their superior goods and better prices, still also dominated the fur trade. As British and American relations deteriorated after 1807, the British attempted to use the northwestern nations, already predisposed in their favor, as aids defending Canada from a possible American invasion. The northwestern nations well understood that American expansion threatened not only their own territory and hunting grounds but also their national political autonomy.

In the southeast, where the Spanish colony no longer actively opposed American expansion, the four major southeastern nations were bound together in a loose alliance to prevent the sale of land to Americans, but they lacked the support of a foreign power to back their efforts to retain territory and political autonomy. In treaties made after 1795, most eastern Indian nations had no choice but to recognize American political supremacy in the region. American hegemony over the eastern United States became more or less complete after the War of 1812, when the British in the Treaty of Ghent ended their military and formal political relations with their former Indian allies in the eastern part of the interior, and in 1819, when the Spanish relinquished control of the Floridas to the United States.

Whereas the British had not deliberately attempted to alter or restructure the Indian societies but had been pleased to allow the Indians freedom so long as they were a labor force for the British, the Americans believed that they should bring economic and social change to the Indian nations. American policy had to concentrate first on curbing hostilities between Indians and white settlers; but beyond that, it sought to regulate and control trade, and then to institute a program for civilization and eventual assimilation. To control trade, the American government started a factory system, which traded goods at cost to Indian hunters. This system, which was in effect until 1822, was designed to keep away foreign traders, prevent trader abuses that might lead to conflict, and satisfy Indian demand for and dependency on manufactured goods. Instead of being in debt to individual traders, Indian leaders were encouraged to incur large debts at the goods factories, and when these debts accumulated, the Indians were persuaded to cede territory to pay off their own and the private debts of tribal members.

To promote civilization, American agents were sent to selected Indian nations to teach agriculture and domestic arts and to inculcate the ideals of alliance and peace. The Americans also demanded that the Indian nations honor the terms of treaties, which, by outlining collective responsibility for the actions of individuals, induced the Indian nations to strengthen internal coercive controls, if only to prevent military retaliation from the increasingly powerful Americans. The Indians were supplied with limited quantities of plows, axes, hoes, spinning wheels, and looms, and tools for blacksmithing, and carpentry, as well as hogs and cattle. The idea was that if Indian hunters would turn to subsistence farming, that would free large hunting territories for American expansion. If the Indians only gave up hunting, then they would no longer feel compelled to defend their hunting territory, and the Americans could buy it—preferably as cheaply as possible and without fighting.[1]

Up until 1803, U.S. government policy was premised on the consideration that the Indians eventually would be assimilated as American citizens. With the signing of the Louisiana Purchase, which brought vast unsettled territory into the United States, this policy changed. Instead of allowing the Indians to be assimilated in the southeast, President Jefferson suggested that they could be removed west of the Mississippi River, thus leaving their territory for the new American settlers. Indian agents were supposed to use persuasion and material incentives to convince the Indians to migrate west, where, they were assured, they could continue to live by the fur trade and hunting economy.[2] During the years in which this policy of persuasion, not force, prevailed—until 1828—there were no large-scale migrations of southeastern Indians.

Changing World-System Relations

The fur trade had been remarkable for its vigor, but as early as the middle 1760's there were reports by Indian leaders of scarcity of deer and other game. By the early 1800's the trade in the southeast was clearly on the decline. Hunters were having to travel farther and hunt for longer periods in order to get enough skins to repay their debts and satisfy their own material needs. Many causes were involved in the decline of the fur trade: American settlers who established farms on hunting territory, scaring away the game; the decline in fur prices; and, not the least, the depletion of game by overexploitation.[3]

All four of the major southeastern nations were affected by the dwindling fur trade economy during the 1795–1817 period. The Cherokee, though not without resistance and reluctance, were the quickest to turn away from hunting to subsistence husbandry and farming; the Creek for the most part showed overt or fundamentalist resistance to adopting agricultural change; the Chickasaw and Choctaw, for reasons that had less to do with cultural attitudes than with circumstances, made a more gradual transition to husbandry and agriculture than the Cherokee and were less active in opposing economic change than the Creek.

By the end of the first decade of the nineteenth century, most of the Cherokee and Creek were unable to sustain a livelihood in the trade. Between 1795 and 1809 the Cherokee fur trade steadily declined, and the Cherokee, against their inclinations but spurred on by American advice and aid, turned more and more to subsistence agriculture and cattle raising. Most Cherokee males would have preferred to continue their hunting and trading way of life, but the game declined noticeably every year, while the Cherokee demand for manufactured goods gradually rose. By 1805, many Cherokee men turned to raising cattle and horses, which had been introduced by traders during the eighteenth century; these could be bartered for goods in nearby American settlements, and husbandry required little labor, since the river bottoms abounded with cane for cattle feed. Hogs, too, were easy to raise, for the woods were filled with acorns. Corn, a traditional crop, was one that could be expanded, since surpluses could be sold in local markets. After the middle 1790's, many Cherokee women also cultivated cotton and wove it into cloth, though that was mostly for household use rather than for market or trade.[4] Between 1800 and 1817, many Cherokee moved out of their villages and established independent family homesteads.

In the Creek country, the fur trade was on the decline as early as 1797, and the Creek, lacking skins for trade and no longer sustained by diplomatic gifts, were becoming increasingly in debt to traders and increasingly impoverished. At the same time, their demand for manufactured goods increased. As the price of furs steadily fell, the American agent to the Creek, Benjamin Hawkins, tried to convince the Creek to turn to agriculture, as the Cherokee were doing. This proved to be very difficult, especially among the upper town Creek. Most Creek still clung to the skin trade, despite the worsening trade conditions. They were not wholly against farming, but they preferred the traditional village-oriented system to the notion of independent family farms.[5]

The Chickasaw and the Choctaw, too, experienced declines in their fur trade economies similar to those experienced by the Cherokee and the Creek, but for them the major impact of the downturn in the fur trade came after 1817. The Chickasaw began turning gradually to agriculture as early as 1801, though on a small scale only. Game had been overexploited in the Chickasaw country and the Chickasaw were accumulating trade debts, but these were relieved by the sale of land to the United States in 1805, and up until 1817 or so, the majority of Chickasaw people continued to live in scattered nonnucleated villages or communities, where they engaged in subsistence farming on a small scale.

The game in the Choctaw country had already declined by the 1790's to the point where it could no longer support the Choctaw trade requirements. Driven by their dependency on trade, the Choctaw stepped up hunting across the Mississippi River, sometimes in semiannual hunts that involved whole families. An accumulated debt to traders was paid off with cessions of land in treaties with the United States in the first decade of the nineteenth century, and thereafter the Choctaw turned increasingly to farming and cattle raising. Stock raising became a primary economic activity among the Choctaw in the Okla Falaya and northeastern districts; most of the more conservative Choctaw in the Six Towns district preferred to live in their villages and tried to retain the hunting and horticultural way of life.[6]

CLASS STRATIFICATION

The decline of the fur trade in the years after the end of the Revolutionary War coincided with the gradual development of a very small entrepreneurial class in the southeastern nations. The large majority of southeasterners, of course, still continued in subsistence skin trade and horticulture or adopted subsistence husbandry and agriculture, but out of the group of mixed bloods and Tory families there had now emerged a small group who were actively engaged in profit making through trade, merchant, and agricultural pursuits. Before 1817 this group amounted to no more than 3 percent of the total family households, but it was a clearly identifiable stratum. Some of these families, sprung from mixed-blood sons of former traders or Tories who had lived and married among the southeastern nations, had acquired their values of private accumulation and profit making, along with property and economic skills, from their European fathers; other families, like the Cherokee Ridge family and some of the Choctaw chiefs, simply followed a European pattern without direct family influence. The model in all cases, however, was that of the southern planter and business community, and particularly among those who were educated in American schools and learned business methods, there was an eagerness to accept American agricultural aid and equipment and to adopt the new American ideals of civilization.

Since land was owned collectively in the southeastern nations and distributed on a usufruct basis, the planters and merchants could not own land, but they did have access to any land in the nation that was not occupied. Planters could maintain several plantations or ranches in different parts of the nation as long as they did not occupy land within a quarter of a mile of another plantation or homesteader. Besides cattle raising, the plantations grew corn and cotton. Because the Indian subsistence farmers and villagers refused to work for wages for the planters, the planters imported black slaves to work their farms and ranches; this had been the custom of the early traders, and also of the Tories, who brought slaves with them during the Revolutionary War. After 1795, slavery as a means of producing agricultural products for export to American markets became an established institution among the southeastern nations.[7]

The entrepreneurial class, or at least those who were sons of traders who had married or cohabited with women from prominent lineages, did have access to village and national political offices, but this was not an overwhelming advantage. Even the Cherokee entrepreneurial class, though it was perhaps the largest, was composed of only a small percentage of the family households in the nation, and the Cherokee entrepreneurs did not have access to coercive means to force change or gain political domination. In no case was the entrepreneurial class large enough or powerful enough to effect its interests directly or gain direct control over the political apparatus.

During this period, however, the large majority of the southeastern households—well over 90 percent—still continued to have no interest in profit making. Though hunting was no longer the main occupation and was done along with farming, the farming of communal fields and/or small private plots of two to five acres was still at a subsistence level, to satisfy family food requirements. Only limited surpluses of skins, cattle, horses, cotton, or agricultural produce were bartered at local trading stores or in American settlements so that the subsistence farmers and hunters could obtain the manufactured goods they had come to rely on. Most southeastern Indians continued to adhere to the nondifferentiated cultural orientations and subsistence labor ethic of their forebears, and on occasion even criticized the acquisitive orientations of their entrepreneurial brethren, whose economic activities and orientations were in direct contrast to and even in violation of traditional economic norms and values.[8]

Cherokee Political Centralization, Unification, and Early Internal Political Differentiation

The sociopolitical order of the Cherokee appears to have made them the most predisposed toward institutional change. Of the four nations, the Cherokee had the most extensive and symbolically integrated kinship system, and their national council was secular and separate from the kinship system. This did not mean that the Cherokee polity automatically became centralized and differentiated. Most Cherokee were conservative, and reluctant to adopt political or economic change, and they did so only under extenuating circumstances. They continued to adhere to nondifferentiated world views and subsistence labor ethics that oriented social action toward preservation of the existing sociopolitical order. They were no more motivated to accept political innovations than were the other south-eastern nations, even though their tradition was of a more differentiated and socially solidary society.

It is true that the motivation for change in the Cherokee nation came from the interests and political actions of members of the emergent planter-merchant class, many of whom had adopted more rationalistic cultural orientations, and from the American threats to land and national political sovereignty. But since the same motivations are to be found in the other three nations, they alone cannot explain the variations in political change. In the Cherokee case, however, external threats to land and political sov-ereignty and the formation of a change-oriented planter-merchant class operated in conjunction with the symbolically integrated national kinship system and a secular polity that was differentiated from the kinship and solidarity system. None of the other southeastern nations had the differen-tiated and solidary features of Cherokee society, and that difference may explain why they did not exhibit similar movements toward increased political differentiation and national political unification during the same time period.

At the beginning of the period of American hegemony, the Cherokee national government exhibited little internal differentiation or political solidarity: clans continued to manage personal judicial matters, and local and regional political loyalties took precedence over national loyalties. By 1810 the Cherokee centralized control over blood revenge, formed com-mitments of national political unity, and created ad hoc committees and more rationalized administration of government. All these changes were adopted in order to strengthen Cherokee ability to keep control over their homeland and preserve their national sovereignty in the face of American land encroachments and threats to national autonomy.

Between 1795 and 1810 the Cherokee were not able to sustain political unity between the two major political cleavages that had emerged at the start of the American Revolutionary War. Although the nation was divided into upper towns and lower towns, these only vaguely resembled the national divisions of the same description before the 1750's. The nucleus of the lower towns was the dissident Chickamauga villages; the upper towns, which contained remnants of the overhill towns and valley towns, were for the most part the villages that had advocated neutrality during the Revolutionary War and in the ensuing border conflicts of 1783–95. After 1795, many of the lower towns, led by traders, Tories, and men who had most strongly resisted the Americans during the 1780's and 1790's, turned quickly to farming and trade. Despite their wartime resistance to the Americans, the leaders of these towns readily accepted U.S. offers of tools and aid for farming. The more conservative upper towns were reluctant to adopt agricultural methods, and the lower towns therefore gained an early agricultural advantage over the upper towns. By 1809 the upper towns were far behind.[9] Also, the chiefs of the lower towns, being more interested in business and commerce, were more predisposed to allow the Americans to build roads through Cherokee country and even more willing to cede hunting land for monetary compensation. The more conservative upper towns, although they were increasingly willing to adopt subsistence agriculture, were generally opposed to the building of roads through Cherokee country, since that would surely bring unwanted American influences and intruders, and they were even more strongly opposed to the selling of Cherokee land.

The upper and lower towns thus formed two distinct political divisions in the nation. The Cherokee principal chief, Little Turkey, was a resident of Wills Town, one of the lower towns. The upper towns usually gathered at Ustanali, and since the two divisions could not agree on a central capitol, they agreed to alternate locations for their irregular national council meetings.[10] The American agent, Return Jonathan Meigs, favored Wills Town as the Cherokee national capital. While the two political divisions remained at odds, the Cherokee did not institutionalize any further changes in political centralization or differentiation of their polity. National political unification appears to have been a precondition for political centralization and for further development of internal differentiation in the Cherokee polity.

EARLY ATTEMPTS TO CENTRALIZE
LEGITIMATE FORCE

The first efforts toward political centralization arose out of the need to curb the practice of blood revenge against American citizens in cases of the murder of a Cherokee by an American. Clan law required retaliation, but the killing of American citizens threatened to involve the Cherokee in war with the Americans. In a similar situation in the 1760's and early 1770's, the Cherokee national council had attempted to assert control over blood revenge in order to preserve orderly relations with the English colonies, but with the outbreak of the American Revolution, it had lost control and was unable to prevent relatives from retaliating against frontiersmen whenever a clansman died in battle.

Treaties with the United States in the 1790's forced the Cherokee council to revive control, because the U.S. government demanded that American murderers of Cherokees be tried in American courts and that blood revenge be considered invalid. Between 1792 and 1803, Chief Little Turkey, who wanted to maintain peaceful and regular relations with the United

States, managed to exert tighter internal control over treaty violators—though he could do little to control the frontier rings of illegal horse stealing and trading. A council at Ustanali reported in 1804 that it was glad to see that there were no blood retaliations by Cherokee against American murderers of Cherokees. The Americans to some extent reciprocated: although between 1800 and 1803 it became clear that no frontier court would sentence an American to death for killing a Cherokee, a situation that the Cherokee councils complained bitterly about over the years as the count of unavenged murders continued to rise. After 1803 American agents paid blood money to compensate Cherokee families for deaths perpetrated by American citizens.[11]

The Cherokee chiefs reasoned that the preservation of their land base, which was guaranteed by treaty, rested on maintaining regular relations with the United States, and because the U.S. government held the Cherokee collectively responsible for the acts of individuals, the Cherokee council very sensibly attempted to extend stronger internal controls over violators of treaty provisions. The centralization of internal control over treaty violators, and especially the curbing of blood revenge against American citizens, was an externally imposed condition that the chiefs accepted, since treaty violations threatened regular trade and diplomatic relations with the powerful United States. The control of blood revenge applied only when American citizens were involved, however: Cherokees could still invoke blood revenge in their internal affairs and against some of their Indian enemies, such as the Osage.[12]

As early as 1797, U.S. agents tried to convince the Cherokee to modify their domestic clan law and blood revenge. They had help from Ridge, a young leader from the upper towns, who advocated the abolishment of blood revenge among the Cherokee and the adoption of judicial procedures similar to American laws. In 1797 Ridge and U.S. agents Silas Dinsmoor and Benjamin Hawkins proposed to the Cherokee national council that the blood law be modified so that accidental homicide was not subject to blood retaliation.[13] Ridge further convinced the council to modify the clan law so that only the murderer, and not a near relative or clansman, had to pay with his life for an act of murder. Two years later the Cherokee national council created national laws to punish adultery and replaced the ancient tradition of seeking protection from blood retaliation in cases of accidental murder in one of the four white towns with the right to appeal to the national council for protection. Also in 1799, the Cherokee national council established a police force, called lighthorse, to recover debts and punish crimes—in a sense reviving an old Cherokee system in which chiefs had commissioned ad hoc groups of warriors to undertake specific tasks. The term lighthorse was symbolic of the civil chief or white chief hierarchy, and the lighthorsemen were considered an extension of the authority of the national council. In 1800 at Ustanali, the seven Cherokee clans agreed that the lighthorsemen would not be subject to blood revenge if they injured or killed a suspect in the course of duty. The fact that the seven clans granted the lighthorsemen immunity from retaliation indicates a further differentiation of kinship and legal prerogatives, in that the clans granted the enforcement of law to the national council and the police force.

There does not appear to be any record of overt resistance on the part of the seven clans against the centralization of law enforcement, and in fact the compliance of the seven clans gave legitimacy to the more centralized legal system. By 1803, Ridge was advocating the total abolishment of blood revenge. He was elected to the national clan council, which still had jurisdiction over blood revenge and other legal matters. Between 1801 and 1808, however, the lighthorse was commissioned on an irregular basis owing to a lack of funds. The 1799 law was committed to writing at Broomstown in 1808, but the blood revenge law was not actually abolished until 1810, and then only after the political unification of the upper and lower town divisions into a single nation. As late as May 1809 the lower towns refused to meet the upper town chiefs in council and declined to abide by the new laws because of general political disagreements as well as specific disputes over the enforcement of the laws that were made primarily by the younger chiefs of the upper towns.[14]

POLITICAL UNIFICATION

Even though the Cherokee had a unified national clan system, national political unity had always been a tenuous and situational affair. The political cleavages between the upper and lower towns now were exacerbated by consistent American pressures for land and for road access through Cherokee territory and by American agents who attempted to exploit Cherokee political divisions. Cherokee national political unification in late 1809 and 1810 was born of a crisis in Cherokee leadership, which failed to protect the Cherokee homeland from American encroachments. The crisis led to national political unification, further political centralization, and the formation of a specialized committee to manage relations with the Americans more effectively. The Cherokee moved to centralize and rationalize their political institutions in order to preserve territory and national political autonomy.

After the first treaties in the late 1790's, the Americans began to solicit land cessions from the Cherokee on a nearly annual basis. American settlers were impatient with the slow progress of government extinguishment of Cherokee land rights and began ignoring treaty provisions and Cherokee boundaries and simply settling on Cherokee lands. Under that pressure, the adjoining states of Tennessee and Georgia petitioned the federal government to extinguish all Indian land titles and claims. Georgia asked for territory from the Atlantic Ocean to the Mississippi River. Starting in the middle 1780's, Georgia had allowed several land companies to sell a total of almost 50 million acres of land in the area of the Yazoo River and the Mississippi River; the federal government would not recognize the sales—the so-called Yazoo Fraud—since Indian title had not been extinguished, but in 1802 the federal government at last agreed to extinguish Indian title by peaceful means if Georgia would accept a smaller area for its chartered state boundaries. Nevertheless, Georgia still claimed land in Cherokee and Creek country, and it pressured the federal government to unencumber its claim by extinguishing Cherokee and Creek rights to territory within its chartered state limits.[15]

By 1800 settlers, states, and the federal government were clamoring for Cherokee land. When the Cherokee still refused to sell, U.S. officials resorted to bribery and intrigue. The lower Cherokee and Chickamauga towns, which were closer to American settlements, were especially harassed and pressured into retreating farther and farther into the interior. As early as 1796 the residents of several of the lower towns had already abandoned their towns. Complaints about encroachment from the national council to American officials were ignored.[16] Under these circumstances, many lower town leaders, certain that the Americans would occupy the land anyway, had concluded that they ought to accept the American offers to remove westward. The upper town leaders were still firmly opposed to removal westward and to any further land cessions to the Americans.

Nonetheless, in the treaty of 1798, the Cherokee ceded to the Americans a large tract of land, and between 1801 and 1805 the Cherokee were pressured to grant a right-of-way for a road and further land cessions. In 1801 the Cherokee council refused to grant a right-of-way for a road that would connect Tennessee and Georgia. In the spring of 1802, the principal chief, Little Turkey, died, and in late summer of the same year Black Fox from the lower towns was elected principal chief. Early in 1803 the Cherokee council again refused U.S. commissioners the right to build a road. Turtle-at-Home, a leading member of the national clan council and a leading chief at the Ustanali or upper town council, delivered the refusal as speaker for the council. But a combination of bribery and fear in the end broke down the resistance. Even though it was generally feared among the Cherokee that intensified relations with the Americans would lead to disruption in the nation, there were some men of property who favored building the road because it would facilitate commerce and trade.[17] Permission to build the road was given in 1803; in 1804 tribal business was delegated to an ad hoc committee of three chiefs—Cheistoya, Broom, and Taluntuskee—who ceded a small tract of land.

The split over the question of ceding land led to a political crisis between the upper and lower towns. In 1805 and 1806, Doublehead, a leading chief among the lower towns who had engaged in business as a trader-merchant since about 1800, and other lower town chiefs were bribed in treaty negotiations with parcels of land. Doublehead then proceeded to rent the land to American settlers. Although Doublehead was held in public disfavor for using his position as chief to gain private financial advantages for himself at the expense of the national domain, he still held the post of leader, and in January 1806 he took a delegation to Washington and ceded more land to the United States. Doublehead, Taluntuskee, Black Fox, and the lower town chiefs received special cash annuities for their assent. Again, early in 1807, Doublehead and other lower town chiefs negotiated a land-ceding treaty in Washington, and this time they decided to keep the proceeds of the transaction instead of distributing them among the upper towns. Representatives of the upper towns protested the treaty so vigorously that it was never ratified by the United States, but Doublehead still hoped to cooperate with American officials. At last the council and will, at least of the upper town chiefs, prevailed: in the summer of 1807 Doublehead was executed for taking bribes during treaty negotiations.[18]

The upper town chiefs were still dissatisfied with the actions of the lower town chiefs, however, and in May 1808 a group of the most conservative upper town chiefs proposed to American officials that the Cherokee nation be divided into two separate nations. Several of the chiefs even proposed that Cherokees should become American citizens and that Cherokee land should be allotted to Cherokee families for farms. Return Jonathan Meigs, the U.S. agent to the Cherokee, opposed the idea. He argued that the allotment of lands to individual Cherokee families would lead to dispossession and impoverishment for most Cherokee subsistence farmers: the Cherokee would sell their land to American settlers and live off the sale for a time, but eventually their lack of land would make them destitute. He recommended instead that the United States should persuade the Cherokee to exchange their eastern lands for western land and move west to territory in present-day Arkansas, where they could continue their hunting way of life. Those who had taken up farming could stay and become American citizens. Some lower town leaders appeared to favor removal, but the upper town leaders, led by Ridge, moved to prevent the lower towns from signing a removal treaty. Most upper town Cherokee were unwilling to leave their homeland, and in the fall of 1808 it appeared that the two divisions would agree to make a separation of territory and nationality.[19]

During November of 1808, the Cherokee council met to depose the principal chief, Black Fox, and some of the other lower town chiefs who were favorable to removal. Black Fox was popular, but Ridge and other leaders were strongly in favor of his impeachment. Early in 1809, Black Fox was replaced by Path Killer, the second principal chief and a resident of the upper towns, a man who owned two farms and also a ferry on the Coosa River near his home village of Turkey Town and was influential among the conservative chiefs and subsistence farmers.[20] The lower towns refused to recognize either the impeachment or the new principal chief, and in May 1809 they refused to meet with the upper towns in council. Turtle-at-Home was delegated the task of settling the differences between the two political divisions, and in July 1809 some 42 Cherokee towns met at Ustanali under the leadership of Path Killer. All 42 towns were unanimous in their rejection of removal and the plan to divide the nation. American officials had expected the lower towns to adopt the removal plan and emigrate, but by July 1809 only about 1,000 Cherokee, all from the lower towns and led by Taluntuskee, one of the deposed chiefs, had registered to remove. The majority of Cherokee did not approve of either the removal proposal or the proposal to allot land and live under American laws. The Cherokee had experienced economic harassment and depredations of their villages and farms by frontiersmen, and they did not believe it would be easy to assimilate into American society and live as citizens with equal rights and protection. They were all too familiar with the slowness of frontier courts to sentence any American to death for the murder of a Cherokee.

The Cherokee national council at Ustanali, reflecting the majority view, rejected both removal and assimilation, and adopted a strategy of national political unification, government centralization, and economic change as a way of preserving their homeland. Meigs, the U.S. agent, proposed to Bloody Fellow, an old chief, that if the Cherokee would remove west they would be free from the constraints of American influences and customs and could perpetuate their own customs with fewer hindrances. Bloody Fellow's answer summarized the prevailing opinion of the national council: "He had no inclination to leave the country of his birth. Even should the habits and customs of the Cherokee give place to the habits and customs of the whites . . . . He was for preserving them together as a people." [21]

In late September of 1809, for the first time in several years, both the upper and lower towns gathered at Wills Town during a Green Corn festival and made a formal declaration of national unity. Over the years, the Cherokee national council had become increasingly secular and was no longer required to meet in a sacred village square, though as late as the fall before the treaty of 1805, Black Fox, the principal chief, had implored the village headmen to attend their annual Green Corn ceremonies in their villages in order to seek spiritual guidance and wisdom in treaty negotiations with the Americans. Earlier, during the reign of Chota (early 1750's–70's), it had been customary for the national council to gather at Chota during the Green Corn ceremony. The Green Corn ceremony, in which all seven clans of the nation participated, did not ordain the form of political organization or uphold special political prerogatives in political decision making, but it did give spiritual guidance, and it contributed to social-cultural solidarity in support of the gathering and decision making of the national council. The gathering of the Cherokee national council during the Green Corn festival at Wills Town to create a stronger national government was certainly no accident. At a time of political crisis and innovation, the Cherokee looked to their traditional symbols of national unity and guidance.[22]

At Wills Town the council, again led by Black Fox as principal chief and Path Killer as second chief, declared that the Cherokee were no longer to be known by their affiliations with upper or lower towns but were now unified as a single nation. In rejecting removal, the council argued that the Cherokee had an indisputable right to their present territory and that to remove would cause conflict with western nations. It rejected the argument that they should remove to continue the fur trade, which was no longer a profitable enterprise in the east. Instead, the council argued that the Cherokee needed their present land to pursue cattle raising and agriculture.[23] The council deliberated over the means of forming a more regular government that would place checks and balances on individual leaders and prevent bribery and mistakes that resulted in unauthorized cessions of land to the Americans.

The council created a thirteen-member standing committee that was delegated the duties of managing national business when the council was not in session. The formation of an ad hoc committee to manage Cherokee government affairs was not an entirely new idea. In 1803 and 1804, a committee of three had managed treaty negotiations, and when the Americans began paying annuities for land cessions made in treaties, ad hoc committees had been appointed to manage the per capita distribution. But the task of managing relations with the Americans had become too complex and cumbersome for a council composed of 50 village delegations, where binding decisions still required unanimous consent of all the villages. The standing committee of 1809 represented an attempt to establish a more permanent committee that was separate from the principal chief and the council of town headmen. The committee's decisions were subject to the approval of the national council, hence no autonomous powers were invested in the national committee. Nevertheless, the Cherokee had found that the old system of government, which required consensus among 50-odd village delegations, was cumbersome, and the appointment of the national committee was an attempt to develop a more efficient means of handling government business and to facilitate more effective and responsive political decision making. The committee and council demonstrated their political unity by rejecting American offers to buy land in present-day Kentucky, formally rejecting removal, and refusing the U.S. government a road right-of-way from eastern Tennessee to the Coosa River. Between 1809 and 1815, the national committee was delegated management of the lighthorse, resolution of claims by Cherokees against the national annuities, distribution of the national annuities gained in treaties with the United States, and regulation of economic matters. Until 1815, the Cherokee had made appropriations out of the national funds to pay debts incurred by Cherokees, but the national committee ruled in October 1815 that it would no longer pay private debts. This act represented a further rationalization of the Cherokee government, since private economic affairs were now differentiated from the public affairs of the nation, and thereby indicated a further differentiation of polity and economy in Cherokee society.[24]

Younger planter-merchants from the upper towns predominated in the national committee; they were thought to have the experience with and knowledge of American institutions necessary to negotiate effectively with American officials. They could not, of course, act without the approval of the general council of village chiefs. Chiefs who had played a prominent part in land sales or had advocated removal were not elected to serve on the national committee. The movement toward national political unification was an effort to organize a stronger defense against unauthorized cessions of land and to prevent removal, and the decisions of the Wills Town council of 1809, in formally rejecting the removal proposal and creating a standing committee to manage relations with the United States government, were a step toward greater Cherokee national political integration and increased internal political differentiation.[25]

CENTRALIZATION OF LEGITIMATE COERCIVE FORCE

Between 1810 and 1816 the Cherokee were continually harassed by American intruders and pressured by American officials to cede land. Small groups of dissident Cherokee decided to remove west, but most

Cherokee continued their efforts to unify and rationalize their government. In 1810, at a council at Ustanali, the seven clans unanimously agreed to abolish blood revenge and to make the killing of a fellow clansman a capital offense. This action represented the formal delegation of the use of legitimate force to the Cherokee national council, and met a major criteria for the formation of a state political structure. Turtle-at-Home marked the document. As the representative for the seven national clans, Turtle-at-Home had been a prominent political leader among the upper towns since at least the early 1800's; on several occasions he was speaker for the national council, and he was a member of the national committee that was appointed in 1809. He was strongly opposed to the building of roads through the Cherokee nation and to land cessions, and his opinion lent support to the argument that the national clan council approved and gave legitimation to Cherokee innovations in political centralization and unification that were designed to facilitate resistance to removal and land sales. The seven clans gave direct and explicit legitimation to the centralization of judicial affairs in the national council and to the delegation of law enforcement to the Cherokee lighthorse. The delegation of control over blood revenge indicates both a centralization of coercive power in the national polity and the further differentiation of kinship and judicial institutions.[26]

Some writers have given credit to American officials for the abolishment of blood revenge, but as we shall see, in the other southeastern societies there was no similar voluntary centralization of blood revenge during the same time period. Therefore the mere encouragement of American officials is not sufficient to explain the Cherokee action. American officials had tried as early as 1797 to convince the Cherokee to abolish blood revenge, but those suggestions did not become institutionalized in Cherokee society until the seven clans agreed to delegate their judicial prerogatives to the national council in an effort to facilitate national preservation. Others have argued that the growth of Cherokee commerce and of the planter-merchant class gave rise to state sponsored adjudication and regular and stable law administration, and thus to the centralization of the Cherokee court system.[27] Certainly the interests of the planter-merchants are important for understanding the overall centralization of Cherokee judicial law—for example, as early as 1800 the lighthorse were assigned to collect debts and protect private property. Nevertheless, the delegation of coercive authority to the national government arose not from the forced usurpation of judicial control by the planter-merchant class but rather from the gradual development of consensus and consent of the seven clans, who historically were invested with judicial prerogatives.

After 1810 the role of the seven clans in judicial proceedings faded into the background, but it did not entirely disappear. Even after the removal, as late as 1839, there were major judicial events that still required the approval of the seven clans. After 1810 judicial proceedings were invested in the national council and lighthorse police, but the judicial proceedings of the national council were still attended by representatives of the national clans, and the clan leaders were asked to give informal consent to judicial actions by the national council. Clan and community norms and values continued to inform the judicial procedures of the national council and the later court systems. Community sanctions and threats of ostracism and withdrawal continued to be major forces of social control over individual behavior. In the judicial proceedings the cases were managed more on Cherokee norms of justice than on Anglo-Saxon judicial procedures. For example, in the period before the American Civil War there was little concept of intent in cases of murder or injury. The judges and jurors were interested primarily in whether the accused had performed the deed; there was no legitimate plea of self-defense.[28]

THE CHEROKEE FUNDAMENTALIST
MOVEMENT OF 1811–12

The first visions and the beginnings of the Cherokee fundamentalist movement were reported in early February 1811. There does not seem to have been any significant precipitating event, except perhaps the pressure and distress experienced by a significant number of Cherokee who were troubled by the economic, political, and legal changes that the national council had recently adopted. Though the movement appealed to conservative Cherokees, who were dissatisfied with the changing conditions and wanted to return to the old religious, medicinal, and economic practices, not all conservatives accepted the message of the leading prophet, Charley, a mixed blood from Coosawatie; it was in fact rejected by the conservative mountain Cherokee of Charley's home area, but he found more followers at a religious gathering at Ustanali. All the Cherokee prophets and visionaries were generally fundamentalist, and blamed the loss of game and their ancient lifestyle on the failure of the Cherokee to adhere to the ancient religious beliefs and practices. Charley's special message was that the spiritual "mother of the nation" had abandoned the Cherokee because they had adopted the agricultural practices and the grain mills of the Americans. The Great Spirit was also displeased that the Cherokee had not kept out American intruders and had not protected Cherokee holy sites at Tugaloo and Chota, and furthermore had been harsh in using whipping as punishment of lawbreakers. Charley told his audiences that if they returned to their horticultural methods, returned to hunting, excluded Americans from Cherokee country, and abandoned the clothes and material goods of the Americans, then the Great Spirit would send sufficient game for them to live as they had formerly lived. Charley's most extravagant prediction was that those who did not believe would be destroyed in a hailstorm, and he designated an area on the highest peak of the Smoky Mountains as a safe refuge for believers. Hundreds of believers went to the mountain-top refuge, but the prediction failed to materialize and Charley was discredited.[29]

During 1811, several conditions provided a context for a temporary revival of the movement. The fur trade continued to decline, and more Cherokee were required to move into husbandry and agriculture. The principal chief, Black Fox, died early in the year and was replaced by Path Killer, while Toochelar of the lower towns became second chief. There was famine during the summer; there were rumors of war; and during the summer, the Shawnee chief Tecumseh came to the southeastern nations with his anti-American and fundamentalist message. In February of 1812, prophets reported a second vision in which the Great Spirit was still angry with the Cherokee and told them that they should turn their attention to reclaiming their sacred towns of Tugaloo and Chota and restore the religious dances and ceremonies, and also should have confidence in their traditional medicines. Several prophets rose, made predictions of world destruction, and then lost credibility when the predictions failed to materialize.

By late April 1812, both the national council and Meigs, the U.S. agent, considered the movement ineffectual, and it disintegrated without the use of force or explicit repression by either Meigs or the council. The planter-merchant class had on the whole opposed the movement, and Ridge had actively opposed the prophet Charley. Ridge's argument was that a strongly fundamentalist and anti-American posture would bring defeat and destruction to the now relatively tiny Cherokee nation, whose population was about 20,000. Ridge and the planters opposed the prophets and favored alliance with the Americans in the War of 1812, and also in 1813 when the Red Stick War erupted among the Creek. In July 1813, when the Creek lower towns asked for Cherokee assistance against the Red Stick fundamentalists, although the older Cherokee chiefs favored neutrality, the younger chiefs favored supporting the Creek lower towns because they thought the fundamentalist movement could revive fundamentalist sympathies in the Cherokee nation and threaten Cherokee national security.[30]

William McLoughlin argues that the Cherokee movement was not merely a fundamentalist movement but rather an attempt to reconcile change and tradition. Many Cherokee were attempting to reconcile the events of the political crisis of 1808–10 and faced the problem of reconciling political and economic change while retaining their national identity. In the end, the Cherokee movement did not become an institutionalized feature of Cherokee society, but it did indicate that a significant portion of the Cherokee were distressed by the agricultural, cultural, and material changes that were affecting their lives. Most Cherokee retained non-differentiated cultural orientations and conservative orientations toward change.

In the ancient world view, deviation from the sacred norms and laws spelled potential disaster and this-worldly misfortune. Similar themes ran through the visions of the prophets, who blamed Cherokee misfortunes, including the scarcity of game, on their failure to adhere to the old ways of life. Only by returning to the ancient modes of hunting, horticulture, and religious adherence would the Cherokee rid themselves of the pressing American threats to land and the need to adopt alternative economic and political institutions. When the predictions of the prophets failed to come true, the prophets and their notion of this-worldly retribution for experiments in political and economic change were discredited, and, indirectly, the political and economic changes that were in process in Cherokee society were acknowledged as legitimate.[31]

CAUSES OF SOCIAL CHANGE

The external threats of removal, pressures for land sales, and American intruders onto Cherokee land would seem to provide an explanation for Cherokee political unification and increased centralization and differentiation. Yet these threats were not unique to the Cherokee: the other southeastern nations faced similar threats, but did not respond by increasing political centralization, differentiation, or unification. Though the Cherokee unified their nation and centralized and differentiated the polity as a means of fighting removal threats and land threats, the external geopolitical pressures are not sufficient to explain Cherokee institutional change.

Further, though many writers have argued that the Cherokee planter-merchant class led in the political and economic changes in Cherokee society,[32] relatively similar class structures emerged in the other three societies without bringing political change, and the Cherokee planters and merchants did not dominate the Cherokee polity. Throughout the 1795–1817 period, Cherokee norms of political authority, egalitarianism, accountability, and consensus decision making predominated. Men like Doublehead who attempted to assert political control were rebuffed by the Cherokee political community. The chiefs who advocated removal became very unpopular. Wealth could not be translated directly into political power, and those who tried failed. In 1810 planters attempted to gain political control of the government, which caused some instability. The Cherokee community controlled their leaders by means of normative and community sanctions. Leaders who did not conform to the wishes of the majority were deposed from political office, even, in the case of Double-head, who flagrantly defied the Cherokee community by his direct personal benefit from treaty negotiations, executed. When the principal chief Black Fox advocated removal, he was deposed from office by a large majority of the Cherokee villages. James Vann, who was the richest planter-merchant among the Cherokee and was influential among the younger planter-merchant chiefs of the upper towns, could not assume an overt position of national political leadership for fear of losing his life.[33]

Cherokee political community and consensus prevailed over class position and personal charisma. Leaders who took a position on treaties that went against the general will of the people were subject to dismissal or, in unusual cases, to execution. The chiefs were not free to sell land without the consent of the national council, and it was unpopular to speak in favor of land sales. The Cherokee chiefs did not form a political aristocracy. Rather, there were about 60 to 70 chiefs who shared a diffuse authority through negotiated consensus formation. The chiefs did not have coercive powers, and no important business was concluded without consulting the sentiments of the Cherokee community at large. Even the U.S. agent Meigs commented that the political power in Cherokee government was held by the conservative chiefs: "The chiefs never conclude any very important business before they find the popular sentiments of their people."[34] The small class of Cherokee planters and merchants occupied prominent political positions partly because the more conservative leaders needed their skills in language and business and their knowledge of U.S. customs, and they kept their influence so long as they were loyal to the nationalistic goals of the more conservative chiefs. Lacking the means to rise to positions of direct control of the Cherokee polity, they had to be content with their role as important members of the national committee, knowing that ultimate authority resided in the national council of village chiefs. The planters did not challenge the political order directly and did not attempt to assume direct political control of the polity, but they did try to bring about change by appealing to the nationalist sentiments of the conservative chiefs, offering a means of preserving Cherokee nationality and land base through economic and political change.

The Cherokee, faced with threats of loss of land and removal to new territory, created a national committee to regularize and rationalize government administration. The formation of the national committee met little institutional opposition because kinship and religion prerogatives did not interpenetrate political organization, and the national committee was formed after the Cherokee were nationally unified and mobilized to preserve territory and national political autonomy. Forming the national committee did not involve overturning religious world views or the rights of kinship groups or the loyalties of regional political groupings. The Cherokee societal community, or kinship-ceremonial complex, did not create a political nationality, before or after the removal crisis, but the Cherokee societal community did legitimate political unification, differentiation, and centralization. Leaders of the national clan system were instrumental in the whole process of forming a unified political nationality, centralizing political and coercive power in the polity, and increasing internal differentiation of the polity. Under threats of removal and loss of political autonomy, the relatively solidary Cherokee societal community, which was differentiated from the political sphere, provided the Cherokee with an institutional basis that helped them form a stronger and more unified political nationality and a more centralized and differentiated national government. External threats and a market-oriented planter class were, indeed, major forces for change, but once the Cherokee leaders and population in general understood that change was necessary, the political changes in Cherokee society were legitimated by consensus within the Cherokee societal community. Furthermore, the differentiation of the Cherokee clan-ceremonial complex from political relations allowed the clan system to provide social legitimation for and support of the new, more centralized political institutions. At the same time, it did not present institutional obstacles for change, because of the separation of kinship and religion from national political relations.

Limited Choctaw Political Centralization

Between 1795 and 1817, the Choctaw did not make any significant steps toward national political unification or develop any further differentiation of national political institutions. The only major change in government organization came in 1812 when blood revenge against American citizens was abolished, and even this change was the result of pressures from American agents and Choctaw treaty obligations; among the Choctaw themselves, blood revenge continued into the 1820's. The Choctaw did not follow the Cherokee path of political unification, political centralization, and increased political differentiation, though they were subject to similar pressures for cession of land to the United States and similar pressures from American settlers; they also experienced a similar decline in the fur trade economy and the emergence of a small planter-merchant class.[35] The Choctaw's localistic and decentralized kinship system, which was not differentiated from regional and national political relations, was a significant political and social difference. The local iksas and three major political divisions in Choctaw society retained particularistic political rights that inhibited national political unification and any movement toward political centralization and internal political differentiation.

The Choctaw occupied large areas of fertile land in the south and also held a strategic position between the United States and the Spanish colony in the Floridas, and beginning in 1800 American settlers put steady pressure on Choctaw territory. Since there was little central government among the Choctaw, each of the three district divisions acted as independent nations. The three districts gathered occasionally in a national council, but binding decisions required unanimous consensus among the divisions, which had a history of political and military antagonism, and therefore few decisions were possible and there was little national political unity.[36] In a treaty in 1801, the Choctaw ceded 2.6 million acres of land to the United States and agreed to the right-of-way for a road through their territory. Unlike the Creek and the Cherokee, the Choctaw had no objections to the building of roads through their territory, but they reserved the right to establish inns and to supply travelers. In 1803, when the three districts could not agree on selling land to the United States, the southern district on its own ceded 853,000 acres of its land in order to pay off debts of chiefs and individual Choctaw that were owed to traders. Some of the newly ceded land was settled quickly by American planters. Fear that national political autonomy and territory were rapidly disappearing exacerbated internal political cleavages among the Choctaw. After a treaty in 1805 ceded 4.1 million acres of southern land to the United States, a violent antitreaty party arose and the southern district chief Pushmataha was challenged to personal combat. Even so, the 1805 treaty was ratified by the United States four years later.[37]

Unlike the Cherokee and the Creek, the Choctaw did not produce a fundamentalist movement. All three districts, except a small disaffected group, sided with the United States during the Red Stick War and fought with the United States against the British in the War of 1812. And in 1811, when Tecumseh visited the Choctaw with a message of alliance with the British and prophetic teachings of his brother, the Shawnee Prophet, the Choctaw refused to join the anti-American alliance. Some reports indicate that many of the younger Choctaw, who were disturbed that the treaties were taking away land and threatening political autonomy, favored Tecumseh's message, but the Choctaw chiefs declined to join Tecumseh's military alliance and fundamentalist movement because they believed it was unwise to challenge the increasingly powerful Americans militarily and felt that to do so would end in military defeat and further loss of land

and national independence.[38] Despite pressures for ceding land and increasing American hegemony, the Choctaw did not respond with increased political unification, as had the Cherokee under similar conditions. The three Choctaw political districts remained politically independent, and local kinship groups remained a central feature within Choctaw political institutions. The Choctaw exhibited little movement in the direction of either political unification or differentiation of polity and kinship.

American officials found the tradition of blood revenge among Indians both distasteful and disruptive, and in treaty agreements with the southeastern nations they always dictated that blood revenge be curbed against murderers who were American citizens. In 1812 the Choctaw council officially abandoned blood revenge against American murderers of Choctaws, although among the Choctaw themselves, blood revenge remained in practice into the late 1820's. Between 1812 and 1816, the families of Choctaw murder victims of Americans demanded payments for the deaths of relatives, since Americans were rarely if ever convicted in American courts for murdering a Choctaw, but after 1817 the United States discontinued such payments.

The centralization of control over blood revenge in 1812 by the Choctaw council was largely a change imposed by American officials and by the need to maintain peaceful and regular relations with the American government. Unlike the Cherokee, the Choctaw did not show much interest in institutionalizing governmental control over the kin-based law of retaliation. The abolishment of blood revenge in 1812 was largely a curtailment of blood revenge against American citizens and involved negligible centralization or differentiation of internal Choctaw judicial and kinship relations.[39]

Chickasaw Resistance to Political Change

The Chickasaw did not make any significant changes in political organization during the 1795–1817 period. There were no movements toward increased national political unification or differentiation of political institutions. Since the late 1790's, the king of the Chickasaw had been Chinibee, whose hereditary leadership derived from the old French and Spanish faction; the first war chief, who held the title of Piomingo, or Mountain Chief, was the leader of the American party, consisting of planters and merchants. Though the king held only nominal political power, the same was true also of the Chickasaw council, which in 1805 was no longer meeting in a village sacred square or village town house. There was, in fact, little positive law. Community normative sanctions were the primary means of social control.[40]

By 1805, many of the mixed blood Chickasaw planters and merchants had gained access to high political office. Some, like the second-ranked chief Isaac Albertson, were traders and hereditary chiefs; others, like Levi Colbert, head of the large and influential Colbert family, held honorary chieftain rank because of past service to the nation and held important positions in the national council because of their business skills and knowledge of English and American institutions, which were increasingly necessary in the transactions with the U.S. government. The conservative Chickasaw chiefs were willing to pay thousands of dollars to induce the merchants and planters to help them in their councils. In fact, in 1805 the Chickasaw council agreed to a treaty with the United States to cede land in order to raise funds of which half, about $10,000, eventually were used by Chickasaw merchants to pay their private debts to the trading company of John Forbes.[41]

Like the other southeastern societies, the Chickasaw were subject to changing geopolitical and economic conditions. By 1805 game was declining as a result of overexploitation, and more Chickasaw were being forced to turn to cattle raising and agriculture, although the rapid transition toward agriculture did not come until the 1820's. Between 1796 and 1817 the Chickasaw negotiated several treaties that ceded land to the United States. In the treaties of 1801, 1805, 1816, and 1818, the Chickasaw ceded their extensive lands north of the present state of Mississippi. The treaty of 1801 provided for the building of a road through Chickasaw country, and Chickasaw merchants quickly set up stands to sell merchandise and agricultural products to travelers. The Colberts, George and Levi, helped write and negotiate the treaties with an eye toward promoting Chickasaw-owned economic enterprise, and toward excluding American traders and entrepreneurs from the nation. Also, between 1801 and 1815 the Chickasaw council occasionally asked for American economic aid in the form of tools, hoes, plows, spinning wheels, and other agricultural equipment.

By 1809, despite the land sales, the remaining Chickasaw territory was besieged by American squatters and by thefts of timber, and the Chickasaw council demanded that the intruders be removed. Again in 1816, the council complained of intruders and of loose American cattle. The council was greatly dissatisfied with existing territorial boundaries and upset about American pressure for cession of land south of the Tennessee River.[42] Nonetheless, though the Chickasaw had sufficient cause for grievance, they did not fall in with Tecumseh's idea of a militantly fundamentalist alliance against the Americans. When Tecumseh came to Chickasaw country in 1811, the Colberts and other planters and merchants there would have nothing to do with his fundamentalist and militant message, and they also showed no sympathy for the Creek "Red Stick" fundamentalists during the Red Stick War of 1813–14. Even the conservative leaders were not willing to join the cause of the fundamentalist movements, and the Chickasaw supported the United States with troops and sales of agricultural products.[43]

Despite the changing economic and geopolitical situation, the Chickasaw did not make any significant centralization or differentiation of their political institutions during this period. Though U.S. agents were able to end blood revenge against Americans, they could not convince the Chickasaw to abandon blood revenge against their own people. Despite efforts of agents to substitute payments, the Chickasaw law of blood continued into the late 1830's. By 1805 the Chickasaw were leaving off the old tradition of taking the life of a near relative if a murderer had escaped, but even murder by accident still required taking the life of the murderer, and the norm that the murderer must surrender voluntarily and allow himself to be executed remained in effect throughout the period.[44]

CLASS AND POLITICAL COMMUNITY

Some scholars believe that between 1800 and 1818 the planter-merchant class, especially members of the Colbert family, gained de facto political control over the Chickasaw government. The planters and merchants were acquisitively oriented and quickly accepted American agricultural aid. They established farms and plantations, imported slaves, and promoted schools for their children, and many became wealthy. By 1818 the Chickasaw had a class-stratified society, consisting of a very small group of slaveholders and merchants and a large majority of hunter-farmers.[45] Accounts by American agents of the period make it clear that the Colberts led a clique of merchants and planters who manipulated the old chiefs and controlled the kin-based government to augment the material interests of their class. Scholars have argued that the slaveholder clique gained political power while the conservative chiefs and the mass of Chickasaw withdrew from politics, and the planter clique thus was free to manage the government for their own private interests by means of treaties and laws that promoted economic enterprise. In this view, the Chickasaw chiefs are considered the pliable tools within the hands of the planter clique, who, since the death of the last strong traditional chief in 1795, had control over the national chief and council.[46]

There is no question that the planters gained significant access to Chickasaw leadership and manipulated the government toward promotion of commercial ends; the records of U.S. agents clearly show this. But the records quite understandably overrepresent the actions of Chickasaw planters, since they were the ones the agents dealt with; there is no basis for concluding that the more conservative and less market-oriented Chickasaw chiefs and other men actually abdicated rule in favor of the planters. The principal chief, Chinibee, and his more conservative national council led the majority in the nation and were actively opposed to any changes in the national political order. The planters could not introduce more political centralization or differentiation into the Chickasaw polity because the chief and the majority were strongly opposed to political change. The U.S. agent noted in 1826, "So far from endeavoring to adopt the manner of the whites, if one of them insofar as shows a disposition to conform to them, say in dress, he is forced to abandon them or subject himself to frequent insult and his influence amongst them [is] completely destroyed. They still maintain their old customs, and no argument, however cogent, can induce them to depart from them."[47] Thus, although the planters used the national council to promote their business interests, they were not strong enough politically, and did not control the coercive powers, to be able to restructure the Chickasaw polity. Some planters, like George Colbert and his son Pittman Colbert, actively sided with the conservative chiefs and did not overtly favor change in the political system. They operated within the traditional Chickasaw political framework, and they had to act in the national political interest of the majority of Chickasaw conservatives or else be deposed from office. For all their economic and political success, the Chickasaw planters had few ways of introducing political innovations, and they were well aware of a consensus against change in the Chickasaw political order. All this is consistent with the theoretical argument that less differentiated societies should show strong resistance to institutional change.

For their part, the conservative chiefs were willing enough to promote the material interests of the planters as a way of getting them to help manage Chickasaw relations with the U.S. government. Since the Chickasaw nation held land collectively and there were large surpluses of farming land for the small fields of the subsistence farmers and for the large plantations of the planters, the promotion of commercial enterprises for a handful of planters did not directly harm the subsistence farmers. The two groups were not economic competitors, nor did the planters monopolize the land as private property or exploit the labor of the other Chickasaw. The conservative chiefs induced the planters to help manage increasingly complex and threatening relations with the U.S. government; in return, the chiefs were willing to pay off the debts of the merchants and planters, as they did in the 1805 treaty, and allow the planters to benefit personally from treaty arrangements, if that ensured that the planters would help protect the nation from American political and territorial encroachments. This arrangement was mutually beneficial to both conservatives and planters, and it took place within the Chickasaw political structure; the conservatives demanded that the structure remain intact, and the planters were unable to challenge it overtly.

Creek Fundamentalism and Coerced Centralization

During the 1795–1817 period, the Creek did not form a stronger national political unity or a more differentiated polity, but after military defeat in the Red Stick War of 1813–14 and the associated massive surrender of land, the Creek centralized national control over blood revenge and held the remainder of their land as a collective group. Between 1797 and 1813, the U.S. agent Benjamin Hawkins attempted to induce the Creek national council to centralize internal control over blood revenge and to create a more regular national government. But his efforts, though complied with, did not become institutionalized by a consensus among the Creek until 1814–18, after the defeat of fundamentalist opposition in the Red Stick War, which forcibly eliminated much of the opposition to change and convinced the remaining opposition to agree to the new laws. Of the major southeastern nations, the Creek showed the strongest overt resistance to political and economic change, although by 1818 the Creek had a more centralized legal system than that of the Choctaw and Chickasaw, who continued to adhere to the kin-based law in internal relations.

Throughout the 1795–1817 period, the competition for political leadership continued between the major red and white towns. American agents preferred to support the leaders of the two major red towns, Coweta and Tuckabatchee, although Fushatchee Micco of Cussetah, the central white town of the lower town Creek, was a major national figure in the 1790's. In 1799 Cussetah Micco was the speaker of the national council, and thus Cussetah was still centrally involved in the national government even though American officials favored Efau Hadjo of Tuckabatchee as Creek principal chief between 1795 and 1803. Since his temporary incarceration at the treaty of Shoulderbone in 1787, Hoboithle Micco of Talisee was disgruntled with the Americans and participated with the loose and shifting coalition of fundamentalist towns that opposed American proposals for economic change and for regularizing and centralizing the national council. United States agents ignored Hoboithle Micco's claims to Creek national leadership, because of his anti-Americanism, and this further alienated him from the Americans.[48]

Beginning in 1797, the strongest effort to restructure the Creek government came not from the Creek themselves but from the U.S. agent Benjamin Hawkins. Hawkins proposed a plan of civilization for the Creek, and in particular tried to convince the Creek national council to centralize control over law and regularize its own meetings. He also tried to reconstruct the Creek economy by introducing plows, spinning wheels, and looms, and by subsidizing agricultural production with smiths. Hawkins proposed that the national council regulate blood revenge and punish crimes perpetrated by individual Creeks against American citizens. Between 1797 and 1799, the Creek national council acquiesced to Hawkins's plan for centralizing and regularizing the Creek government, after Hawkins made it clear to the chiefs that violations of treaty infractions, especially for horse stealing and murder, had to be punished by the Creek government, for if they were not, the United States would hold the entire nation responsible for crimes committed by individuals. The Creek chiefs realized that the safety of the nation was at stake and that only centralization of control over treaty violations would prevent American retaliation.

In 1798 the chiefs agreed to curb blood revenge against Americans and to accept payments for the murder of Creek; in 1799 and 1800 Hawkins insisted that the Creek appoint lighthorse police to maintain order in the towns.[49] But even though the national council agreed to abolish blood revenge and punish treaty violators, it was loath to enforce the law because the Creek chiefs as well as the lighthorse police were afraid that the clans of the punished individuals would retaliate against them. At least until 1814, the chiefs acted to enforce the law often only under direct threats from the U.S. agent; there was no national consensus over centralization and the differentiation of law from clan relations.[50]

Some Creek villages showed overt and conscious opposition to Hawkins's civilization and political centralization plan. As early as 1797, Hoboithle Micco of Talisee led an anti-American and fundamentalist group of towns in opposition to Hawkins's proposal for political and economic change. In 1799, when Hawkins demanded punishment of several leaders of Talisee for raiding and stealing supplies from a Spanish and American team that was surveying the American-Spanish border in west Florida, the Creek chiefs at first refused to take any action against the raiders. Hawkins pressured Mad Dog, the principal chief, into punishing the raiders, and for their part in the incident several prominent men from Talisee, a white town and a town of refuge, were whipped and publicly humiliated, but the whippings only created more resentment at Talisee and stiffened opposition to the new plans for change.[51]

More fundamentalist opposition was generated by demands from the state of Georgia for more land cessions and for rights-of-way for a road through the Creek country. By 1802 the lower town Creek were being harassed by American squatters, and lower town chiefs were reluctant to cede land to the Americans for fear that their men would join the forces of Augustus Bowles, an American Tory who had influence among the lower towns and Seminoles and had been organizing raids on the Spanish since the early 1790's. In the treaty of 1802, the lower town chiefs compromised by selling Georgia a tract of land and declaring that they could not gain support to sell any more tracts. Georgia still pressed for more land, and in 1803 Talisee, the Mikusuki, a central Seminole town that had formerly been associated with the Creek lower towns, and Broken Arrow, a daughter town of Coweta—all of which opposed the Americans—ceded land to the Forbes Trading Company in order to pay debts. The unauthorized sale of land to Forbes made the national council furious, but little action was taken.[52]

In 1803 Hoboithle Micco of Talisee challenged the American-supported Efau Hadjo of Tuckabatchee for leadership of the Creek national council. This challenge failed for lack of support, and Efau Hadjo, who was old and wanted to retire as chief, then designated Hopoie Micco of Hickory Ground as his successor. The passing of leadership from Tuckabatchee, the major red town of the upper town Creek, to Hopoie Micco of Hickory Ground signified a return of leadership to a white town. Hickory Ground was a town of refuge, "the holiest town in the nation," and a daughter town of Talisee, which was struggling for national leadership. But Talisee was strongly fundamentalist and anti-American and therefore was not likely to be recognized by the American government. Furthermore, Hopoie Micco favored the economic and political civilization plan and was willing to use force to suppress opposition. He enforced the national laws to punish violators of treaty agreements with the United States.[53]

Hawkins's innovations tended to exacerbate Creek political cleavages. Between 1803 and 1805, Cussetah and many of the lower towns that were opposed to Hawkins tried to confine him to his friends at Tuckabatchee and the allied upper towns. Hoboithle Micco of Talisee vowed to chase Hawkins out of Creek country and advocated the restoration of the old political order and customs. The fundamentalist villages were, in fact, so strongly opposed to the new economic innovations that they threatened to kill anyone who adopted use of the plow. In the summer of 1804, when Hawkins proposed a new treaty to the Creek council that would allow the Creek to cede land to pay their increasing trade debts, the opposition rejected the plan and many opposition villages refused to attend the meeting. Later in the year Hawkins secured an agreement from the Creek, but the Creek demanded such a high price for the land that the United States Senate would not ratify the treaty. From 1805 to 1814, despite continued American pressures, the Creek held steadfast in their refusal to sell land.[54]

In the winter of 1805–6, two men from Cussetah murdered Hopoie Micco, the principal chief. The record does not indicate whether the murder resulted from a private matter or from political motives, but Cussetah,

a white town, was opposed to Hawkins and the civilization plan that
Hopoie Micco had embraced. In June 1806, in session for choosing a
principal chief, the national council could only agree on Alex Cornells, a
mixed blood who lived at Tuckabatchee. Cornells was a close associate of
Hawkins. Perhaps because he feared that he would meet the same fate as
Hopoie Micco, Cornells declined to serve as principal chief. The council
could not come to any further agreement, and from then until the outbreak
of civil war in 1813, the Creek were much divided and unable to agree on
a single leader for principal chief, even though the position carried largely
nominal authority. Both the lower towns and the upper towns emerged
with their own independent chiefs. In 1806 Big Warrior of Tuckabatchee
was reported chief of the upper towns, and Hoboithle Micco of Talisee
was the leader of the upper town villages that were opposed to the civilization plan. In 1807, Little Prince of Broken Arrow, a daughter village of the
major red town of Coweta, and Tuskegee Tustenuggee of Cussetah were
the leaders of the lower towns. Between 1808 and 1810, the fundamentalist Hoboithle Micco of Talisee was recognized as principal chief by the
lower towns and some of the upper towns, but he was actively opposed
by Big Warrior of Tuckabatchee, a politically ambitious slaveholder who
was in favor of the civilization plan.[55] Big Warrior's opposition created a
split between the upper and lower towns, and Big Warrior then sought
Spanish support and an alliance to back his bid for national leadership;
the council, however, warned the Spanish that Big Warrior should not be
regarded as a principal chief.

Fundamentalist opposition to the economic and political civilization
plan gained momentum as economic conditions worsened; though game
became more scarce and fewer hunters could supply their material needs
through the fur trade, many of the Creek, especially in the more conservative upper town villages, still refused to turn to agriculture and husbandry.
In May 1811 the Creek were internally divided over political leadership.
The lower towns were in favor of the system of separate chiefs for the
upper and lower towns, while the upper towns were internally divided,
with some villages dissatisfied with the American-backed government and
others demanding a return to the old form of government, in which the
white towns assumed leadership.

Hawkins, still hoping to unify the Creek politically under a national
government, persuaded them to adopt a national executive committee
consisting of nine chiefs from the upper towns and four chiefs from the
lower towns; the committee was to meet alternately at Tuckabatchee and
at Coweta. Big Warrior of Tuckabatchee, who favored the civilization plan
of the Americans and therefore was a more acceptable leader to the Americans than the fundamentalist leaders at Talisee, was made speaker of the

council. Hoboithle Micco of Talisee was excluded from any claims to be principal chief; Hawkins also got the chiefs to depose Hoboithle Micco of Talisee from national office. In order to accomplish this, Hawkins overtly supported the political aspirations of both major red towns, Coweta and Tuckabatchee, while excluding the major white towns, Cussetah and Talisee, from direct leadership. This event began a 50-year period of American support of the major red towns over the white towns in internal Creek political affairs.[56]

THE CREEK CIVIL WAR

The events of the Creek civil war are not of direct importance here, but the conditions that led to the war are illustrative of the cleavages and conflicts within Creek society. Numerous conditions created stress and discontent in Creek society before the outbreak of the civil war. Between 1807 and 1811, the Americans imposed taxes on the Alabama towns for transporting their agricultural produce to settlements down the Alabama River, something that they had formerly done quite freely. In 1811, when the Americans asked permission to build a road through the Creek nation, the Alabama and other upper town villages refused, fearing that the road would bring American settlers and result in a further decline of hunting and loss of land, but the Americans began the road anyway. There were also increasing numbers of American intruders on Creek land and hunting territory, and the Forbes Trading Company laid claim to Creek land in payment for debts. In the background were rumors of war between the Americans and the British. All these were contributing conditions to civil war, but they were not the primary cause.

In September 1811, Tecumseh visited the Creek upper towns. He gave his militaristic and fundamentalist message to the Creek, and although Big Warrior of Tuckabatchee rejected Tecumseh's plan, many of the fundamentalist and anti-American upper towns were willing to listen. Tecumseh was not asking for immediate military action but told his adherents to remain quiet until the British were ready with aid.[57] Soon several prophets emerged among the Creek, at first mostly among the disgruntled Alabama towns, all giving the message that the present difficulties of the Creek were caused by their failure to adhere strictly to the teachings of the Great Spirit. The Creek must reject the civilization plan, though they could continue to trade and accept some material changes. Since many of the upper town Creek already opposed the American political and economic civilization plan, Tecumseh's message, coupled with a military alliance with the British, merely accentuated already existing fundamentalist orientations.

Oral tradition says that the primary cause of the Creek civil war or

Red Stick War was the rejection of American insistence on abolishment of blood revenge and other innovations in government.[58] Hawkins had systematically imposed a plan of economic and political change—the introduction of the red town-dominated executive committee in 1811, and the insistence that the Creek council punish violators of treaty stipulations concerning murder, thefts, and other crimes—and in doing so he had created much resentment among the upper town Creek. He had particularly alienated the Talisee, the long-time fundamentalist white town and claimant of national leadership, and the disgruntled leaders of Talisee embraced the new prophets movement, and also embraced Tecumseh's doctrine of executing chiefs who were compliant with the American civilization plan. Thus, although the leaders of Talisee were in many ways no different in orientation from the majority of fundamentalist upper towns, they also saw the new movement as a means to regain national leadership and punish the compliant pro-American chiefs, and reestablish the old political order.

The event that precipitated the Red Stick War involved the rejection of the chief's authority to administer justice outside clan law. The executive committee of the upper towns complied with American requests that murderers of Americans be executed and that robbers be publicly whipped. Hawkins demanded punishment by the national council; if the murderers were not executed he would hold the chiefs directly responsible. In the summer of 1812 six Creek were executed for their crimes, and although one suspect sought protection at Talisee, a traditional place of sanctuary, the armed guards executed him and thereby perpetrated a breach of traditional norms and values.

The Creek civil war erupted after the execution of Little Warrior of Wewocau and a group of his followers. On a return trip after consulting with Tecumseh in the north, Little Warrior, believing that war had started, killed seven families of Americans in Ohio. In March 1813 Little Warrior appeared before the national council to argue that the Creek should join the British and ally with Tecumseh's Indian confederacy in the War of 1812. The national council refused. When word of the murders in Ohio reached the Creek, Hawkins insisted on the execution of Little Warrior's band, which included several prominent upper town leaders. The Creek council complied with Hawkins's demands. The members of Little Warrior's band from the white towns of Wewocau and Tuskegee were executed and one man was executed at Hoithlwaucee, the ancient red war town. Little Warrior sought protection at the holy white town of Hickory Ground, but the Creek lighthorse carried out the death sentence without regard for the protections given in that sacred sanctuary. In addition, at about the same time two men from Oakfuskie were executed for stealing. Men from the red towns of Tuckabatchee and Coweta were prominent participants in the executions, while most of the victims were from white towns.[59]

The executions exacerbated the already hostile relations between the chiefs and the majority of the conservative upper town Creek villages, who refused to recognize the right of the American-backed executive committee and chiefs' council to use force in the executions. There were demands for revenge against the leading chiefs such as Big Warrior of Tuckabatchee, and William McIntosh, a merchant, planter, and head warrior of Coweta, and calls for the death of Hawkins. The conservatives also demanded the destruction of Coweta and Tuckabatchee, the two major red towns, which Hawkins supported for Creek political leadership. The fundamentalists demanded execution of the American-supported chiefs, attempted to restore Hoboithle Micco of Talisee to national political leadership, made their own laws, and plotted to destroy the civilization plan.[60]

The outbreak of the civil war did not divide the nation into red towns against white towns, although the Americans supported the two major red towns, Coweta and Tuckabatchee. The conflict took a more regional form, with lower towns dividing against the majority of upper towns. The fundamentalists or Red Sticks were composed of a combination of both red and white towns, and they composed a majority of the upper town villages. The leading villages for the Red Sticks were the white towns of Talisee, Oakfuskie, and Tuskegee and the red town of Atasi. Only the Yuchi among the lower towns defected to the fundamentalists of the upper towns, while the upper towns and some individual towns were internally divided. The ancient white towns of Coosa and Abihka and nearby associated towns rejected the fundamentalist movement, while Tuckabatchee, the major red town, and a few other associated villages sided with the lower towns. Regional considerations were a stronger criterion for political alliance in the civil war than white or red town affiliation.

The Red Sticks, though a majority, eventually suffered a severe military defeat in the conflict, mainly because the less numerous lower towns got military support from the Americans, the Cherokee, and the Choctaw. The British continued to support Talisee and Hickory Ground for leadership of the Creek confederacy even after their military defeat, but with the defeat, the American-allied red towns of Coweta and Tuckabatchee gained political ascendancy in the nation. The leaders of Hickory Ground and Talisee fled to Spanish territory. The terms of the treaty signed at Fort Jackson in 1814 were harsh: the American negotiator, Andrew Jackson, demanded nearly half of Creek territory, and even the pro-American Creek allies were traumatized over the harshness of the treaty terms.[61]

CENTRALIZATION OF CREEK LAW

After the treaty of 1814, the pro-American Creek gathered on the banks of the Okmulgee River and made national laws and appointed officers to enforce the laws. Having lost half their territory, the Creek wanted to centralize collective ownership of the land that remained and prevent blood revenge from again creating conflict that would jeopardize national territory and political autonomy. Land was now considered under the control of the national council, and the penalty for unauthorized cession of land was death. A law was passed extending the right of other towns to enforce the national laws if one town was delinquent in executing the law against its own town members. After the war, the Creek executive committee continued to have the support of the American agent, and when necessary, had access to U.S. troops to arrest and apprehend violators of the peace.[62] Little Prince of Broken Arrow, a daughter village of Coweta, was principal chief when the council met in the lower towns, and Big Warrior of Tuckabatchee was chief when the council met in the upper towns. Hawkins died in 1816, however, and without his presence the executive committee system that he instigated faded into disuse and did not become institutionalized as a central feature of Creek political structure.

The Creek political structure did not become appreciably centralized, since the upper and lower towns retained separate head chiefs and independent councils. Political loyalties were stronger within regional groupings and primary loyalties were given to villages rather than to the national council. The major change in Creek political organization during the early hegemonic period was the formalization of national laws in the control of the national council between 1814 and 1818. In 1817, all the laws adopted by the Creek were written down and clan revenge was formally superseded by the national council and appointed law officers. The Creek national council began to take on more regularly the duties of a legislative body that made laws for national protection and material well-being.[63] In 1818 the Creek confirmed the earlier abolishment of blood revenge, or in other words confirmed the centralization of use of legitimate coercive force in the national council. The code of 1818 also protected and regulated private property, trade, and theft and provided for rules of inheritance through the male line, all of which encouraged the accumulation of private wealth.

With strong American support and the effective elimination of overt fundamentalist opposition, the major red town leaders moved to formalize political centralization of law and the promotion of economic change and commercialism. The prime leader involved in making the legal changes was a wealthy planter and head warrior of Coweta, William McIntosh.

Big Warrior and a few other leaders of Tuckabatchee were also slave-holders, and although there were scattered large slaveholders among the villages of the upper towns, the largest concentration of planters and merchants was located among the lower towns. The large majority of Creek remained subsistence villagers and hunters who continued to resist economic change despite worsening economic conditions for the hunting and trading economy.[64] Most Creek accepted the new national laws, and when some refugee Red Sticks returned from Florida, where they had fled, they accepted the centralization of national law because they understood the futility of trying to resist the American-supported central red towns. The abolishment of blood revenge was also legitimated by a concern that the invocation of blood revenge had been a major cause of the Red Stick War, which had resulted in American intervention and loss of nearly half of Creek land. The centralization of national laws was a means of ensuring greater internal political controls and preventing incidents that might result in further intrusions on Creek political sovereignty and territory by the American government.

Comparisons

During the early period of American hegemony, the Cherokee responded with political unification and some limited internal political differentiation. American officials put pressure on all four southeastern societies to centralize control over blood revenge, and though all four societies abolished blood revenge against Americans, only the Cherokee and the Creek went as far as abolishing the clan law among themselves. Even so, the Creek centralization of law and differentiation of law from kinship organization was the result of external American pressures and defeat of the resistance movement in the Red Stick civil war. Thus the centralization of the legitimate use of force for the Creek involved considerable use of coercion, which sharply contrasts with the consensual abolishment of the clan law among the Cherokee.

The differences in political change between the Cherokee and the other three southeastern societies cannot be explained by differences in world-system or geopolitical context. The Cherokee, like the other southeastern nations, were subject to a declining fur trade, and all four societies were encouraged by the U.S. government and by the incentive of changing economic conditions to make a transition to agriculture and husbandry. Furthermore, all four nations were subject to American demands for land and were harassed by American intruders. The Cherokee alone were subject to a removal threat in 1809–10, but as will be seen, when the Choctaw, the Chickasaw, and the Creek were subject to much stronger removal threats in the 1820's, none responded with political unification. Class structures emerged in all four societies, and planters and merchants were influential political actors in all four societies. Nevertheless, even in Cherokee society, the planters could not challenge the political order directly and introduced change through preexisting political institutions. The fact that the Cherokee planters were more successful at achieving political change than the planters in the other three societies had more to do with the differences in social-political organization among the four societies than with the characteristics of the class structures.

Though the planters showed rationalistic economic orientations, the large majority of people in all four societies retained nondifferentiated cultural orientations and subsistence economic orientations. Hence most southeasterners held conservative attitudes toward institutional change. The Cherokee were not different from the others in this respect, and therefore differences in cultural orientations cannot be the cause of the Cherokee propensity for consensual acceptance of political change. The major difference between Cherokee society and the other three societies was that the Cherokee had a national clan system that was ceremonially integrated and differentiated from national political institutions. The ceremonially integrated national clan system helped legitimate the political unification of the Cherokee while the Cherokee were under external threats to surrender territory and national independence. Similar threats among the other societies did not lead to political unification. Among the Choctaw, the Chickasaw, and the Creek, either there was no national kinship system and/or the kinship system was not differentiated from the organization of the national council. Thus particularistic and local orientations interfered with the formation of national political commitments when the societies were under external threat. Cherokee national political commitments were supported by the consensus of the national clan system in 1809, when the Cherokee declared themselves a unified nation, and in 1810 when the national clan leaders surrendered control of clan law to the national council. The Cherokee had an institutional mechanism for forming a national social consensus, but at the same time the national clan system did not have political prerogatives and therefore did not form an obstacle to national political unification and further differentiation of the Cherokee national government.

A combination of conditions is necessary to explain Cherokee political unification and differentiation. External threats to land and political sovereignty and the presence of a change-oriented and economically rationalistic planter class were necessary conditions for the formation of national political unification and differentiation in the polity, but these conditions did not effect the same result among the Chickasaw, the Creek, or the Choctaw. The presence of the culturally integrated national clan system that was differentiated from political relations was the most critical condition for explaining Cherokee national political unification, political centralization, and increased political differentiation. Cherokee national social integration provided a basis for forming a national political consensus for accepting changes introduced by the planters in the political sphere that were designed to preserve Cherokee territory and national integrity.

The Creek centralized national laws and lawmaking, but the more centralized polity was formed without national social or political consensus. External threats, changing economic conditions, and the formation of a small planter class were not sufficient to unify the Creek; they retained their political allegiances to villages and regions. The Creek political centralization was achieved by the use of force by a minority of the Creek towns, supported when necessary by American arms. Thus the Creek did not centralize their legal system by any consensual procedure. The Creek showed much more overt and sustained fundamentalist resistance to political and economic change than did the other three societies. The Creek national polity, though differentiated from kinship organization, was the least secular of the four southeastern nations at the turn of the nineteenth century. The American plan for a transition from communal village horticulture to small-scale homestead agriculture and the proposed changes in political organization challenged the particularistic religious cultural organization of the villages and the symbolic red-white political organization of the towns. In the struggle between the red and white towns for political leadership, the Americans supported the major red towns because their leaders favored the American civilization plan. The American proposals for economic and political change were resisted because they required the differentiation of culture from political and economic relations, but for most Creek the village remained the primary social, political, and cultural unit. Even the economically rationalistic Creek planters and merchants conducted their political affairs within Creek political institutions and were either unwilling or unable to challenge them. Thus it was difficult to achieve either national political unification or further differentiation of the Creek polity. The nondifferentiation of cultural order from political and village organization helps to account for the strongly fundamentalist orientations of the conservative Creek.

5 THE REMOVAL CRISIS

AFTER THE END OF the War of 1812 and the agreement by the Spanish to relinquish control of the Floridas in 1819, the American government established undisputed control over the entire southeast. In addition, the price of cotton advanced as demand in the English textile industry made cotton farming increasingly profitable. By 1818 the fur trade was an unreliable economic base and the southeastern nations turned to agriculture and cattle raising, which resulted in internal stratification between small-scale subsistence farmers, or villagers in the Creek case, and slave-holding large plantation owners. American settlers and states stepped up their demands for the extinguishment of Indian land titles, and after 1830, official American policy—removal policy—brought the forced relocation of most of the indigenous southeastern nations to lands west of the Mississippi River. This objective was more or less accomplished by 1845.

To all these intense pressures for removal and in the context of changing relations in the world economic system, the four major southeastern nations responded in varying ways. The Chickasaw and the Creek attempted to cope by clinging to their preexisting political institutions. Between 1826 and 1830, a small group of Choctaw planters gained leadership positions and attempted to unify, centralize, and increasingly differentiate the Choctaw polity, but failed, owing in part to the predominance of regional loyalties. The Cherokee showed the most active institutional response to removal pressures. By 1817 the Cherokee had the most extensive and well-integrated social organization; they had a secular polity that was differentiated from kinship; they had centralized the use of legitimate force in the national council and had declared themselves nationally unified as a means of resisting earlier removal attempts; and they had already institutionalized some aspects of internal political differentiation. During the decade 1817–27, the Cherokee proceeded to adopt increased internal differentiation that resulted in the formation of a differentiated constitutional government modeled after the American constitution.

Why was it that of all the four southeastern nations, which were subject to much the same geopolitical pressures and changing world-economic system relations, only the Cherokee formed a highly differentiated polity? This chapter will attempt to answer this question by describing the formation of the Cherokee constitution, the failure of the Choctaw centralization, and the resistance to change by the Creek and Chickasaw.

The Geopolitical Context: Removal Pressures

After the War of 1812, American settlers streamed into Indian country. Settlers saw arable land for cultivation and reasoned that, not only was agriculture a better use for the land than hunting but also the Indians had more land than they could possibly use for hunting. The federal government was unable, and at times unwilling, to restrain settler encroachment on Indian land, and squatters found little difficulty in evading treaty-based restrictions on settlement of Indian territory. After the rapid rise in the price of cotton, land seekers clamored for the opportunity to establish plantations in the southern interior. Southern planters, politicians, and land speculators lobbied Congress for extinguishment of Indian title and removal of the southeastern nations to locations west of the Mississippi River.[1] The presence of the Indian nations, which claimed large tracts of fertile and arable land, was regarded as a major impediment to the economic integration and development of the southern export economy.

Since only the federal government had the constitutional authority to manage relations with the Indian nations that occupied territory outside the borders of the original thirteen colonies, southern state governments put pressure on the federal government to extinguish Indian title within their chartered state limits, and when the federal government did not act quickly, the states, pressured by the planters, accused the federal government of indecisiveness and slowness. Until 1828 the federal government was still following a policy of peaceful removal, and it interpreted state interference in land and treaty negotiations with the Indians as an infringement on federal constitutional powers and refused to bow to state pressure to remove the southeastern nations.[2]

This policy, and the whole policy on states' rights, changed after 1829 and the succession of Democrat Andrew Jackson to the presidency. John Quincy Adams had lost support on the frontier and in the southern states for refusing to act quickly on the removal and title questions, whereas

Jackson only reflected popular opinion when he argued that the Indians must not stand in the way of American national and economic growth. In his view, the resistance of the southeastern Indian nations was an obstacle to American economic integration, political expansion, and geopolitical security in the lower Mississippi Valley.[3]

As a strong states' rights advocate, Jackson was quite agreeable to the wishes of the southern states to extend their laws over Indian territory and extinguish the right of the Indian governments to function. The states had no desire to incorporate the Indians into their populations; they just wanted them to move out, somewhere west of the Mississippi River, so that their old lands could be put to agricultural use and make work for a growing white (and slave) population. The Indian Removal Act, passed by Congress in 1830, made it official American policy to remove all eastern Indian nations. No effort was made by the federal government to curtail the efforts of the states to pressure the Indians into removal; Jackson and the succeeding Democratic administrations did not protect the Indian nations because the potential conflict between federal jurisdiction in Indian affairs and states' rights issues threatened the political unity of the American government. From 1830 to 1845 most eastern Indian nations were either induced or forced to cede their eastern territories and remove west. Though the removal policy had its basis in land and export economy interests, the issue that determined the policy was that of states' rights, and the states were the primary instruments by which the southeastern nations were dispossessed and removed from their homelands.

Under the removal policy the bulk of the Choctaw agreed to remove in 1830; they resettled in present-day Oklahoma. The majority of Cherokee finally were forced to remove in 1838–39. The Chickasaw initially agreed to remove in 1832 but did not make the resettlement until 1838–39. The bulk of the Creek were removed between 1832 and 1837.

The removal policy constituted a direct threat to Native American territory and political sovereignty. The Cherokee succeeded in adopting a differentiated constitutional government in 1827, several years before pressures to remove had intensified. The formation of this government was in fact a direct counterthreat to the southern states in that it raised the possibility of permanent and quasi-independent Indian nations within the chartered limits of the states, and it not surprisingly precipitated more direct and coercive action on the part of Georgia, Alabama, and Tennessee to pressure the southeastern Indians to remove. The Choctaw in 1830, faced with even more direct pressures than the Cherokee had faced when they adopted a constitutional government, did not institutionalize a centralized government or unify the three major political districts. Throughout the whole period of removal pressure, though both the Chickasaw and the

Creek resisted, they did so within the framework of their existing political institutions and did not make any concerted efforts to differentiate or further centralize their political systems.

Changing World–Economic System Relations

The steady decline of the fur trade from the start of the nineteenth century on had forced most southeastern Indians to find another source of barter to trade for manufactured goods. The Cherokee began the transition to agriculture and husbandry around 1805; the Chickasaw and Choctaw held off until the 1820's. Among the Creek, although there emerged a small class of slaveholders and planters, most Creek, especially among the upper towns, were reluctant to adopt small-scale family farm agriculture and preferred to remain in their villages and work the communal fields, despite worsening economic conditions. Many Indian slaveholders and merchants, like the southern slaveholders in general, took advantage of the rise in the price of cotton and turned to more extensive production of cotton for the export market.

Under the collective land ownership system of the southeastern nations, by which anyone could occupy land and cultivate a farm or plantation as long as he did not interfere with the farming activities of his nearby neighbors, the resident family owned only the improvements on the land, and if a family abandoned its improvements for longer than a year, the first family to occupy the improvements had the right to claim them. Since most southeastern Indians were engaged in subsistence husbandry and farming or village horticulture, usually farming small plots of five to seven acres or less, there was considerable surplus land available, and the slaveholders and merchants, who were strongly market oriented and materially acquisitive, could claim several choice locations for establishing plantations, free of taxes.[4] With some reason—though not wholly accurately— American agents argued that the main group resisting removal was the Indian planters who sought to preserve their material advantages of free access to large amounts of land.

The planters relied on imported slave labor because the subsistence farmers and villagers would not sell their labor, and therefore the planters did not compete for land directly with other members of the nation nor did they exploit the labor of other members of their nation. Though they exploited the labor of imported black slaves, slaves were not considered social or political members of the southeastern Indian nations, and the Indian planters' adoption of coercive labor practices that were common in the southern export economy did not have direct or immediate consequences for internal political relations between the subsistence-oriented majority and the planters. The subsistence farmers and villagers were not in direct competition for land, nor were there conflicts between the planters and subsistence farmers over the use and exploitation of slave labor. The subsistence farmers were economically independent of the planters and also maintained their political autonomy.

But what had begun as only a small economic core was by the 1820's and 1830's a deepening stratification. In 1835, about 8 percent of the Cherokee families were slaveholders; 42 families owned ten or more slaves. The majority of Cherokee still retained subsistence labor ethics; they engaged in the production of cotton, cattle, or agricultural produce not for exchange or trade but primarily for domestic consumption, and they marketed only limited quantities of produce to obtain necessary goods that could not be manufactured domestically. Among the Choctaw, economic stratification was similar. By 1830 the Choctaw were a nation composed primarily (90 percent or more) of subsistence farmers and cattle raisers; cotton was exported by Choctaw plantation owners. A similar pattern of stratification was present among the Chickasaw also. The large majority of the Chickasaw turned to subsistence farming and husbandry during the 1820's; a relatively small number, significantly less than one-fourth, of the Chickasaw families were engaged as planters and merchants. In the mid-1830's, there were 4,914 Chickasaw and 1,156 slaves in the nation. The Creek at this same time, especially in the upper towns, were still village oriented in a way of life that combined religious, political, social, and economic aspects. They retained subsistence economic orientations. Slaveholders were scattered throughout the upper towns, and some of the leading chiefs at Tuckabatchee were slaveholders, but the slaveholders were concentrated mainly in the lower towns. Although many central features of the preexisting social order still remained, changing market relations and the rise of opportunities for export of cotton and development of a plantation economy were slowly creating class stratification within the southeastern societies.[5]

The Internal Political Differentiation
of Cherokee Society

By the end of the War of 1812, the Cherokee had adopted numerous changes in structural organization that gave them a greater potential than the other southeastern nations for further developments in political differentiation and centralization. Before 1817, the Cherokee had declared themselves a unified nation, had centralized control over judicial affairs in the national council, and had differentiated judicial relations from clan relations, while embarking on some initial internal differentiation of the polity with the formation of the national committee. None of the other southeastern nations had comparable levels of social integration, political unification, political centralization, or differentiation of the polity from kinship and culture, and only the Cherokee formed a differentiated constitutional government during the removal crisis.

THE REMOVAL CRISIS OF 1817–19

American threats to Cherokee territory came immediately with the conclusion of the Red Stick War with the Creek. At the Treaty of Fort Jackson in 1814 the Americans took claim to 2.2 million acres of land from the Creek that the Cherokee claimed as their own. The Cherokee had fought with the American militia against the fundamentalist Creek in the Red Stick War, and they naturally protested against the treaty terms that were costing them their land. In compensation, the United States offered to pay for the 2.2 million acres. This offer brought out the old political cleavage between the Cherokee upper towns and lower towns, the lower towns favoring the sale of the land and the upper towns opposing it. The Cherokee were able to avoid ceding land this time, but American officials continued to press Cherokee leaders for land cessions and again raised the issue of Cherokee removal west of the Mississippi River.

In 1815 a Cherokee delegation to Washington agreed to grant a right-of-way for an American road through the Cherokee country, but again the Cherokee refused to sell. Most Cherokee chiefs did not wish to remove and did not wish to cede more land to the United States. But American pressures and disputes over ownership of land were making it urgent for the southeastern nations to make explicit their national boundaries and territorial claims, and to that end the four nations met at Turkeytown, the village of Path Killer, the Cherokee principal chief, in October 1816.[6]

Nonetheless, under pressure from American officials, in September 1816 a small group of Cherokee chiefs, acting without the approval of the Cherokee national council, agreed to cede to the United States 2.2 million acres of land north of the Tennessee River. A Cherokee delegation composed largely of lower town chiefs was sent to the Chickasaw capitol at Pontotoc to observe treaty negotiations between the United States and the Chickasaw in order to make certain that the Chickasaw did not sell land that the Cherokee claimed. Since the early 1800's the Cherokee and Chickasaw had disputed land sales in the present state of Kentucky. At the Chickasaw council, Andrew Jackson, the main American treaty commissioner, used a combination of threats and bribery to induce the fifteen member Cherokee delegation to agree to the land cession.

In early October, the treaty of 1816 was ratified illegally by the chiefs of only four towns after the Cherokee national council refused to ratify the agreement. Although the national council informed the War Department of the manner in which the treaty had been ratified, the government proceeded to have the treaty ratified by the Senate, and the Cherokee were forced to cede the 2.2 million acres that Jackson originally claimed in the treaty of 1814. Of the Cherokee nation, only the lower town chiefs favored the land cession, for the reason, they said, that the ceded land already was occupied by American settlers and there was little hope of the Cherokee ever recovering it.[7]

In the spring of 1817, the Cherokee were informed that another American commission would arrive in the summer to negotiate Cherokee removal and buy more land. Many of the lower town chiefs were predisposed to sell land and remove west. The lands of the lower towns were the most directly affected by American intruders and the lower towns were subject to economic harassment from the American settlements; furthermore, a drought in the spring of 1817 killed much of the crop on the frontier, and this fact, combined with American bribery to remove west, disposed the lower town leaders to sell land and remove. The upper towns, the large majority, favored remaining in their eastern homeland.

The combination of American pressures for land and removal and the internal regional cleavages between the upper and lower towns led the Cherokee leadership to meet and discuss ways to prevent removal and land sales by a small group of chiefs. Early in May 1817 the Cherokee national council, consisting of representatives from 54 towns, met at the village of Amoah to discuss further changes in government that would make it easier for the nation to resist American pressures for land and for removal. At the Amoah council, the Cherokee expressed their distress over the impending treaty negotiations and the recent failure to prevent unauthorized cessions of land.

The planters and merchants attempted to convince the council that further political centralization and delegation of powers were necessary to strengthen Cherokee resistance to removal and to preserve the remainder of the national domain. The arguments of the planters were particularly important in the national council's decision to centralize the Cherokee government in order to resist American treaty pressures and to prevent minority factions and local chiefs from making unauthorized sales of land.[8]

In their turn, the national women's council recounted the history of the progressive loss of the once extensive Cherokee territory, voiced their concern over the possible loss of more land, and stated their opposition to removal west. The women's council was composed of an elected member from each of the seven clans. In ancient times, they had the right to override the decisions of the chiefs if they thought a different decision was in the best interest of the nation. In the early 1800's, a place was

reserved for the women in the council house; although they were not permitted to vote, they could express their views on special issues. In this
time of national peril, the women's council favored economic and political
change in order to maintain Cherokee political independence and rights
to their ancient homeland, they advised their "children" to enlarge their
farms and plant corn and cotton in their present homeland rather than
return to the hunting lifestyle that the American commissioners thought
the Cherokee would prefer in the western hinterlands. They were willing
to suspend their ancient privilege of addressing the national council, and
favored a constitutional government modeled after the male-dominated
American system if it would enhance the nation's capacity to resist removal and preserve the Cherokee homeland. Nancy Ward, a member of
the wolf clan from Chota and an affluent innkeeper, farmer, and slaveholder, was the spokeswoman for the women's council. She resigned from
the highest female rank of War Women to show her support for a written
constitutional government.[9]

The Amoah council decided to centralize the government and adopted
the first organic laws for the Cherokee nation. In order to prevent further
loss of their collectively owned land, the village delegations unanimously
agreed to adopt a six-article constitution. The new laws created an elected
thirteen-member standing committee for a term of two years. The standing
committee was to be delegated the management of the Cherokee annuity
and treaty negotiations with the United States, but its acts were subject to
the consent of the national council. It was, in effect, a form of bicameral
legislature. Cherokee leaders who could read and write in English were
expected to fill the seats on the national committee, since one of the committee's primary tasks was to manage treaty and diplomatic relations with
the American government more effectively.[10]

But Cherokee efforts to centralize their government in order to prevent sale of land or agreement to removal by local or regional chiefs did
not prove effective during the treaty negotiations the following summer.
Once again, the Cherokee national council was bypassed by the U.S. treaty
commissioners, who then negotiated a treaty permitting removal and cession of land with a group consisting primarily of lower town chiefs. The
treaty concluded on July 8, 1817, required the Cherokee either to remove
westward to present-day Arkansas or to remain in the east but take individual land allotments and live under the laws of the American states.[11]
The Cherokee also ceded two tracts of land totaling about 650,000 acres
in present Georgia and Tennessee in exchange for land to be occupied by
the western emigrants.

Andrew Jackson, the chief American negotiator, was adamant that the
Cherokee either remove or be assimilated as small farmers under Ameri-

can law. He threatened that if they did not comply and negotiate a treaty with the U.S. government, the government would withdraw its protection of Cherokee lands from frontier intruders and would cease to pay treaty annuities and give technical assistance. Under this combination of threats, bribery, the drought during the spring and summer of 1817, and economic harassment by American intruders especially in the lower towns, many of the lower town chiefs gave up all hope of resistance. Toochelar, the second principal chief, Chief John Rogers of the lower towns, and Chiefs Jolly and Glass were among the thirteen prominent chiefs who accepted the American treaty terms for removal. That summer and in 1818, about 1,000 Cherokee decided to emigrate west; the majority, at least 12,000, chose to stay in the east. The lower town chiefs who decided to remove took their local kinsmen and villagers with them; many of them were slaveholders who intended to continue the plantation economy in the west and not return to hunting and the fur trade, as American officials had suggested.[12]

At the national council meeting at Etowee in September 1817, Toochelar and the other lower town chiefs were dismissed from office for favoring removal; those who were willing to remove were considered traitors to the nation. Charles Hicks, an English-speaking Cherokee and wealthy trader and planter from the upper towns, was elected second chief, while Path Killer remained principal chief. The Cherokee council sent a delegation to Washington to inform the government that the 1817 treaty had been negotiated by a disaffected minority of chiefs and did not have the approval of the nation, the majority of whom wished to remain in their traditional homeland, where the bones of their ancestors were buried and where the Great Spirit had directed them to settle, and to continue the civilization program that the government had initiated in the preceding two decades.[13]

The treaty had only whetted the appetites of the land grabbers. For the remainder of 1817 and during 1818, American agents, settlers, and the states of Tennessee, Georgia, and Alabama continued to pressure the Cherokee to remove west. The Cherokee must either emigrate or assimilate. Neither choice would leave the Cherokee as they were before, and though most Cherokee wished to remain in their traditional homeland, they realized that assimilation was never a real possibility because the states and the frontier populations did not want the Cherokee to remain in the east as citizens. Moreover, the Cherokee did not believe they would be granted equal civil rights or social status under American state laws.[14]

In response to the removal pressure, the Cherokee remained committed to their own institutions, while seeking further centralization and attempting to renegotiate the 1817 treaty. The inability to prevent land sales convinced the leaders that even more political centralization and control were necessary to protect national political autonomy and territory, and the influential Cherokee planters, whose counsel was equally important, were convinced that the nation could be saved only if the Cherokee continued with economic improvements and political centralization. Centralization offered the more conservative Cherokee a way of preserving their home- land and their independent nationality. Chiefs who favored removal were dismissed from office and new members who were opposed to removal and assimilation were elected.

A month after the September 1817 council meeting at Etowee, the coun- cil met again to appoint regulators to suppress stealing and to protect private property. The council also agreed to allow American missionaries to establish schools within the nation. During 1818, further steps were taken to consolidate the nation. In February, Cherokee laws were recorded and copies were printed and distributed to the heads of families through- out the nation. In June, the women's council again addressed the national council and strongly stated their opposition to removal, while expressing their approval of the plan for economic and political change. In Novem- ber, the council determined a fine of $100 and 100 lashes for anyone who brought American families into the nation for purposes of labor or tenant farming. The council rejected the removal proposals of the 1817 treaty and passed a law imposing the death sentence on any Cherokee who sold land without the council's permission. One member of the national committee, a slaveholder, was dismissed for initiating negotiations with U.S. officials without permission of the national council.[15] In December, the council informed American officials that the Cherokee were strongly attached to their institutions and homeland and that the council would send a dele- gation to Washington to negotiate closure of the issues of removal and assimilation.

In February 1819, the Cherokee delegation secured a compromise treaty, which superseded the removal or assimilation treaty of 1817. The Chero- kee delegation persuaded the U.S. government to rescind the 1817 treaty and gained assurances that American intruders would be removed from Cherokee territory, but the delegation was required to cede 6,000 square miles of Cherokee land. In return, the Cherokee received guarantees of protection for their remaining territory, money to finance schools, and technical assistance for agricultural development. The 1819 treaty also allowed Cherokees to take private allotments of 640 acres and become American citizens. In 1819 and the early 1820's, about 230 Cherokee fami- lies, many of them well-off even by southern American standards, chose to take allotments. Virtually all these families, however, eventually returned to the Cherokee nation owing to economic harassment by local settlers and the failure of the states to recognize the validity of the allotments and to provide the Cherokee with civil protections. Even where assimilation into American society had been a choice, it proved an impossibility. Disappointments such as these further intensified nationalist orientations and efforts to reorganize Cherokee economy and polity.[16]

FORMATION OF THE CHEROKEE CONSTITUTIONAL GOVERNMENT

From the point of view of the Cherokee, the treaty of 1819 was a final settlement with the United States. The Cherokee resolved to sell no more land. Between 1819 and 1835 the Cherokee held fast, despite pressures for land cessions and removal far more intense than those that had been exerted on them in the period before 1819. Georgia increased its pressure on the federal government and on the Cherokee for the extinguishment of Cherokee title within Georgia's chartered limits, and Georgia state officials even went so far as to try and encourage the federal government to use force if necessary to induce the Cherokee to remove. In 1824 the Georgia government argued that the Cherokee were only tenants-at-will on Georgia territory and threatened forcible removal, since they regarded the Cherokee presence to be impeding the progressive development of the state. During the early 1820's Cherokee land was encroached upon extensively by American intruders, who were removed sporadically and with great difficulty. The American agent to the Cherokee, R. J. Meigs, writing in 1822, commented that state pressures for Cherokee removal from Georgia, Tennessee, and Alabama were so strong that the Cherokee would never be able to hold on to their homeland. It seemed as if the states and their populations could not be restrained.[17] Almost annually, state and federal officials attempted to persuade the Cherokee to cede more land.

The intensified pressure for removal and land cessions in the early 1820's had the effect of uniting the Cherokee in their resolve to preserve their nation and homeland. In 1822, a poll of the Cherokee nation reported by the national council stated that the entire nation unanimously rejected land sales and opposed removal.[18] The Cherokee were still politically united against removal, and in several stages between 1819 and 1827 they worked out a more differentiated political system that culminated in the constitution of 1827.

In the national councils of 1819 and 1820, the Cherokee discussed the question of whether to adopt American economic and political institutions or instead continue in the ways of their forebears. The planters and other influential men argued that the nation could be preserved only by further agricultural and political improvements. The question was deliberated in the national councils and determined in favor of adopting the plan of civilization. The council then set out to organize a civil government modeled after American political institutions. The new government was to create a national legal code that would preserve the rights and liberties of its citizens, protect freedom of religion, and encourage morality and education. Although the plan was not necessarily favored by all Cherokee, most acquiesced because they believed the plan was a means of preserving national rights and territory. The Cherokee no longer were motivated by the desire to preserve hunting grounds; rather they adopted a patriotic commitment to national and territorial preservation.[19]

The national council moved to strengthen collective resistance to removal pressures in 1819. John Ross, a planter and merchant and personal secretary to Path Killer, the principal chief, was appointed president of the national committee. Ross was influential with the conservatives and placed a strong emphasis on national unity and preservation. The national council also forbade the use of American labor as farmhands or plantation managers. Although the conservative subsistence farmers, who were the majority in the nation, did not use American farm laborers or plantation managers, they were afraid that the American population in the country would soon outstrip the Cherokee population and thereby threaten Cherokee nationality. The council also excluded American merchants from the nation, which gave a monopoly on retail trade to Cherokee merchants.[20]

In October 1820, the national council approved several major changes in the organization of Cherokee government. It divided the nation into eight districts and organized a standing legislative body, which was to meet each October at Newtown, the newly created Cherokee capital village. The legislature was composed of two bodies. The national committee of 13 members formed the upper house, while the lower house was reduced to 32 members, four elected from each district. The upper house was given power to inspect the expenditures of the treasury, to hear claims against the Cherokee government, and to initiate legislation. The members of the national committee, or upper house, were elected by the national council, and the decisions of the national committee were subject to the approval of the national council.[21] The two houses elected the two head chiefs, or executive branch, for terms of four years, and all laws needed the approval of both houses and the two head chiefs. Each of the eight district divisions had a council house where the elected officials met twice a year and where district and circuit courts were held. The council also appointed a national treasurer.

The Cherokee also created an independent judiciary. Since the relinquishment of judicial affairs in 1810 by the seven clans, the national council heard all judicial cases, but this procedure became cumbersome and time consuming. Thus in 1820 a separate judiciary branch was created to handle most criminal cases. Each of the eight districts had a district judge. There were also four circuit judges who presided over two districts. All the district courts held trial by jury, and were assigned a marshal, constables, and district officers. The Cherokee laws were few, but order was maintained according to the treaty agreements, which were designed to keep the peace on the frontier. In addition to criminal codes, Cherokee laws regulated intermarriage with Americans, the employment of American free labor, and the rental of Cherokee land to Americans; they prohibited sale of land to Americans; they also regulated taxes, debt, the licensing of American merchants in the nation, and the duties of the officers of the government.[22]

The political innovations of 1820 embodied major efforts at further internal and external differentiation of the Cherokee polity. The reduction of the national council to 32 elected members constituted further differentiation of the polity from society. Previously, each of the 50 to 60 villages had sent official delegations of five or six men to the national council, which then was made up of 200–300 men. In the interest of rationalizing political decision making, the Cherokee villages, no longer recognized as the primary political units within the polity, surrendered their rights to send a delegation to the national council. The formation of distinct and autonomous judicial and legislative branches indicates further specialization of judicial affairs and separation of police and judicial functions. Previously the lighthorse often acted as police, judge, and executioner; now, many criminal and civil offenses were delegated to the district and circuit courts and decided by juries. Furthermore, the Cherokee polity increasingly regulated economic activities with laws regarding American free labor, construction of roads, slave labor, debts, and contracts.

Between 1820 and 1826 the Cherokee national council continued to accept the advice of the small group of planters, chiefs, and mission-educated Cherokee who proposed further changes in the government. During this period there were no strong or overt movements by conservatives to inhibit or rescind the proposed changes in political organization, and reports generally observe that the Cherokee population complied with the new laws and the modified form of government.[23]

In 1822, a Supreme Court was established that functioned as a court of appeals for the district and circuit courts. The council also enacted laws against gambling and intemperance. In 1823 the national committee was given powers to review the actions of the national council, which created a greater balance of power between the two houses. In 1824 a law was passed that prohibited intermarriage with blacks. In 1825 the council declared that the Cherokee nation was common property and prohibited its sale under any conditions without authorization from the national council. The national council was formally delegated control over all land, public property, treaty annuities, and payments. Individual chiefs were divested of all rights to dispose of any land, to make treaties, or to overrule the decisions of the national council. Though planters and merchants were the majority in the national committee, conservative leaders were the majority in the national council, which continued to retain ultimate decision making authority in the Cherokee government. In 1825 the council declared that the judiciary was independent of the council, thereby formally ensuring checks and balances between the judiciary and other branches of government. Despite the increased differentiation and centralization of the Cherokee polity, the Cherokee government could not enforce laws that were rejected by the general population. For example, when the Cherokee council created a poll tax law in 1820, most Cherokee refused to pay. Consequently, the government's finances were underwritten by treaty payments and annuities, and were dependent on the American government's willingness to uphold its treaty obligations.[24]

Early in 1826, Georgia succeeded in imposing a treaty on the Creek nation that extinguished Creek title to all land within the chartered limits of the state of Georgia, except a small fragment that was exempted by mistake. The treaty had resulted from a fraudulently negotiated treaty in 1825, for the negotiation of which William McIntosh had been executed; though President Adams had vetoed that treaty, Georgia managed to secure the second treaty a few months later, and this success emboldened Georgia to turn its attention to the Cherokee, who were now the primary holders of land in the territory claimed by Georgia. Georgia officials put pressure on the federal government to secure a treaty of removal from the Cherokee. The Cherokee, of course, were well aware of the implications of the Creek cession in Georgia, and they knew that Georgia state officials did not look favorably upon the political changes in the Cherokee government. Georgia argued not only that the Cherokee impermissibly sought to establish a separate government within the chartered limits of Georgia but also that the Cherokee occupation of territory claimed by the state was an infringement of Georgia's state rights.[25]

The intensified clamoring by Georgia as well as by the states of Alabama and Tennessee for Cherokee removal created a crisis that kindled Cherokee nationalistic orientations toward economic change, education, and political change, which Cherokee leaders and planters exploited as a strategy for national survival. American pressure for removal was a major factor that mobilized the Cherokee to centralize and differentiate their government institutions further; Georgia's threats of removal provoked the Cherokee into forming a constitutional government. Since both Georgia and Tennessee claimed that the Cherokee were a barbarous nation without rules or laws, the Cherokee decided to adopt a constitutional government modeled after the American constitution, and to proceed with

agricultural development and education in order to prove that the Cherokee were capable of living under the rule of law. The establishment of a
Cherokee constitutional government was an attempt to put the Cherokee
political system into a form comparable to that of the surrounding American state governments. On November 12, 1826, the Cherokee national
council passed a resolution authorizing the election of delegates and the
formation of a constitutional convention. The election was set for May
1827 and the convention was scheduled to start on July 4, 1827. In December the Cherokee national council asserted its national independence by
rejecting an American proposal to build a canal through the Cherokee
country. The Cherokee demanded the right to regulate their own internal
affairs and argued that the building of an American canal through their
territory would infringe upon Cherokee political sovereignty.[26]

Several events intervened before the constitutional convention. In late
February of 1827 the principal chief, Path Killer, died, and within two
weeks the second chief, Charles Hicks, also died. Until the national council could be convened in October, temporary leadership of the government
was delegated to John Ross, the president of the national committee, and
to Major Ridge, the speaker of the council. Both Path Killer and Hicks
had strongly opposed removal, and their deaths encouraged Georgia and
North Carolina to seek more land sales from the Cherokee, in hopes that
Cherokee resistance to land sales and removal would soften.[27]

Indeed, after the deaths of the two chiefs, several leaders, including Ki-
li-tsu-li and a fundamentalist chief named White Path, rose in opposition
to the new Cherokee laws and to proposals for further political change
and centralization. White Path, an old and respected chief from the village
of Ellijay, had been evicted from the national council in 1825, perhaps
for opposing the changes in the Cherokee government. The conservatives
under White Path preferred the old council, composed of delegations from
each village, and wanted to destroy the new government and drive out
the missionaries. Though they organized in seven of the eight districts and
created laws of government, they did not go so far as to insist on the enforcement of its laws, and from an initial surge of popular support it began
to decline from lack of systematic organization and cohesive leadership.[28]

In May the elections were held for certifying delegates to the constitutional convention. Ki-li-tsu-li, now the main leader of the opposition,
was elected as a delegate, but the well-to-do planters represented the large
majority of the elected convention delegates. In late June the opposition
leaders, but not including White Path, and a committee of the national
council met to reconcile their differences. The committee was composed
largely of planters and mission-educated Cherokee leaders, including John
Ross, Major Ridge, Elias Boudinot, and Going Snake. Ki-li-tsu-li denied

that the opposition had intended to overthrow the government, insisting
rather that the opposition had only protested against certain laws that he
said had been instituted by the planters. Most of the opposition leaders
agreed to unite behind the government and proceed with the constitutional
convention, and they promised to desist from rebellious activities and
bring their grievances about objectionable laws to the national council.
Nevertheless, the committee issued a warning against unlawful assembly
and threatened to mete out 100 stripes on the bare back to anyone found
in unlawful meetings that threatened to disrupt the peace and tranquillity
of the nation. A few days later, two of the opposition leaders, including
Ki-li-tsu-li, were installed as duly elected representatives to the national
council.[29]

Thus, with the opposition mollified, the Cherokee convened the constitutional convention on July 4, 1827, at New Echota, a location not too
distant from Ustanali, which had been the central meeting place for the
upper towns since the abandonment of Chota in 1788. Georgia commissioners were present at New Echota with an offer to buy more Cherokee
land, but the council postponed meeting with them until the fall. There
were 24 elected convention delegates—three from each of the eight districts, which were subdivided into three precincts for voting purposes. The
national committee and national council nominated up to ten men from
each district, and the election by adult males was done by open voice vote,
not by secret ballot. About twenty of the elected delegates were planters
with the ability to speak English.

The convention decreed that the new constitution was not to impair the
existing rights and freedoms of Cherokee citizens, and could not change
the fundamental laws that were already approved. On July 4, John Ross,
who had been a leader in advocating political and legal change since at
least 1819, was elected president of the convention. On July 6, the convention appointed a committee of eight, consisting of one delegate from
each district, and asked the committee to report a draft of a constitution. Although there is no record of all the events and discussions at the
convention, it is reported that the early drafts of the new constitution
raised significant opposition from the older and conservative Cherokee.[30]
The early opposition to the new constitution eventually was overcome,
however, and the convention came to a final agreement on July 26, 1827.

The new constitution formalized greater internal differentiation of the
Cherokee polity. It created the separation of powers among legislative,
executive, and judicial branches. The general council was bicameral, with
both houses having elected members. Whereas the national committee had
formerly been appointed by the council, now each district elected one
member to the committee and three members to the national council. The

general council elected the principal chief and the second chief every four years. The court system was maintained and a code of criminal law was defined. The constitution strengthened the relative positions of both the executive and the national committee against the traditional plenary authority of the national council: the committee was put on equal legislative footing to the national council and could veto decisions of the national council or lower house, and the chief now had a more active role in vetoing legislation and in implementing the law.

A bill of rights granted freedom of religion and the right to trial by jury. The document established Cherokee boundaries and set down a statement of common ownership of land and the right of citizens to own improvements on the common domain. A slave code excluded blacks from political participation. Laws were passed that strengthened law enforcement, encouraged economic accumulation, encouraged schools and education, and consolidated the investment of coercive powers in the central government.[31]

The next year, the constitution was ratified by the national council. Missionary reports state that between 1828 and 1832 the Cherokee were strongly united behind the new constitution. Even White Path's opposition party came to see the wisdom of having national unity and a strong government if the Cherokee were to preserve their national sovereignty and territory in the face of ever-increasing pressure. The people obeyed the new laws and participated in the new political system in an orderly manner. In the first election under the constitution in October 1828, the English-speaking planters dominated the national committee, while the national council was composed predominantly of respected conservatives. Many leaders who were active in securing the changes between 1818 and 1827 were elected to offices under the new government; even White Path was elected to national office. Many of those who were elected to the national committee were the educated and market-oriented Cherokee who had English-language skills and experience with American government and institutions. William Hicks, the brother of Charles Hicks, and John Ross had been appointed acting principal chief and second chief in the fall of 1827, but in the 1828 election the national council passed over William Hicks for principal chief in favor of Ross and elected a well-known conservative, George Lowrey, as second chief. Hicks was bypassed because he was suspected of favoring removal. In an effort to maintain political unity, Ross appointed Hicks to the executive committee, but Hicks refused to participate and in the early 1830's helped form a pro-removal party.[32]

American agents and observers believed, as several contemporary scholars argue now, that the Cherokee constitutional government was formed by a clique of the Cherokee planter class led by John Ross primarily to promote the planters' material interests. The planters who controlled the national committee, so this argument goes, introduced political innovations and dominated the Cherokee government in such a way as to facilitate their further accumulation of wealth. One observer lists about 80 planters who were prominent in initiating changes in Cherokee political structure and creating laws that fostered economic accumulation, and who then dominated the new Cherokee political institutions. In the opinion of American agents, the major resistance to removal came from the planters, who enjoyed free access to land (many had several plantations) and freedom from taxes. Furthermore, over 200 planter families had tried to assimilate onto farms in the neighboring states in accordance with treaties between 1817 and 1820, but had failed because of the policy of the local states not to recognize Cherokee civil and property rights. This meant that most Cherokee planters were excluded from holding land in the United States and could maintain their property and wealth only within the confines of the Cherokee nation. Other scholars argue that the Cherokee constitution was designed primarily to control slave labor and promote the accumulation of wealth. Indeed, 40 percent of the laws passed under the new constitution were designed to protect private property and to regulate markets and contracts, and for this reason some argue that planter class interests were the most important element in the formation of the Cherokee state, because the planters needed to regulate slave labor and ensure a profitable economic environment.[33]

The class domination argument does not agree with the oral tradition and with other evidence, however.[34] Certainly the planters and the missionary-educated Cherokee played a major role in the construction of the Cherokee constitution. The planters were the advocates of American political models, and they proposed the innovations in government organization and new laws for regulating the economy. The majority of Cherokee were subsistence farmers who still retained nondifferentiated cultural world views and had little experience or knowledge of American political institutions, and because they were not oriented toward producing for profit, they had little direct use for the new laws regarding contracts and private property. Unquestionably, the new laws and constitutional government created a stable legal and political environment in which the planters could continue their efforts toward greater profit making.

It is unlikely, however, that the planters were ever in direct or total control of the Cherokee government. The political innovators among the Cherokee could not have gained acceptance of new laws or more differentiated forms of government without the approval of the traditional elders and people of the nation.[35] The Cherokee planters did not have control over sufficient means of force to impose their views on the large majority.

The economic and political innovations were not accepted by all Cherokee, or accepted evenly, but the achievement of the planters was not so
much the formulation of constitutional laws and government as the persuasion of the more reluctant and conservative Cherokee to accept and
comply with the program of political and economic change. The Cherokee planters were successful in institutionalizing their plan of political and
economic change, but they did so with the support and consensus of the
Cherokee political community. The planters offered their more conservative countrymen a strategy for preserving their homeland and political
sovereignty. From the point of view of the conservatives, the new constitutional government was legitimated as an instrument of political unity
and centralization that would enhance Cherokee chances of resisting more
land cessions and removal from their homeland.

Though the planters led the way in political and economic institution
building, they did so only within the context of a negotiated consensus
and approval by the conservative majority, which held a diffuse but ultimate authority over Cherokee national affairs. The arguments of class
domination tend to relegate the Cherokee conservative majority to an
uninformed and inert mass that was easily led and manipulated by the
planters. The Cherokee conservatives were in fact politically active and
mobilized, especially after the removal crisis of 1817. The power of the
Cherokee political consensus can be seen most clearly in the dismissing
of leaders who favored removal or other policies that were contrary to
the will of the conservative majority. The examples of the execution of
Doublehead in 1807, the dismissal of the second chief Toochelar and
other lower town chiefs in 1817, and the failed re-election bid of the acting principal chief, William Hicks, in 1828 are indicative of the Cherokee
political community's demand that their leaders reflect the consensus of
the majority. The missionary Samuel Worcester observed that chiefs and
planters did not politically overawe the people; rather, popular opinion
and consensus ruled: "They are not overawed by the chiefs. Individuals
are overawed by *popular opinion* but *not by the chiefs*. On the other hand,
if there were a chief in favor of removal, he would be overawed *by the
people*. He would know that he could not open his mouth in favor of such
a proposition, but on pain, not only of the failure of his re-election, but of
popular odium and scorn. The whole tide of national feeling sets, in one
strong and unbroken current, against removal to the west." [36]

It had always been true that planters were welcome to serve in the
government at strategic posts, since their education, experience, and language skills were considered necessary and useful for protecting the nation
against the land and removal demands of the American government; but
the conservatives were always the majority in the national council, and the

national committee, which was dominated by planters, could not make decisions without the approval of the national council. The conservative leaders monitored and approved the actions of the planters in the national committee. The constitution of 1827 put the council and the national committee on more equal terms, although the council continued to be led by conservatives and the committee by planters. Between 1819 and 1832 the planters and the conservatives generally were unified in their resistance to removal, and there was little overt conflict between the two groups.

Despite the introduction of constitutional government and administrative districts, the conservatives maintained informal political loyalties to villages and village chiefs and to the principal chief. Between 1810 and 1827 the conservative majority rallied behind Path Killer, the principal chief, and when John Ross inherited the support of the conservative majority and was elected principal chief in 1828, he continued to ask the opinions of the conservative leaders and to act in the interests of the conservative majority. Had he done otherwise, he would have been removed from office. Ross was seen as an honest leader and a man who had repeatedly resisted the bribes of American treaty commissions, and therefore could be trusted by the conservative majority.[37]

The class domination argument does not seem to hold for this period of Cherokee history. The acceptance of the political innovations that led to the formation of the constitutional government of 1827 and the role of planters in leadership positions were dependent on the consent of the conservative majority, who accepted the new government because it held out the promise of preserving Cherokee political nationality and protecting the Cherokee homeland from American threats of removal. The planters were invited to lead the new government as long as they served the interests of the conservative majority. The planters, too, wanted to preserve Cherokee territory; though they secured passage of laws that were more in their interests than in the interests of the subsistence farmers, they introduced political innovations and laws within the context of consent by the broader Cherokee political community.

CHEROKEE REMOVAL

The formation of the Cherokee constitutional government had the effect of increasing hostile pressure from the surrounding states to convince the Cherokee to remove west. The election of Andrew Jackson to the presidency in 1828 further encouraged the southern states to use more coercive measures to induce the southeastern Indians to remove and relinquish title to their territories. Between the beginning of 1829 and June 1830, the states of Georgia, Tennessee, and North Carolina declared their intention to extend their state laws over Cherokee territory and block the operation of the Cherokee government, except for the negotiation of treaties of land cession or removal. In 1832 the state of Alabama also extended its laws over Cherokee territory. The discovery of gold in the Cherokee nation in 1828 led to the rapid influx of American prospectors, and according to oral tradition was the primary event forcing the Cherokee to remove west.[38] Since under the laws of the southern states a Cherokee could not testify in court against an American, intruders caused depredations and forcibly assumed control of Cherokee farms, plantations, and property, all of which caused economic hardships for both the Cherokee small farmers and the planters.

Cherokee leaders, hoping to obtain redress, brought two cases before the Supreme Court of the United States. The Cherokee petition in the first case, *Cherokee Nation v. Georgia,* was denied because the court refused to allow the Cherokee to bring a case as a foreign nation. The second case, *Worcester v. Georgia,* was decided in 1832 in favor of the Cherokee. The Supreme Court denied that Georgia had the right to extend its laws over the Cherokee nation, since according to the American Constitution only the federal government could extinguish title to Indian land. But though the Court's decision was a legal victory for the Cherokee, President Jackson refused to enforce the decision, and the Court did not impose an injunction against Georgia to withdraw from Cherokee land. Soon after the Worcester case, Jackson met with John Ridge, the son of Major Ridge, and informed the Cherokee that he would not enforce the Supreme Court's decision. Jackson argued that the Cherokee could not stay in the east under the pressure from the larger surrounding states, and that the federal government could not intervene for fear of dividing the states of the union over the issue. Jackson implored the young Ridge to convince the Cherokee to remove west, out of the jurisdiction of the southern states.[39]

Ridge returned to the Cherokee nation and attempted to convince the Cherokee leaders of the necessity of removal, but removal was still very unpopular among the conservative majority and Ridge's arguments were in vain. From then until 1835, Cherokee society was split into two major "parties": the treaty party, consisting mainly of planters who were convinced that they faced economic and political loss if the Cherokee continued to resist removal, and the conservatives, led by John Ross and a small group of planters, who favored remaining in the east in spite of American economic and political pressures for removal. The conservatives were unyieldingly opposed to any suggestion of removal, and at a national council in August 1834 they again demonstrated their political strength by proposing impeachment for all government officials who favored removal. Several members of the treaty party were assassinated, perhaps by members of a militant segment of the secret Keetoowah Society, and the killings were only stopped by the intervention of John Ross.[40]

The Keetoowah Society was presumably a revival of an old Cherokee religious society, perhaps dating to the 1700's, that seems to have surfaced in Cherokee political affairs only during times of crisis. The conservative Night Hawk Keetoowah version claims that the society was organized when the seven leaders of the seven clans came together to pray for the resolution of a national crisis. Although the historical record suggests that the Keetoowah Society was organized formally as an active political organization only in 1858, when the Keetoowahs wrote an organizational charter, oral tradition indicates that the society was active politically during the 1830's in the campaign to prevent removal, when the elder and conservative leaders of the society mobilized the members to fight national betrayal by the planters and other young educated Cherokee. The old conservatives thought that the planters and young leaders were smart men but that their education and emphasis on accumulation of wealth had changed their morals and values; some of the young leaders had learned graft, they said, and were prone to immorality, corruption, and a willingness to sell Cherokee national territory in return for American bribes.[41]

The Keetoowah Society was a highly religious and moral order, and membership was strictly limited to those who were considered qualified in terms of moral and religious discipline and especially, honesty, which was considered a defense against the bribery and corruption that had led to the loss of Cherokee land to Americans. Meetings were held secretly in the woods and maintained the traditional sacred fire. In the 1830's, at least, the society functioned as a mutual-protection organization against threats to Cherokee treaty and land rights.[42]

Though the treaty party had failed to gain support from the Cherokee government, and in fact represented only one-tenth of the Cherokee nation, it considered itself powerful enough to act on its own, and in late 1835 the treaty party signed a removal treaty with the United States government. Over the next two years most of the planters, who were the majority of the treaty party, migrated west to present eastern Oklahoma. The conservative majority or Ross party refused to honor the treaty on the grounds that it had not been confirmed by the Cherokee government and had indeed been negotiated fraudulently by an unauthorized minority. Nevertheless, the U.S. government held the entire Cherokee nation to compliance. And when the conservative majority still refused to recognize the treaty, despite continued economic harassment and the loss of civil and political rights under state laws, the U.S. government responded by sending soldiers in the summer of 1838 to round up the Cherokee and forcibly march them to what is now eastern Oklahoma. Since most Cherokee were gathered into camps during the summer, the Cherokee leaders decided that it was futile to resist; after agreeing to remove west, they were granted permission to organize and command the march. Before leaving, the Cherokee leaders agreed to reestablish the constitutional government when they arrived in the west.

Choctaw Regionalism

By 1817, the Choctaw polity was largely secular, but there was still little internal political differentiation; regional, local, and particularistic political identifications predominated and blood revenge norms continued. Nonetheless, the strategy adopted by the Choctaw chiefs and planters was similar to the strategy of political and economic change adopted by the Cherokee as a means of resisting removal pressures and retaining their traditional homeland. Like the Cherokee, the Choctaw came under direct pressure for removal after the War of 1812, at a time when the fur trade was steadily diminishing as an economic base for the bulk of the Choctaw. In the 1820's the Choctaw made rapid strides toward adopting agriculture and husbandry, and the response of the Choctaw leaders, like that of the Cherokee, to removal pressures and changing economic conditions was to work toward political, economic, and cultural change. Unlike the Cherokee, however, the attempts by Choctaw leaders to establish a constitutional government did not lead to enduring centralization or differentiation of Choctaw political relations.

REMOVAL PRESSURES AND POLITICAL CHANGE, 1817–26

In a treaty in 1816, the Choctaw had ceded to the United States territory east of the Tombigbee River, but in 1818 U.S. commissioners were again pressuring the Choctaw for more land cessions. All three district chiefs refused to sell. The Choctaw council was willing to allow schools and missionary teachers into the nation, but it was not willing to sell more land. American settlers had poured into the Choctaw interior after the War of 1812 seeking land that could be put into the production of cotton; settlers continued to clamor for Choctaw land, and there was intense pressure by settlers, land speculators, and state and federal officials for more cessions of Choctaw land. Mississippi became a state in 1817; its borders surrounded much of the Choctaw territory. In 1819, acting as U.S. treaty commissioner, Andrew Jackson attempted to persuade the Choctaw to cede land in the east and migrate west of the Mississippi River. Jackson argued that the game was getting increasingly scarce in the Choctaw country and that many Choctaw in the Six Towns district, which had resisted taking up agriculture, were destitute and would not be able to support themselves. The three Choctaw district chiefs again refused to cede land and rejected the removal proposal. They stated that the Choctaw would rather remain in their homeland and adopt the plan of civilization than migrate west of the Mississippi River.[43]

The following year, 1820, Andrew Jackson led a commission to treat with the Choctaw at Doaks Stand in the Choctaw nation. The chiefs were opposed both to selling any land and to exchanging their eastern territory for land west of the Mississippi River; any chief who was willing to sell or exchange land was threatened by his own people with death. Nevertheless, by using threats and bribery, the American commissioners succeeded in their quest to acquire more Choctaw land. Special presents were made to a few chiefs and influential men, and the commissioners threatened that if the Choctaw would not cooperate, the Americans would turn to a small group of Choctaw who had already migrated to live west of the Mississippi River and would take land in the east acre for acre for the lands that were occupied and hunted by the western Choctaw group. Furthermore, if the Choctaw continued to resist land cessions, the U.S. government would stop protecting the Choctaw from the encroachments of local settlers and territorial designs of nearby states, and Congress would assume control over Choctaw affairs and cede the desired land to the United States.

Reluctantly, the Choctaw agreed to the treaty of 1820, which ceded six million acres of Choctaw territory in the present state of Mississippi to the United States. Apushimataha, chief of the southern district, spoke for a secret council of chiefs and agreed to an exchange of land in the east for a similar sized portion of land west of the Mississippi River. Moshulatubee, the chief of the northeastern district, also was agreeable to the proposal. The United States pledged to support all Choctaw migrants to the western territory with equipment and rations for one year, and also to support Choctaw schools with money from the sale of land. Apushimataha suggested that a permanent border be created for what was left of Choctaw territory, where the Choctaw could live undisturbed until they built homes and acquired educational and agricultural skills that would put them on equal footing with the American frontier communities; eventually the Choctaw would become American citizens. The treaty marked the intention of at least two Choctaw district leaders to oppose removal and adopt a strategy of education and agricultural transition. But as in the Cherokee case, the plan of assimilation did not prove possible owing to the attitude of the surrounding southern states, which preferred that the Choctaw remove west and not remain as citizens.[44]

Not all the Choctaw district chiefs were agreeable to the treaty of 1820; Apuckshunnubee, the aged chief of the northwestern district, left the council ground in disgust. Many young mixed-blood planters and cattlemen also strongly opposed the cession of land, thereby raising their standing within the general Choctaw political community. There was a difference, however: whereas the large majority of Choctaw remained small-scale subsistence farmers and villagers, the Choctaw planters and cattlemen had acquired the values of their fathers regarding wealth, material accumulation, and active participation in trade, export agriculture, and cattle raising. Like the subsistence-oriented Choctaw, the mixed-blood planters wanted to remain in their homeland, but their nationalism was change-oriented rather than conservative. Under the terms of the 1820 treaty, American agents, missionaries, and the planters attempted to introduce schools and promote agricultural development. The decline of the fur trade economy and the pressures by the Americans for land cessions, combined with the nationalist orientations of both the planters and the subsistence-oriented and culturally conservative Choctaw, created conditions under which the Choctaw leadership was willing to promote agricultural change and accept schools.[45]

During the 1820's many Choctaw made the transition to husbandry and subsistence agriculture, although the pattern was uneven among the three major districts. The southern or Six Towns district, the most conservative, was set against adopting cattle raising and agricultural innovations, and many Choctaw remained in their local communities and tried to continue with hunting and horticulture. In the northeastern and northwestern districts there was less resistance to economic change, and most Choctaw moved out of their local communities and villages and took up cattle raising as their primary means of trade and subsistence. Yet well over 90 percent of the Choctaw families still continued to produce only limited surpluses of cattle or animal furs for trade. The large majority were not interested in accumulating wealth by producing a surplus for the cotton, cattle, or other agricultural markets; the norms of sharing food and essential goods and reliance on female horticultural labor continued to predominate. By 1830 there were an estimated 200 Choctaw households—only about 4–5 percent of the total—that held extensive properties, including black slaves, and produced cotton, cattle, or other agricultural products such as corn for export and market.

Slaveholding became an accepted practice among the Choctaw. Even a few conservatives held slaves, although slave labor among the conservative Choctaw was not usually exploited for market production. Among the Choctaw district chiefs, Moshulatubee of the northeastern district, an economic conservative, was a slaveholder; Apuckshunnubee of the northwestern district by 1816 was engaged in the production of cotton for marketing and was pressing the Americans to supply a cotton gin; Apushimataha of the conservative southern district was quite poor and had little interest in the personal accumulation of wealth.[46] During the decade 1820–30, the Choctaw became increasingly stratified according to economic and cultural criteria, which resulted in a relatively small class of market-oriented merchants, planters, and cattlemen, while most Choctaw remained subsistence-oriented small farmers or villagers.

American missionaries, who arrived in the Choctaw country after 1817, were among the strongest promoters of legal and constitutional change. Not all the influential mixed-blood leaders were eager for Christianity, but most of them wanted schools for their children, and in general the missionary schools were attended disproportionately by the children of mixed-blood families. This fact of course tended to accentuate the class and cultural cleavages in Choctaw society that were already in evidence.[47]

The changes in the Choctaw polity during the early 1820's were primarily legal and normative, and they were enacted within the framework of the prevailing system of district chiefs and the 30 captains or local iksa leaders who made up the district councils. There was little in the way of national political authority, and no attempt was made to bring national political unification or significant differentiation of the national polity. Most of the changes that did occur took place within the district governments. In 1820 a code of written laws was adopted by some districts. In October 1821, the northeastern district authorized a ten-man lighthorse patrol to enforce the collection of debts and to execute the law regularly. In 1822, the northeastern district council passed laws against intemperance in order to stem an active whiskey market. Laws were enacted and enforced against the practice of infanticide. Planters in the southern district advocated new laws, which were first enacted in the fall of 1821. By 1823, two districts had passed laws preventing the introduction of whiskey, had formed lighthorse police to curb the execution of persons for witchcraft (still commonly practiced), and had adopted laws against infanticide. In many instances the officers of the lighthorse acted as police, judge, jury, and executioner, although some cases were brought before the national council. The lighthorse guard was generally composed of mixed bloods, who were interested in the enforcement of laws against indebtedness and laws that would create a stable legal framework for the promotion of commerce.[48]

THE FAILURE OF POLITICAL CENTRALIZATION

A series of crises in 1825 and 1826 led to a rebellion by the younger mixed-blood chiefs. The trouble began when a Choctaw delegation negotiated a treaty in Washington in 1825 whereby the Choctaw agreed to cede back to the United States 5.5 million acres of land that had been exchanged in the west under the 1820 treaty. In return, the Choctaw received a $6,000 annuity for twenty years to support schools, though they rejected offers to sell land in the east and rejected removal. During this trip to Washington, Apuckshunnubee and Apushimataha, the chiefs of the northwestern and southern districts, died. Robert Cole, Apuckshunnubee's nephew, became chief of the northeastern district and continued to participate in the negotiations; later in the summer, Apushimataha's nephew Tapenahoma succeeded to the chieftainship of the southern district. Both these successions proceeded according to Choctaw custom, whereby nephews have the right to inherit the positions of their maternal uncles. The treaty caused an uproar in the Choctaw nation, however. After the delegation returned, Moshulatubee, the nominal principal chief, on several occasions had reason to fear for his life. David Folsom, a planter, accused the chiefs of immoral conduct and drinking during the negotiations, but Moshulatubee in order to regain the favor of the men in his district introduced a one-month moratorium on the prohibition of whiskey, an act that the pro-Christian planters used to discredit Moshulatubee's leadership further.

News of the William McIntosh incident also added to the anti-cession sentiment. Choctaw planters who were strongly opposed to land cessions openly exulted in the execution of McIntosh and other Creek chiefs who had illegally sold Creek land to the United States in early 1825; but when news came early in 1826 that a Creek delegation in Washington had been forced to cede nearly all remaining Creek lands in the chartered limits of Georgia, the opposition of the Choctaw planters to their own chiefs hardened. Chiefs whom they had trusted they now accused of incompetence and corruption that potentially threatened to jeopardize the remainder of the Choctaw domain.[49]

In April 1826, Moshulatubee was dismissed from office by unanimous agreement within the district council; the charge against him was not that he had ceded land in the treaty of 1825 but that he was intemperate, ignorant, tyrannical, and capricious in the disposition of treaty monies. In the council, the young pro-Christian planter David Folsom argued that the events within the Creek nation indicated that the Choctaw were subject to the same dangers and that in order to avoid them they should choose respectable men to guide their political affairs. The district council was determined that "a second McIntosh should not rise up among them, and dispose of their lands."[50] The northeastern council then determined that the district chief should be elected to four-year terms, and unanimously elected Folsom as district chief for the first four-year term.

Two months later the young mixed-blood Greenwood LeFlore, one of the biggest slaveholders in the nation, secured the dismissal of Robert Cole as chief of the northwestern district. The slaveholders did not like Cole, who was uneducated and, they said, not capable of adequately defending the territorial and political rights of the nation, and they accused him of accepting bribes in former treaties and cited the McIntosh example as reason for change toward a leadership and government that would demonstrate stronger resistance to American land and removal threats. Cole tried to muster his political allies to regain his position, but he was greatly outnumbered and in the end had to accept defeat. Moshulatubee formed a group to oppose the new slaveholder leaders and argued that the new leaders ultimately would prove unreliable; both he and Cole believed that they had been removed from office by unorthodox political procedures.[51]

The two new chiefs got considerable support from the conservative majority, to whom they promised that they would reject every proposition for removal and land cessions. The recent events among the Creek had precipitated concern within the Choctaw councils that the old chiefs were not the most appropriate people to muster effective resistance against American territorial demands and removal threats and that the planters, English-speaking Choctaws, and American-educated men were more capable of defending the nation, especially when the planters were overtly and strongly opposed to removal and land cessions. With conservative support, the new leaders embarked on a plan of political, economic, and cultural reorganization to strengthen Choctaw capabilities to resist removal. They encouraged continuing the transition to an agricultural economy, the promotion of Christianity, and the building of schools. In particular, the two new chiefs proposed strengthening and centralizing Choctaw government with a national constitution. The new slaveholder leadership argued that change was a precondition for effective resistance to removal and the safeguarding of the Choctaw homeland.[52]

Without delay, then, in August 1826, under the leadership of the northwestern district chief, Greenwood LeFlore, the Choctaw adopted a constitution. The constitutional government, however, differed very little from the old decentralized government: it kept the division into three districts, and it kept the system of district and national councils composed of local iksa leaders, though it did end the hereditary district chieftainship by making the district chief an elected four-year office. Perhaps the major innovation in government structure was the formation of a national committee that, in combination with the national council, was delegated legislative powers to initiate and enact bills that would become the law of the land. The national committee was organized by eight members from each district, for a total of 24 members, and was composed primarily of men from the English-speaking slaveholder class. The committee also was delegated the duties of assisting in the negotiation of treaties and relations with the U.S. government. The national council was composed of the captains or leaders of the local iksa and one additional member from each local iksa. The national council now was obligated to meet annually. The three district chiefs formed the executive, and unanimous consent among the chiefs was necessary for a binding decision. The council adopted a written code of laws and proposed new laws pertaining to inheritance through the male line, lawful enclosure of the common domain, discouragement of polygamy, and the regularizing of the lighthorse police.[53]

For the next four years the new leadership continued its efforts to strengthen Choctaw resistance to removal. Laws were passed to encourage schools, commerce, and temperance, to protect private property, and to curtail blood revenge and the killing of witches. In 1827 the Choctaw government resisted American efforts to buy more land and effect Choctaw removal. In October 1828, the chief of the southern district was removed for intemperance and for allowing the consumption of whiskey and was replaced by a slaveholder, John Garland, who was unanimously elected to a term of four years. Under Garland's leadership the southern district began to pass laws comparable to laws of the other two districts. Generally in all three districts the slaveholder leadership began to push harder for further economic, political, and even religious change. Until the summer of 1828, the Choctaw had tolerated American Protestant missionaries in the nation primarily as a means of supporting the school system; even the slaveholders, though many were Christians, tended to value the schools solely for the education of their children in arithmetic, reading, and discipline—skills necessary for business. But from mid-1828 through 1829, hundreds of Choctaw began attending revival meetings and were converted into at least nominal, churchgoing Christians. The slaveholder leadership encouraged the movement, which they saw as one more step in the transformation of Choctaw society, and in this they had the general support of the majority conservative community. Among anti-Christian district captains like Moshulatubee, the formation of Christian groups that were closely associated with the slaveholder leadership began to rankle. Moshulatubee, of course, still resented his removal from office, but he got a measure of support from a group of anti-Christian and politically disaffected Choctaw who advocated removal west.[54]

Nevertheless, as long as the slaveholding Christian planters held to their policy of absolute resistance to land sales and removal, they kept their position of leadership. By early 1830, however, under increasing pressure for removal, the leadership views began to change. In the summer of 1829 the U.S. agent to the Choctaw warned that the state of Mississippi soon would extend its laws over the Choctaw nation and that the federal government, led by recently elected Andrew Jackson, would not protect the Choctaw. Though the district chiefs held to their position of resistance to removal, the deposed chiefs accepted the American rationale that the Choctaw could not survive as a nation if it were surrounded by American settlers who were eager to acquire Choctaw land and that it was therefore better for the Choctaw to migrate west and live under their own laws than to live under the American state laws, which were not of their own making. Following his own argument, the deposed chief of the southern district, Tapenahoma, migrated west in the fall of 1829.[55]

In an attempt to harass the Choctaw into removing, Mississippi extended its laws over the Choctaw nation in January 1830, and a few months later the U.S. Congress passed the Indian Removal Act, which made removal the official federal policy toward Indians residing east of the Mississippi River. The district chiefs decided that it was no longer possible to resist removal. Greenwood LeFlore, who learned of the difficulties the Cherokee were having in their effort to resist removal, was convinced that any resistance would lead to the disruption and disintegration of the Choctaw nation. The chiefs therefore decided that it was up to them to negotiate the best possible treaty, and in March 1830 they convened a national council. The council was attended primarily by men from LeFlore's district, with only a few representatives from the other two districts. The chiefs of the southern and northeastern districts thereupon resigned, and the council elected LeFlore as principal chief. Supported by Methodist missionaries who helped write the Choctaw treaty proposals, the council then signed a relatively favorable removal treaty with the United States. With their change in attitude toward removal, the planter leaders attempted to centralize the Choctaw government and eliminate the autonomy of the three traditional political divisions; LeFlore's argument was that the division of the government into three districts inhibited coherent government decision making and also inhibited the uniform enforcement of and compliance with the law.[56]

The removal treaty and the elimination of the three traditional chiefs and political districts greatly angered the conservatives and the old leaders of the northeastern and southern districts. They charged the missionaries and the Christian converts with being instruments of American society who were scheming to deprive the Choctaw of their land and heritage. Moshulatubee declared that the removal treaty was unauthorized because there were not enough council members present from two districts to permit ratification, and he denounced the attempt to centralize political authority under one chief: "The extinction of the two council fires, and the bringing of all the Choctaws under one government and one chief were acts of usurpation not to be endured." [57]

In April, Moshulatubee and Nitakechi, a conservative chief of the southern district, held a council and, in defiance of LeFlore, organized their own election as chiefs of the northeastern and southern districts. Moshulatubee and Nitakechi were "strongly determined to have a chief in each district and have a government of their own as usual," and they asked the United States to protect them from LeFlore's warriors, who threatened to use force to gain the compliance of the two dissident districts with the new centralized government.[58] This development meant that LeFlore's political influence was restricted to his own northwestern district. Both Moshulatubee and Nitakechi strongly opposed the influence of missionaries, whom they blamed for the removal treaty and the attempt at political centralization. Folsom was, of course, removed as chief of the northeastern district, although he retained the loyalty of the Christian captains in his district; in the southern district, all Christian captains were removed from office. LeFlore offered Moshulatubee recognition as chief of the northeastern district if he would agree to the removal treaty, but Moshulatubee refused to sign the treaty and attacked LeFlore as a tyrant and for arbitrarily eliminating the ancient tripartite political organization of the Choctaw nation.[59]

In May, after receiving estimates of the cost of removing the Choctaw and paying allotments, the U.S. Senate rejected the treaty. Although the Choctaw were not now forced to move, the political unrest in the nation did not abate. Opposition to LeFlore's political leadership and concern over pressures for removal still continued, and when during the summer of 1830 the United States pressed for another removal treaty, negotiations had to be postponed because of Choctaw reluctance and internal political turmoil. The two Christian district chiefs who had resigned in March and the Christian captains in the same districts who were removed from office by the conservative opposition formed small parties in northeastern and southern districts and were re-elected chiefs by their constituencies. The fight was now between the Christian and "pagan" parties. Moshulatubee, in seeking American support, called his followers the "Republican" party and LeFlore's party the "Despotic" party. Whatever the designations, civil war almost erupted between the rival groups. An oral tradition recounts that armed forces of several hundred men on both sides met in an open field but withdrew without bloodshed after a discussion between the leaders. It is clear, however, that LeFlore could not command sufficient force to gain compliance with the centralized government and that the districts were willing to fight to maintain their political autonomy and independent governments.[60] The attempt to form a centralized Choctaw government had failed.

REMOVAL

In September 1830, at Dancing Rabbit Creek, American commissioners once again came to the Choctaw nation to negotiate a removal treaty. This time the Choctaw were represented by the three district chiefs and their advisers from the district councils. As was the custom, as many Choctaw as wished to attend came to observe the proceedings. Most Choctaw opposed removal, and in the initial negotiations, the Choctaw leaders refused to agree to removal. After stating their opposition to removal, many Choctaw withdrew from the treaty grounds believing that there would not be an agreement to a removal treaty. The American commissioners, however, were not to be denied; they resorted to bribery and threats of military force to browbeat the Choctaw leaders into accepting removal. If the Choctaw remained in the east, the commissioners warned, they would be subject to the taxes, courts, and laws of Mississippi and the federal government, and they would never be allowed to maintain an independent government.

Thus pressured, the Choctaw chiefs decided that under the circumstances they could only try to negotiate the best possible terms. They agreed to accept a large territory in what is now central Oklahoma, an annuity, payment for the costs of removal, and one year's subsistence in the new country. Article 15 of the treaty represented an attempt by the Americans and the Christian leaders to engineer political change among the Choctaw by stipulating that the Choctaw would adopt a constitutional government with a single executive when they arrived in the new country; this gave the Christian leaders the support of the United States government in centralizing and changing Choctaw governmental institutions, but as will be seen, even the alliance of American officials and the Christian planters was not enough to create a centralized government among the Choctaw in the early postremoval period. The treaty also gave the U.S. government the right to intervene in Choctaw political affairs so as to maintain order, and it provided annual stipends for Choctaw chiefs and captains.[61] In return, the Choctaw agreed to remove west in two years' time.

News of the treaty was not well received by either the conservatives or the Christians, and many openly voiced their opposition to removal. As opposition to the removal treaty increased, steps were taken to depose the three district chiefs. First, Greenwood LeFlore, on October 23, 1830, was removed from office as district chief and replaced by George Harkins, elected for a term of two years or during good behavior. There were numerous complaints against LeFlore: that he was unfit to rule because he sold the territory of the nation against the will of the people, that he had spent money on weapons and had organized a force of four or five hundred men to suppress the southern and northeastern districts, and that he had made oppressive laws and had tried to centralize the government. Early in January 1831, Moshulatubee attempted to resign his northeastern district post in favor of his nephew, Peter Pitchlynn, who had sided with the conservatives during the political turmoil of 1829–30. Folsom was elected chief by the Christian captains in the northeastern district, but his constituency was a minority. In April 1831 in the southern district, the council argued that Nitakechi had not been elected officially by a majority of captains of the southern district and that during the period of political difficulties in early 1830 he was recognized by Moshulatubee without full consent of the southern district council. In Nitakechi's place the southern district council elected Joe Nail, a chief from Chickasawhay, a major iksa in the district.[62]

However, the American government refused to recognize the new chiefs and insisted that it would transact business only with the district chiefs who had signed the treaty at Dancing Rabbit Creek. The three district chiefs were to be recognized until the Choctaw formed a centralized constitutional government in the west after removal. The action of the federal government was sufficient to keep the removal chiefs in official authority, although the majority of Choctaw continued to resist removal, and many local iksa or communities made their own decisions whether to remove or to stay in Mississippi under state laws. The Americans recognized LeFlore as principal Choctaw chief until at least 1833. Between 1831 and 1833, about three-fourths of the Choctaw migrated to present Oklahoma; the rest decided to stay in the east.

REMOVAL AND CHOCTAW POLITICAL CHANGE

Despite intense removal pressure, a class structure, a Christian revival movement, and the constitution of 1826, there was little significant institutionalized change in the Choctaw polity during the removal crisis. The Choctaw polity remained decentralized in three politically autonomous districts that were further subdivided into local particularistic communities or iksa. The district councils were formed by leaders of local kin-based communities. The Choctaw polity was not differentiated from kinship, and it did not form a unified political nationality in which loyalties and commitments to the national government superseded loyalties to the region, local communities, and kin groups. The attempt by LeFlore to centralize authority failed as the district governments reclaimed their traditional authority. Throughout the 1820's political decision making in the district and national councils required unanimous agreement. Until the Americans bolstered the district chiefs who agreed to the 1830 removal treaty, Choctaw political leaders were directly accountable to their political communities, and chiefs and captains were impeachable if they acted contrary to the will of the community. The attempt by the constitution of 1826 to create a national committee did not survive the political crisis of 1830, and little permanent internal differentiation of the national government resulted. There were some changes, but these were not in increased national unity, centralization, or differentiation but rather in the legal sphere, in the form of numerous laws pertaining to the right of private property and several Choctaw practices that the Americans found offensive. The Choctaw national council heard judicial cases, which were traditionally the domain of the local iksas. But many of the normative changes were repudiated during the conservative reaction to the removal treaty, and the attempts to curtail blood revenge and the execution of witches by a police force were not completely successful. The conservatives continued to adhere informally to the norms and beliefs of blood revenge, and most retained a nondifferentiated world view.[63]

In the end, although the removal crisis instigated a change-oriented alliance between the planters and the conservative majority, this alliance unraveled when the planters decided that resistance to removal was no longer possible. The political innovations of the planters became casualties of the reassertion of autonomy by regional and local communities. For the Choctaw, the removal crisis did not result in major changes in political differentiation, political centralization, or political unification, and the planters were not able to retain political leadership or effect their program of political change.

Chickasaw Resistance to Political Change

In the Cherokee case, a ceremonially integrated kinship system, combined with a secular polity that was differentiated from kinship ties, facilitated political unification, centralization, and increased political differentiation during the removal period. In the Choctaw nation, which had regional and local political identities and nondifferentiation of polity and kinship, the pressures of the removal period did not lead to the institutionalization of significant political centralization, unification, or increased differentiation of the polity. The Chickasaw society had a tradition of national kinship-religious integration, but its national political system was not differentiated from the national kinship system or religious system. In both the Cherokee and Choctaw cases there was mobilization for change in response to removal pressures, but in the Chickasaw case there was overt resistance to political and cultural change, and during the removal period the Chickasaw introduced and institutionalized only a few minor changes in political organization, while retaining their old government based on iksas and hereditary chiefs.

REMOVAL PRESSURES AND CHANGE DURING THE 1820's

For the Chickasaw, the period following the War of 1812 brought economic changes much the same as those experienced by the Choctaw— the disappearance of game and a swift decline in the fur trade economy to the point where it could no longer sustain the entire nation. After 1818 most Chickasaw were more or less forced to turn to agriculture and husbandry for subsistence and for production of goods that could be traded for manufactured goods. The decade 1820–30 saw a rapid increase in farming among the Chickasaw, and although many conservatives were reluctant to abandon the fur trade, most were forced to adopt subsistence farming by 1830. The number of Chickasaw planters and merchants increased; they turned more to cotton farming and slave labor in the postwar period. By 1818, Chickasaw society evinced a definite class structure, which deepened as the decade progressed and the mixed-blood sons of former traders showed increasing material acquisitiveness and readiness to accept American agricultural aids and education. The major portion of the Chickasaw—more than three-fourths of the total Chickasaw population of four to five thousand—retained subsistence economic orientations and continued to adhere to nondifferentiated world views. They raised crops, cattle, and cotton mainly for home use, and traded limited surpluses in order to buy manufactured goods and other products that they regarded as necessities and that could not be locally produced.[64] They were willing to accept limited change in the economic sphere, but they were overtly resistant to cultural and political change.

Pressure for land cessions and removal came soon after the end of the War of 1812. By a treaty in 1816, the Chickasaw ceded all their territory south of the Tennessee River and west of the Tombigbee River. During the negotiations for a second treaty in 1818, the United States pressed for land cessions and for Chickasaw removal west and it withheld the annuity payments promised in 1816 as a way of softening Chickasaw resistance. The Chickasaw council refused to move west, but, after initially declining to sell land, the chiefs did agree to cede all their territory north of the present boundaries of Tennessee. This meant that from 1801 through 1818, in four treaties, the Chickasaw ceded twenty million acres of land to the United States.[65]

The sale of the land led to great dissatisfaction with the chiefs among the Chickasaw warriors, and perhaps on that account the Chickasaw for the next twelve years resisted any further land cession and removal, despite mounting pressure from federal commissioners, local settlers, land speculators, and the states of Mississippi and Alabama. At the same time, Chickasaw leaders informed American officials that they were anxious to adopt agriculture and have schools built for their children. By 1820, both the planters and the conservatives welcomed teachers and the building of schools in the nation. As in the Cherokee and Choctaw cases, the new schools were attended disproportionately by the children of planters, a situation that tended to accentuate the class and cultural cleavages that already had emerged between the planter-merchants and the conservative subsistence farmers and hunters. The Chickasaw planters, like planters elsewhere, were interested primarily in education as a means to enhance the business skills of their children and showed little interest in the religion of the missionary teachers; generally, throughout the removal period, the Chickasaw stood aloof from Christian proselytizing. The Chickasaw conservatives welcomed teachers, but they were skeptical of, even hostile to, Protestant missionaries and preachers.[66] By 1829, there were only about 100 Christian converts and the missions were generally failures. The schools, too, closed down by 1834, having had little effect on Chickasaw society in general, although many of the Chickasaw who were educated in mission schools during the 1820's and early 1830's became national leaders in the postremoval period.

The Chickasaw political structure changed very little during the 1820's. The Chickasaw national council continued to be based on representatives from local iksas, chiefs from four major districts, and several hereditary warrior and civil chiefs. Several prominent planters and merchants held district and tribal chief posts. A new king, or principal chief, Ishtehotopa, the nephew of the old Chickasaw principal chief Chinibee, was installed in July 1820. He owned a ferry; the second chief, Tishomingo, was the owner of a well-kept and productive farm. Several members of the prominent Colbert family of planter-merchants were advisers, and Levi Colbert was variously speaker of the national council and an honorary chief. The national council encouraged the participation of the planters and the merchants because they had language skills and the experience to manage treaty and diplomatic negotiations with the American government more effectively, and they were willing to let the planters and merchants get

material benefits from the treaty negotiations in the form of special economic privileges and gifts. Nevertheless, throughout the removal crisis
period, the planters and the merchants, who had a secure place in the kin-
based political system, did not overtly suggest major change in the political order. They understood that they could act for the Chickasaw nation
but only insofar as they protected the national interests and rights of the
conservative majority, and they never directly challenged the kin-based
Chickasaw political order.[67]

The McIntosh incident among the Creek, which in early 1826 led to
the cession of Creek territory in present Georgia, precipitated movement
toward a more centralized constitutional government among the Cherokee, and the eventual deposing of all three district chiefs in the Choctaw
case. The response of the Chickasaw national council in early 1826 to the
difficulties among the Creek was a resolution that prohibited any person
from receiving a private reservation of land from any territorial cession
to the Americans. This law was designed to remove a major incentive for
any Chickasaw chief to sell Chickasaw land and reserve a special plot of
land for himself either for subsequent sale for private profit or for settling
upon and assimilating into American society.[68] The law appears to have
been aimed mainly at the more materially oriented mixed-blood planters
who might be tempted to betray the nation.

The Chickasaw council in 1826 refused to consider removal, and a majority within the national council were opposed to introducing American-
style national laws in the nation. American agents had for some time been
actively attempting to convince the Chickasaw to abolish blood revenge
but without success. In 1829, however, a group of influential planters convinced the national council to adopt a written code of laws that enforced
the protection of private property and facilitated commercial activity. A
lighthorse police force of 100 mounted men was created to enforce the
new code of laws. The Chickasaw council created few laws, but those laws
were easily understood and strongly enforced.[69]

CHICKASAW REMOVAL

The state of Mississippi, bent on destroying the Chickasaw nation,
between 1819 and 1829 progressively enacted laws that finally abolished
the Chickasaw government and brought the Chickasaw under Mississippi
state jurisdiction. Though the Chickasaw withstood pressure from the U.S.
government after 1826 to cede the remainder of Chickasaw land in the east
and remove west of the Mississippi River, settlers increasingly intruded
into the Chickasaw country and farmed land on speculation of Chickasaw
removal, while others drove off stock and stole slaves, horses, and cattle.

In August 1830 President Jackson informed a delegation of Chickasaw chiefs that the Chickasaw must either remove west or, if they stayed in the east, surrender their political autonomy and submit to the laws of Mississippi. In other words, the federal government was not going to prevent the southern states from extending their laws over the Chickasaw nation, and therefore if the Chickasaw wished to preserve their nationality they should migrate west. If the Chickasaw did so, the American government was authorized by the newly passed Indian Removal Act to pay the expenses of removal and provide support for one year in the new territory.[70]

Like the conservatives among the Cherokee and Choctaw, the Chickasaw had long argued that the Great Spirit had given them their land, it was the land where the bones of their ancestors lay, and they did not wish to move to a new land. But the new conditions of increased American pressures and the extinguishment of Chickasaw nationality by the states of Alabama and Mississippi convinced most Chickasaw to accept the removal proposal. The American offer of assimilation under state law did not seem realistic, and few conservative Chickasaw believed they would be granted equal civil rights as American citizens: the state laws were made and implemented by the Americans, and the Chickasaw felt that they were unskilled in American law and in law suits and reasoned that they would inevitably be dispossessed if they stayed and lived under state law. The Chickasaw therefore concluded that it would be better to migrate west and try to preserve their nationality and live under laws of their own making than to stay and lose everything in the east. At the treaty negotiations during the summer of 1830, when the Chickasaw finally agreed to move, it was decided that the Chickasaw would buy land in the west from the Choctaw who had already become established there. But the Choctaw refused to sell, and the treaty could not be ratified. During 1830 and 1831, efforts were made to find a western homeland for the Chickasaw among the Caddoes and the Osages in roughly the same area, but no agreements were forthcoming.[71]

Even with this question undecided, American commissioners were determined to force a removal treaty, and negotiations were undertaken in 1832 at Pontotoc, the Chickasaw capital village. The commissioners threatened to leave the Chickasaw to the mercy of state law if they did not agree to a treaty, and they offered terms to the mixed-blood Chickasaw planters and merchants that allowed them private reservations in the east. The commissioners said that if the conservative chiefs would not negotiate a treaty, they would negotiate a treaty with the planters and merchants.[72] Once again, and for the same rationale that it would be better to remove west and preserve their nationality and political freedom than to submit to the laws of Mississippi, the Chickasaw gave in.

This time, however, the conservative Chickasaw objected strongly to the treaty terms, which were clearly favorable to the planters and merchants since they knew the best land and could make better bargains with the Americans for allotments than could the conservatives. Led by Levi Colbert, the conservatives appealed for a revision of the 1832 treaty to stipulate that the Chickasaw land would be sold as a whole and the money divided per capita. The American commissioners denied the petition. Meanwhile, the Choctaw were again refusing to sell land to the Chickasaw and were only willing to incorporate the Chickasaw into a fourth district within the Choctaw nation; the Chickasaw rejected this proposal, and so the matter rested.[73]

In the spring of 1834, the Chickasaw renegotiated another removal treaty to modify the 1832 treaty. This treaty retained the condition of dividing the Chickasaw land into allotments, which were to be sold by individual Chickasaw, but it provided that a commission would be formed to validate the sales before removal. The formation of this national commission was the most significant change in Chickasaw political organization during the removal period, and over the next decade the commission was delegated the major tasks of government. The original commission was composed of the king Ishtehotopa and several district chiefs, most of whom were prominent planters; when men died or retired, they were replaced by others, usually men with planter and/or merchant backgrounds. The commission's authority, directly based on the 1834 treaty, included managing the finances of the nation, distributing treaty annuities, finding a western homeland, and generally serving as mouthpiece for the nation.

Though Mississippi state law had abolished the old kin-based political structure of the Chickasaw, men who were captains or leaders of local kin-based communities continued to lead in their customary fashion and gave deference to the nominal principal chief. Since the men who became commissioners were also prominent district chiefs or influential planters, the authority structure of the old kin-based political system was incorporated into the new national commission. The district and local chiefs and captains continued to manage local affairs, although the national council itself appears not to have met often, or at all, because of the state laws prohibiting the operation of the Chickasaw government, except on the business of facilitating removal.[74]

Between 1835 and 1837, some 2.4 million acres of Chickasaw land were allotted to individual Chickasaws and eventually sold to Americans. The Chickasaw country became inundated with American speculators who wanted to buy Chickasaw allotments, and also with settlers who just moved in. The Chickasaw found it increasingly difficult to maintain their national character and maintain control over their own people. No homeland had been decided upon, there were no immediate plans for removal, but the pressure to sell was hard to resist, and many Chickasaw now without land and soon without money, became homeless and destitute. A Chickasaw delegation that tried again to buy land from the Choctaw in 1836–37 was refused. Finally, in desperation, the Chickasaw at Doaksville in 1837 agreed to join the Choctaw nation in present-day Oklahoma. They agreed to become Choctaw citizens and to form a fourth district of the Choctaw nation and submit to the laws and political organization of the Choctaws.[75]

The terms of this agreement required the Chickasaw to surrender their political sovereignty. Many conservative Chickasaw, led by the king Ishtehotopa, for the moment kept quiet about their losses. The planters seemed more willing to embrace the government of the Choctaw, which by 1837 required election of the district chief and of representatives to the national council. Between 1837 and 1839, the Chickasaw migrated west to become part of the Choctaw nation.

The Chickasaw removal crisis did not precipitate a movement toward political change. While members of the planter and merchant class remained part of the kin-based political structure, they neither overtly attacked the old political system nor organized support for significant changes in political centralization or differentiation. And when the extension of state law over Chickasaw country abolished, *de jure*, the Chickasaw government, the king, district chiefs, and local village and iksa leaders remained influential in local affairs, and so the old political system was not destroyed. After 1834, the state and federal government ignored the old Chickasaw political system and refused to recognize it as representing Chickasaw national affairs. The Chickasaw Commission was recognized as the official organization that managed Chickasaw affairs with the Americans, although the commission did not have internal governmental prerogatives.

The 1837 agreement to join the Choctaw nation as citizens further contributed to the decline of influence of the old kin-based Chickasaw polity. In accordance with the 1837 agreement, the Chickasaw people voluntarily forfeited their government and nationality to join the Choctaw nation. Thenceforth the U.S. government refused to recognize the old Chickasaw government in any governmental capacity and instead recognized the Chickasaw only as one of four political districts within the Choctaw nation. Treaty business was managed by the commission created in 1834. Thus the old Chickasaw kin-based political system was officially abolished by the events of the removal crisis, though it remained the informal political organization for a group of conservatives who represented a small majority within the Chickasaw population. In the end, the removal pressures did not precipitate any major changes in political centralization or differentiation of the Chickasaw polity. The Chickasaw remained resistant to the internal reorganization of their nondifferentiated polity, even when the course of removal events led to the abolition of an independent Chickasaw government and nationality.

Creek Institutional Fundamentalism

As in the Chickasaw case, the Creek response to removal did not result in significant national political unification or differentiation of the polity. Immediately after the War of 1812, the Creek abolished blood revenge and centralized the legitimate use of force in the national council. Nevertheless, the Creek polity was organized by religious symbolism, by red and white towns, and by locally and religiously particularistic villages or tribal towns. Furthermore, regional identifications between upper and lower town regions continued to take precedence over national identifications and loyalties. Though the Creek national council in a sense resembled the Cherokee council (though not the councils of the Choctaw and Chickasaw) in that the Creek national polity was differentiated from kinship, the altogether different response of the Creek indicates that differentiation of the polity from kinship does not guarantee an increase in differentiation and solidarity as a response to removal pressures. The Creek polity remained decentralized and the polity was not differentiated from cultural and religious symbolism, an institutional configuration that inhibited Creek national political unification as well as further political innovation or differentiation of the Creek polity.

LAND PRESSURES AND CREEK CONSERVATISM

After the defeat of the Red Sticks in 1814, the United States and Georgia exacted a penalty on the Creek of over 10 million acres of land. In 1818 the Creek ceded two more tracts of land in Georgia, and in a treaty made primarily by the lower town Creek in 1821, the state of Georgia gained another five million acres. The upper town Creek did not consent to the cession in 1821 and regarded it as an illegal minority-approved transaction.

More or less at American instigation, the American-supported red towns of Tuckabatchee and Coweta abolished blood revenge after the defeat of the Red Sticks and adopted a written code of laws. One of the laws decreed death for any Creek who sold land without the authorization of the national council. William McIntosh was the head warrior of Coweta and also the owner of two plantations. He had fought effectively against the Red Sticks, and besides being influential in Coweta, he had a strong following both among lower town planters and among conservatives in lower towns that were allied with Coweta. McIntosh was influential in signing the 1821 treaty, an act that, according to the newly formalized Creek law, was an offense punishable by death. In response to threats made on his life, McIntosh argued that the land sale was necessary because the Creek were in debt to Georgia and the sale would clear the debt. The argument silenced the criticism for the moment, and McIntosh then agreed that hereafter the death penalty should be invoked for unauthorized sale of land. Though the upper town Creek grew to distrust McIntosh, who had been accused of embezzling national funds in 1819–20 and also of having gained two private reservations of land in the 1821 treaty, the flurry over the 1821 treaty did not alter the political status quo. The independent chiefdoms in the upper and lower town districts continued as before, and the national council continued to meet alternately in the upper and lower towns. The only specific result of the controversy was an affirmation of the law against land sales as a defense against unlawful cession of land.[76]

The Creek had made significant economic progress in the aftermath of the destruction caused by the Red Stick War. Much of the change reported by American agents was restricted to the resurgence of the planters, who accumulated slaves and plantations in order to exploit the new favorable market conditions for cotton and other agricultural products. Most of the planters lived in the lower town districts, and many were politically associated with McIntosh and the red town of Coweta. Although some of the prominent leaders of the upper towns were slaveholders, there were on the whole few slaveholders in the upper towns. Both Big Warrior and his political successor and assistant, Opothleyoholo—the two most influential chiefs at Tuckabatchee—were slaveholders, but they nevertheless adhered to the political culture and customs of their village, as did most of the planters, who as a group did not have any formal recognition or legitimacy within Creek political organization. Therefore, the planters operated within Creek political institutions and, like the Chickasaw planters, did not challenge the old order.

The large majority of Creek, however, were not interested in taking up American-style agriculture or acquiring wealth by market participation. Most Creek remained in their villages and continued to work the communal fields and small private plots, which were cultivated primarily by women. The large majority of Creek, at least 90 percent, remained primarily subsistence oriented and sold only enough goods to buy manufactured goods that they were dependent on and could not produce themselves. After 1824, the increasing pressures and disruptions of land cessions and removal led to economic decline and marginalization among the Creek villagers. The fur trade increasingly declined, but the conservative Creek were reluctant to adopt American agriculture; most preferred to continue to hunt despite dwindling economic prospects.[77]

The general Creek resistance to American-inspired change extended beyond agriculture to religion and schools. Unlike the Choctaw, the Chickasaw, and the Cherokee, the Creek flatly rejected American missionaries in the 1820's. At Tuckabatchee, Creek leaders openly spurned Protestant missionaries, declaring that their own religion and worship were sufficient. In the Creek world, political and social institutions were not differentiated from religion and cultural world view, and therefore the new religion of the Americans constituted a threat to the fundamental cultural legitimacy of the Creek institutional order. The other southeastern nations had had difficulties with missionaries, but they had tolerated them after a fashion. The Creek rejection of the missionaries was unique in its vehemence and effectiveness: Creek who adopted Christianity were openly persecuted, and missions and schools made little headway. Even the group most favorable to schools and to missionaries in the other southeastern societies, the planters, were against the missionaries; according to the Creek planters, the missionaries were dangerous because they taught spiritual equality, which implied equality between slaves and their masters. Even the leading Creek slaveholders in the removal period preferred to adhere to the ancient religion of the village square rather than adopt Christianity. Thus schools and missionaries had little impact on Creek society during the removal period. There were few schools, and planters who wanted to educate their children sent them to American schools outside.[78]

THE McINTOSH INCIDENT

Within this context of a shrinking land and general distrust of Americans and the U.S. government, the removal crisis came to a head. In late 1824, American commissioners were pressing the Creek for removal and for the cession of what remained of their land within the chartered limits of the state of Georgia. During the negotiations at Broken Arrow, the village of the lower town chief Little Prince, William McIntosh was forced to flee for his life after word got out of his having possibly engaged in secret negotiations with the Americans. The national council then forbade McIntosh any official capacity in the national council, and it declared that it would neither remove nor sell any more land to the Americans.

But still the Americans persisted, and in February 1825 they met with a group of Creek town delegations near an inn owned by McIntosh. McIntosh, who was quite ready to negotiate, tried to convince his fellow Creek that it would not be possible to continue to live in the east and that in order to preserve the nation they must remove west and abandon the old territory. The large majority rejected this argument, saying as before that the Creek could not abandon the homeland given to them by the Great Spirit, the land under which the bones of their ancestors lay. The chiefs ordered the towns to withdraw from the council and to decline to negotiate, since other negotiations could be held later in the year. But McIntosh and his faction went on with the negotiations, lured by large bribes and assurances of protection from the opposition Creek, and proceeded to give up Creek lands in Georgia, claiming that Coweta and the lower towns had the right to do so. Over the next few months McIntosh invited Georgia to implement the treaty by sending surveyors to mark out the Creek cession.[79]

The Creek national council refused to acknowledge the treaty. For their part in the fraudulent treaty negotiations, McIntosh and a brother-in-law of McIntosh were executed. According to Creek law, a defendant accused of a major crime could have his case argued before the national council; since late 1824, however, McIntosh had refused to appear before the national council for fear of his life and so he was condemned without an appearance. In such cases of conviction in absentia, the condemned man's town, Coweta in this case, was supposed to carry out the sentence; but because Coweta was under McIntosh's influence and could not be relied on to perform the execution, Creek law permitted the organizing of warriors from other towns to carry out the will of the national council. The Creek had centralized legitimate use of force in the national council and had differentiated judicial functions from kinship relations, but Creek judicial institutions were not differentiated from the national council or from the town governments.

Although some of the towns that were delegated the task of execution were white towns that had been enemies of Coweta and McIntosh during the Red Stick War, the execution was ordered by the national council, after the approval of both leading chiefs of the upper and lower towns. Warriors from Oakfuskie and Talledegas, both white towns and former Red Stick towns, led in action that resulted in McIntosh's execution. Most town chiefs who had signed the 1825 treaty quickly recanted, and those who did not were dismissed from office. A very small group, perhaps 2 percent of the Creek population, remained defiant of the national council under the leadership of McIntosh's brother and son. The American ratification of the 1825 treaty led to a national crisis among the Creek; the Creek, however, did not respond with any further political national unification or differentiation but attempted to resist from within their prevailing political institutions.[80]

The protests and controversy that followed the treaty of 1825 led to an

immediate investigation that convinced President Adams that the treaty
was fraudulent, having been signed by only a small minority of Creek. A
Creek delegation was called to Washington in the fall of 1825 to negotiate a new agreement and to reconcile the nation with the McIntosh
faction. Though the delegation was determined not to cede any more land,
Georgia insisted, and in January 1826 the Creek delegation ceded most
of their remaining land in Georgia, except for a small tract and other
small territories that were left by mistake. This new treaty of 1826 forced
the lower towns to resettle in present-day Alabama, much nearer to the
upper towns. The McIntosh faction was compensated for damages and
allowed to remove west. About 1,300 Creek, mostly prosperous planters,
removed to present-day Oklahoma in 1828. Others left when Alabama
threatened to extend its laws over the Creek, and by 1830 between 2,000
and 3,000 Creek had emigrated and settled in the west. The more conservative members of the lower towns remained in the east and between 1827
and 1830 resettled in Alabama, although they suffered considerable social
disruption and economic hardship.[81]

ATTEMPTS TO PRESERVE THE POLITY

In response to the increasing pressure for removal and the events of
1825–26, the Creek national council looked for ways to resist American
demands more effectively. Since many of the educated Creek were associated with the McIntosh faction, and since the means of gaining access
to political leadership in Creek society required years of study and participation within Creek religious and ceremonial activities, there were few
educated Creek who had direct access to positions of national leadership.
Between 1824 and 1829, the Creek occasionally adopted the services of
the mission-educated Cherokees David Vann and John Ridge, the son of
Major Ridge; both men were members of the Cherokee planter class and
had been educated in New England. The two Cherokee acted as advisers
and also interpreters to the Creek, since the Creek did not wish to trust
the translations of American officials.

The two Cherokee suggested that the Creek should adopt a written
constitution and centralize authority and financial control as the Cherokee
had done during the same period in response to similar removal and land
pressures. The Creek were interested in strengthening their political structure, and although they watched the developments in the Cherokee nation
with interest, the national council, which was composed of localistic, kin,
and religiously particularistic villages, rejected adoption of further differentiation and national unification of their political relations. In 1826 the
Creek national council continued the process of centralizing and ratio-

nalizing national law with a revised written legal code that extended the legal code that was developed in 1814–18. The national laws only rarely infringed on the self-government of the individual towns, however, and clashes of authority between the national council and the local towns were avoided. Furthermore, the legal code was enforced according to Creek norms and views of justice. The upper towns and lower towns continued to have separate chiefs and councils. The crisis of land loss and threatened removal did not lead to national political unification or further differentiation of the Creek polity. The Creek attempted to strengthen their polity not by increased political unification and differentiation, which threatened the political autonomy and prerogatives of the village governments, but by adopting a more extensive legal code within the existing level of differentiation and within the existing form of symbolic-political integration.[82]

Between 1826 and 1830, American pressures for removal intensified. Early in 1827 the state of Alabama extended its laws over part of the Creek nation and threatened to extend its laws over the rest. Two years later, Alabama completed the process of extending its laws over the Creek and prohibited the Creek government from legally operating. Despite the pressure, the Creek who remained in the east were still strongly opposed to removal. In the spring of 1829, the aged Little Prince of Broken Arrow, who was the principal chief of the lower towns, died; the following year Eneah Micco of Cussetah was appointed to replace him. Most of the McIntosh faction and the allied towns of Coweta had migrated west, and now the more conservative white towns again became dominant politically among the lower towns, making the lower town chief the nominal chief of the nation. Eneah Micco's opposition to removal and land sales appealed to the remnant conservative lower town villages.

In the upper towns, Big Warrior had died in 1825 and had been replaced by his son, Tuskeneah of Tuckabatchee. Tuskeneah tried to rule with a small clique of chiefs but disregarded the will of the many, and in early 1827 he was removed on grounds of immaturity; he was told that he could observe and learn from the experience and knowledge of others. The office of principal chief was given to two men, one of whom was Nehathie Hopia of Tuckabatchee. Tuskeneah's primary political opponent was Opothleyoholo, who had been second in command to Big Warrior and was now the most influential leader in the nation. Opothleyoholo was, like Big Warrior, a prosperous slaveholder who had fought with the Americans against the Red Stick fundamentalists, but he was respected for his knowledge of Creek religion and ceremony—a precondition for high political rank during this period of Creek history—and he had the support of the conservative Creek for his strong stand against removal and for his articulation of the conservative position that, according to treaty, the Americans guaranteed the Creek their land rights and that the American government would not break their treaties. The Creek conservatives believed that the Creek had a religious and historical right to their territory, and they did not want to cede it or exchange it for unknown lands in the west. Early in 1827, Opothleyoholo was appointed "prime minister or chief councillor of the nation" with the assignment to assist the principal chief. In 1830, Nehathie Hopia, or Little Doctor, was appointed principal chief, although in late 1831 Tuskeneah was again reappointed principal chief of the upper towns.

Thus it appears that, although the Creek did not make major changes in their institutional order, they attempted to appoint better, more competent, and trustworthy leaders. They were quick to dismiss leaders who would not or could not resist removal and be accountable to the demands of the general interests of the conservative majority. As removal pressures increased, the Creek council remained conservative and did not seek change in the institutional political order.[83]

For most Creek, political and economic conditions continued to decline over the 1826–32 period. Although Creek planters continued to be prosperous and suffered little economic distress, most Creek refused to adopt American agriculture, and the game necessary for subsistence and for exchange in the fur trade was inadequate to support the population. Alabama continued to harass the Creek by withdrawing civil rights, hoping in that way to force the Creek out of their territory altogether. Furthermore, American settlers increasingly settled on Creek-claimed territory, and although according to treaty the American government was obligated to protect Creek land and remove intruders, it made little effort to protect Creek lands permanently from the determined settlers. The Creek leaders appealed to the protections guaranteed in past treaties, but the federal government under Andrew Jackson refused to interfere with the actions of the state governments and repeatedly asked the Creek to remove in their own interests. Nevertheless, despite increasing economic marginalization and political harassment, the Creek resolved to remain in their ancient homeland and not cede any more land or remove west.[84]

Creek resistance was broken in the summer and fall of 1832, when a drought destroyed Creek crops and brought many in the nation to the point of starvation and impoverishment. Desperate for aid, the Creek leadership, Eneah Micco of Cussetah and Tuskeneah of Tuckabatchee and the national council, agreed to submit to American demands for a treaty. The Creek, still not wanting to remove west, asked that each town be granted a special land reservation where they would be allowed to retain their customs and local self-government; they were willing to accept Alabama laws if they could preserve the ancient political autonomy of the villages. In this way the Creek hoped to continue living in their home-land, maintaining the fundamental institutions of the individual towns. In addition, the Creek were given an annuity, money to pay their collective private debts, and support for those who wished to emigrate west.[85] For this, the Creek ceded the remainder of their land in Alabama, except the land to be reserved for the towns.

From the point of view of the Creek, the treaty of 1832 was a failure. The treaty did not guarantee the Creek legal or political equality within the state of Alabama, and the subsequent use of coercion and fraud soon dis-possessed the Creek villagers of the remainder of their land. By early 1834, all the village reservations had been surveyed and assigned, but the towns were overrun by land speculators who by fraudulent means bought much of the land comprising the village reservations and effectively dispossessed the Creek. By 1835 the Creek leadership began to consider removal west. Hostilities broke out in the spring of 1836, when some dispossessed and starving members of the Yuchi village stole food and attacked some Ala-bamians. Residents of several lower towns who did not want to remove and wished to remain undisturbed in the east according to treaty guaran-tees joined the hostilities. The lower town principal chief, Eneah Micco of Cussetah, and Neahmathla of Hitchiti were the primary leaders of the opposition, which was composed primarily of white towns. The resistance was broken quickly by American troops with the aid of some upper town Creek; ironically, the hostile villages were not the old fundamentalist Red Stick villages but villages that had supported American troops during the Red Stick War. After the several rebellious lower towns were brought into submission, most of the Creek nation—about 14,000 people—migrated west to present-day Oklahoma.[86] Even the failure of the 1832 treaty did not bring the Creek council to implement any further efforts toward national political unification or differentiation of the polity.

Removal and Political Change

For all four southeastern nations, the removal crisis was prolonged and painful and in many ways much the same. The four nations were subjected to similar economic pressures, and the pressures by the state governments and the federal government, and by settlers and land speculators, were all too distressingly of the same pattern. It is evident, however, that external political pressures and competition by themselves cannot explain why the responses in terms of political change among the Cherokee, the Choc-taw, the Chickasaw, and the Creek varied so greatly. All four societies also were subject to American programs of social and economic change, had access to missionaries, experienced similar declines in the fur trade, and developed similar class stratification based on cotton export and slave labor. How, then, can we account for the early acceptance of political differentiation among the Cherokee, while the other three societies either failed to institutionalize political differentiation and unification or were strongly resistant to change in political unification and/or differentiation? Given the similarities of conditions experienced by all four nations during the removal period, an explanation for the differences in institutional response to removal must be sought in the differences in sociopolitical organization.

Although the planter class varied in size and political orientation in the four nations, it was in all cases small relative to the entire population, and before removal none of the planter classes had control over police or military that would enable them to extend their class interests and political innovations over the other members of the society. Therefore, since each of the planter groups was confronted with consensual polities, the critical variable becomes how the planters mobilized the nation for change—assuming that the planters wanted to change the polity. In such a situation, unless the planters or other change-oriented groups can use coercion to break down institutional barriers to change, then the group must mobilize change within the existing institutional framework.

In a similar way, the role of charismatic individuals in effectuating institutional change must also be set within their institutional contexts and relations to the major groups in the society. For example, we can accept that William McIntosh of the Creek, John Ross of the Cherokee, and James and Levi Colbert of the Chickasaw (and many others) were influential leaders and that their actions were very important elements in the responses made by the Cherokee, the Creek, and the Chickasaw. But we cannot assume that influential men (or groups or classes, for that matter), though they may be catalysts for change (or for conservatism, as the case may be), can by themselves create and maintain new political institutions: the stability of the new political order ultimately depends on the willingness of at least a majority in the society to agree to participate and give their time and commitments to the new institutional arrangements. For example, among the Choctaw, the Christian-planter leaders during the late 1820's could not create a centralized government because of the hostile attitudes of regional leaders who moved to restore the old decentralized polity of three districts. Among the Creek, the efforts of the American agent Benjamin Hawkins to change Creek political organization had minor success and were at least partly responsible for the outbreak of the Creek civil war in 1813–14. Again, the charismatic William McGillivary's conscious efforts in the 1780's and 1790's to reorganize and unify the Creek confederacy did not lead to any permanent changes in the Creek polity.

Any attempt to bring about significant and permanent social change in a major social institution such as government requires more than charismatic advocates, since, barring coercion, it ultimately requires the consent of most other members of the society—that is, of social classes or groups, not just individuals, since no consensual change can be induced by the influence of one person without cooperation, support, and commitments from major segments of the society. Indeed, the argument based on groups and their orientations toward change, and the level of political differentiation and social and political solidarity in the society, is directly opposed to a view that influential persons are directly responsible for significant change in political order. Significant institutional change in a society is either a consensual event involving most members of the society, or it is imposed and maintained by force and manipulation by a segment of the society. In the removal periods of the four southeastern nations, individual and group actions were important, but that action must be considered within their historical and institutional contexts and can be only one part of a broader explanatory argument. The possibilities for change are constrained by a society's configuration of institutional differentiation and social and political solidarity.

At the beginning of the removal period, the Cherokee polity was the most differentiated, centralized, and unified. By 1817, the Cherokee already had adopted significant innovations in the centralization of legitimate force in the national government; they had adopted some early elements of bureaucratic organization and had declared themselves a unified nationality. Between 1817 and 1827, in response to removal pressures, the Cherokee worked out a highly differentiated constitutional government. These political changes, which encountered some resistance and doubt, were formed and legitimated by widespread consensus among the Cherokee elders and conservatives, although the innovations were introduced largely by the planters and American-educated Cherokee. The Cherokee exhibit a relatively rare example of predominantly consensual political institution building. The secular, non-kin-based Cherokee polity and the national political unification in opposition to removal were central features of Cherokee political organization that facilitated the institutionalization of significant changes in political differentiation.

In the Choctaw case, the planters attempted the same plan as the Cherokee, but the Choctaw did not institutionalize the differentiation of polity from kinship, significant internal political differentiation, or national political unification. The attempt to centralize and politically unify the Choctaw nation in 1830 failed because of regional, local, and kinship allegiances and identities. Lacking the differentiation of kinship and polity and the national political unification of the three segmentary political districts, the Choctaw leadership could neither institutionalize any further significant differentiation of the polity nor unify the nation politically and centralize the government against removal pressures.

The Creek and the Chickasaw both responded to removal without much change in their political institutions. The Chickasaw, like the Cherokee, had a tradition of a symbolically unified nation, although not necessarily a politically unified nation. The Chickasaw, although unified and centralized by their traditions and kinship system, did not respond to removal pressures with further political unification or further centralization or differentiation. The nondifferentiation of kinship and national symbolic integration within the Chickasaw polity proved highly resistant to change and innovation: the Chickasaw were resistant to Christianization and overtly rejected suggestions for change in their existing sociopolitical order. Finally, the Creek, too, were resistant to political change and responded to removal from within their institutional order. The Creek national polity was differentiated from kinship, but it was the least secular of the southeastern nations and was based on a loose coalition of religiously particularistic and kin-based villages. Although the Creek villages and government were integrated symbolically into red and white villages, there was little politically unified nationalism; regional and local political allegiances took precedence over national political loyalties and identities. Without a politically unified nationality and because of the symbolic-religious nondifferentiation of the Creek polity, the Creek were unwilling to adopt further secularization or further internal differentiation of their national government and/or to institutionalize a national political identity despite the intense pressures of the removal period.

The experience of the southeastern nations during the intense political competition of the removal period indicates that the formation of a national political identity and unification are preconditions to further developments in political differentiation. Without national political unification, neither the Creek, the Chickasaw, nor the Choctaw adopted significant changes in differentiation of their polities. The Cherokee formed a nationally unified polity in 1809–10 and soon thereafter centralized legitimate use of force in the government and adopted further changes in internal differentiation that led to the constitutional government of 1827. The Creek centralized legitimate force between 1814 and 1818, but without national unification and with a large measure of American and planter coercion that was the result of their victory over the fundamentalist Creek Red Sticks. Political centralization in the Creek case was therefore achieved without national political unification, but was institutionalized by coercive means rather than by the consensual means that determined political centralization and differentiation in Cherokee society.

The primary motivation for change came not from internal cultural or group tensions but from American territorial threats, from the differentiated political models that the planters borrowed from the Americans, and from the economic interests of the planters. Nevertheless, the latter motivations for change were not strong enough to overcome institutional barriers to national political unification and further political differentiation. In the societies with nondifferentiated polities and localistic or particularistic political loyalties, either the movements for further political unification or political differentiation failed, or no mobilization for change occurred in the face of strong institutional fundamentalism against unification and political differentiation and in the face of the alternate strategy of responding to American geopolitical threats and world-economic system incorporation from within the preexisting nondifferentiated and politically decentralized institutional order.

The preexisting configuration of political differentiation played a major role in the extent of further differentiation in the polity. By 1817, the Cherokee polity was by far the most differentiated, both internally and externally, and the most politically unified, and showed the greatest capacity for the institutionalization of further differentiation. The Choctaw and Chickasaw polities were not differentiated from kinship organization, and neither of them institutionalized any further significant political differentiation. And the Creek national polity, though it was differentiated from kinship, was tightly interpenetrated by religious organization and cultural symbols, and the Creek were strongly fundamentalist in their opposition to political and cultural innovations. The conditions of national political unification and political differentiation are central for understanding the variation in institutional responses of the southeastern nations to changing world-system relations and intense geopolitical competition.

6 POLITICAL INSTITUTION BUILDING AFTER REMOVAL

ONLY THE CHEROKEE had formed a constitutional government during the removal crisis; after removal, and within a less threatening geopolitical context, the Creek, the Choctaw, and the Chickasaw also formed differentiated constitutional governments. All four nations were removed to present eastern and central Oklahoma and thus their geographical, geopolitical, and world-system contexts remained similar; but the post-removal period was not characterized by the intense political pressures of the removal period. For the time, at least, the isolation of the west protected the four nations from the American population and agricultural expansion in the east, and in accordance with the removal treaties, American agents were assigned to protect the new lands from encroachments by American settlers. American officials continued to promote economic, social, and political change among the migrant nations, and missionaries continued to manage schools and attempted to make converts in each nation.

World-system relations remained similar to the conditions in the east. The planters transported their slaves and established plantations in the rich soil of the river valleys of Indian Territory. Within a few years the planters again were making good profits from exporting cotton and other agricultural goods. The Cherokee had the most slaves, with 1,600 before removal and about 2,500 in 1860. The Choctaw planters had the next highest number of slaves, with about 500 near removal and 2,350 in 1860. The Creek held 902 slaves in 1832 and 1,532 in 1860, while the Chickasaw had the fewest slaves—several hundred near removal and about 1,000 in 1860. The free Chickasaw population, however, was less than one-fourth the size of the Cherokee population, so the per capita slaveholding among the Chickasaw was relatively higher.

In the west, although there were large surpluses of arable land and a ready agricultural market, the large majority of the people of the four nations remained subsistence farmers. Most of them farmed small parcels of land, usually five to seven acres; often, the women worked the fields more than the men. Subsistence farmers who owned slaves used them primarily to help with subsistence farming rather than for market farming. Members of local communities engaged in communal labor such as harvesting and raising houses and barns for newlyweds, and they engaged in a round of community social and ceremonial events such as picnics, fishing parties, horse racing, bullplays, fox hunts, stomp dancing, and church-going. The produce from the small farms was supplemented by hunting for plentiful game and fish, as well as by the husbanding of pigs, cattle, horses, and sheep. The subsistence farmers generally lived in small one- or two-room log cabins with dirt floors and with little furniture. Cooking was done on an open fire. As in the east, the subsistence farmers retained predominantly nondifferentiated world views and preferred to produce primarily for home consumption. They traded only enough goods to give them the means to buy what they needed. In all four societies, the former class stratification system was reproduced in the west, with a long-term gradual trend toward a higher proportion of native southeasterners becoming active market participants.[1]

A major difference between the living conditions during the post-removal period and the conditions in the southeast before removal was the absence of intense political pressures for land and for removal. After removal, the Cherokee reestablished their constitutional government in 1839. The Chickasaw formed an independent constitutional government in 1856, the Choctaw adopted a centralized constitutional government in 1860, and the Creek adopted a constitution in 1867. The pattern of state formation among the Creek, the Chickasaw, and the Choctaw was very different from that of the Cherokee constitutional government, which had had broad support in a nation under threat. The formation of constitutional governments in the postremoval period involved more coercion and was not directly legitimated or created as a response to threats to national existence. Moreover, in the formation of the Cherokee constitutional government, American officials and missionaries did not play a significant role, but in the Chickasaw, Choctaw, and Creek political institution building in the postremoval period, an alliance of American officials who advocated the formation of constitutional governments and a group of planters and mission-educated southeasterners moved to set aside the old governments and establish constitutional governments modeled after the American government. This chapter examines the events and conditions that led to the formation of constitutional governments in the post-removal period. Chapter 7 will discuss the stability or institutionalization and internal political relations of the new constitutional governments.

Cherokee Political Reconciliation

From the fall of 1838 to the summer of 1839, most Cherokee in the east were forced to migrate west. The migration was difficult, and as many as 4,000 Cherokee lost their lives during the move because of disease, age, extreme youth, and inadequate preparation for difficult winter conditions. The "Trail of Tears" reinforced the bitterness that the conservatives held toward the treaty party for their sale of land in the east. When the immigrant Cherokee arrived in the west, in present-day northeastern Oklahoma, they were officially welcomed by the Old Settlers, the former Chickamauga and lower town dissidents who, despite criticism, had chosen to move west in 1810 and 1817. The Old Settlers had formed a constitutional government in 1824, with an elected chief and a legislature, and when the eastern Cherokee arrived, the Old Settlers argued that they should submit to the prevailing leadership and government. The Ross or national party, which had the loyalties of at least two-thirds of the Cherokee population, rejected this idea and instead proposed that the Old Settlers unite with the immigrants to form a unified nation and write a new constitution modeled after the Cherokee constitution of 1827.

The leaders of the Old Settlers, mainly planters, initially refused the national party's offer to form a new government, and in this they had support from the treaty party, also composed primarily of planters, who were in disfavor with the conservative majority. American agents and policy also supported the position of the more cooperative Old Settler and treaty party leaders, and American officials worked to discredit the political claims of John Ross, a small group of like-minded planters, and the conservative majority.

The conservative majority was organized informally by community leaders and maintained their loyalties to John Ross, who was the principal chief under the constitution of 1828. A further element in the organization of the national party was the secret Keetoowah Society, which had been mobilized for political ends to prevent removal in the east and now had migrated west with its membership. It is not clear whether John Ross was a member of the Keetoowah Society before 1858, when the Keetoowahs established a chartered organization, but many Keetoowahs were bitter toward the treaty party for their betrayal in the east, and the society remained organized to pursue its political opposition. Keetoowahs still blamed the treaty party for breaking Cherokee moral codes of honesty and trust and for taking bribes to sell their eastern homeland.[2] Many of the eastern immigrants, not just Keetoowahs, were bitter over the loss of relatives during the Trail of Tears and held the treaty party at least partly responsible.

Therefore the immediate political problem for the Cherokee in 1839 was to reunify the three major political groups and to adopt a common government. The form of government was not the central issue: all three major parties were in agreement that the government would have a differentiated constitutional form. The struggle was largely over control of the government, and over which government would prevail, the constitution of the Easterners or the government of the Old Settlers. There were class elements in this struggle also, since most of the planters and merchants were aligned with the treaty party and with the Old Settlers, whose leadership was composed primarily of planters, even though most Old Settlers were subsistence farmers. Being in the clear minority, the Old Settlers and the treaty party enlisted and received American support for their claims to political leadership. Hence the Old Settlers and the treaty party, backed by American support, were arrayed against the conservative majority or national party.

The national party continued to operate under the government and officers of the 1827 constitution until a new constitution could be agreed upon. In the spring of 1839, negotiations were initiated for political unification, but interference by the leaders of the treaty party angered the members of the national party, who thought the treaty party was attempting to prevent national unification and the formation of a new majority-rule government. On June 19, 1839, a convention between the national party and the Old Settlers failed to reach an agreement on forming a unified government. On June 21, about 300 conservatives met in secret to discuss the interference of the treaty party leaders and decided to execute several of them. According to the Baptist Missionary Evan Jones, who in later years was closely associated with the Keetoowah Society, the leaders of the treaty party would have been spared if they had been conciliatory during the early negotiations for political reunion. At the meeting, the leaders of the treaty party were tried according to clan procedures: the seven clans were represented and the clans of the condemned men gave permission for their execution and promised not to invoke blood revenge against the executioners.[3]

According to the oral tradition, many men who were present at the meeting were members of the Keetoowah Society. The Keetoowah Society was divided into three overlapping sections. There was the general Keetoowah Society, which encompassed the whole membership. The Nighthawk Keetoowah, or religious segment of the society, was oriented toward preserving Cherokee traditions and religion and considered the Keetoowah more a sacred institution than a political organization. The Nighthawks openly identified as a group only after 1895 when they broke ranks with the rest of the Keetoowah Society. A subgroup within the conservative Nighthawk Keetoowahs was called "pins." The pin organization was formed in the postremoval period, primarily as an organization to execute "the crooked and corrupt" Cherokee who had betrayed the nation in the east. Oral tradition says that members of all three sections of the Keetoowah Society were present at the secret trial of the treaty party leaders; some pins were selected to carry out the assassinations, and they did so the very next day, except for several men who were warned by relatives and escaped.[4]

The assassinations polarized the conservatives and the treaty party into armed camps and set off a sequence of internal political turmoil among the Cherokee that lasted until the fall of 1846. In July 1839, the national party passed an Act of Union that was intended to unite the Cherokee nation, but few Old Settlers agreed and the treaty party boycotted the meetings. The following September 6, the national party held a constitutional convention and adopted a constitution that closely paralleled the constitution of 1827. In an effort to placate the Old Settlers, the national party promised them proportional representation in the new government and access to high office for at least the first election. Ross was chosen as principal chief, but the second chief and the speakers of the house and senate were Old Settlers. Nevertheless, most Old Settlers and treaty party members boycotted the new government. American officials, who continued to lean toward recognition of the government of the Old Settlers, then ordered a plebiscite vote by the Cherokee to ascertain their government of choice. The convention of November 1839 was again boycotted by the two dissident parties, who refused to recognize what they called a "mobocracy" government. American officials, sympathizing with the treaty party, demanded the arrest of the assassins and attempted to oust Ross from political leadership under the assumption that he had participated in the murders. Finally, on June 26, 1840, General Matthew Arbuckle, the local American military commander, mediated negotiations for the unification of the national party and the Old Settlers, under terms that entailed American recognition of the constitution of 1839 and of the government led by the national party.

Most of the Old Settlers accepted the treaty terms, and over the next several years the Old Settlers increasingly participated in the new government led by the national party. Some of the discontented Old Settlers migrated to Texas or Mexico, however, and another small group of Old Settler discontents, along with the treaty party, refused to submit to the new government. The treaty party insisted that the national party had overthrown the Old Settler government by force, intimidation, and sheer weight of numbers, and it did not forget the assassinations of their leaders, for which they had been unable to obtain redress either from the Cherokee or from the American government. In frustration, the treaty party leaders took revenge against the assassins of their kinsmen and friends. These acts of revenge led to counter acts from the conservatives, in a series of intermittent political and revenge murders. Though the revenge murders resembled the old clan obligations, the clans were no longer operable in these affairs: political party membership now claimed stronger loyalties than clan affiliation.

The national party governed from 1839 to 1846 and increasingly won American recognition as the official Cherokee government, despite the continuing internal political violence. During this period of political instability, the Keetoowah Society, which was active in different communities, selected leaders and councillors, and held regular meetings at which it made plans for carrying on the conflict against the treaty party. By 1843 some Old Settlers were outspoken in their repudiation of the American-mediated unification of 1840. Appealing to the American government, the Old Settlers asked for an independent government and a separate territory on the grounds that they were the victims of political oppression at the hands of the conservative national party. The treaty party allied with the dissident segment of the Old Settlers, and they, too, complained of political harassment, loss of property, and repressive use of the lighthorse police by the Ross government. The political difficulties intensified during the election in the fall of 1845. The Cherokee lighthorse executed several treaty party members for murder and conspiracy; the treaty party responded with arms, and in the ensuing events perhaps as many as 35 people were killed. Many treaty party members and their families fled the nation, and the Old Settlers appealed for redress to the American President, James Polk.[5]

In January 1846, the treaty party and a group of Old Settlers decided to ask the American President to divide the Cherokee nation among the three parties, believing that the Cherokee could not live in peace. All three parties sent delegations to Washington to negotiate; President Polk, agreeing, sent a bill through Congress proposing to divide the Cherokee nation. The Ross party strongly opposed the action and expressed a willingness to compromise in order to preserve the national domain. During the negotiations, war broke out between the United States and Mexico, and the President and government turned their attention away from Indian affairs.

The negotiations were left to officials of the Office of Indian Affairs, who opposed the division among the Cherokee. Official reports indicated that the large majority of the Cherokee supported the national party government and that the Old Settlers were well represented in the government. A bill proposing the division of the nation was presented to the Old Settler delegation, but the Old Settlers decided not to pursue a separation. The treaty party delegation now found itself alone. In addition, some of the strongest advocates of separation had recently died. Ultimately, the treaty party delegation decided to seek reconciliation with the Ross party. A treaty was signed in August 1846 that gave amnesty to all combatants and laid the foundations for an end to the political antagonisms of the last seven years.[6]

The period 1846–60 was relatively peaceful for the Cherokee. The Old Settlers and the treaty party were incorporated into the government and held a disproportionately high number of offices. The conservative subsistence farmers led by John Ross, however, continued to hold the majority of the electorate, and the national party won all the elections for principal chief and dominated the government through the electoral process. But if the planters of the treaty party and the Old Settlers did not gain control of the government directly, Cherokee laws and the constitution facilitated the realization of the planters' material interests by providing a slave code to control slave labor, access to large sections of the public domain, and no taxation.[7]

Political relations between the conservative subsistence farmers and the planters remained relatively quiet until the late 1850's, when the United States was sliding toward civil war over the slavery issue. The Cherokee planters avidly sided with the South and began to persecute and exile American missionaries who advocated abolition. In 1858–59, conservative leaders and Evan Jones, the longtime Baptist minister to the conservative old valley town Cherokee—many of whom were also members of the secret Keetoowah Society—decided to revive and strengthen the long-dormant Keetoowah Society. Since most members of the Keetoowah Society were subsistence farmers and not strongly attached to the institution of slavery, they had little difficulty accepting abolition. Protestant missionaries among the conservative Cherokee preached abolitionism, and the conservatives readily adopted the doctrine as a weapon in their struggle against the entrepreneurial and acquisitive treaty party. In the spring of 1859, the Keetoowah Society adopted a charter and organized along the principles of a voluntary association. Previously the meetings of the Keetoowah Society had been conducted according to the rules of Cherokee councils; the revived Keetoowah Society of 1859 was a predominantly Protestant Christian organization formed to protect Cherokee national and land rights and to preserve Cherokee customs. The pins, the more militant and conservative wing of the Keetoowah Society, controlled certain parts of the country and harassed the slaveowners by burning their property, killing their slaves, and attempting to assassinate specific slaveholders.[8]

By the summer of 1861, Union troops abandoned Indian country in present Oklahoma and Southern agents attempted to rally the major Indian nations in the Indian Territory to the Southern cause. The differences in the Cherokee parties carried on: the majority national party wished to remain neutral, while the planters, known thereafter as the Southern party, were strong advocates for an alliance with the Confederates. At a mass meeting, Ross argued that the Cherokee would not be able to stay out of the conflict, but he urged the principal parties to remain unified as a nation and to ally with the South because of their institutional ties to the South and because of their precarious geographical location. Ross's argument that the Cherokee could be overwhelmed by nearby Confederate states if they were not allies persuaded the Cherokee to make a treaty with the South and to supply the Confederate army with troops. Most conservatives, many of whom were members of the antislavery Keetoowah Society, either refused to acknowledge the treaty with the South or joined the Confederate forces temporarily as a political expedient. By the spring of 1862, the conservatives had defected to the Union, and again the Cherokee nation was divided, largely along class and cultural lines: with a few exceptions, the entrepreneurial slaveholders sided with the South, and the conservative subsistence farmers sided with the North. One of the persuasive reasons for the conservatives was that by maintaining an alliance with the Union they would safeguard their treaty guarantees to national political autonomy and territory. For the next three years, while the major battles were waged farther east, the Cherokee in Indian Territory waged a civil war of their own that rekindled old political cleavages and feuds and devastated the Cherokee nation.[9]

In the postremoval period, the chief problem for the Cherokee was not the continued centralization or differentiation of the polity but political integration. The conflict between the dissident treaty party and the Old Settlers had its origins in responses to the removal crisis in the east, but it also involved class and cultural cleavages, pitting the planters and the American-educated Cherokee of the treaty party and the leadership of the Old Settlers against the conservatives, who were well organized within the secret Keetoowah Society and maintained traditional allegiances to community headmen and the principal chief. Throughout the pre–Civil War period, the conservatives were the large majority and dominated the Cherokee polity, but the planters, though never in control, were increasingly incorporated and represented in the government. After a period of relative internal peace, the events of the American Civil War broke the Cherokee into political cleavages similar to the earlier class and cultural cleavages that erupted during the removal crisis.

Choctaw Political Centralization and Differentiation

The Choctaw formation of a centralized and differentiated constitutional government was a process that took place over a long period. In a series of constitutions beginning in 1834 with an alliance of the American government and several Choctaw large landholders, the Choctaw, after many conflicts and compromises between the three traditionally autonomous political districts—and ultimately, again, after an American-planter alliance—finally in 1860 formed a centralized constitutional government.

The Choctaw reestablished their old tripartite political districts as soon as they arrived in Indian Territory. Although the nation had dismissed the chiefs who signed the removal treaty in 1830, the American government, by refusing to recognize any other leaders and supporting the removal chiefs and captains in their political offices, kept alive the old political conflicts that had existed in the east. As before, Christians and planters, the minority, elected their own chiefs, while the conservative majority adhered to different chiefs. Neither party wished to be governed by the leaders of the other party.[10]

In 1833–34, the American agent to the Choctaw encouraged the planters and districts to adopt constitutional governments. Some educated Choctaw and planters favored formation of a national government during the early 1830's and now were active in organizing the new constitutional government. In February 1834, one district and parts of the other two districts met to consider the adoption of a new constitution. The American agent insisted that the Choctaw form a constitutional government according to Article 15 of the 1830 treaty; he threatened that if they did not do so, he would intervene and assume management of Choctaw national business. The northeastern district formed a constitution and submitted it to the other two districts for adoption; the southern district accepted it, but the northwestern district did not and proceeded to elect a principal chief directly. Two groups in the northeastern district added to the excitement by electing two different chiefs, after which the American agent felt compelled to intervene and threatened to quell the political disturbances with military force if necessary. The American agent insisted that the Choctaw adopt majority rule as the procedure for voting on the constitution, and he also denied the claims of the northwestern district for political leadership over the other two districts. The conservatives in the northwestern district were led by George Harkins, a slaveholder, who was opposed by

Greenwood LeFlore's cousin, Thomas LeFlore. The American agent re-fused to recognize any chiefs who were elected before the adoption of a national constitution. If the old northwestern district continued to quar-rel over elections, the agent warned, the United States would intervene to restore peace.

In a letter dated March 25, 1834, the agent instructed the members of the old northwestern district to meet with the other two districts and form a government: "I called on you . . . to meet and make a government and laws for yourself to live under. This is expected in the Treaty that you all have signed . . . A council such as called for in the treaty must assemble . . . When you meet have the Constitution read, and if you take it, take a vote and adopt it by a majority of all present . . . a factious minority cannot be tolerated by the 5th article of the treaty, which compels the U. States to protect the Choctaws from domestic strife; Therefore it is useless to quar-rel about your elections. Should your controversy bring about a serious difficulty among you, the Government is bound to interfere." [11] The agent stated that the new constitution would become valid when a majority of the three chiefs and 99 captains who signed the constitution written in February 1834 approved it.

In early June of 1834 the Choctaw formally adopted a new constitution. This constitution, modeled after the constitution of the state of Missis-sippi, introduced innovations in the centralization of legitimate force and external and internal political differentiation, but it continued the au-tonomy of the three political districts, and it made a formal differentiation between polity and kinship. Where the national council formerly was com-posed of 30 captains or iksa leaders from each of three districts, the new constitution decreed that each district would have ten elected delegates invested in a unicameral national council. The trauma and disruptions of removal, and the new political allegiances based on class, culture, and religion, had weakened particularistic iksa and village political identifi-cations. In some communities, captains or iksa leaders continued to be influential in local affairs and occasionally pressed issues of national con-cern. There were no major disturbances over the weakening of local and kinship power and prerogatives in favor of stronger district and national councils.[12]

The formation of a judicial branch and a police force constituted a formal differentiation of kinship and judicial affairs. Blood revenge was abolished and the government now controlled the legitimate use of force. Informally, however, Choctaw court procedures and legal norms in many respects continued to conform to the rules that governed kinship groups. For instance, there were no jails in Choctaw country and defendants were obliged to appear freely for their own trials. A man condemned to death for murder was set free to arrange his family affairs and was obligated to appear on an appointed day for his own execution. To fail to do so would bring dishonor to himself and his family, and, it was believed, even prevent his family from gaining access to a pleasant afterlife. Reports indicate the Choctaw invariably honored the rules of the legal order, which resembled the old iksa obligations.[13]

In terms of internal political differentiation, the constitution provided for a bill of rights, separation of powers, trial by jury, and majority rule. The executive branch was composed of the three district chiefs, who were elected to four-year terms; all three chief executives had veto power over legislation. The constitution allowed for three judges and eighteen elected lighthorsemen, although the duties and jurisdictions of the judicial system were not well defined. All Choctaw males over the age of sixteen were given the right to vote, and candidates were elected by voice vote. Unanimous consent no longer was required in the national council to make binding decisions or to approve laws. According to the treaty of 1830, the instrument by which the Americans induced the Choctaw to adopt a constitutional government, the Choctaw were supposed to elect a fourth chief, who would be the central executive of the new government. But the Choctaw refused to accept one central executive and chose instead to divide the salary intended for the central chief among the three district chiefs. Most Choctaw preferred to preserve the political autonomy of the three districts, in which the three district chiefs managed their own internal district affairs and had no jurisdiction outside their own districts. It is clear that it was more difficult for the Choctaw to accept national political unification and administrative centralization than changes in centralization of legal authority and changes in differentiation of polity and kinship.[14]

Over the next several years, the constitution of 1834 restored order to the Choctaw polity, which had been disrupted by the removal crisis, and the succeeding constitutional reforms led to the further rationalization and differentiation of the Choctaw political sphere. In 1838 a new constitution was adopted, primarily to incorporate the Chickasaw as a fourth district in the nation, but the Choctaw took the opportunity to make further changes in the government, chief among which was the apportionment of district representatives to the national council on the basis of population. Apuckshunnubee, the old northwestern district, received thirteen delegates, and Moshulatubee, the old northeastern district, and Pushmataha, the old southern district, were apportioned nine representatives each. The new Chickasaw district also received nine representatives. In addition, the 1838 constitution established a military department, with a general from each district. In the event of war, a commander-in-chief was to be elected. A supreme court was established and greater guarantees of judicial independence were given. The new legal code affirmed collective national ownership of land. The executive now consisted of four chiefs—the three Choctaw district chiefs and the Chickasaw district chief. Throughout this period, only men who were trusted by the conservative majority in each district were elected to the office of district chief; the Christian planters were not trusted in high political office because of their actions during the removal period, and though the planters maneuvered to influence events informally in their interests, they turned most of their attention to economic accumulation.[15]

In 1842, another constitutional convention adopted a constitution that righted what three of the districts regarded as an unfair feature of the 1838 constitution, that is, the numerical majority of representatives in the national council enjoyed by Apuckshunnubee district. The 1842 constitution established a bicameral legislature with an upper house or senate composed of three delegates from each district, and a lower house composed of delegates apportioned according to population, each district to have one representative for every 1,000 people. The revised constitution abolished the military department; it also stipulated that appointments to the supreme court were to be made by the national council, though it was unclear as to the jurisdiction over district and local courts, which still jealously maintained their local autonomy.[16]

Changing and increasingly complex economic, social, and political patterns in the 1840's led Choctaw leaders in 1850 to convene a constitutional convention in order to make adjustments that would facilitate orderly growth. The major innovation in the 1850 constitution was the formation of nineteen counties across the four political districts. The new county system rationalized the administrative and juridical system within the traditional districts. The judicial system was more clearly defined and expanded to include county, circuit, and supreme courts, and all judicial actions were withdrawn from the lighthorse and delegated to the courts. In addition, the constitution of 1850 increased pay to senators, introduced tax on property, and established rules for constitutional amendment.[17]

At least some Choctaw continued to be dissatisfied with the organization of the government, and during the early 1850's there were several efforts to modify the constitution and write a legal code. An opportunity to rewrite the constitution came in 1855, when the American government mediated a treaty between the Choctaw and the Chickasaw for the withdrawal of the Chickasaw district from the Choctaw government. The Chickasaw had campaigned for independence since the late 1840's, but the Choctaw refused to grant independence until American officials intervened in the Chickasaws' behalf. The treaty of 1855 removed the Chickasaw district from the Choctaw nation in exchange for monetary compensation, and the following year the Chickasaw wrote their own constitution and reestablished their political independence from the Choctaw.[18]

The secession of the Chickasaw laid the basis for another revision of the Choctaw constitution. This was authorized by the general council in November 1856, and in January 1857 a convention at Skullyville adopted a new constitution that eliminated the Chickasaw district. The most radical change in the new constitution, however, was the centralization of the executive branch under a single principal chief and the elimination of the three district chiefs who had been politically autonomous. Although all national legislation had required the approval of a majority of the several district chiefs, the district chiefs were not concerned with and did not have jurisdiction over governmental affairs outside their own districts.[19] The new constitution drew strong opposition from the Choctaw conservatives and eventually from the large majority of the Choctaw population.

The framers of the 1857 constitution were predominantly American-educated, affluent planters who wished to create a more efficient and powerful centralized government that eliminated the trappings of tribal society. The opposition consisted of some slaveholders and mission-educated Choctaw, but most were conservative Choctaw subsistence farmers, who were the large majority in the nation. They feared that the new constitution would create a government that could be incorporated easily into the American government as a territory; they did not wish to surrender their independent national status and their right to self-government, and they did not wish to be forced to assimilate socially, politically, and economically into American society. The conservative opposition particularly objected to the abolishment of the offices of the three traditional district chiefs as an attempt to destroy old Choctaw laws and customs.

One of the arguments put forward by the conservative opposition was that the 1857 convention was empowered only to frame a new constitution and not empowered to place the constitution into effect, for the constitution required a referendum vote and approval before it could be considered legal and binding. This argument was supported by the American missionaries. In the 1830's and 1840's, the planters had welcomed the missionaries for bringing Christianity and for their financial sponsorship of and provision of teachers for schools, and the children of slaveholders and largeholder cattlemen had benefited disproportionately from the mission-administered schools. But in the 1850's, the conservatives, who had been less willing to send their children to schools in which English was the language of teaching, began to be allied with the missionaries after disagreements over the issue of abolitionism turned the planters against the predominantly New England Protestant missionaries. Throughout most of 1857 and 1858, there was controversy over the legitimacy of the 1857 constitution and the nation was nearly on the brink of civil war.[20]

To show their opposition to the 1857 constitution, two of the largest districts, Apuckshunnubee and Pushmataha, which contained three-fourths of the population, held elections under the constitution of 1850. Except for some scattered precincts, no elections were held under the new constitution in the two largest districts. Yet in spite of the opposition to the new constitution, its supporters organized elections and met in October of 1857 in legislative assembly. Alfred Wade, a Christian minister and entrepreneur, was elected governor, the title given to the chief executive. The opposition argued that the new government was organized by a small minority and that the majority of Choctaw refused to recognize the new government and demanded that the new constitution be submitted to the people for a referendum vote. When the Wade government refused to give any concession to the opposition, the opposition decided to organize a new constitutional convention and draw up a constitution that would be submitted to a vote of the people. An American agent was sent to investigate and mediate the internal political conflicts among the Choctaw, but this only resulted in an endorsement of the legality of the 1857 constitution.[21]

In January 1857, Governor Wade resigned in face of the opposition to the new centralized government; the legislature appointed Tandy Walker, a slaveholder and president of the Skullyville constitutional convention of 1857, in his place. Six months later, at Doaksville, the dissident Choctaws adopted a constitution, which was to be voted on in a national referendum. Not surprisingly, the Walker administration interpreted the framing of a rival constitution as a rebellious act and passed legislation to support repressive measures against the dissidents. Any elections other than those under the 1857 constitution were declared illegal and the number of lighthorse was increased. The right to bear arms was suspended, except for weapons carried by officers of the law. If the opposition wanted change, they would have to seek it through the mechanisms that were available under the constitution of 1857.[22]

Meanwhile, although the Doaksville party had majority support within the nation, the Skullyville constitution continued to enjoy American legal recognition, and annuities from past treaties were delivered to the Walker government. In August 1858, the Doaksville party moved to establish its countergovernment. The American agent threatened to station a contingent of American troops in the Choctaw country to maintain order between the rival governments, but in early October, during the regular legislative session, American agents mediated discussions between the contending parties. American officials wanted a quick and amiable settlement of the controversy, and they threatened to use force to crush the opposition party if they would not negotiate their demands with the Walker government. The Doaksville party demanded a constitutional referendum. The Walker-Skullyville government, after initially refusing to make any concessions at all and still insisting that any changes would have to pass through the constitutional mechanisms of the 1857 constitution, reluctantly suggested that it would support amendments to the Skullyville constitution during the next regular election. This was hardly satisfying to the Doaksville party, but since the American officials supported the Skullyville party as the lawful authority and regarded the Doaksville government as invalid and treasonous, there was little that the Doaksville party could do.[23]

After reassuring the Skullyville government of American recognition, the American officials suggested that it could make concessions to appease the disaffected party by submitting to a vote whether or not to call a new constitutional convention, and at a minimum restore the offices of district chief with small salaries and limited powers in order to placate the "ancient prejudices of the people." After due deliberation, the Skullyville officers agreed not only to allow a national referendum concerning the validity of the 1857 constitution but also to reestablish the three district chiefs. To American officials, the fact that the 1857 constitution abolished the three district chiefs and the Doaksville constitution restored them (and accepted a central chief) was merely trivial; they thought the whole controversy was largely an attempt by opposition leaders to gain political power and control over governmental resources. The American government also thought that after the Choctaw legislature enacted the compromises into legislation, it was justified in using military force to defend the Skullyville government if the opposition continued.[24]

After gaining the concessions for the reestablishment of the three district chiefs and setting a referendum vote on the constitution for December 1858, the opposition leaders agreed to the new terms. District chief offices were offered to, and accepted by, leading opposition leaders. The concessions restored political order to the Choctaw nation. The result of the national referendum on whether to convene a new constitutional convention was an overwhelming vote in favor of writing a new constitution. The constitutional convention was scheduled for January 1860. In the meantime, in an election in August 1859, Basil LeFlore, a candidate from the opposition party, was elected governor by a handy majority, and other leaders of the opposition were elected to prominent positions in the government.[25]

In January 1860 the Choctaw adopted a constitution that would last until forced political dissolution in 1907. The 1860 constitution was in many ways similar to the 1857 constitution: it contained a declaration of rights and the limitations and separation of powers among the executive, legislative, and judicial departments; the legislative branch continued to be divided into the three traditional districts and further subdivided into counties and precincts for administrative and voting purposes; the Supreme Court of three men, one from each of the three districts, also reflected the traditional political divisions. Each political district also had a circuit court, and the old kin-based norms of submission to arrest and sentences continued.

The new constitution, however, restored the offices of the three district chiefs and instituted the office of "principal chief," who was given control over the bureaucratic administration of the national, district, and county levels of government. The principal chief commissioned the police officers of the nation and had the right to dismiss government officers for nonperformance of duties. Though the district chief offices were largely symbolic, they had control over the district militia and nominated police officers, who were appointed and administered by the principal chief. In practice, the district chiefs were usually men of outstanding leadership, who were elected in order to balance the influence of the principal chief. The new constitution also eliminated the county police boards, county justices of the peace, and constables that were created after 1857 and were believed to have been used for political purposes by the Walker administration. The district chiefs were instructed by the constitution to attend the meetings of the circuit courts in their districts and to "address the people on the importance of obeying, and enforcing the law and maintaining good order" and to admonish the people to practice temperance, industry, and morality. Aside from limited control over the lighthorse police, the district chiefs did not have direct access to the central bureaucratic administration, and therefore they had little power, but their presence within the framework of the centralized government at least gave a certain legitimacy derived from traditional political symbols and assured a measure of peace and order within the three traditional political districts.[26]

The constitution of 1860 represented a compromise between traditional political organization and the effort by the planters to centralize the government and judicial administration. It outlined a centralized and differentiated government, which, though it continued to rely on traditional Choctaw political symbols, norms, and organizational divisions, invested the main administrative controls in the national offices. The 1860 constitution went further than previous constitutions in defining and protecting rights to private property, but at the same time it gave fewer guarantees of humane treatment to slaves than the 1857 constitution. Nevertheless, although the constitution promoted commercial enterprise and control of slave labor, it rejected American suggestions to divide the Choctaw common domain into privately owned sections and continued to keep land as a collectively owned good. As in the past, the improvements and profits made from working a section of land belonged to the farmer, but the land itself belonged to the nation. The Choctaw leaders argued that allotment of land into private sections would most likely lead to the dispossession of the smallholder subsistence farmers, many of whom would sell their homestead out of necessity or because they lacked secure legal protections.[27] Keeping the land as a common domain was one way of safeguarding the nation against American encroachments.

As the American Civil War approached, the Choctaw were divided over which side to ally with. The issue was hotly debated. Many conservative Choctaw argued that in order to maintain their treaty rights they would have to remain loyal to the Union; to counter the Union treaties, the Confederacy offered even more liberal treaties to the Choctaw, and the planters quickly advocated a Southern alliance. The conservatives initially were inclined to remain neutral. In the spring of 1861, Union troops withdrew from Indian Territory and the Choctaw found themselves surrounded by Arkansas and Texas, both Confederate states. Given their geopolitical location, the influence of the planters, and Southern inducements and threats, most Choctaw decided to side with the South, while only a few hundred allied and fought with the North. During the war, the Choctaw government continued to operate, led largely by members of the planter class.[28]

Over the period 1834–60, the Choctaw, influenced by American government officials and planters, incrementally centralized and increasingly differentiated their government institutions. The constitution of 1834 entailed the differentiation of polity and kinship, centralization of legitimate use of force, and increased internal political differentiation. Subsequent constitutions led to further rationalization of the Choctaw polity, but the most difficult change was the centralization of executive authority. The Choctaw planters proposed the centralization of executive authority in the 1857 constitution and this government was supported by the American government against massive opposition from the Choctaw subsistence farmers. Even with American military support, the centralized planter government had difficulty maintaining itself in the face of the majority conservative opposition. The compromise government of 1860 bowed to the demands of the conservative majority by reinstating the district chiefs, primarily as traditional symbols of political legitimation. In the new government, the planters realized their interests in executive centralization and administrative rationalization and secured laws that more clearly defined protections of private property and promoted and regulated economic accumulation. For their part, the conservatives gained assurances of the continuity of tribal institutions and symbols and of the collective ownership of land, both of which were important to them as defenders of national political autonomy.

Chickasaw Nationalism and Political Differentiation

The signing of the treaty of 1837 at Doaksville granted the Chickasaw citizenship in the Choctaw nation and permitted them to organize a fourth district in the Choctaw nation. In so doing, it also formally abolished the old Chickasaw government based on iksas and ended any recognition by the American government of the king and council as representative of Chickasaw government affairs. Thereafter, the U.S. government recognized only the district chief and elected councils of the Choctaw constitutional government as the official government of the Chickasaw. The removal migration led to a general disruption of Chickasaw life. Because of hostilities from Plains Indians who saw the Chickasaw as invaders, few Chickasaw went to live in the Chickasaw district, the westernmost territory of the Choctaw nation; most settled at scattered locations in the three Choctaw districts. Many Chickasaw turned to subsistence farming and incurred debts to traders in anticipation of payments for the land sold in the east; about one-fourth of the Chickasaw did not start farming at all but lived on credit in anticipation of their land payments.[29] Land payments were not made until 1844, and by 1842, many Chickasaw were economically destitute and debt-ridden.

Though they lacked any status as a nation, most Chickasaw were reluctant to give up their national independence or change the old kin-based political order. The king and the council continued to meet and make laws and rules for the Chickasaw and elected commissioners to manage treaty funds and unfinished business from the 1834 treaty. The planters and some of the younger Chickasaw favored reform and the framing of a constitutional government, but during the 1840's hereditary chiefs still held office until they died; nephews were the preferred successors, and there were no elections for political office within the Chickasaw government.

The Chickasaw also, though they were included in the Choctaw government according to the constitution of 1838, were slow to participate in Choctaw political institutions. Only in 1841 did the Chickasaw form a government in their district by electing a chief and ten members to the Choctaw national council. The government in the Chickasaw district was formed largely by planters who increasingly moved to the Chickasaw district.[30] The planters now publicly rejected the old government and denied legitimate political authority to the old regime, and in this they had the support of the American government.

Many conservative Chickasaw had unwillingly surrendered their nationality in order to join the Choctaw nation. This group, which still looked to the old king for political leadership, soon became dissatisfied with Choctaw government institutions. Under the system of proportional representation, three-fourths of the national council were Choctaw and one-fourth were Chickasaw; furthermore, the Chickasaw felt that they were never completely incorporated into the Choctaw nation, because the Choctaw conservatives always voted for Choctaws, which *de facto* excluded Chickasaw from political office outside their own designated district.[31]

Between 1841 and 1845 there were three Chickasaw political groups contending for American recognition and political power. In accordance with the treaty of 1837 between the Chickasaw and the Choctaw, both nations kept their financial relations independent. Part of the struggle between the rival Chickasaw political groups was simply to get control over treaty annuities and land payments. The king, the iksa council, the conservatives, and a few planters formed the conservative party, which had a small majority of adherents within the nation. The second contending group was the Chickasaw Commission, which was authorized to manage the administrative details of the treaty of 1834, including the verification of land sales and management of the financial affairs of Chickasaw who were declared orphans or incompetent. The Commission took the position that, according to the treaty of 1834, it was the constituted authority of the nation. Although the king and some of the hereditary chiefs were also members of the Chickasaw Commission, it was dominated by planters and merchants. The third rival political organization consisted of the elected district chief and representatives to the Choctaw national council.[32] The first elected district chief was also a hereditary chief and a member of the Chickasaw Commission.

In 1845, a rift over control of the Chickasaw annuity payments led to a major disruption in Chickasaw political affairs. Because the American agent refused to recognize the king and old council, in 1844 the Chickasaw annuity payments were distributed by the Chickasaw Commission. But the king and conservatives complained that most Chickasaw did not live in the Chickasaw district, where the annuity was distributed, and that the previous year's distribution had caused much dissatisfaction. In July 1845, the Chickasaw held a general council and the members of the Chickasaw Commission agreed to resign, with the understanding that no more commissioners would be appointed. But the king's party went ahead and appointed new commissioners and requested that the annuity be paid to the king and council. American officials ignored this development and continued to recognize only the elected district chief and the elected captains of the district government as the constituted authority of the Chickasaw. At this point the planters took the opportunity to repudiate the old government and declare themselves in favor of assimilation into the Choctaw polity.[33]

The conflict over control of the annuity continued into late 1846, when the king's party demanded that the annuity be paid to Edmund Pickens, a respected conservative, but the district chief's constituency asked that the U.S. agent distribute the annuity. The conservatives, who declared that it had never been their intention to assimilate into the Choctaw constitutional government, sent a delegation to Washington in the fall of 1846 to negotiate a separate territory and an independent government for the Chickasaw. They argued that American recognition of the Chickasaw district chief as controller of Chickasaw national finances was oppressive, since most Chickasaw did not live in the Chickasaw district, and that Chickasaw financial matters should be decided by the majority of local captains. That October, at a convention called by the district council, the Chickasaw adopted a constitution. This first constitution was a simple statement of intent to guard liberties and property within the Chickasaw nation.[34]

In April 1848 both the conservatives and the planters sent delegations to Washington. The conservatives, or King Ishtehotopa's party, most of whom lived scattered within the three Choctaw districts, wanted to emigrate out of the Choctaw nation, secure an independent land, and reestablish their old government. The Chickasaw district leaders preferred to remain under Choctaw laws and government and were in favor of only minor modification of Choctaw laws.[35] American officials again supported the position of the district government.

In November 1848, the leaders of the Chickasaw district government drafted a more elaborate constitution that established laws for the administration of Chickasaw finances and funds. The constitution created a two-department government, with legislative and executive branches. Judicial functions remained in the hands of the Choctaw government, although the Supreme Court of the Chickasaw district presided over the district and precinct elections. The constitution created a unicameral legislature of 30 elected "captains," and created several national officers and rules for the passage of laws. The council members were elected to two-year terms; seventeen seats were allocated to the Chickasaw district and thirteen to the Chickasaw who lived in the three Choctaw districts. The constitution stated that the Chickasaw council was to have absolute control over the distribution of the Chickasaw treaty monies and annuities.[36] The executive branch of the new government was given to the district chief, who was elected, for a term of two years, to represent the Chickasaw in the

Choctaw government. Thus, with American support, the planters of the Chickasaw district consolidated the adoption of a constitutional government, obtained control of Chickasaw finances, and rejected the ancient Chickasaw government.

After 1848 the Chickasaw held regular sessions of national government, but between 1849 and 1851 some important changes and compromises were made between the king's party and the planters of the Chickasaw district, who, because more conservative Chickasaw had moved to the Chickasaw district, were now the minority group and were in danger of losing control of the government. The planters changed their position from support of assimilation and citizenship in the Choctaw nation to the nationalist and separatist cause of the conservatives. But the conservatives, too, were forced to make significant concessions. Since the American government would not recognize the king's government as an authority in Chickasaw affairs, the conservatives were obliged to accept the new constitutional form of government.

To accommodate the new political consensus, a new constitution was written in 1851. This constitution separated the executive or principal chief, now called the Financial Chief, from the district chief of the Choctaw government; the office carried the duties and responsibilities of managing Chickasaw internal affairs and treaty funds. (The first Financial Chief, Dougherty Colbert, actually assumed office after being elected by the general council in November 1850; the constitution of 1851 formalized the duties of the Financial Chief and granted him a salary.) The conservatives, though they accepted the new constitutional government form, disassociated the office of principal chief from the Chickasaw district chief in the Choctaw government; since they refused to assimilate into Choctaw society, the creation of an independent Chickasaw chief furthered their nationalist plans of secession from the Choctaw government. The district chieftainship was retained, but he served the Choctaw government; national affairs of the Chickasaw were delegated to the Financial Chief, and therefore the district chief became of secondary importance.[37]

The constitution of October 1851 was a separatist document that symbolized the political unification of the conservatives and the planters in their intention to withdraw from the Choctaw government and form an independent government. The new constitution invested control over treaty monies in the general council, which was now bicameral and composed of thirteen elected captains and thirteen representatives. Captains were elected every four years; representatives were elected annually. Two conservative leaders were granted lifetime seats on the council. The Financial Chief was elected by the General Council for a two-year term, and other national officers were elected by the General Council. The constitution explicitly encouraged schools and economic development and set as an informal priority national separation from the Choctaw government. A special committee was appointed by the General Council to seek ways of securing Chickasaw political independence.[38]

For the next four years the Chickasaw steadily sought separation from the Choctaw. During this time there were numerous boundary and jurisdictional disputes with the Choctaw government. The Chickasaw complained not only about their minority political status in the Choctaw government, where the Choctaws controlled three-fourths of the vote, but also about discrimination in the Choctaw judicial system, and unequal enforcement of laws and sentencing. The Choctaw not only would not grant the Chickasaw independence, they also recognized only the district chief as an official of the Chickasaw government and demanded that the Chickasaw treaty annuities be paid to the district chief and not to the Chickasaw Financial Chief. As early as 1851, American officials were sympathetic to the Chickasaw efforts to gain independence, and after the Chickasaw council unanimously voted in 1853 in favor of separation from Choctaw society and set aside funds to buy the Chickasaw district, the American government intervened on behalf of the Chickasaw. Negotiations between the Choctaw and the Chickasaw in 1853–54 were only resolved by the American government, and at last, in June 1855, a treaty was signed that granted the Chickasaw the right to organize an independent government.[39]

In accordance with the treaty of 1855, the Chickasaw organized a constitutional convention and adopted a new constitution in August 1856. The Financial Chief and the captains elected under the Chickasaw constitution of 1851 were seated at the convention, and delegates were elected from ten precincts. The new constitution contained a bill of rights that guaranteed the people the right to reform the government whenever they deemed it necessary, political equality, freedom of religion and freedom of speech, trial by jury, freedom from unreasonable searches, the right to assembly, freedom from laws that might impair contracts, and freedom from imprisonment for debt. The second article framed voting procedures and rights, and the third article outlined the separation of powers among the executive, legislative, and judicial branches. The legislature was bicameral, with a Senate and a House of Representatives. House members were elected to one-year terms and senators to two-year terms. The chief executive was now called "Governor" and served a two-year term but was not eligible to serve more than four years in any six-year period. The governor controlled the national treaty funds and annuities and determined the mode of expenditure or distribution. The constitution described the duties and offices of other national officials such as national secretary, treasurer, auditor, and attorney general. The judiciary was divided into the Supreme Court, district courts, and county courts. The constitution promoted public education. It contained a slave code that prevented the government from emancipating slaves without full payment for the value of the slave, although it allowed the legislature to pass laws that obliged slaveowners to treat their slaves with humanity and provide for their safety and sustenance. The nation was divided administratively into four counties, which corresponded to the four counties created by the Choctaw government in 1850, also to the four ancient districts of the Chickasaw nation in the east.[40]

With the passage of the constitution of 1856, the Chickasaw adopted a highly differentiated, centralized, and unified form of government. The new Chickasaw polity was differentiated from religion and from kinship, and was internally differentiated with the separation of powers, and specialized rules and procedures for political and legal decision making. The judicial system was differentiated from kinship organization and kinship prerogatives. Thus blood revenge was no longer in effect, and the legitimate use of force was reserved for the agents of the government. Nevertheless, the norms of kin group law persisted among the Chickasaw. As among the Choctaw, there were no jails, and men accused of crimes were expected to attend their trials voluntarily and submit voluntarily to whatever punishments were prescribed, even execution. Above all the Chickasaw evinced a strong sense of nationalism and national unity, which had developed in the struggle for independence against what the Chickasaw interpreted as the oppressive political domination of the Choctaw. After 1850, both major political groups—the planters and the conservative subsistence farmers—were united in the struggle for national independence, and this nationalist political unity lasted until the early 1870's.

Dougherty "Winchester" Colbert had served as the Financial Chief from late 1850 to August 1856. In the first election under the new constitution, several candidates campaigned but none won a majority of the votes, and so in accordance with the constitution, the election was decided by the legislature. Cyrus Harris won in the legislature by a small margin and became the first governor, serving from 1856 to 1858. Over the next decade, Harris and Colbert traded places as governor: Colbert was elected governor in 1858, Harris in 1860, Colbert in 1862, Harris in 1864. Both these men were planters and large-scale ranchers who had strongly supported the Choctaw district government before 1850; they represented the interests of the planters and the commercial groups in the nation. As long as the Chickasaw leaders and government protected the nationalistic interests of the conservatives, the planters received conservative support for the political leadership. The conservatives themselves did not elect a governor until the 1870's, but prominent conservative leaders were incorporated into leading positions within the new government. For example, Pittman Colbert, a close associate of the old king Ishtehotopa, served as president of the Senate and was an influential member of the government and a participant in many delegations to oversee Chickasaw business in Washington.

The events of the American Civil War did not provoke strong internal political turmoil among the Chickasaw. The planters were strongly pro-Confederacy, and the combination of their location near the Confederate states of Arkansas and Texas, the withdrawal of Union troops from Indian Territory, and Southern inducements led the Chickasaw to ally and fight with the South. Only a few Chickasaw fought on the Union side.[41]

Political change among the Chickasaw in the postremoval period involved direct coercion by an alliance of planters and American officials who actively worked to destroy the old government. While the Chickasaw planters tried to assimilate into Choctaw society, the conservatives struggled to maintain Chickasaw political autonomy and the old government form. Between 1848 and 1851, the two dominant political groups forged a national political consensus, which entailed dropping the ancient form of government in favor of a constitutional government and a struggle for national independence. As long as the planters and conservatives held differing views of political order, the Chickasaw polity was unstable: The conservatives struggled for national independence and preservation of the old form of nondifferentiated kin-based political relations; the planters struggled for a constitutional government, and hoped to achieve their end with American support and through assimilation into Choctaw political institutions. The Chickasaw national consensus was formed with the compromise that the conservatives would abandon the king and iksa government in favor of a constitutional government, and in return the planters would work toward national independence. The conservatives were willing to sacrifice the ancient form of government in order to achieve the goal of national independence. The nationalist movement laid the basis for secession, which was effected only with American intervention and force, and provided a new national political consensus for the formation of a differentiated, centralized constitutional government. Without the compromises that led to a national consensus over secession, the Chickasaw would not have formed an independent, differentiated constitutional government.

Formation of a Constitutional Government
Among the Creek

Between 1828 and 1833, most of the lower town Creek planters migrated
west and settled in the northeast section of Creek land in Indian Territory.
The early Creek migrants were led by the red town of Coweta. The more
conservative lower town villages that were associated with the leadership
of Cussetah, the major white town, migrated west after the brief hostilities of 1836. The upper towns, led by Opothleyoholo of Tuckabatchee, a
red town, also migrated in 1836–37. As the residents of the towns prepared to leave their old homeland, they performed rituals to carry the
sacred fire and sacred objects with them to the new country. The Creek
migrated west as villages, carrying with them the unique sacred objects
that gave each village a particularistic covenant relation with the Great
Spirit, and in the new country they resettled as village groups and preserved the rituals and socioeconomic organization that the villages had
in the east. Except for some of the lower towns, the Creek preserved the
local government and local religiously particularistic organization of the
villages. They continued to reckon social, religious, and political membership not by a concept of national citizenship but rather by matrilineal
kinship and town. Within the village governments, religious organization,
kinship, and political organization remained nondifferentiated, and nondifferentiated cultural world views continued to predominate among most
villagers.[42]

When the upper towns arrived in the new country they deliberately
settled in a segregated area in the southern section of the new Creek country, which became the Canadian district. The settlements of the lower
towns became known as the Arkansas district. The lower towns that were
allied to Cussetah resettled in the Arkansas district and rejoined the lower
towns that had migrated earlier. However, when the villages of Cussetah
and Hitchiti, two central white towns and leaders in the 1836 hostilities
against the Alabamians, arrived in the Arkansas district, American officials forced them to recognize Coweta as the leader of the lower towns.
Tuckabatchee claimed leadership of the upper towns, and even claimed
to be the center of the entire nation, although the Americans preferred
the more amenable planters of the Coweta leadership.[43] Thus from 1836
until 1859, with American support, the two red towns, Coweta and Tuckabatchee, continued to dominate political relations within their respective
districts. The white towns played a secondary leadership role in national
politics and in relations with the American government.

The formation of the Arkansas and Canadian districts, corresponding to the old lower and upper town divisions, recreated the old segmentary organization of national and regional government. Both districts formed a council and had chiefs and managed their internal affairs independently. Between 1836 and 1840, the two Creek district governments did not meet. The Creek had never had strong national integration, and in the new territory, tradition, old feuds, and hostilities dating back to the William McIntosh execution inhibited friendly relations. Although American officials actively sought to unify the two districts and finally succeeded in convincing the Creek to reestablish meetings of the national council in 1840, it was not until after the American Civil War that the two districts interacted on anything but an occasional basis.[44]

At a meeting of the national council in 1844, the representatives adopted a written code of laws that extended the laws that had been adopted in the east. Before 1840, each of the district councils heard criminal cases. The law was enforced by the lighthorse police. After 1840, the national council heard criminal cases on appeal from the district councils. In civil cases, the village councils heard the cases and passed and executed judgments. As in the Choctaw and Chickasaw cases, the clan norms of submission to arrest and sentence, even execution, persisted among the Creek. The Creek court system remained nondifferentiated from the legislative branch. The general council made laws that extended over the towns, but the towns remained the primary political units. Many of the laws passed in the succeeding years reflected conservative Creek values and norms: for example, in 1845 the national council passed a law providing fines for Creek who did not attend town ceremonies. The national laws supported the religious integration of the local Creek towns and left the ancient customs of the nation intact. They were concerned primarily with the regulation of criminal offenses and the definition and regulation of private property of individuals and of villages. The Creek affirmed the collective ownership of all land, and also affirmed the right of Creek to claim usufruct rights to tracts of land on the common domain. A slave code was adopted that prohibited intermarriage with black slaves, prohibited the harboring of runaways, regulated slave debts, and defined criminal acts of slaves. As the American Civil War approached, the slave code increased in severity. Most conservative Creek, however, either did not own slaves or owned only a few to help with subsistence farming.[45]

Until 1858, there was little institutional change in Creek national government. The most far-reaching change was the increased extent and rationalization of the legal code and judicial institutions. Nevertheless, the courts remained linked to the district, national, and village councils and did not show much differentiation from the legislative branch at the village, district, or national level. In 1842 the Creek national council was composed of the two principal chiefs, the town chiefs, and a committee of "lawmakers." A judge was appointed to each district. As time passed, the committee exercised increasingly important executive and legislative functions. In 1855, in response to American agents who were agitating for reform and centralization of the Creek government, the Creek centralized control over annuities and treaty monies in the hands of the general council, created a national treasurer, and reduced the members of the national council to 500—still a good many but less than the 800 or so from the Creek villages and daughter villages who formerly attended a national council. Decision making still remained under the rule of unanimous consent, a system that American officials found cumbersome and continued to try and change.[46]

Throughout the 1840's and 1850's, Roley McIntosh (a brother of William McIntosh) was the principal chief of the lower towns. McIntosh retired from office in 1859 on account of old age, and in the same year the Creek wrote a short constitution allowing for the election of principal chief and assistant principal chief in the two Creek political districts. The constitution of 1859 retained much of the old political order. There were two districts, each entitled to a principal chief and an assistant principal chief; the principal chief of each district appointed a speaker for the district council; and an extensive legal code was adopted that regulated slave labor and tenant labor, ensured payment of debts, guaranteed trial by jury, and levied a tax on imported American labor. Court trials were managed by the district and national councils, which also acted as courts of appeal over the decisions of village councils. In no way was the constitution to be construed as infringing on the ancient political autonomy of the town governments. In July of 1859, the Creek held their first elections for principal and assistant chief in each district.[47]

The 1859 constitution did not satisfy the American agent to the Creek, and in 1860 he introduced his own version that outlined a highly differentiated polity. The constitution of 1860 unified the two Creek districts and provided for a single principal chief for the nation. It provided for the separation of powers among the executive, legislature, and judiciary and instituted judges and trials by jury. Four districts were created from the earlier two, and a bicameral legislature was created with 16 elected members in the committee or upper house and 24 elected members for the House of Warriors or lower house. The constitution reaffirmed collective ownership of land. The constitution of 1860 was formally adopted by the Creek council, but it was largely ignored by the Creek and never was put into effect. The highly differentiated and centralized polity did not become institutionalized among the Creek, and the two autonomous political districts continued to manage Creek government affairs as before.[48]

The new constitution came at an inopportune time. The storm clouds that were gathering during the prelude to the American Civil War brought out new disagreements between the lower towns or Arkansas district, which contained most of the Creek planters, and the upper towns or Canadian district, which contained mostly conservative villagers. The planters were strongly in favor of slavery and were willing to ally with the South. When war broke out, the conservatives of the Canadian district, who had little interest in slavery, rallied to Opothleyoholo, the old speaker of the Tuckabatchee council, and the central red town of the Canadian district. Like the conservatives elsewhere, the Creek conservatives preferred neutrality or an alliance with the Union so that they could safeguard their treaty guarantees with the federal government. During the war, most people in the Canadian district sided with the Union, and, with some notable exceptions such as the Coweta Micco, the Arkansas district fought with the South. There were some exceptions—a few hundred in each district crossed over—but in the main, the two districts divided along their ancient regional lines. But the division also indicated an emerging class cleavage, because the more change-oriented planters predominated in the lower towns, and the more fundamentalist conservative subsistence farmers predominated in the Canadian district. The war divided the two districts, and the fighting that took place left many dead and the country in ruins.[49]

The war marked the end of the domination of the red towns in Creek government. Since a few years before the Red Stick War in 1813, the American government had supported Coweta and Tuckabatchee as the dominant towns. When Opothleyoholo died early in the American Civil War, leadership of the conservatives or loyal Creek passed to Oktarsars Harjo, or Sands, who was a member of Abihka, the ancient central white town of the Creek upper towns. Sands was elected second chief of the Canadian district in the 1859 election and was declared principal chief by the conservatives early in the war after the Arkansas district sided with the South. Among the southern or lower town Creek, Samuel Checote, a Methodist preacher, member of the tiger clan, and member of the Hitchiti village of Sawokla, which was also a white town, became the principal chief. For the rest of the period of Creek political independence, men from the white towns occupied the leading political positions in the nation. Coweta declined in political influence just before and during the American Civil War, and the leadership of Tuckabatchee was ignored in the re-formation of the Creek government after the war.[50]

The immediate problem in the postwar period was to bring about a peaceful reconciliation between the conflicting parties and form a national government. There were three contending groups. The Southern party favored national reconciliation but steadfastly refused to return to the old government of chiefs and instead proposed a constitutional government. The conservatives were divided into two groups: the elected and white town leadership of Sands led the majority of conservatives from the Canadian district, and Spokokee of Tuckabatchee led a group of about 500 Creek who refused to join the Sands party and wanted a return to the old chief government. When Opothleyoholo died, Spokokee was advanced to Opothleyoholo's position of speaker of the Tuckabatchee council. During Opothleyoholo's political career, speaker of the Tuckabatchee council was also speaker of the upper town council, and Spokokee claimed the same leadership prerogatives as his predecessor; he also claimed that no government or political reconciliation was possible without Tuckabatchee's approval. The American government and the other Creek ignored Spokokee's claims and attempts to reestablish the old government by chiefs, and for several years Tuckabatchee and allied villages refused to participate in Creek political relations. This nonparticipation only served to weaken the position of the Canadian district and the conservatives against the planters of the Southern party.[51]

National reconciliation and political reconstruction were in the end brought about by the groups led by Sands and Checote. In late 1866 the Creek came to an agreement to resettle the devastated Creek country peacefully. Discussions were opened over the formation of a Creek government. The Southern party was adamantly opposed to a return to the old government by chiefs, but during the war, both Creek divisions had gained intensive experience with Americans and with American bureaucratic and military organization, and some, though not all, of the fundamentalist resistance to change in the political institutional order had softened. The Southern party argued that the old government was inadequate to cope with changing economic and political conditions. They were dissatisfied over the code of laws, which they thought tended to lead to a proliferation of lighthorse police; there were too many government officers; the administration was inefficient; duties of officers were ill-defined; and salaries were allocated arbitrarily. The party also complained about the slowness of change in the government and its unwillingness to promote education. The Southern party was confident that it had the support of a majority across the nation and could gain control of an elected national government; furthermore, it had the support of American officials. Sands, the elected leader of the conservatives, was one of the leading framers of the constitution, but he and his party were equally confident of the support of a clear majority in the nation and expected to win control of the new government.[52]

In October 1867, delegations from 47 Creek towns, including three new towns of freedmen, adopted a constitution. The convention hotly debated the advantages and disadvantages of the old government and the new proposed constitutional form of government. A group of fundamentalist Creek from both districts, a minority according to American officials, opposed the new constitution and boycotted the constitutional proceedings. During the convention, leaders from the white towns were the central actors in the framing of the new constitutional government. Besides Sands, from Abihka, there were also Samuel Checote, Pleasant Porter and the Perrymans from the Hitchiti towns of Sawokla and Okmulgee, and Roley McIntosh from Tuskegee, an ancient white town from the upper towns.[53]

The new constitution was modeled after the American government. There was a bicameral legislature, including a House of Kings, which was composed of a member elected from each town for a four-year term. The lower house, called the House of Warriors, had a membership apportioned at a ratio of one member for every 200 people within a village. More so than any of the constitutional governments of the southeastern nations, the Creek constitution did not differentiate village political units from the national polity. The authority of the Creek constitution did not interpenetrate or challenge the leadership of the village governments, which remained localistic and religiously integrated collections of clan segments. The religiously integrated and kin-based villages remained the primarily political unit in the Creek polity.

The new national government was, however, a significantly more differentiated polity than previous Creek governments. An independent judiciary was created that was differentiated from the district and village councils. There was a separation of powers among the judicial, legislative, and executive branches. The principal chief was elected at large and had the power to veto legislative bills and powers to reprieve and pardon. The nation was divided into six judicial and administrative units: Eufaula, Deep Fork, Wewocau, Okmulgee, Muskogee, and Coweta. Each of the districts was assigned a lighthorse police force, a judge, and a district attorney, and Creek citizens were entitled to a trial by jury. The new national government separated church and state, and even espoused some Protestant Christian religious doctrines. Elections were called for November 1867. The new constitution remained in effect from 1867 to 1907, but in the succeeding years the new Creek government encountered considerable difficulties from fundamentalist Creek who tried to return the old chief government to power.

Comparisons

The formation of differentiated constitutional governments in the post-removal period exhibits a pattern different from the formation of a constitutional government among the Cherokee during the removal crisis.

The Cherokee formed their new government under intense external political pressures, and though the planters were the carriers of the models of constitutional government, they succeeded in their efforts only after convincing the conservatives that the chances of preserving nationality and territory would be enhanced by the adoption of the new government form. In the postremoval period Cherokee political conflicts did not focus on fundamental change in political institutions but rather centered on political struggles for control of the government. The well-organized majority of Cherokee conservatives forced the planters and the dissident Old Settlers to participate in the constitutional government that was based on the 1827 constitution.

The formation of more centralized and differentiated governments by the other three southeastern nations in the postremoval period did not result from a direct nationalist movement against intense American threats, since there was little American pressure for land and few threats to political autonomy in the postremoval period before 1860. Yet the formation of constitutional governments in the postremoval period occurred with greater coercion of a different sort: among the Chickasaw, the Choctaw, and the Creek, an alliance between the planters and American officials served the purpose of breaking down the ancient form of political organization. In all four societies the planters were a political minority, which relied on American recognition, material aid, and threats of military intervention to support their plans for adopting constitutional governments and for abandoning the ancient political forms. In the Cherokee case, before removal, the alliance between the planters and American officials was not strong enough to maintain the planters in political power over the highly politically mobilized Cherokee conservatives.

The American and planter class alliance was most effective in forcing the abandonment of the ancient political forms, but in none of the societies could the planters institute a more differentiated polity without the agreement and consent of the conservative majority. Among the Chickasaw, the ancient government was formally abolished, but the Chickasaw did not form a differentiated polity until agreements were made to pursue a nationalist separation from the Choctaw. The Chickasaw nationalist unification preceded the formation of a differentiated and centralized polity. This pattern is similar to the Cherokee national unification of 1809–10, which also preceded the further centralization and differentiation of the polity. Among the Choctaw, the planter-American alliance supported a centralized and differentiated constitutional government that did not have widespread support among the conservatives. The planters and American officials felt compelled to make institutional concessions to the conservative majority in order to gain their support for a centralized constitutional government. The Choctaw conservatives resisted the imposition of a government that did not include ancient political symbols and forms of organization. The Choctaw constitution of 1860 gained the broad support of the Choctaw nation only after it included the district chieftainships and other aspects of ancient regional political organization. In the Creek case, though they showed little receptiveness toward political change until after the American Civil War, Creek planters, American officials, and a large group of conservatives combined to reject the ancient form of national government and agree to a constitutional government. Thus, although class interests and geopolitical coercion played a significant role in the disruption of the ancient government forms and in the proposal of new political models, the formation of the proposed constitutional governments in the postremoval period was contingent on the support and consent of the conservative majority.

7 STABILITY AND DECLINE OF THE CONSTITUTIONAL GOVERNMENTS

THE GEOPOLITICAL AND world-system relations of the nations in Indian Territory changed rapidly and drastically after the American Civil War. Because of their alliance or partial alliance with the Confederate states, the Choctaw, the Chickasaw, the Creek, and the Cherokee were forced to make major concessions in land and political autonomy to the Union government in the postwar Reconstruction treaties. The Americans forced the Indian nations to accept two railroad rights-of-way through their territory, to accept in principle the allotment of their common domain into private farms, and to make preparations for the organization of a territorial government and their eventual incorporation into the American political system. Congress retained plenary power to legislate laws for the Indians as it deemed necessary. The rights-of-way were granted to railroad companies that were induced to build the rail lines by grants of alternate sections of land along the route of the railway. The land grants were contingent on the extinguishment of Indian title, and from the early 1870's until the late 1890's the railroad companies engaged in incessant lobbying in Congress for the territorialization and extinguishment of Indian title in the present state of Oklahoma. American settlers, miners, and railroad workers began to take up squatter's rights in Indian Territory in the 1870's, in anticipation of extinguishment of Indian title. After 1880, the American government no longer made a significant effort to remove the intruders, and soon the American citizens outnumbered the Indian citizens in Indian Territory.[1]

During the late 1860's and early 1870's, American policy toward the Indians continued to involve the forced migration of many nations to Indian Territory. In 1871 Congress decided to make no more treaties with the Indian nations, and no longer to recognize the Indian nations as independent for purposes of making treaties. Several migrant nations in Indian Territory found the environment inhospitable and struggled to return to their own territories and habitats. After the late 1870's, policy no longer attempted to move the now-subdued Indian nations to Indian Territory. Rather, reservations were created for the tribes on or near their ancient homelands. The reservation period was to be short. In the late 1880's, a new, more aggressive policy of rapid assimilation and destruction of Indian cultures was initiated. The General Allotment Act of 1887 authorized the President to allot and survey the common domain of most Indian nations. The land was to be divided into private tracts and the remainder made available for sale to American settlers. The purpose of the act was to break up the collectively owned tribal domains and to encourage the Indians to become American citizens and small independent farmers.

The Cherokee, the Choctaw, the Chickasaw, the Creek, and the Seminole escaped inclusion in the Allotment Act of 1887, primarily owing to the political strength of the association of cattle ranchers and their corporate backers, who did not want to lose the large open ranges in Indian Territory that were leased to them by the Indian governments and private owners. Between 1885 and 1889, the American court system extended its jurisdiction over Indian Territory, an act that directly infringed upon the rights of self-government of the Indian nations. The respite from the allotment and assimilation policy ended in 1898 with the passage of the Curtis Act, which decreed the abolishment of the Choctaw, Cherokee, Chickasaw, and Creek governments and the allotment of their collective domains into privately owned tracts of land. Much of the political activity in the 1880's and 1890's within the Indian Territory governments was focused on opposition to American threats to national political autonomy and threats of allotment and involved discussion and conflict over the best means to preserve self-government and national territory.[2] The American government eventually forced the Indian governments to accept formal dissolution, despite the opposition of many of the citizens within the Cherokee, Choctaw, Chickasaw, and Creek nations.

While American threats to national autonomy intensified over the post–Civil War period, economic and market relations deepened and became more diverse. The building of railroads in the early 1870's led to a rapid pace of economic change and increased integration into the American national market system. After the Civil War, the demand for beef increased rapidly in the industrial northeast, and Texas cattlemen drove their herds from Texas across Indian Territory to Kansas, where the cattle were shipped east by rail. The long cattle trail, however, led to the loss of cattle and to loss of weight by the cattle that survived. After the railroads were built through Indian Territory, Texas cattlemen started to lease large ranches and tracts of land in order to fatten their herds on the grasses of the Indian Territory prairies. After being driven or taken by rail to Indian Territory and fattened on the ranches, the cattle were then transported by train to Kansas and then to the eastern markets. Thus cattle ranching became a primary economic activity in Indian Territory. Although some of the former Indian planters were heavily engaged in the cattle business, the Texas cattlemen were the primary entrepreneurs in the industry. Between 1866 and 1900, the ranches formed the basis of a large export economy in Indian Territory.

The railroad construction also facilitated the extraction of minerals, especially coal, from Indian Territory. By 1901, there were 39 coal corporations extracting coal from the Choctaw nation; by 1907, there were 50 companies mining Choctaw coal. Coal and cattle became the primary exports of the Indian Territory economy, although hogs, corn, cotton, and lumber also were exported. Miners, railroad workers, and tertiary industry workers flocked to the Indian Territory, and new market towns sprang up rapidly along the railroad lines. Muskogee, Vinita, Tulsa, Eufaula, Atoka, and other towns quickly became trade centers, while old trade centers such as Doaksville, North Fork Town, and Boggy Depot, which were not on the railroad lines, quickly faded into ghost towns. The Indian governments leased land for cattle and for mineral extraction and financed government programs, such as schools and education, with the lease and royalty monies. Most Indians participated very little in the management of the cattle and coal industries, and most Indians did not seek employment as ranch hands or miners. The new trade communities and workers in the cattle and coal enterprises were primarily Americans, often recent European immigrants.[3]

The Cherokee, the Choctaw, the Chickasaw, and the Creek remained internally stratified primarily between large landholders and small-scale subsistence farmers. The immediate effect of the end of the American Civil War was the emancipation of the slaves. The former slaveholders were now deprived of their main labor source, but they soon turned to hiring American citizens as tenant farmers. The freedmen took up small-scale farming. Although many of the freedmen were more entrepreneurial than the conservative Indian subsistence farmers, they were restricted to relatively small tracts of land and had little chance of challenging their former masters economically. Land was in surplus in all four nations and was collectively owned and distributed on a use basis; those who made claims to land and made improvements had use of the land until they voluntarily abandoned the farm. But because the subsistence farmers needed relatively little land and were not in competition for land with the more entrepreneurial class, the former slaveholder entrepreneurs could organize several farms throughout the nation and have them worked by American tenant farmers. The large holders engaged in large-scale ranching and in cotton production, and after the 1850's they increasingly concentrated on the production of hard grains such as wheat, oats, and barley. After the 1880's, technological innovations led to the increased use of machinery and increased commercialization of agriculture. The tenant farm system made it possible for the entrepreneurs to control large tracts of land not only for agricultural and cattle production but also for lease to Texas cattlemen. And under the system, the large landholders could claim usufruct rights to the farms, ranches, and improvements that were built by the imported American tenant farmers.[4]

The regulation of tenant farm labor became a major issue of conflict between the market-oriented large holders and the conservative subsistence farmers. The subsistence farmers regarded the importation of American labor as an invitation to American squatters on the common domain, and therefore a threat to national political autonomy, because too many Americans settling on the common domain would surely make it difficult for the Indians to keep self-government. The struggle over the importation of American tenant farmers can be seen in the debates and legislation on the permit laws that imposed a tax on imported labor. The subsistence farmers sought to raise the tax in order to discourage tenant farmers, while the large holders tried to lower the tax, if not abolish it altogether.[5]

During the 1870's and 1880's, the economic stratification in all four nations became more diversified, with the appearance of doctors, lawyers, teachers, and other professionals who were the products of the early missionary and public schools that were formed in the postremoval period. Most of the professionals were sons and daughters of the large landholders, who had benefited disproportionately from the public school system in Indian Territory and had then attended college back east. By and large, their political views and economic orientations were much the same as those of the class from which they sprang.

At the same time, a significant portion of the populations within the four nations in Indian Territory—by one estimate, at least 50 percent in 1875—remained subsistence farmers, and they persisted as a major social and political group throughout the period until the formal dissolution of the national governments in 1907. Despite the availability of large tracts of often much more fertile land on the common domain, the subsistence farmers continued to occupy small tracts of land, on which they raised crops for home consumption with very little beyond that toward the end of accumulation of wealth through sale. Since game was plentiful until the first decade or so of the twentieth century, most subsistence farmers preferred to hunt for food, while the women often cultivated and cared for the small fields, mainly of wheat, corn, cotton, beans, and pumpkins. Besides hunting and fishing, the farmers could supplement their incomes by gathering nuts and berries and by raising horses, hogs, cattle, and sometimes sheep. A fur trade was carried on with local merchants, but the price of furs was so low that trading furs was not a major economic enterprise during this period.

Most subsistence farmers were not integrated into the money economy and used barter to satisfy their material needs. They continued to exhibit traditionalistic labor ethics—that is, if they received treaty payments, they preferred to engage in the round of community social and ceremonial activities and put off work until it was required to supply their customary necessities of life. Where a community had turned to Christianity, the church became the center of community meetings and social life. In the "pagan" communities, the ancient ceremonies and social gatherings remained the focus of community life. Many subsistence farmers continued to hold a world view that prohibited disruption of the physical environment by the overexploitation of game animals or the wasteful taking of more provisions than were necessary for healthy consumption. They did not engage tenant farmers for domestic or market production, and they did not themselves seek employment from the large holders, the mining companies, or the railroad companies; instead they remained culturally and socially insulated and isolated from the increasingly commercialized economy of Indian Territory.[6]

The conservative subsistence farmers continued to hold nondifferentiated world views. They continued to believe in the efficacy of magic, in witchcraft, in the significance and efficacy of supernatural omens and signs, and in the abilities of doctors who used herbal medicines and sacred incantations to heal the sick. The conservatives maintained a strong sense of moral community order. They engaged in communal labor for building, for harvesting, and for helping the sick and crippled. They believed in sharing food with anyone who needed it, and they expected everyone to contribute as they could in community social and ceremonial events. In the spirit of the old traditions, the conservative Indians placed community service and moral commitment to norms of generosity, honesty, sharing, and redistribution of material wealth above any accumulation of private wealth. Rituals still had to be correctly performed in order to have positive effects, and incorrect ceremonial procedures would have unhappy consequences. The conservatives continued to entertain the belief that ceremony, causality, morality, and religion were tightly interrelated or nondifferentiated. The large holders and professionals, on the other hand, for the most part held world views that were more rationalistic in economic and cultural terms, and they were on the whole less resistant to the American policy of assimilation. The conservatives were opposed not only to change in their way of life but also to railroads and to the allotment of the common domain. They were not particularly interested in education, but they were extremely interested in maintaining their cultural, political, and economic independence from the Americans.[7]

Although the United States increasingly attempted to incorporate politically the nations of Indian Territory, and the economic relations of Indian Territory became more complex and integrated into the emerging American national economy, the primary issue set before the Indian Territory governments was not further significant political differentiation, but political stability and national survival. The changing economic and political conditions resulted in increasing rationalization and elaboration of legal codes to manage the new economic relations and increased bureaucratic rationalization. By 1867, all four nations had adopted relatively differentiated constitutional governments. The Creek government was the least formally differentiated polity since it included the religiously integrated and kin-based villages as the primary political unit. The Choctaw government also included the symbols and offices of the district chiefs as part of the constitutional government and thus evinced less differentiation of polity and society than the Cherokee and Chickasaw governments, where locality, villages, and kinship were formally differentiated from the polity. From the post–Civil War period until formal political dissolution in 1907, the Cherokee, Chickasaw, and Choctaw governments were stable in the sense that no significant political or social groups challenged their legitimacy. Political conflict in the Cherokee and Chickasaw polities involved struggles for power between large holders and conservatives. The Choctaw polity was comparatively peaceful until the 1890's, when political conflict erupted over the issues of allotment and national political dissolution. The Creek government was the most unstable; there were numerous challenges to the constitutional government, and several rebellions, and different groups formed alternative governments that were meant to restore the ancient government of village chiefs. During the difficult period of the 1890's and early 1900's, all four governments encountered resistance from conservatives who refused to accept American demands for political dissolution and the privatization of the common domain.

Cherokee Political Stability and Conflict

No major changes occurred in the Cherokee polity in the postwar period. Most of the changes involved increased bureaucratic rationalization as well as rationalization and extension of the legal system, and these were accomplished within the mechanisms of the existing institutional framework to meet the demands of increasingly complex economic and political conditions. The Reconstruction Treaty with the United States in 1866 led to several amendments to the Cherokee constitution. After 1866, the Cherokee upper house was known as the Senate and the lower house was known as the Council. Representation in the Council now was determined by population in each of the eight, soon to be nine, Cherokee administrative districts. Until the 1890's, when the issues of national survival and allotment of the common domain became paramount, the major events in Cherokee political relations were focused on a struggle for political power between the entrepreneurial large landholders and the conservative small farmers.

In the immediate years after the Civil War, the primary political task was the reconciliation of the Southern party and the loyal Cherokee. The war caused great bitterness between the predominantly Southern slaveholders and the conservative small landholders. Indian Territory was a shifting battlefront during the war, and many were killed on both sides; the military action left Cherokee country devastated. Property belonging to the former planters was confiscated by the militant pins of the Keetoowah Society, who wanted to keep the Southern party out of the Cherokee polity. Many members of the Southern party feared returning because they might be assassinated by the conservatives. The Southern party, supported by the American government, seriously contemplated a division of the national domain and the formation of a separate national entity, and this possibility brought the majority national party to make concessions in the form of assurances of personal protection, return of private property, and political inclusion in the Cherokee government for the Southern party.[8]

Political reunification was further encouraged by a new political party, called the Downing party after its leader, Lewis Downing, which included selected members of the Southern party and many Christian conservatives of the Keetoowah Society. Lewis Downing was a popular Baptist minister, whose church at Delaware Town was the center of the Baptist mission to the Cherokee nation and the site of large gatherings of Christian Cherokee. He was a close associate of Evan Jones and his son John Jones, the two Baptist ministers who had made many converts among the conservative valley town Cherokee back east and had established the Baptist church at Delaware Town in the early 1840's. The two Joneses had helped initiate the revival and reorganization of the Keetoowah Society in 1858–59. During the war, while chief John Ross spent most of his time in the northeast, Lewis Downing was the acting principal chief of the loyal Cherokee. In 1866 the Joneses, Downing, a majority of the Keetoowah Society, and certain members of the Southern party joined together and formed a party of national reconciliation. John Ross, who had been principal chief since 1828, died in 1866 shortly before formation of the new party, and national party leadership passed to his nephew, William P. Ross, who had a college degree from Princeton and had served the Cherokee government since the early 1850's. William Ross served as acting principal chief for fourteen months, until the election of 1867 when he was defeated by Downing. Downing was reelected two years later thanks in great part to the support of the well-organized Keetoowah pins, who made political speeches and stored weapons in each district of the nation. Downing also had the support of the Southern party and many from the national party.[9]

The major issues during the Downing administration were postwar economic reconstruction, national and political reunification, railroad rights-of-way, and the freedmen. Economic reconstruction proceeded rapidly, and the Downing party was able to restore political stability to the nation. Though Downing himself, who expressed the views of his conservative supporters, opposed the building of railroads demanded by the Americans in the Reconstruction treaty of 1866, he was powerless to prevent the coming of what the conservatives correctly foresaw as the destroyers of their political independence. In 1869, the Cherokee adopted tough anti-allotment laws against Cherokee citizens who advocated division and private ownership of the public domain. They also tried to organize a Cherokee-owned railroad company to satisfy the conditions of the 1866 treaty, but this was vetoed by the American government. Leading members of the Southern party of course favored the building of railroads for economic reasons, as a way of integrating Indian Territory into the American economy and creating business opportunities. The Downing party also differed with the Southern party over the granting of citizenship to the former slaves. The former slaveholders of the Southern party wanted the freedmen to be settled on land in western Oklahoma, because if they stayed in Cherokee territory they would ally politically with the conservatives, which they in fact did over the next two decades. In 1870–71 the Downing and national parties moved to adopt the freedmen as Cherokee citizens.[10]

In 1872 Lewis Downing and the second principal chief died in quick succession, and the general council appointed William Ross to complete the term of office. Ross's legislative election led to some open hostility and disturbances by the Downing party, but Ross continued a policy of representing the nationalist interests of the conservatives. He opposed American efforts to form Indian Territory into an American territorial possession, opposed allotment, and worked to preserve Cherokee national independence. In 1875, Ross was defeated in the election for principal chief by the Downing party candidate, Charles Thompson, or Oochalata. Thompson, like Downing, was a Baptist minister and successful merchant who lived in the Delaware district, eleven miles from the Delaware Town Baptist church. He had a close association with the Keetoowah Society, which was still influenced by the two Baptist ministers, Evan and John Jones. Thompson appealed to the conservatives in his campaign by advocating higher permit fees on American labor and tenant farmers and by opposing tenant farming, and during his administration he attempted to uphold Cherokee national political sovereignty. In 1876 he helped revise the legal code, and he authorized the leasing of unused land to American cattlemen. Evan and John Jones both died in 1876, however, and with their deaths the Downing coalition dissolved. Although the landlords and merchants of the Southern party adopted the Downing party name and thereafter campaigned as the Downing party, most conservatives and the Keetoowah Society realigned with the national party.[11]

In the elections of 1879 and 1883, Dennis Bushyhead was elected principal chief on the national party ticket. Bushyhead, who had the support of the Keetoowah Society, was a Baptist minister and owned a large cattle ranch; he had served for many years as national treasurer. During his administration Bushyhead opposed territorialization, opposed the influence of cattle associations and railroads, and sought to provide education to the conservatives. Under increasing American demands for allotment and political dissolution, the Keetoowah Society and the national party became more and more nationalistic and began advocating Cherokee citizenship by blood. This position alienated groups of Delaware, Shawnee, and freedmen who had been incorporated into the Cherokee nation after the Civil War. Heretofore, most freedmen as well as the Baptist Delaware and Shawnee had allied with the conservatives, but during the election of 1887, the Cherokee minority groups started to gravitate toward the Downing party, which was now led by the big landholders and merchants of the former Southern-treaty parties and Old Settlers.[12]

The election of 1887, in which the Downing party won control of the principal chieftainship and of both legislative houses, signaled a major shift in political power in Cherokee society. Until 1887 and throughout the previous Cherokee state period, the conservatives of the Ross party–national party–Keetoowah Society had controlled the principal chieftainship and usually held the majority in the legislature. For the first time in Cherokee history, the reins of political power passed to the large holders. Rabbit Bunch, the candidate for the national party, was the second chief under Bushyhead; he was well educated and a successful farmer. He campaigned against allotment and upheld the conservative position of trying to preserve national independence. The national party accused Joel Mayes, the Downing party candidate, of being backed by real estate and mineral companies.[13]

There is a conservative tradition that says that Rabbit Bunch won the election but that the American government supported Mayes and the Downing party. Whatever the truth of this story, when Mayes and the Downing party arrived at the Cherokee capitol at Tahlequah in the fall of 1887 to take office, Chief Bushyhead and the national party refused to vacate the national government buildings and both sides took up arms. The Downing party appealed to the U.S. government, and an American representative called a joint session to count the votes for election of the principal chief. When the American official did not get an immediate response, he threatened to bring in American troops and assume control over the Cherokee government. Under pressure, the rival parties met to count and verify the vote of the election. Mayes was declared the winner and was placed in office. The national party was forced to accept the decision, and in the following years political relations became increasingly bitter and divisive.[14]

From 1887 to political dissolution in 1907, the Downing party controlled the executive offices of the Cherokee nation. In the early 1890's, a major issue emerged over whether the Cherokee should allow the building of more than the two railroads that were mandated by the 1866 treaty. Over the opposition of the conservatives, the national council voted to allow more railroads to be built across the Cherokee nation. In the early 1890's, parts of Oklahoma were opened to settlement by American citizens, and in 1893 a large tract of land called the Cherokee Outlet was opened to American settlers. Also in 1893, Congress created the Dawes Commission with the intent of extinguishing Indian title and Indian government in Indian Territory and allotting the land in private tracts averaging about 160 acres of average-quality land; excess land was to be made available to American settlers.[15]

With the increasing American pressure for allotment and political dissolution, the Cherokee conservatives began to lose their political grip, and the Keetoowah Society, which for some years had maintained a solid front, broke into two somewhat antagonistic organizations, further weakening the ability of the conservatives to manage internal political events against the increasingly dominant Downing party. In the early 1890's, Red Bird Smith revived the old nucleus of ultraconservative Nighthawk Keetoowahs as a strongly fundamentalist, apolitical group that honored old clan identifications and ancient Cherokee rituals and religion. The Nighthawks of the 1890's were against schools, intermarriage with Americans, allotment, assimilation into American society—against anything they regarded as an American threat to Cherokee national autonomy. The established, more politically organized Keetoowah Society was still willing to work within the Cherokee government and reluctantly accepted American decisions about allotment and political incorporation. It opposed the allotment policy, but after the policy went into effect, it turned to providing legal and political protection to the Cherokee conservatives during the difficult transition to private land holdings and incorporation under American laws.[16]

With the Curtis Act of 1898, Congress formally mandated abolition of the Cherokee government by March of 1906 and mandated that the Cherokee domain be allotted by July of 1902. The Downing party won the principal chieftainship in 1899, and the new chief favored allotment. The Cherokee general council voted to accept the provisions of the Curtis Act, but Wolf Coon, the national party leader and candidate for principal chief, appealed to the United States to call for a national referendum because the council did not properly represent the position of the conservatives. A national referendum was called, and the vote went for allotment. The conservative tradition maintains, however, that the majority of Cherokee opposed allotment and that the proposition passed only because the Nighthawks boycotted the election.[17]

Between 1902 and 1907, the Cherokee land was allotted and the Cherokee government was formally abolished. The Nighthawks, true to their convictions, refused to register and accept allotments. Both the Keetoowah and the Nighthawks continued as organizations after 1907, and both are still active today. After 1907, the Cherokee principal chief was appointed by the American government to manage business relating to the Cherokee domain. Since the early 1970's, the Cherokees again have been allowed to elect their own chiefs. Many of the large landholders were incorporated into the economy and power structure of eastern Oklahoma after it became a state. At least 10,000 to 12,000 conservatives continue to live in communities in eastern Oklahoma.

Between 1866 and 1907, although the Cherokee government was relatively stable in the sense that there were no major challenges to the organization of the government or attempts to create alternative forms of government, there were struggles for political power within the constitutional framework, primarily between the conservative parties, with the Keetoowah Society behind them, and the Cherokee big landholders and professionals in the Downing party. If there was any challenge to the Cherokee polity, it came from the fundamentalist, apolitical Nighthawk Keetoowahs. The political alienation of the Nighthawks was not so much a challenge to Cherokee political institutions as it was a realization that the Downing administrations would not protect the nationalist interests of the conservative Cherokee.

Choctaw Political Rationalization and Stability

Aside from some elaboration and rationalization of laws and bureaucracy in order to regulate increasingly complex economic relations, there was little change in the Choctaw constitutional government from the post–Civil War period to political dissolution in 1907. The completion of the railroad through Choctaw country in 1872 destroyed the Choctaws' relative isolation and led to their rapid economic integration into the American national market. In the 1870's and 1880's, the Choctaw government passed new laws to regulate the building of railroads, to tax the railroad companies, to regulate tenant farming, to regulate the importation of American labor, and to impose national control over leasing and regulation of the export of coal and national resources. Other laws were designed to regulate the influx of American citizens who flocked to Choctaw country following the opportunities created by the railroads. In accordance with the 1866 Reconstruction treaty, the American government was supposed to remove all noncitizens as intruders, and the Choctaw tried to define citizenship so that they could identify persons who were not eligible to reside in the nation. But in the early 1880's, the Choctaw lost the right to regulate American citizens, and the American government was no longer exerting itself to remove illegal American settlers. As a result, so many American citizens came to live in the railroad and mining towns in the Choctaw nation that they soon constituted a majority. By 1907 there were 185,000 Americans in the Choctaw nation, but only 11,000 to 12,000 Choctaw citizens.

After the Civil War, although the Choctaw national government became increasingly centralized and the principal chief, or governor, held more authority, the largely symbolic and integrative role of the three district chiefs still remained. An attempt to abolish the offices of the three district chiefs in 1880 failed; but in 1885 the pay for holding the office was reduced by two-thirds, to $50 per year. Thus over the half-century after the American Civil War, the Choctaw government became more centralized and bureaucratically rationalized, and extended its laws to regulate an increasingly complex export economy and to protect national economic interests.[18]

During the late 1860's and 1870's, the Choctaw government was influenced strongly by the conservative majority, who effectively used the government institutions to protect their nationalistic and cultural interests.

Although the Choctaw had been divided since the 1820's into a conservative majority and a minority of entrepreneurs and Christians, who were
more willing to accept American values and customs, these groups never
formed standing political parties; the conservatives were divided into their
local communities and districts, where their primary political loyalties lay,
and the big landholders also maintained strong district and local political affiliations. After 1866 and up to 1880, the conservatives used their
strong representation in the national government to oppose the building of
railroads, to oppose joining the United States as part of a territorial government, to prevent the allotment of the public domain into private tracts,
to exclude American intruders, and to regulate the influx of American
labor and tenant farmers—all of which the conservatives thought threatened the longterm independence of the Choctaw nation and their own
way of life.

Against great pressure from the Americans throughout the 1870's, the
conservative-influenced Choctaw administrations rejected both allotment
and territorialization, but the conservatives could not prevent the building
of railroads or the influx of American laborers. In 1877, in Moshulatubee district, conservatives went so far as to tear up the railways, but the
movement was repressed by local police. A lawsuit against the operation
of the railroads also failed. The large holders favored the building of railroads as a means of obtaining new economic opportunities, and they also
differed with the conservatives over the importation of American labor
and tenant farmers. Whenever the conservatives passed legislation that
prohibited leasing of land and enacted permit laws that highly taxed the
importation of American labor, the landlords acted to annul or minimize
the labor permit fees and to annul and evade the laws aimed at constraining tenant farming. The leasing and permit laws changed often, depending
on which group could muster a majority in the national government during any given legislative session. There was agreement on the question of
freedmen; the Choctaw did not favor adoption of the freedmen as citizens, and they asked the American government to transport the freedmen
to western Oklahoma, in accordance with the treaty of 1866. Many of
the freedmen had established small and mid-sized farms in the Choctaw
nation and refused to leave, and in 1885 the American government forced
the Choctaw government to grant the freedmen citizenship.[19]

During the 1880's, as the two loose political groupings of Christian
large holders and conservatives began to differ more vehemently over the
major issues of allotment and dissolution, there were movements on both
sides to form party organizations in order to elect men of their own persuasion to national political offices. The large holders, most of whom lived
like Americans, began to favor private allotment of the Choctaw public

domain and American political and economic incorporation. They had the support of other Choctaws who saw the futility of trying to resist incorporation into American society as more American citizens continued to move into the Choctaw nation. Believing that the Choctaw nation could not survive as an independent entity, the large holders and their supporters argued that the nation ought to accept allotment and attempt to negotiate the best possible terms for national political dissolution. The large holder party was often called the Eagle party, but after 1885 it became more formally known as the Progressive party.

The conservatives continued to insist on preserving Choctaw national political independence and cultural autonomy. Their position was that Choctaw nationality was guaranteed by the treaties of 1830 and 1866, and that the majority of the Choctaw small subsistence farmers were not socially, culturally, economically, or politically prepared to enter into American society. The conservative leaders feared that statehood and allotment would lead to taxes on land and dispossession of the small subsistence farmers. They also feared that the Americans would class the conservatives by color and that the conservative Choctaw would not gain full social and political inclusion into American society. The national party, often called Buzzards, formed in the late 1880's when the American government was planning to open large tracts of Oklahoma to settlement by Americans.[20]

The elections of the 1890's were hotly contested between the two parties and on several occasions erupted into violence. In the elections of 1890 and 1892, both won by the Progressives, the major issues were whether to accept allotment and whether the Choctaw should allow more than two railroads in their nation. The conservatives campaigned on a platform that opposed the building of more railroads and the incorporation of the Choctaw into American society. After the 1892 election, groups from the two parties exchanged skirmishes in the "Locke-Jones War," and American troops had to be sent to restore order and prevent further bloodshed. Locke was an American large holder who had married a Choctaw woman and supported the conservative party; Jones, a farmer with large holdings, was the gubernatorial winner in 1890 and 1892.

More political violence erupted in September and October 1893, when a group of conservative leaders plotted to assassinate a large number of progressive leaders who, the conservative leaders claimed, had won office fraudulently. Several progressive leaders were in fact assassinated before the plot was discovered and the progressive party defended their men and arrested the conservative party leaders. The leaders of the revolt were tried in the Choctaw courts and executed. An oral tradition relates that the condemned national leaders conducted themselves according to

Choctaw judicial procedures and norms: they were tried and sentenced, then allowed out on probation for six months to set their private affairs in order. On the appointed day, they appeared voluntarily for their execution.[21] The uprising of 1893 was a serious challenge to the Choctaw government, and it was managed within the framework of Choctaw constitutional government. It was no more than a challenge to the political leadership, however; it did not propose an alternate form of government or any major modifications in the constitutional government.

A conservative candidate won the election for governor in 1894, but two years later the election was won by the candidate of the Tuskahoma or progressive party, a large holder and merchant named Green McCurtain. The McCurtain family had a long association with the progressive or Eagle party, and two of McCurtain's brothers were former principal chiefs. McCurtain ran on a platform that openly advocated assimilation into American society and allotment and Choctaw incorporation into the projected state of Oklahoma. The opposition conservative national party totally rejected incorporation into the projected state of Oklahoma and wanted to expel all Americans who were not legal residents of the nation. The Tuskahoma administration accepted their victory as a mandate to start negotiations for allotment and the dismantling of the Choctaw government, and in 1898 McCurtain and the Tuskahoma party won again, this time against the Union party, which was a coalition of opposition groups who now accepted the inevitability of the loss of Choctaw self-government but wanted to obtain better terms in the negotiations. In 1898 the Curtis Act set a timetable for the abolishment of Choctaw government and allotment of the common domain, to which the Choctaw government promptly agreed.[22]

In the election of 1900, McCurtain was not eligible to run for governor, and a progressive candidate, Gilbert Dukes, won against the Union candidate. Two years later, McCurtain ran and won, but Dukes refused to hand the government over to McCurtain and instead favored the Union candidate. McCurtain had to be verified as winner of the election and placed in office with the help of American marshals and troops. McCurtain then served as governor from 1902 until his death in 1910. In 1903 and 1904 the Choctaw lands were allotted among the Choctaw, although many conservatives still refused to accept allotments. One group, called "Snakes," that did not accept allotment tried unsuccessfully to negotiate emigration to Mexico. The Snakes, numbering several hundred, were mainly subsistence farmers, strongly fundamentalist, who not only wanted to maintain the Choctaw government but declared they were not ready or willing to enter American society and live under American laws. Most of them passively resisted allotment by refusing to take private land allotments, although American officials arbitrarily assigned land to many of them.[23]

In 1907 the Choctaw government was formally abolished and thereafter the U.S. government appointed the governor, whose primary business was to manage the remaining estate and legal affairs of the Choctaw nation. In 1934 the Choctaw accepted the Indian Reorganization Act, which enabled them to form an advisory council for management of their legal and governmental affairs. Since the mid-1970's, the Choctaw have enjoyed limited self-government within the framework of the administration of the Bureau of Indian Affairs.

Despite the sporadic election violence in the 1890's and later, the Choctaw constitutional government in the post–Civil War period was relatively stable. No major social or political groups challenged the legitimacy of the constitutional government or actively sought to construct an alternate form of government; the major changes had to do with greater centralization and rationalization of bureaucratic organization and the creation of a more elaborate legal code to regulate an increasingly complex export economy and to protect against threats to national autonomy from American intruders and growing numbers of imported workers and tenant farmers. The formation of political parties in the late 1880's also indicated a further internal differentiation of the Choctaw polity, reflecting the intense nationalist orientation of the conservatives as against the more resigned assimilation platform of the progressive party. Conservative-progressive cleavages had existed in Choctaw society for most of the nineteenth century, but the political mobilization and action were galvanized by the threat of forced political dissolution and privatization of the common public domain.

Chickasaw Institutional Stability and Political Conflict

The Chickasaw constitutional government did not undergo any major changes in organization during the period 1866–1907. The new constitution adopted in 1866 differed little from the constitution of 1856, except that the slave code was deleted. The Chickasaw did not adopt the freedmen as citizens until 1885, and only under American pressure. For the Chickasaw, as for the Cherokee and the Choctaw, the post–Civil War period was a time of increasing economic incorporation into the American national economy, and the Chickasaw government created laws to regulate the importation of American labor, tenant farmers, railroads and railroad construction, and the cattle industry and mineral extraction. These incremental legal changes were accomplished within the framework of the constitutional government and were the result of efforts by the Chickasaw to accommodate to a changing political and economic environment. Nevertheless, the most significant change in the Chickasaw polity was the formation of political parties in the early 1870's.

Up until 1873, carried on by the spirit of the nationalist movement of the early 1850's, the leaders of the Chickasaw government, who were mostly large holders, enjoyed a relative unity of political orientation with the conservative majority. But between 1870 and 1873 a major split emerged between the conservatives and the large holders over the question of allotment of the Chickasaw common domain. According to the treaty of 1866, the Chickasaw were free to allot their common domain if the nation agreed to that purpose. In 1872, acting under strong pressure from railroad companies and settlers to open up the Chickasaw nation for settlement, the Chickasaw government asked the Department of the Interior to proceed with private allotment of the Chickasaw nation. The Secretary of the Interior stated that allotment could not be done without the consent of the Choctaw nation.[24] The Choctaws, who retained an interest in the Chickasaw domain from the treaties of 1855 and 1866, refused to allow the Chickasaw to proceed with allotment, something that conservatives in both nations opposed as a weakening of national defense against American plans for territorialization and extinguishment of national autonomy.

In 1873, Benjamin Franklin Overton, a Chickasaw senator, started campaigning against the allotment policy of the Chickasaw leadership. He argued that the large majority of Chickasaw did not want allotment and that the allotment policy was engineered by a small group. In the election for governor in 1874, Overton organized the conservatives into the national or Pullback party. The large holders formed their own party, usually called the Progressive party. Cyrus Harris, the incumbent governor, ran against Overton. Both parties developed national machines with platforms, national chairmen, and local managers; there were public meetings and campaign speeches. The Pullback party campaigned in favor of schools and in favor of preserving Chickasaw nationality by restrictions on American labor and tenant farmers, exclusion of noncitizens, and rejection of allotment and territorialization. The Progressive party favored leasing land to tenant farmers and Texas cattle associations, importing American labor and tenant farmers, and further commercialization of the Chickasaw economy. Although several of the elections were close and controversial, the conservative Pullback party won the governorship in the 1874 election and controlled the governorship from 1874 to 1896, except for 1886–88 when it was held by a Progressive candidate.[25]

B. F. Overton, the organizer and leader of the Pullback party, served as governor for four terms (1874–78 and 1880 until his death in 1884). The 1878 election was won by a surrogate candidate, Overton's son-in-law, Benjamin Burney, because of the two-term law. During these years, the Pullback party rejected American plans for territorialization and allotment and took measures to restrict tenant farming, to exclude noncitizens, to restrict entry of American laborers, and to restrict the number of land-holdings on the common domain. Between 1876 and 1878, the Overton administration changed the permit law that regulated American labor and tenant farmers by raising the tax from $5 to $25 per year for each laborer. The intention was to deny the large holders access to labor and also to discourage Americans from entering and settling in the country, since any noncitizen without a permit was considered an intruder and was sub-ject to deportation by the lighthorse or the American government. The $25 permit proved unenforceable, however, despite the personal efforts of Overton, the Chickasaw militia, and the lighthorse, and it was lowered to its former level in 1878; this reduction was followed by massive entry of outside labor in the 1880's.[26]

The ranks of the Progressive party were strengthened in 1876 when the Chickasaw government enfranchised intermarried citizens—Ameri-cans who married Chickasaw citizens. Most intermarried citizens were large-scale farmers and ranchers whose political interests and cultural and economic orientations were much like those of the Chickasaw large holders who belonged to the Progressive party, and very unlike those of the Chickasaw subsistence farmers. In 1879, after the failure of the per-mit law, the conservative Chickasaw administration passed a law limiting to two the number of farms or ranches that a Chickasaw citizen could maintain on the common domain. Overton was quite willing to enforce the law, but the large holders easily evaded it by putting farms under the names of relatives or plural wives.[27]

The election for governor in 1884 was won by Jonas Wolf, the Pullback party candidate. He carried on the policies of Overton and the Pullback platform of preserving nationality and political independence by opposing allotment and American intruders. He refused to enfranchise the freedmen and imposed restrictive measures on the issuance of permits to Ameri-can traders and doctors. Wolf lost the nomination of the Pullback party in 1886 to William Byrd, a large holder and merchant who was now the leader of the Pullback party. Wolf ran as an independent. The Progressive candidate was William Guy. None of the three candidates won a majority, and when in accordance with the constitution the legislature decided the election, Guy won by a single vote, and had to face a hostile national council. During the Guy administration a major controversy arose over American efforts to secure an additional railroad right-of-way through the Chickasaw nation. Guy called a special legislative session to consider the proposition, but the conservatives in the legislature, who strongly op-posed the introduction of more railroads, instead took up the question of Guy's impeachment. The impeachment effort failed to carry, but the ses-sion broke up without considering the railroad question. The Secretary of the Interior commanded Guy to make an agreement for the railroad right-of-way and to proceed without the approval of the national council. After the arrangements were made, the Chickasaw refused to accept payment for the sale of the right-of-way.[28]

The Pullback party won the next four elections for governor—first William Byrd (1888, 1890), then Jonas Wolf (1892), and then Palmer Mosely (1894). During a dozen years of power for the Pullback party of conservative subsistence farmers and a few large holders, conditions in the Chickasaw nation steadily worsened. Between 1885 and 1890 alone, 25,000 American citizens entered the nation, outnumbering the Chickasaw citizenry by several times, and the pace increased rapidly during the 1890's. At the same time, pressures for allotment and extinguishment of Indian title to land mounted, and in the early 1890's large tracts of land in Oklahoma were opened to American settlement. In the election of 1888, the Progressive candidate, Guy, tallied twenty more votes than the Pullback candidate, Byrd, but the national council, which was controlled by the Pullback party, claimed that some of Guy's votes were fraudulent and threw out enough votes to allow the Pullback candidate to win. The Progressive party challenged the decision and briefly took over the capitol by force of arms, but American officials supported the Pullback claims, and the national council refused to recognize the Progressive candidate as governor. The new Pullback administration called an extra session of the legislature and passed an amendment to the constitution that disenfranchised all intermarried and adopted citizens. Since the intermarried and adopted citizens were allied primarily with the Progressive party, the new amendment effectively weakened the ability of the Progressive party to compete in the electoral process.[29]

The conservative Pullback administrations between 1888 and 1896 passed several measures that were supposed to evict American intruders, regulate and restrict the use of the common domain by the big landholders, tax American cattle grazing on Chickasaw land, and strengthen enforcement and administration of the permit laws, but many of these new laws, as well as efforts at enforcement, were simply ignored by the resident American population and by the large holders. The government was powerless to prevent the exploitive use of the common domain by the big cattle ranchers and landlords of tenant farmers. The leasing laws, permit laws, and tax on imported cattle were widely abused and evaded. By 1893 there were 40,000 noncitizens in the nation, while the Chickasaw population, excluding freedmen and intermarried citizens, was never more than 6,000. The capitalistic large holders increasingly became dissatisfied with the conservative-dominated government and judiciary, which they argued did not adequately protect private property and individual liberties; the entrepreneurial class complained that the Chickasaw courts and laws were not adequate to manage the increasingly complex commercial relations. For these reasons, the large holders began to think it would be better to incorporate under American jurisdiction than to remain under what they regarded as the stultifying leadership of the conservative Chickasaw majority.[30]

The Dawes Commission hearings of 1895, together with the growing tide of American settlers, increased the pressure on the nations in Indian Territory to come to an agreement for abolishment of their independent governments and the allotment of land and sale of excess lands to the settlers. More and more Chickasaw were coming to believe that preservation of an independent nationality was futile. In 1896, a Progressive party candidate, Robert Harris, one of the largest landholders and richest men in the Chickasaw nation, was elected governor, and from then on until political dissolution in 1907, the Progressive party controlled the governorship, although some of the elections were close and disputed. In 1897 the Progressive party administration negotiated an agreement for allotment and abolishment of the Chickasaw nationality, but a referendum vote in December 1897 rejected the agreement. The Curtis Act of 1898 forced the Chickasaw to reconsider allotment, and the Chickasaw resigned themselves to American demands with a confirming referendum vote.[31]

In the election of 1902, the Pullback party made a concerted effort to regain control of the government and avert the allotment and political termination agreement. William Byrd, the former governor and still a leading figure in the Pullback party, ran for governor against Palmer Mosely, who had been affiliated with the Pullback party during his first term as governor from 1894 to 1896 but was now a well-off banker and had switched his political loyalties to the Progressive party. Byrd gathered the most votes in a close election, but the returns were contested and were sent to the Progressive-dominated legislature for certification. The legislature disqualified the votes from Pontotoc County, a Pullback stronghold, and Mosely was declared governor. The dispute almost broke into armed conflict, but American officials intervened and confirmed Mosely's election. Mosely's Progressive government then pushed through the allotment and termination agreement. The Chickasaw domain was allotted in the early 1900's, and the government was officially dismantled by 1907. About 300,000 acres of land were opened to purchase by American settlers.[32]

As among the other nations of Indian Territory, the passing of the Chickasaw constitutional government did not necessarily imply the passing of the Chickasaw as a nation or people. From 1907 to 1963, the President of the United States appointed the Chickasaw governor, who managed what remained of the affairs of the Chickasaw state. Since 1963, the governorship has again been elective, and the Chickasaw have adopted a constitution and government organization, which are subject to the oversight of the Bureau of Indian Affairs.

The Chickasaw constitutional government was institutionally stable during the post–Civil War period. At the same time, the Chickasaw polity became more internally differentiated, with increased bureaucratization, and elaboration of legal codes and the formation of political parties. The major political conflicts within Chickasaw society were not struggles over the rules of organization of the polity; the two major social and political groupings in Chickasaw society both accepted and participated in the constitutional government. Rather, the major political conflicts emerged over the struggle for political power, which reflected the class and cultural cleavages of Chickasaw society. Once organized, the nationalist conservatives controlled the leadership of the Chickasaw government against the economic interests and competition of the commercial large holders. But the combination of the capitalist interests and orientations of the large holders and American economic expansion and assimilation policies was too powerful, not only for the conservative party but for the national autonomy of the Chickasaw government.

The Instability of the Creek Government

Of the four transplanted southeastern nations, the Creek had the most unstable constitutional government. In all the nations, there was a cleavage between conservatives and large landholders, but in the Creek case, a group of conservatives not only challenged the authority of the constitutional government on numerous occasions but formed a countergovernment that was meant to reestablish the old regime of chiefs. The several attempts by conservatives to change or overthrow the Creek constitutional government failed, but only because the American government supported the Creek government with force when necessary. The Creek government remained in power with more use of overt coercion and with considerably more negotiation and conflict over the fundamental rules of political order than in the Cherokee, Choctaw, and Chickasaw cases.

The Creek constitutional government had the least differentiated polity of the four nations. Although the new Creek government was formally differentiated from religion, in that it allowed freedom of religion, the principal chiefs often made reference to God in their annual addresses, and at least two of the principal chiefs after 1866 were Christian ministers who used Christian symbols in their addresses; but in the villages the Creek continued to honor the ceremonies and world view of the religion of the town square. Even rich, well-educated large holders participated in the religious ceremonies of the towns. In the post–Civil War period, there was a return to the dominance of the white towns of Cussetah, Abihka, Nuyuka, Okmulgee, and others; the symbolic division of red and white towns was not recognized formally by the Creek constitutional government, but throughout the post–Civil War period Creek national leaders on both sides—those who favored the constitutional government and leaders of the opposition—were men from major white towns. The return of political dominance of the white towns and the continuity of the religious-political organization of the Creek towns underscores the continuity of nondifferentiated symbolic and political institutions in Creek society, despite the formal adoption of the constitution of 1867.[33]

Although the new Creek constitution organized the nation into six administrative districts, the primary political units were, as before, the tribal towns, and the governments of the tribal towns, based on kinship and religious integration, continued to have primary responsibility over local political affairs and were seldom interfered with by the national government. Therefore, since the tribal towns remained the primary political units under the new constitution, the formation of six administrative districts did not represent a differentiation of polity from the local kin-based and religiously particularistic tribal towns. Each town sent one representative to the upper legislative house, or House of Kings, and sent representatives to the House of Warriors according to the town's population. The town chief was not automatically elected to the House of Kings, and when he was not he continued to lead the town government, with the assistance and advice of the elected member to the House of Kings. The towns jealously protected their local political and cultural autonomy, and town and regional loyalties continued to take precedence over national loyalties. Political and social membership continued to be identified with the town ceremonial square and clan of one's mother; the concept of national citizenship was secondary, if not nonexistent. Consequently, Creek national political unity remained tenuous, and relations between polity and society were relatively nondifferentiated. Several attempts to revise the constitution in order to reduce the number of town representatives to the national legislature failed to change the importance of the towns in the Creek polity.[34]

The Creek constitutional government framed the separation of powers among the judiciary, the legislature, and the executive. The legitimate use of force was centralized in the executive and judicial branches. The Creek did not hold condemned men in jails but, in the traditional way, released them with instructions to return on an appointed day to stand for their execution. Lesser crimes were punished by whipping. In the post–Civil War period, as the economy in Indian Territory became more complicated, the Creek government passed more elaborate and rationalized laws and legal codes to regulate railroad building and railroad traffic, the employment of American workers and tenant farmers, the leasing of land to Texas cattlemen and American citizens, and the operation of mining enterprises.[35] The adoption of the Creek freedmen as citizens was accomplished with little controversy. The freedmen organized three towns, which were incorporated into the government with the same rights as the other Creek towns. The new laws aimed at regulating economic relations and protecting the Creek public domain from American intruders were secured within the framework of the constitutional government.

The new constitution ran into difficulties at the first election in late 1867, and nearly every national election in the post–Civil War period was contested by the conservatives. In the first election, the parties still represented the regional loyalties: the Sands party represented the upper town or loyal Creek, the Checote party represented primarily the lower town Creek. The Southern party set out to build a national ticket by inviting Micco Hutke, White King, the chief of Tulsa (Talisee), the ancient upper white town, to run as second chief. Micco Hutke accepted in the name of national reconciliation, although the conservatives considered him a traitor for doing so. Samuel Checote, who ran for principal chief for the Southern party, was a Methodist minister at Okmulgee and a member of the Hitchiti white town of Sawokla. Sands, from the white town of Abihka, ran as principal chief for the upper town or loyal Creek; his running mate for second chief was Cotchoche, Little Tiger, from the fundamentalist white town of Wewocau. Checote won the election, but the Sands party, believing that with the freedmen's vote they were the majority, claimed that the election for principal chief was won by fraud; they said that the secret ballot led to easy fraud because many of the conservative Creek were not literate and the educated members of the Southern party understood the new laws and political apparatus better than the conservative Creek villagers did. The conservatives refused to acknowledge the election of Checote because traditional election practices were not used, where a candidate stood for office on election day and his supporters lined up behind him, and the man with the largest number of supporters won the office.[36]

For the next four years, until the next election of 1871, the Sands party caused political turmoil by refusing to recognize the legitimacy of the elected members of the constitutional government. Twenty-three loyalist towns joined in the opposition; many refused to send delegates to the national legislature. The conservatives now said that the constitution went further than they intended, and that they wanted a return to the old form of government. They were also very dissatisfied with the method of direct distribution of national funds to schools and government administration rather than to the town chiefs, who traditionally redistributed the funds to members of the village community. Some men were disgruntled because the new government required and hired fewer administrative and elected officers than they thought it should. The American government recognized the constitutional government and the Checote administration as the legitimate Creek government and turned over national funds to Checote, and it was quite willing to use troops and U.S. marshals to defend the constitutional government and maintain order against the disaffected conservatives. Seeing this, the Sands party withdrew and formed a rival government with elected officials, but not with American recognition.[37]

By 1869 there was a breakdown in political consensus between the Sands party and constitutional party. The Checote administration offered a compromise by amending the constitution, but the Sands party still refused to participate in the constitutional government and maintained its opposition government at Nuyuka, a white town and a daughter town to the ancient central white town of Oakfuskie. The political crisis led to several political murders, and the Checote government passed a series of laws to strengthen the lighthorse police and the courts against the action of the anticonstitutionalists. The Sands party and government remained aloof from the Checote administration and waited until the elections of 1871, which they were determined to win so that they could restore the old chief form of government.[38]

Early in October of 1871, the Sands party descended on Okmulgee, the new Creek capital, and forced an election for national officers according to the old rules of counting the number of men standing behind the candidate of their choice. The Sands party candidate for principal chief was Cotchoche; Sands intended to reserve for himself the traditional and more active position of speaker of the council. The Checote administration asked American officials to intervene in the election controversy, and the American agent refused to accept any election procedure except the one that was written into the Creek constitution. American officials oversaw the counting of the election ballots and declared Checote principal chief. At Okmulgee the conservatives accepted this decision, but they soon complained again of election fraud, and again Sands refused to recognize the constitution as Creek law. In June 1872 a special American commission held hearings on the controversy. The opposition party accused the government of having excluded qualified voters from the election count, and they complained of inappropriate use of national funds and misdirection in government and the constitution. The conservatives also complained that American recognition of the constitutional government prevented them from changing the new government and returning to the old form. American officials estimated that the conservative opposition held a slight majority over the Checote party, although many towns were split.[39]

Several leading members of the conservative party, including Sands himself, died in 1871 and 1872. The new principal chief of the conservative anticonstitutional government was Sands's assistant, Lochar Harjo of Nuyuka, the white town where the conservatives held their meetings. Acting on the advice of the American agent, the Checote government hardened its posture toward the conservative countergovernment in 1871–72 by passing a series of repressive laws against subversive anticonstitutional action—including restrictions on freedom of assembly and the right to bear arms, on the carrying of messages that were subversive to the constitution, and protection of the lives of officers of the government; the lighthorse police was strengthened. In late May 1873, American officials, anticipating an outbreak of factional hostilities, moved to support the constitutional government by stating that it would recognize only that government and would use whatever force was necessary to put down any resistance to the recognized government. The conservatives protested, but they did say that they would submit if the special commission decided that the constitutional government was the proper Creek government. And indeed, after the report of the special commission supported the constitutional government and recommended that the Creek conservatives accept it, the conservatives, in 1873, formally recognized the constitutional government, and all the towns except Wewocau, a white town and former Red Stick town in the war of 1813–14, sent elected delegates to the national legislature.[40]

Two years later, Lochar Harjo defeated Checote by a margin of two to one, but in late 1876 Harjo was impeached for failing to carry out the laws of the legislature and instead trying to repeal the permit law that allowed large landholders to hire American laborers and tenant farmers. Starting in the early 1870's, many Americans had come into Creek territory along with the railroad construction and were living in the trade centers that had grown up along the railroad lines. Here again, there were clear differences between the conservatives, who considered the American residents a threat to the continuity of their nation, and the large holders; it was the latter who led the impeachment proceedings in the Creek legislature, and some conservatives joined them.[41]

The second chief, Ward Coachman, served the remaining three years of Harjo's administration. Coachman was a member of Alabama Town, a religiously conservative town with a mixture of populace that was adopted into the Creek confederacy. The Coachman administration was occupied with threats of territorialization organized by the railroad interests, the problem of American intruders, regulation of labor, and discussions over revision of the constitution. In 1878, discussions over revising the constitution to reduce the number of members in the legislature failed owing to conservative opposition. The Creek government was also plagued by high debt and near bankruptcy, but no significant changes were made.[42]

The fundamentalists reacted sharply to Harjo's impeachment and the movement was revitalized. Harjo's supporters demanded an explanation for his impeachment and demanded his return to office. Harjo, in September 1877, even contemplated convening the national council and having himself reinstated as principal chief. Nothing came of this idea, but the fundamentalists led by Harjo did resume their old position of opposition to the constitutional government. The conservative opposition was now divided into two major groups: the old regional alliances of lower towns or southern Creek against the upper town or loyal Creek had become less salient as men from the upper towns began to side with the constitutional party, and some large holders and members of the lower towns now sided with the loyal Creek. The conservatives now had the Muskogee party, led by Ward Coachman, which consisted predominantly of Creek freedmen and conservatives who were willing to accept the constitutional government, and an ultraconservative fundamentalist party led by Lochar Harjo. In 1878 Harjo's party withdrew from national politics and organized its own government at Nuyuka. The fundamentalists retained nondifferentiated cultural world views, opposed economic inequality, and upheld a norm of sharing of material goods; they rejected the constitutional government and opposed allotments. They did not believe that Christianity or schools were suited to the Creek, and wished to return to the custom and social order of their forebears.[43]

In the election of 1879, Samuel Checote ran for principal chief under the auspices of the Constitutional or Progressive party and won in a close election over Ward Coachman, the candidate of the Muskogee party, and a third candidate running on the Loyal party ticket, the politically disaffected Isparhechar, from the white town of Cussetah. According to Checote, the major problems confronting the Creek were securing obedience to the constitutional law, meeting the need for stronger national political integration, paying the national debt, managing increasing numbers of American intruders, and effectively defending against American threats of territorialization and allotment of Creek territory. Measures were passed pertaining to American labor and tenant farmers, private contracts with railroad companies, and cattle grazing and cattle drives on the Creek domain. In 1882 a law was passed that withdrew the citizenship rights of intermarried Americans. After 1881, the American government was no longer seriously interested in restricting intruders in Indian Territory, and efforts to exclude intruders fell more heavily to the local governments.[44]

Along with these other problems, the Checote administration of 1879–83 had to deal with the fundamentalist Creek. The trouble began immediately after the election, when the Loyal party, led by Isparhechar, charged irregularities in the election procedures. The party attempted to prevent Checote from taking office; men took up arms on both sides and skirmishes occurred at various points throughout the nation. Sporadic conflict, called the Green Peach War, went on until 1883. Isparhechar had sided with the South at first in the American Civil War but later turned his alliance to the loyal Creek and became a leader among them. He was elected to the national council in 1867 but accepted a position as a judge, from which he was removed by impeachment. Embittered by his experience, he joined the fundamentalist party at Nuyuka and after the death of Lochar Harjo became the leader of the fundamentalists.[45] Isparhechar's leadership inspired the fundamentalists to pursue more actively the restoration of the old form of government by town chiefs and to topple the progressive or constitutional party from political leadership.

On several occasions between 1881 and 1883, American troops had to be sent to the Creek nation to restore and maintain order. The major conflicts came in 1882, when the fundamentalists declared their willingness to challenge the constitutional government with force, but the Checote administration, the party of the entrepreneurial large holders and American-educated Creek, was capable of mustering more men in the field than the fundamentalist party could command. After the American army intervened, Isparhechar's men were forced out of the nation into the Fox and Sac country and were eventually arrested. The Americans then opened negotiations to settle Creek political affairs. Isparhechar's men wanted political separation, which the American government would not grant, and after months of negotiation, and because of the urging of their spouses and kinsmen, the fundamentalists agreed to swear allegiance to the Creek constitution and returned to the Creek nation.[46]

Isparhechar ran for principal chief in the election of 1883 in a three-way contest with Checote of the Constitutional party and J. M. Perryman of the Muskogee party. Perryman, a member of the progressive Hitchiti white town of Okmulgee, won a plurality of the vote and was sworn in as principal chief. Isparhechar challenged the results, claiming that the election was not fair and that, according to the constitution, the principal chief was to be elected by a majority vote, not a plurality. He asked for new elections and managed to convene the national council and get himself appointed principal chief. Though the council was largely opposed

to Perryman, the American government reviewed the controversy and decided that Perryman had been duly elected and should be installed as
principal chief. John Perryman was a big landholder who had many tenant
farmers and grew cotton on a large scale. The second chief was Coweta
Micco, the chief of the major red town. Perryman's administration passed
legislation to exclude American intruders, to levy taxes on Texas cattlemen driving herds across Creek land, to regulate the export of coal, and
to resist further inroads by railroad companies.[47]

More controversy over election procedures arose in the next two elections, of 1887 and 1891. The winner in both elections was Legus C. Perryman, who was also from the progressive Hitchiti white town of Okmulgee.
L. C. Perryman was the candidate of the new Union party, which was
organized by a coalition of Checote and Isparhechar supporters after both
candidates lost the election of 1883 to the Muskogee party. Isparhechar,
who failed to get the nomination of the Union party for principal chief
in 1887, ran independently on the basis of his conservative support. The
freedmen rallied to the Union party, and their votes helped tip the elections of 1887 and 1891 in favor of the Union party candidate; Isparhechar
disputed both elections, but his protests did not lead to reconsideration of
the election results. L. C. Perryman identified several major issues during
his administration: revision of the constitution, payment of the national
debt, and prevention of enclosures on the public domain by American
cattlemen. In 1893 the Creek council put an end to election controversy
by reforming the rules in favor of election by plurality; it also reduced
the number on the national council from 166 to 94. The council also considered and debated legislation to remove American intruders, to regulate
American labor, and to prohibit tenant farming. A referendum to adopt a
new constitution in 1894 was not supported by the Creek electorate. The
Creek council also strongly opposed the efforts of the Dawes Commission
to allot the Creek public domain and liquidate the Creek government.[48]

Resistance to allotment and territorialization was a major issue in the
Creek election of 1895, following the Dawes Commission hearings. From
a field of six tickets, Isparhechar and Roley McIntosh of the white town
of Tuskegee were elected principal chief and second chief. (Perryman had
been impeached late in his second term for misuse of funds, and the impeachment proceedings disrupted the Union party coalition.) Isparhechar
and McIntosh ran on a nationalist platform of stronger resistance to allotment and liquidation of the Creek government, and the Isparhechar administration did what it could to stop all American efforts at allotment
and territorialization and to preserve Creek national independence and
government. As late as 1897, the Creek government refused to approve
allotment, but after the Curtis Act of 1898 decreed the allotment of land

and abolishment of the governments of Indian Territory, the Creek government had no choice but to comply.[49]

In a show of last-ditch opposition to the forced allotment of the Creek land and the abolishment of the Creek government, the fundamentalists set up a countergovernment. Isparhechar, ill and in despair after losing the battle for Creek independence, had retired to his farm and leadership of the fundamentalist Creek had passed to Chitto Harjo, often called Crazy Snake, who was a close confidant of Isparhechar. Between 1897 and 1901, the fundamentalists, called Snakes, formed a "snake" government or shadow government. Chitto Harjo was declared hereditary chief and the Snakes formed their underground government at Hickory Ground, the holy white town and daughter town of ancient Talisee. (Chitto Harjo was himself a member of the central white town of Abihka.) The Snakes stood by the fundamentalist conviction that the Creek should continue to adhere to the government form and the relationship with the American government that were outlined and guaranteed by the treaty of 1832. Thus the Snakes rejected the constitutional government and demanded of the American government that the Creek retain independent government status and common ownership of land as guaranteed to the Creek nation by treaty. They refused to recognize the American right to abolish Creek sovereignty and to allot the Creek domain into private sections.[50]

The elections of 1899 and 1903 were won by the progressive candidates, Pleasant Porter and Motey Tiger, against numerous tickets. Porter was a member of Okmulgee, Motey Tiger was a member of the once influential red town of Tuckabatchee. The Porter ticket campaigned on a platform of accommodation to the demands of the Curtis Act, and his administrations carried out the provisions of allotment and dismantling of the Creek government. The Snake candidate, Chitto Harjo, ran for principal chief in the 1903 election but received only half as many votes as Porter. The Snakes under Chitto Harjo still refused to obey the laws of the constitutional Creek government, and on several occasions between 1900 and 1909 American troops and marshals were called in to arrest Snake leaders, quell unrest, and repress their meetings. The Snakes adopted the tactics of passive resistance and collected funds to hire lawyers to pursue their cause and interests in Washington. Many Snakes refused to have anything to do with the allotment, and allotment officials often assigned less desirable arable land to the Snakes, who refused to stake out claims and denied the legitimacy of the entire process of allotment. Several years after formal dissolution of the Creek government in 1907, Chitto Harjo was wounded in a skirmish with U.S. marshals who were attempting to break up a Snake meeting, and he later died of his wounds. After his death, the Snake movement faded away.[51]

The Creek government continued after 1907 largely as a financial corporation to manage the remainder of the Creek estate after allotment and sale of what was left to American settlers. The principal chief was appointed by the American President, although in the middle 1930's the Creek organized a government subject to the regulation of the Bureau of Indian Affairs and the Indian Reorganization Act of 1934. Many Creek villages survived both politically and ceremonially and were again the primary political units of the reorganized Creek government.

The Creek constitutional polity was the least differentiated and the least politically integrated of the four transplanted southeastern nations, and the Creek polity was the least stable in the post–Civil War period. The locally autonomous kin-based and religiously integrated villages remained the primary political units within the Creek government and represented the continued nondifferentiation of polity and society. Furthermore, the political leadership of both the constitutional parties and the opposition was dominated by men from white towns, which indicates a continuity of nondifferentiation of symbolic order and political organization. There were significant periods during which there was little agreement between major social and political groupings over the legitimate rules of organization of the government. Throughout the period, the ancient regional cleavages between the upper and lower towns continued to exist—the upper white towns of Abihka, Nuyuka, Oakfuskie, Hickory Ground, and Wewocau being the centers of fundamentalist opposition to political and social change. For significant periods, the loyal or predominantly upper town Creek did not accept the legitimacy of the constitutional government, did not participate willingly in the government, and established a separate government based on the less internally and externally differentiated political structure of the ancient Creek council. The lower towns and the entrepreneurial large holders favored the constitutional government and were willing to use repressive measures and force to maintain its prerogatives. That the Creek constitutional government was not modified significantly over the 1867–1907 period was due in large measure to an alliance between the constitutional party and the Americans against the efforts of the fundamentalists to return to more traditional Creek political forms. The Creek political parties were struggling for political power, but they were also struggling over a definition of the basic rules of political organization. The need for repressive measures and the use of force to defend the constitutional government indicated the absence of political consensus and normative institutionalization of the constitutional government among the fundamentalist opposition.

Comparative Political Stability

There is no doubt that the Creek polity was the least politically integrated and the least differentiated of the four transplanted southeastern nations, and it showed the least normative institutionalization of a constitutional government. Only the use of force by the Creek and American governments kept the Creek conservatives from abolishing the constitutional government and reestablishing the less differentiated Creek polity of village delegations and rules of succession. A combination of overlapping conditions inhibited the institutionalization of the Creek constitutional government. Far more than the other societies, the Creek were politically divided into antagonistic regional, class, and symbolic loyalties. The Choctaw, the Chickasaw, and the Cherokee also had regional loyalties, but in Creek society, because the lower towns contained the preponderance of large holders, class and region overlapped more strongly than in the other cases. Both the Cherokee and the Chickasaw formed nationalistic orientations before the Civil War, and regional cleavages were not major issues in the normative institutionalization of their constitutional governments in the post–Civil War period. Regional loyalties were more important among the Choctaw, whose constitution incorporated the three district chiefs as traditional symbols of political unity; but though the conservative Choctaws were opposed to a centralized political administration, their attempts to abolish the district symbolism of the Choctaw government failed. The post–Civil War Choctaw government, like those of the Chickasaw and the Cherokee, had the support of more nationally unified polities than those of the Creek government; the Creek government's instability was largely the result of the tenuousness of its support in a society in which local and regional loyalties were stronger than national loyalties.

The political organization and interests of the conservatives in the four nations also differed significantly. The Creek fundamentalists saw the differentiated polity as an illegitimate political form, and although the Creek adopted a formal constitution in 1867, the conservatives would not agree to a government that eliminated the kin-based and religiously integrated and particularistic villages from a primary role in the Creek polity. The symbolic order of red and white towns continued to be relevant informally in political affairs, as the white towns gained political supremacy in the post–Civil War period, and the fundamentalist movement among the Creek centered among the traditional leading white villages of the Creek upper towns. Thus the Creek polity was not differentiated from social organization and symbolic order. The fundamentalist Creek organized themselves and their underground governments according to the

ancient Creek political order, and one of their main objectives was to restore the old political order, especially the old rules of political election
and succession.

Among the Cherokee and the Chickasaw, the conservatives were well
organized into political parties that were able to control the government
apparatus through the electoral process for fairly long periods. The Cherokee and Chickasaw polities were more differentiated than the Creek polity,
because the Cherokee and Chickasaw constitutional governments made
no formal concessions to local villages as primary political units and differentiated polity and society from the village organizations by creating
political as well as administrative districts. The Creek had created administrative and court districts, but they retained the political primacy
and autonomy of the towns. In the more differentiated Chickasaw and
Cherokee polities, the well-organized conservative parties accepted and
participated in the constitutional government and did not challenge the
legitimacy of the constitutional government; the reestablishment of the old
political order was not a significant issue for them. The Chickasaw conservatives abandoned the struggle for continuity of the old political order
in the nationalistic compromises that led to national unification and independence in the late 1840's and early 1850's; when they mobilized into a
political party in the early 1870's, it was for the purpose not of changing the
government per se but of trying to influence its direction when they saw it
going against nationalist interests. The Cherokee conservatives, organized
by the Keetoowah Society, were politically prominent until the late 1880's
and were well integrated into the Cherokee polity until the 1890's, when
the forced dissolution of the Cherokee government ended the nationally
protective role of the constitutional government. Thus in the differentiated
and nationally unified Chickasaw and Cherokee polities, the conservatives
did not challenge the legitimacy of the constitutional government, but accepted and participated in the governments, while most political conflict
focused on struggles for political power between the primary class and
overlapping cultural cleavages.

The Choctaw conservatives were less well organized and less politically
effective than the Cherokee and Chickasaw conservative parties, mainly
because of the strength of regional and local allegiances. When the conservatives did organize, in the late 1880's, it was in response to American
threats to national survival. The conservative Choctaws did not challenge
the legitimacy of the constitutional government or advocate a return to the
ancient political form but sought political power on an equal basis with
the progressive element; in this, the struggle for power resembled similar
class and cultural cleavages among the Cherokee and the Choctaw.

The Creeks' difficulties in normatively institutionalizing their constitutional government were the result of the Creek conservatives' defense of cultural-normative codes of nondifferentiated political order and particularistic identifications with towns, regions, and symbolic political order. Yet the Creek conservatives were hardly different from the Choctaw, Cherokee, and Chickasaw conservatives in their strong nationalism, their subsistence-oriented economic behavior, and their continuing respect for the old normative order and nondifferentiated world views. The Creek, the Choctaw, and the Chickasaw all continued to adhere to the old kin-based norm of voluntary surrender for punishment for crimes, even if it meant execution, and the world view of the conservatives of all four nations was traditionalistic.

Where the Creek fundamentalists differed from the Cherokee, Choctaw, and Chickasaw conservatives was in the forms of differentiation that were incorporated into the Creek cultural and normative codes. The Creek fundamentalists continued to adhere to nondifferentiated codes of political order, where red and white symbolic order determined the organization of the polity and where the religiously integrated and kin-based towns were the primary political units. The Creek constitution did not abolish these political forms, and the nondifferentiated political order continued to shape the political action of the fundamentalist Creek, if not most Creek. Because the nondifferentiated political order was embedded within the Creek constitution, the Creek conservatives had an alternate model for political organization when they became dissatisfied with the elections and procedures of the constitutional government. Any attempts at the further differentiation of the Creek polity would have challenged the fundamental institutional order of Creek society, in which villages were culturally and politically autonomous and symbolic order defined political hierarchies and relationships. Despite the formal differentiation of polity and symbolic order in the constitutional government, the Creek continued to look to men of the leading white villages for political leadership, while the red towns faded into secondary political importance. In the post–Civil War period, none of the Cherokee, Choctaw, or Chickasaw conservative political parties collectively adhered to normative codes that determined social and political order according to religious or symbolic order. Only the Creek conservatives did that. Nor did the Cherokee, Choctaw, and Chickasaw conservatives challenge their constitutional governments with proposals and political action aimed at restoring a less differentiated political order. The nondifferentiation of polity from symbolic order, and of polity from society, and the continuity of regional and local political cleavages inhibited the formation and normative institutionalization of a differentiated Creek constitutional government.

8 THE FORMATION AND INSTITUTIONALIZATION OF DIFFERENTIATED CONSTITUTIONAL GOVERNMENTS

THE PRECEDING HISTORICAL narrative analyzed the conditions for the formation and institutionalization of constitutional governments among the Cherokee, Choctaw, Chickasaw, and Creek. The analysis considered a variety of conditions and arguments, such as incorporation into the world-system, geopolitical context, culture, differentiation, and social and political solidarity. Now we are in a position to evaluate the relative contributions of the various arguments to an explanation of the formation and stability of a differentiated polity.

The Conditions: Similarities and Differences

GEOPOLITICAL ENVIRONMENTS

The history of the four southeastern nations suggests that a competitive geopolitical environment is not decisive in determining the formation or institutionalization of a differentiated polity. Significant centralization or increased differentiation in the political orders of the four societies did not occur in the eighteenth century. The major change during this period of geopolitical competition was the increased secularization of political institutions, which meant the exclusion of priests and ritual from national political decision making.

The formation of constitutional governments came not during the periods of competitive political relations but during the period of American political hegemony. Nevertheless, hegemonic political relations were not decisive in determining the formation of the differentiated polities, since the Cherokee formed a differentiated polity, while during the same period the Choctaw failed to establish a centralized and differentiated polity, and there was little political change among the Creek and the Chickasaw. Furthermore, the Creek, Choctaw, and Chickasaw formed differentiated polities under conditions of less intense American political and territorial pressure in the postremoval period. Nor does the hegemonic argument help explain the variation in normative institutionalization of the differentiated polities. The intense pressures of the removal period were a major condition in the formation of the Cherokee constitutional government, but under similar conditions the other nations did not follow the same path as the Cherokee. This fact suggests that other variables and conditions are necessary to explain the variation in political change among the four cases.

WORLD-SYSTEM INCORPORATION

All four nations were incorporated into the world-system through a similar sequence of markets and economic conditions. The southeastern nations were subject to a sequence of incorporation into the fur trade and southern plantation export economy, and in the post–Civil War period they were incorporated into a more diversified agricultural, cattle, and mineral export economy. Certainly, trans-societal markets strongly interpenetrated and influenced the economic, social, and political relations of the four nations. Starting with the early fur trade, the households of the four nations became dependent on a variety of imported manufactured goods, which in time superseded and destroyed the traditional crafts. The strategies of balance of power and alliances with European colonial powers during the fur trade and competitive periods in the eighteenth century were largely dictated by the dependency on European trade goods. Furthermore, the intense removal pressures in the first decades of the nineteenth century were to a large extent dictated by the rise in the price of cotton and the desire of Americans to exploit the interior lands for the production and export of cotton. In the second half of the nineteenth century, increased commercialization and a deepening of the export economy in Indian Territory contributed to the further economic incorporation of Indian Territory into the American national economy and spurred the efforts of railroad and mining corporations to extinguish Indian title and political independence in Indian Territory. This economic incorporation into wider and more diversified markets contributed to the ultimate dissolution of the constitutional governments in Indian Territory. World-system economic incorporation did not, however, determine the variation in rate of formation or stability of the differentiated polities. All four nations experienced similar sequences of market incorporation, but nevertheless there was considerable variation in the timing of formation and in the stability of the constitutional governments.

A major influence on political change deriving from incorporation into the world-system was the formation of class structures associated with the cotton market. For all four societies, the pattern was the same: during the fur trade period of the eighteenth century, economic classes did not arise, although the fur trade led to the increased commercialization of goods and labor and increased specialization of labor, most hunters remained subsistence oriented. The rise of an entrepreneurial planter class was associated with the interpenetration of entrepreneurial and acquisitive values among the offspring of the European traders who lived and married among the southeastern nations. When the price of cotton rose after the War of 1812, the trading families moved into cotton production, large-scale farming, and cattle raising. But still the large majority of southeasterners continued to adhere to nondifferentiated world views and continued to exhibit subsistence economic orientations despite the availability of lucrative export markets and large surpluses of fertile land. Since the pattern of economic class stratification was the same for all four societies, the process of economic stratification cannot explain the variation in political change.

In all four cases, members of the entrepreneurial class were the major carriers of differentiated models of political order. That this occurred was not a predetermined outcome of world-system relations. The fact that the entrepreneurs, when maneuvering against the old regime, adopted the differentiated American model derives from the context of American cultural and political hegemony. The southeastern planters were educated in American institutions; they were influenced by American missionaries, and they were pressured by the American government to adopt constitutional governments modeled after the American national government. In other societies, an agricultural entrepreneurial class would not necessarily be expected to advocate an American model of differentiated political order. In other societies, everything else being equal, it would be more difficult to establish a differentiated polity, because the dominant class might favor less differentiated or more coercive models of political order. In our case, the American government supported the political efforts and political changes of the planter class with political and military resources whenever planters moved to adopt a differentiated polity.

Nevertheless, the presence of an acquisitive entrepreneurial class as carriers of models of differentiated political order was not central in determining the timing of the formation or institutionalization of the differentiated constitutional governments. The Cherokee planters were successful in mobilizing support for the centralization, unification, and differentiation of a constitutional government during the removal period; the Choctaw attempted a similar plan, but failed owing to regional and local political loyalties and organization. During the removal period, the planters among the Creek and Chickasaw did not attempt to institute major changes in political differentiation because conservative resistance to such efforts was so strong as to make failure certain; the planters did, however, manage to influence their governments to pass legislation that regulated markets and promoted economic accumulation, despite the continuity of the nondifferentiated political structures. Among the Creek, Chickasaw, and Choctaw, only when the planters received American political support that led to the abolishment of the old political regime did they move to institute differentiated polities. In none of the four nations was the planter class strong enough to force change on the conservative majority; the planters either had to mobilize a national political consensus, as in the Cherokee case, or else had to exploit the American-planter alliance and secure the abolishment of the old political order.

The combination of geopolitical, world-system, and class arguments helps to explain the forces that destroyed the old political orders among the Chickasaw, Creek, and Choctaw, but it does not help to explain the largely consensual political institution building of the Cherokee, nor does it explain the process by which the differentiated constitutional governments were accepted or institutionalized by the majority of conservatives among the Chickasaw, the Cherokee, and the Choctaw.

POLITICAL CULTURE

In the early 1700's, at the time of significant European contact, the four southeastern nations had similar democratic and egalitarian political cultures. There were no coercive political hierarchies nor was there political domination by a class or status group. Political decision making in the national councils required unanimous consensus. Negotiation and compromise continued until a decision was agreed upon; otherwise there was no nationally binding decision. Men gained political influence by means of personal charisma, age, service to the nation, and oratory abilities.

Thus in the eighteenth century the southeastern nations already had a form of democratic political organization, although institutional relations between polity, society, and/or culture were largely nondifferentiated. The ethnographic evidence from the southeastern societies suggests that democratic political cultures can be institutionalized under a variety of levels of differentiation of the polity, although what is now considered a modern democracy requires significant internal and external differentiation of the polity, where a bill of rights and separation of powers are designed to protect individual liberties. The early southeastern democratic forms were not necessarily designed to protect private property or individual freedom in the Western sense, but were more directed toward not infringing upon individual autonomy and the right to participate in consensual decision making. Normative and religious sanctions were the primary deterrents against breaking the law. The principles of egalitarian and noncoercive political authority relations continued in all four nations until formal political dissolution. The form of democratic culture was modified by the adoption of new rules and procedures such as majority rule decision making, court procedures, and bills of rights that accompanied the internal differentiation of the southeastern polities.

It cannot be said, then, that the democratic and egalitarian political cultures of the southeastern nations were major obstacles to the formation and institutionalization of democratic governments. In societies in which political culture is hierarchical and coercive, for instance in feudal societies, it would be expected that the incongruity of nondemocratic political culture would present obstacles in the way of the formation and institutionalization of a democratic government. Since the four southeastern nations had similar democratic political cultures, the variation in the rate of formation and institutionalization of differentiated democratic polities cannot be attributed to variation in the form of democratic political culture. Egalitarian and consensual norms of political action in the southeastern nations were favorable conditions for the formation of differentiated democratic polities, but an argument based on the presence of democratic political culture cannot explain the variation in political change among the cases.

TRADITIONALISTIC WORLD VIEWS AND VALUES

Most members of the four nations adhered to nondifferentiated world views. The conservative members in all four nations adhered to a belief in the efficacy of magic, ceremonies, and incantations that could cure or cause harm, and believed that breaking ceremonial rules could cause bad luck or harm. These world views largely determined the subsistence economic orientation of most conservatives and also their emphasis on institutional fundamentalism, for it was the ancient prescriptive belief in the southeastern religions that breaking the sacred laws and norms would lead to this-worldly retribution. Since the conservatives in all four nations exhibited traditionalistic labor and institutional orientations, the presence of traditionalistic orientations is not sufficient to explain the variation in political change, or such characteristics as the Cherokee's willingness to adopt political innovations and the institutional fundamentalism of the

Creek. The Creek and the Cherokee held similar traditionalistic orientations toward the universe, toward their institutional order, and toward
economic accumulation. Neither society was more traditionalistic than
the other.

To explain the variation in political change and institutionalization, a
more compelling argument has to examine the cultural codes and normative orders prescribed by the different southeastern traditions. In particular, to what extent do the cultural orders specify relations of differentiation
and nondifferentiation between the political sphere and the other major
institutions in society: culture, normative order, and economy? The significant point here is not that the Cherokee conservatives were less traditionalistic than the Creek conservatives, but rather that the Cherokee cultural
and normative order specified more highly differentiated relations between
polity and religion, between polity and institutions of social and political
integration, and between polity and kinship. The Cherokee conservatives
were traditionalistic, and they attempted to preserve an institutional order
that was far more differentiated than the Creek institutional order—that
is, the Cherokee conservatives were traditionalistic toward and defended a
relatively differentiated and socially and symbolically integrated political
order, whereas the Creek conservatives defended a socially and politically
segmentary political order that was tightly nondifferentiated from religion
and symbolic order. Both groups of conservatives defended their institutional orders, but the Cherokee society, with its institutions of national
social integration and externally differentiated polity, had fewer institutional obstacles in the way of accepting a more differentiated polity.

Similarly, the Chickasaw conservatives adhered to and defended a
polity that was relatively unified socially and politically and was not significantly differentiated either from the institutions of social and political
integration or from religion and kinship. Choctaw conservatives defended
a polity that was divided into three autonomous political regions and was
not differentiated from local kinship relations. Consequently, the mere
presence of traditionalistic cultural orientations explains little. A more
effective understanding of social and political change must examine the
norms of social and political integration and the rules of differentiation
and nondifferentiation that govern the relations between the major institutions in the society. Having a traditionalistic cultural orientation does
not necessarily imply resistance to change, since some traditions that have
cultural-normative codes of a more socially integrated and differentiated
political order will have greater tolerance and capability to accept change
than less differentiated and segmentary societies. The traditionalistic argument is more effective for understanding the social action of conservatives
and institutional change in societies where the cultural-normative order

specifies less differentiated and segmentary social and political orders, which have fewer possibilities for consensual institutional change.

SOCIAL AND POLITICAL SOLIDARITY

The Cherokee, with their ceremonially unified seven national clans, had the most nationally integrated institutions, which were differentiated from national political relations that were not dependent on kinship. Nevertheless, the social and symbolic integration of Cherokee society did not translate into political unity: villages and regions continued to demand stronger loyalties than the national polity. The political unification of the Cherokee nation occurred in 1809 and was a response to American threats to territory and national survival. Thus, although the ceremonially integrated clan system helped legitimate the new national political consensus, the Cherokee political nationality was not formed on the old cultural and normative principles but rather was legitimated by the new requirements of national defense and preservation. Cherokee national political unification preceded the major developments in centralization of legitimate use of force and further internal differentiation of the Cherokee polity. Since the Cherokee polity by 1810 already showed differentiation of kinship and polity and was differentiated from religious and cultural prerogatives, the Cherokee planters, who advocated the new model of political differentiation, did not have to break down major structures of a nondifferentiated polity before proposing further changes in political organization. A national political consensus that was mobilized to preserve political autonomy and territory, combined with an externally differentiated polity, allowed the Cherokee to adopt a differentiated constitutional government with relatively little use of force and coercion.

The Chickasaw, like the Cherokee and unlike the Creek and Choctaw, had a tradition of a nationally integrated ceremonial and kinship order. The two societies with the most centralized and extensive forms of national social-cultural integration—the Cherokee and the Chickasaw—were the first to form secular political nationalities. In the Chickasaw case, however, the institutions of national cultural-kinship integration were not differentiated from the polity, and before the 1840's, the Chickasaw were highly resistant to political change and did not form a secular political nationality. The formation of a Chickasaw secular political nationality that was differentiated from the old nondifferentiated polity emerged during the 1840's under American and planter pressure to abandon the old political order combined with the mobilization of the Chickasaw conservatives to regain national political independence. That the formation of national political unification among the Chickasaw was slower and required more coercion than in the Cherokee case was a consequence of the institutional obstacles inherent in Chickasaw society owing to the nondifferentiation of culture, polity, and kinship.

The formation of the Chickasaw constitution was directly related to the formation of a national political consensus that was mobilized to ensure national independence and survival. In the middle 1840's the conservative Chickasaw abandoned the old kin-based political system and elected to pursue national independence from the Choctaw. The new nationalist consensus was formed when the conservatives agreed to accept a constitutional form of government and the planters agreed to abandon assimilation into Choctaw society and united with the nationalist conservatives to pursue national independence under a constitutional government. The lateness of the formation of the Chickasaw constitutional government compared with the Cherokee can be explained by the resistance of the conservatives, who wanted to preserve the kin-based political system and refused to accept significant internal or external differentiation of political relations before the middle 1840's. The strength of the alliance of Chickasaw planters and American officials, who actively opposed the reconstitution and recognition of the old kin-based government, convinced the conservatives that the traditional government was no longer possible under American hegemonic conditions.

Among the Choctaw, on the other hand, the adoption of a constitutional government preceded the formation of national political unification. Choctaw attempts to form a centralized government during the period of removal pressures failed owing to regional loyalties and autonomous regional political organizations, and when a constitutional government was adopted under American influence and coercion in 1834, the Choctaw refused to accept an administratively centralized government and retained the three traditionally independent political districts. Despite the incremental internal and external differentiation of the Choctaw government after 1834, the three regional districts remained virtually independent for almost a quarter of a century, until an alliance between American officials and Choctaw planters forced the conservative Choctaw majority to accept a compromise constitution in 1860 that symbolically integrated the district chiefs into a centralized and differentiated constitutional government. With the aid of legitimation by way of traditional political symbols, the centralized Choctaw constitutional government achieved relative political stability. The Choctaw case exhibits a different path to a stable constitutional government from that of the Cherokee and Chickasaw, where national unification preceded or was concomitant with the formation of a differentiated constitutional government. Among the Choctaw coercion was used to establish the centralized constitutional government, and, after strong resistance, traditional political symbols were manipulated to legitimate and institutionalize the new political order.

Creek society was divided into symbolically legitimated regional cleavages that inhibited national unification. Not only did the Creek form a constitutional government last, but also the government proved more institutionally unstable than the other three constitutional governments. The evidence on national unification indicates that, although national unification need not necessarily precede the formation of a differentiated constitutional government, the use of coercion is more likely where there is still an absence of national loyalties and consensus over the form of government. If differentiated governments that are imposed on societies without national political unity and loyalties choose not to use regional or traditional symbols to legitimate the new government, they are obliged to quell regional dissidence with force and coercion in order to retain their political power. The southeastern societies that formed movements of national unification used less coercion, were more willing to accept change, and had more normatively stable differentiated constitutional governments than the societies that had not formed a unified secular political nationality.

DIFFERENTIATION OF THE POLITY

By the early 1800's the Cherokee had the most externally differentiated polity—differentiated from religion, kinship, and the institutions of social and symbolic integration. After the secular national political unification of 1809, the Cherokee exhibited the earliest adoption of a differentiated constitutional polity and achieved the new political form with the least amount of direct coercion. The "Ghost Dance" and White Path Rebellion fundamentalist movements against proposed political changes either failed or were incorporated into the new political order. In the Cherokee case, by 1800, there were no major external nondifferentiations of the political order that provided institutional obstacles to the consideration of further differentiation and centralization of the polity. The nationalist movement of 1809 united and mobilized the Cherokee in an effort to preserve their nationality. Thereafter, the major institutional issues were centralization of coercive force in the government and further internal differentiation of the polity, these were achieved under the leadership of the planters but with the consent and consensus of the conservative Cherokee majority.

With the combined conditions of national political unification and an externally differentiated polity, the Cherokee formed a normatively stable differentiated constitutional government. Although Cherokee society was not devoid of political conflict, the major political struggles were determined by overlapping class and cultural cleavages, where conservative subsistence landholders effectively challenged the entrepreneurial large landholders. The major political conflicts were over political power and control of the constitutional government, and not over differences in the form or organization of the government. At times the intensity of internal Cherokee political conflict threatened to disrupt the political order, but the contenders did not challenge the legitimacy of the differentiated constitutional form of government.

In the Creek, Choctaw, and Chickasaw societies, in which political institutions were less externally differentiated than in Cherokee society, differentiated constitutional governments were formed at a much slower rate, with greater fundamentalist resistance, and with more direct coercion. Moreover, these societies formed their constitutional governments in the postremoval period, under pressures from allied planters and American officials. Planters and American officials used coercive measures to abolish the kin-based Chickasaw political institutions. Among the Choctaw, American officials and support were instrumental in the formation of the 1834 constitutional government and the formation of the centralized government of 1860. In the Choctaw case the nondifferentiation of kin and polity came about gradually through incremental changes, and the conflict over the formation of a centralized government in 1860 was instigated by conservative regionalist opposition to the centralizing plans of the planters and their American supporters. Among the Creek, large landholders supported by the change-oriented policies of the American government formed a constitutional government, but the defenders of the Creek constitutional government resorted to repressive and coercive measures to maintain an unstable political order. The nondifferentiated political orders presented major obstacles to political change, and among the Creek, the Chickasaw, and to a lesser extent the Choctaw, repressive and coercive means were used by the primary carriers of differentiated political models in order to abolish the nondifferentiated political forms. The societies with externally nondifferentiated political orders had fewer prospects for consensual political change than did the societies with an externally differentiated polity.

In terms of stability, the Cherokee, Choctaw, and Chickasaw achieved stable differentiated political orders after most members of the societies accepted or were reconciled to the norms of an externally and internally differentiated polity. By 1800, the Cherokee conservatives adhered to the norms of an externally differentiated polity, and after the nationalist unification of 1809, the Cherokee conservatives were well organized, active participants, and the dominant political group in Cherokee political affairs until the late 1880's. The Chickasaw conservative majority strongly adhered to the rules of the old nondifferentiated kin-based political institutions until American and planter efforts at change, and the threat of lost nationality, led to national political unification and the adoption of a differentiated polity in the late 1840's and 1850's. After the movement of national political unification and political differentiation, the Chickasaw conservatives no longer insisted on retaining the old political form and accepted a constitutional government as a necessary institution to preserve and maintain national political independence. In the Choctaw case, the external differentiation of the polity preceded the formation of an administratively centralized government. By the late 1830's and early 1840's the Choctaw, in an already secular national government, accepted changes that differentiated polity from kinship. The stability of the centralized government of 1860 required the inclusion of traditional regional symbolism in order to quiet fundamentalist regional opposition to centralization, but with the continuation of the symbolic and integrative offices of the three district chiefs, the Choctaw conservatives accepted and actively participated in the centralized and differentiated polity.

The Creek had the most unstable constitutional government, which was contested by the Creek conservatives, who continued to uphold cultural-normative codes of nondifferentiated religious and symbolic political order. The Creek constitutional government retained the religiously particularistic and kin-based villages as the primary political unit, while most Creek continued to adhere to the symbolically determined political order divided into red and white towns. The fundamentalist Creek continued to adhere to norms that included the nondifferentiation of symbolic and political order and the culturally legitimated autonomy of the village governments.

In their postconstitutional period, the Creek conservatives alone among the four nations continued to adhere to and actively pursue the restoration of a nondifferentiated political order. They struggled over election procedures, formed alternative nondifferentiated governments, at times refused to acknowledge and participate in the constitutional government, and actively sought to restore the old form of government. In the late 1860's and 1870's, they were strong enough, for a time, to overthrow the constitutional government, but they did not in the end succeed in changing it. Although Creek political instability, or absence of normative institutionalization, might also be attributed to Creek regional cleavages, which overlapped with class cleavages, such an argument does not entirely explain the active conservative orientation toward restoration of the old political order. The absence of a unified political nationality among the Creek did contribute to the difficulties of institutionalization of a differentiated constitutional government; but the continuity of norms of non-differentiated political order among the conservatives helps explain the active opposition to the formation of a highly differentiated polity and the absence of normative consensus over the organization of the government. Creek society showed the least amount of national political integration, and the continuity of adherence to a nondifferentiated form of political order by regional conservatives resulted in the most normatively unstable constitutional government, the most frequent use of coercion to protect the constitutional government, and the least differentiated constitutional polity.

Conclusions

The formation, stability, and variation in the four constitutional governments resulted from several different conditions. American cultural and political hegemony, incorporation into the cotton market, the rise of a class structure with change-oriented agrarian entrepreneurs, and the presence of democratic political culture all played some part, but they acted more or less equally in the history of the four cases and therefore cannot be considered effective causal conditions. This is not to say that the controlled conditions are not important. The path of political change in the southeastern nations would certainly have been different if they had not been incorporated into the southern cotton market. In the north, for example, where there was no cotton market, societies like the Iroquois and Delaware did not form agricultural entrepreneurial classes or stable differentiated polities. In other historical contexts and geographical locations, societies that were incorporated into different world-system economic relations and different geopolitical environments, which had different forms of political culture, and had conservative-oriented dominant class structures have usually taken paths of political change significantly different from those that we observe in the history of the four southeastern nations. Since all four nations were subject to American cultural and political hegemony, were incorporated into a similar sequence of world-system market relations, had democratic and negotiated political cultures, and became class stratified, we can consider these conditions necessary for the formation of differentiated polities. Nevertheless, even when taken collectively, these conditions are not sufficient to explain the variation in the rate of change, the extent to which coercion was used in the process of institutionalization, the depth of the institutional changes, and the stability of the new political forms.

Given the presence of the several controlled conditions, the most powerful conditions for explaining the variation in political change were the formation of a unified political nationality and an externally differentiated political order. By 1810 the Cherokee had an externally differentiated polity and had formed a political nationality. The Cherokee were the earliest to form a stable differentiated constitutional government, and the Cherokee government was formed with the least amount of direct coercion. Political change in the less differentiated and less politically unified societies was significantly slower and involved coercive action to destroy the old political orders. The Creek configuration of local and regional political loyalties and nondifferentiated religious, symbolic, and political order proved the most resistant to change; it created the most conflict over the normative institutionalization of a differentiated polity, involved the most use of coercion, and resulted in the least differentiated constitutional government. All else being equal, the external differentiation of the polity and the level of national political integration were the most central conditions accounting for the variation in the formation and stability of the differentiated constitutional governments. The politically unified societies with externally differentiated polities more quickly and more consensually accepted and institutionalized differentiated constitutional governments. The societies that had no national commitments or national political loyalties and in which polities were less differentiated externally required coercive measures to break down the nondifferentiated political order and showed greater difficulties in reaching agreement on institutionalizing a differentiated polity. The histories of the southeastern nations indicate that two primary conditions for consensually institutionalizing a differentiated constitutional government are the formation of nationalistic political orientations—the mobilization for national political survival within the context of a hostile geopolitical environment and competitive world-system—and an externally differentiated polity.

The process of constitution formation is one of building an internally and externally differentiated polity—party formation, separation of powers, specialized rules of political procedure, and centralization of legitimate force. National political loyalties and mobilization combined with an externally differentiated polity provided southeastern constitution-building groups with greater opportunities for mobilizing consensus and fewer institutional obstacles to change than were found in the less socially and politically integrated and less externally differentiated societies. Constitution-building groups in less differentiated and less solidary groups either failed to form constitutional polities, or, if powerful enough, resorted to coercion.

Through the process of historical events, social-political solidarity and societal differentiation are negotiable and changeable. In more linearly positivistic terms, because our dependent variable—differentiation of the polity—is an institution, it also acts as an independent variable. In positivistic terms this may seem like a tautology, but institutional orders are not merely outcomes but are part of the ongoing interaction that makes the stuff of historical process and social change. The institutional order of societal differentiation and solidarity can act as a constraint or facilitator to change, and therefore as a causal argument, but the institutional order itself is an object of change and is acted upon by contending groups and actors. New forms of political solidarity and new configurations of societal differentiation emerge from less solidary and less differentiated configurations. The narratives of the middle chapters of this book have traced out that historical process of change in solidarity and societal differentiation for the Cherokee, Choctaw, Chickasaw, and Creek during the nineteenth century. None of the southeastern nations began with political institutions that closely resembled a differentiated constitutional government. The formation of the southeastern constitutional governments reflect both consensual and coercive modes of change.

What I have tried to explain is not merely the rise of the southeastern constitutional governments, but more specifically the differences and variation in their paths of change. Although many factors—class structure, geopolitical relations, market incorporation, culture and institutional order, as well as group actions—play necessary roles in the processes of change, in this study the latter conditions were controlled, so that we could isolate some central conditions for understanding variation in patterns of change. The different paths to constitutional polities among the southeastern nations in terms of degree of differentiation of the polity, rate of formation, stability, and relative use of coercion are most simply explained by variations in the combined relations of societal differentiation and the degree and form of social-political integration.

NOTES

NOTES

The following abbreviations are used in the Notes:

ABCFM American Board of Commissioners for Foreign Missions Papers, Houghton Library, Harvard University.

CHN Cherokee National Records, Oklahoma Historical Society, Oklahoma City. Microfilm.

CKN Chickasaw National Records, Indian Archives Division, Oklahoma Historical Society, Oklahoma City. Microfilm.

CRN Creek National Records, Oklahoma Historical Society, Oklahoma City. Microfilm.

CTN Choctaw National Records, Oklahoma Historical Society, Oklahoma City. Microfilm.

IPH Indian-Pioneer History Collection, Grant Foreman Collection, Oklahoma Historical Society, Oklahoma City.

M208 Records of the Cherokee Indian Agency in Tennessee, 1801–1835. U.S. National Archives, Washington, D.C. Microfilm.

M234 Bureau of Indian Affairs, Record Group 75, Letters Received by the Office of Indian Affairs, 1824–1881. U.S. National Archives, Washington, D.C. Microfilm.

M271 Letters Received by the Office of the Secretary of War Relating to Indian Affairs, 1800–1823. U.S. National Archives, Washington, D.C. Microfilm.

CHAPTER I

1. Alexis de Tocqueville, *Democracy in America*, 2 (New York: Vintage, 1945), pp. 304–52.

2. Talcott Parsons, *The Structure of Social Action* (New York: Free Press, 1968); Jeffrey Alexander, *Theoretical Logic in Sociology*, 4 vols. (Berkeley: University of California Press, 1983).

3. Talcott Parsons, *The Evolution of Societies* (Englewood Cliffs, N.J.: Prentice-Hall, 1977); Niklas Luhman, *The Differentiation of Society* (New York: Columbia University Press, 1982), pp. 70–88; S. N. Eisenstadt, *Tradition, Change, and Modernity* (New York: Wiley, 1973), p. 47.

4. Paul Colomy, "Revisions and Progress in Differentiation Theory," in *Differentiation Theory and Social Change: Comparative and Historical Perspectives*, ed. Jeffrey C. Alexander and Paul Colomy (New York: Columbia University Press, 1989), ch. 15; Bertrand Badie and Pierre Birnbaum, *The Sociology of the State* (Chicago: University of Chicago Press, 1983), pp. 53, 59; Paul Colomy, "Uneven Structural Differentiation: Toward a Comparative Approach," in *Neofunctionalism*, ed. Jeffrey C. Alexander (Beverly Hills, Calif.: Sage, 1985), p. 131; Jeffrey C. Alexander, *Action and Its Environments: Toward a New Synthesis* (New York: Columbia University Press, 1988), pp. 49–77.

5. The trend toward historical specificity and group conflict in the analysis of differentiation and institutionalization is seen in recent work. See in particular: Neil J. Smelser, *Social Change in the Industrial Revolution* (Chicago: University of Chicago Press, 1959); the articles by Smelser, Richard Munch, Colomy, and Frank Lechner in Alexander, ed., *Neofunctionalism*; also Jack A. Goldstone, "Cultural Orthodoxy, Risk, and Innovation: The Divergence of East and West in the Early Modern World," *Sociological Theory* 5 (Fall 1987): 127–32; N. J. Smelser, *The Theory of Collective Behavior* (New York: Free Press, 1962); N. J. Smelser, "Growth, Structural Change, and Conflict in California Public Higher Education, 1950–1970," in *Public Higher Education in California*, ed. N. J. Smelser and G. Almond (Berkeley: University of California Press, 1974); Edward A. Tiryakian, "On the Significance of De-differentiation," in *Macro Sociological Theory: Perspectives on Sociological Theory*, ed. S. N. Eisenstadt and H. J. Helle (Beverly Hills, Calif.: Sage, 1985), pp. 129–30; Duane Champagne, "Social Structure, Revitalization Movements, and State Building: Social Change in Four Native American Societies," *American Sociological Review* 48 (1983): 754–63; Duane Champagne, *American Indian Societies: Strategies and Conditions of Political and Cultural Survival* (Cambridge, Mass.: Cultural Survival, 1989); Duane Champagne, "Culture, Differentiation, and Environment: Social Change in Tlingit Society," in Alexander and Colomy, eds., *Differentiation Theory*; Colomy, "Revisions and Progress in Differentiation Theory"; S. N. Eisenstadt, "Macro-societal Analysis—Background, Development, and Indications," in Eisenstadt and Helle, eds., *Macro Sociological Theory*, pp. 14–16, 21–22; Gary C. Hamilton, "Configurations in History: The Historical Sociology of S. N. Eisenstadt," in *Vision and Method in Historical Sociology*, ed. Theda Skocpol (Cambridge, Eng.: Cambridge University Press, 1984), pp. 108–9. Articles by Skocpol and Peter Evans in *Bringing the State Back In*, ed. Peter Evans, Dietrich Rueschemeyer, and Theda Skocpol (Cambridge, Eng.: Cambridge University Press, 1985); Daniel Chirot, *Social Change in the Modern Era* (San Diego, Calif.: Harcourt Brace Jovanovich, 1986), pp. iv, 11–28.

6. Emile Durkheim, *The Rules of Sociological Method* (New York: Free Press, 1966), pp. 1–9.

7. Emile Durkheim, *The Division of Labor in Society* (New York: Free Press, 1984), pp. 310–28.

8. Theda Skocpol, *States and Social Revolution* (New York: Cambridge University Press, 1979).

9. Frances V. Moulder, *Japan, China, and the Modern World Economy* (Cambridge, Eng.: Cambridge University Press, 1977), pp. 68–70. See also Max Weber, *The Religion of China* (New York: Free Press, 1951), pp. 42–62.

10. Barrington Moore, *Social Origins of Dictatorship and Democracy* (Boston: Beacon, 1966), pp. 112–13.

11. See Lewis Coser, *The Function of Social Conflict* (New York: Free Press, 1956), pp. 72–75.

12. Max Weber, *Economy and Society*, 1, ed. Guenther Roth and Claus Wittich (Berkeley: University of California Press, 1978), pp. 56, 65. To be fair, Weber also says that a central feature of a modern state is a bureaucratic organization that has norms and rules that are subject to change by a national legislature. This aspect of the state is further developed below in the concepts of separation of powers and internal political differentiation. In *A Law of Blood: The Primitive Law of the Cherokee Nation* (New York: New York University Press, 1970), p. 36, John Reid argues that the critical difference between a nation and a state is the centralization of coercive force in the government. Nations do not have a centralized police to enforce laws. In a similar way, Gearing argues that there are three kinds of political organization: those that are formed by local segmentary kinship groups, those that are a confederation of numerous local kin groups, and those that are formed by a number of local communities or subgroups and have an overall coercive mechanism for controlling the subgroups. Fred Gearing, "Priests and Warriors: Social Structures for Cherokee Politics in the Eighteenth Century," *American Anthropologist*, Memoirs 93, part 2, 65 (1962): 6–7.

13. Theda Perdue, "Cherokee Planters: The Development of Plantation Slavery Before Removal," in *The Cherokee Indian Nation*, ed. Duane King (Knoxville: University of Tennessee Press, 1979), pp. 112, 115–17; M234, roll 222, frame 562: here it is remarked by American officials in reference to the Creeks in 1831: "The half-breeds and chiefs who are in the possession of the wealth and control the government of the tribe, will not probably be induced to yield up those advantages, so long as the tribe can be kept together." This notion that those who control wealth also control the state apparatus (and for that reason the "half-breeds and chiefs who are in the possession of the wealth" wished to preserve the Creek nation in order to protect their material interests) was not unusual at the time. Henry Schoolcraft, in *Indian Tribes of the United States*, 6 (Philadelphia: J. B. Lippincott, 1857), pp. 417–20, argued that Creek resistance to removal and Creek efforts to preserve their government and territory were inspired by class interests: "They not only amassed riches, . . . which led to the introduction of two classes among this [Creek], and other southern tribes, and produced an aversion to transferring their lands to Georgia and emigrating westward" (p. 417). The same view appears in a modern work by Arrell Gibson: "The mixed bloods also dominated the business life of the nation and used their control of the governmental apparatus to legislate special privileges for their group. They were the principal slave owners and emulated the planters on the rim of their nation by developing productive farms and plantations." *The Chickasaws*, (Norman: University of Oklahoma Press, 1971), p. 142.

14. For more on this, see Parsons, *Evolution of Societies*; Luhman, *Differentiation of Society*, pp. 70–88; Emile Durkheim, *Durkheim on Politics and the State*, ed. Anthony Giddens (Stanford, Calif.: Stanford University Press, 1986), pp. 57–58; Talcott Parsons, "Some Considerations in the Theory of Social Change," *Rural Sociology* (October 1961): 237; S. N. Eisenstadt, "Social Change, Differentiation, and Evolution," *American Sociological Review* 29 (1964): 376–77.

15. See works by S. N. Eisenstadt: *Revolution and the Transformation of Societies* (New York: Free Press, 1978), pp. 32–34; *The Political Systems of Empires* (New York: Free Press, 1969), pp. ix, xviii; "Institutionalization and Social Change," *American Sociological Review*, 29 (1964): 235–47; and "Social Change, Differentiation, and Evolution," pp. 375–80. See also Jeffrey C. Alexander and Paul Colomy, "Toward Neo-functionalism," *Sociological Theory* 3 (Fall 1985): 13–16; and Smelser's *Theory of Collective Behavior* and "Growth, Structural Change, and Conflict."

16. For world-system and dependency theory, see Andre Gunder Frank, *Capitalism and Underdevelopment in Latin America* (New York: Monthly Review Press, 1967); Immanuel Wallerstein, *The Politics of the World Economy* (Cambridge, Eng.: Cambridge University Press, 1984); Michael Brown, "A Critique of Marxist Theories of Imperialism," in *Studies in the Theory of Imperialism*, ed. Roger Owen and Bob Sutcliffe (London: Longman, 1972); Andre Gunder Frank, "Sociology of Development and the Underdevelopment of Sociology," in *Dependence and Underdevelopment*, ed. James Cochcroft, Andre Frank, and Dale Johnson (Garden City, N.Y.: Doubleday, 1972).

17. On hegemonic domination, see Otto Hintze, "The Formation of States and Constitutional Development: A Study in History and Politics," in *The Historical Essays of Otto Hintze*, ed. Felix Gilbert (New York: Oxford University Press, 1975), pp. 160–62; Otto Hintze, "Military Organization and Organization of the State," in *Historical Essays*, pp. 183, 215; Goldstone, "Cultural Orthodoxy," pp. 123, 131.

18. Sheldon Stryker, personal communication, 1983.

CHAPTER 2

1. James Adair, *The History of the American Indians* (New York: Johnson Reprint, 1968), p. 10; Charles Hudson, *The Southeastern Indians* (Knoxville: University of Tennessee Press, 1976), pp. 239–313; Fred Eggan, *The American Indian Perspective for the Study of Social Change* (Chicago: Aldine, 1966), pp. 18, 36–37.

2. The descriptions of the societies are reconstructions of social organization in the early 1700's. Reconstructing the social and political organization of the Cherokee, Choctaw, Chickasaw, and Creek for the eighteenth century can be a risky endeavor. Much of the available material is gleaned from the accounts of Western observers—traders, explorers, missionaries, colonial officials, and travelers—and from the oral accounts of the southeastern Indians. Western observers, it must be said, often had their own interests in and purposes for recording the events and social organization of the southeastern nations.

3. Jurgen Habermas, *The Theory of Communicative Action* (Boston: Beacon, 1981), pp. 143–275; Max Weber, *The Sociology of Religion* (Boston: Beacon, 1964); Peggy Beck and Ann Walters, *The Sacred: Ways of Knowledge Sources of Life* (Tsaile, Ariz.: Navajo Community College Press, 1977).

4. Eisenstadt, *Revolution and the Transformation of Societies*, pp. 100–101;

Max Weber, *The Protestant Ethic and the Spirit of Capitalism* (New York: Scribner's, 1958); Weber, *Sociology of Religion*, pp. 138–65, 220–21, 227, 256–57, 268–69; Michael Walzer, *The Revolution of the Saints: A Study in the Origins of Radical Politics* (Cambridge, Mass.: Harvard University Press, 1965), p. 15; Max Weber, *From Max Weber: Essays in Sociology*, ed. H. H. Gerth and C. Wright Mills (New York: Oxford University Press, 1946), pp. 323–62; Max Weber, *Max Weber on Capitalism, Bureaucracy, and Religion*, ed. Stanislav Andreski (London: George Allen & Unwin, 1983), pp. 85–108. Talcott Parsons draws on Weber's argument in *The Evolution of Societies*, pp. 81–85. Joseph Campbell gives more extensive data and a more psychological interpretation to Weber's argument; see: *Occidental Mythology*, vol. 3, *The Masks of God* (New York: Penguin, 1976), pp. 5–6, 24, 109, 179; *Primitive Mythology*, vol. 1, *The Masks of God*, pp. 149–50, 176–79, 404, 421, 466–70; *Oriental Mythology*, vol. 2, *The Masks of God*, pp. 4–7, 21–23, 30, 42, 54, 58, 112–15, 144, 179, 187, 243, 283.

5. *Missionary Herald* 23 (1827): 116–17; IPH 59:63; Thurman Wilkins, *Cherokee Tragedy: The Ridge Family and the Decimation of a People* (Norman: University of Oklahoma Press, 1986), p. 35.

6. Alexander Longe, "A Small Postscript on the Ways and Manners of the Indians Called Cherikkee," ed. David H. Corkran, *Southern Indian Studies* 21 (1969): 10–16; John Payne Papers, Newberry Library, Chicago, 1:149–69; John Payne Papers, 4:150; Hudson, *Southeastern Indians*, pp. 173–74; William C. McLoughlin, *Cherokee Renascence in the New Republic* (Princeton, N.J.: Princeton University Press, 1986), p. 14.

7. John Payne Papers, 1: 9; John Payne Papers, 8: Letter no. 1 by John Ridge, Feb. 27, 1826; Wilkins, *Cherokee Tragedy*, pp. 34–35; McLoughlin, *Cherokee Renascence*, p. 13.

8. Adair, *History*, p. 401; John R. Swanton, *Source Material for the Social and Ceremonial Life of the Choctaw Indians*, Bureau of American Ethnology Bulletin 103 (Washington, D.C.: U.S. Government Printing Office, 1931), p. 227; Alfred Wright, "Choctaws: Religious Opinions, Traditions, Etc.," *Missionary Herald* 24 (1828): 179–80.

9. IPH 20: 228–37; IPH 81: 510–11; Swanton, *Source Material*, p. 216; Wright, "Choctaws: Religious Opinions, Traditions, Etc.," p. 182; David I. Bushnell, "The Choctaw of Bayou Lacomb, St. Tammany Parish, Louisiana," *Bureau of American Ethnology Bulletin* 48 (Washington, D.C.: Smithsonian Institution, 1909): 28–29; John R. Swanton, ed., "An Early Account of the Choctaw Indians," *American Anthropological Association Memoirs* 5 (1918): 65; John A. Watkins, "The Choctaws in Mississippi," *American Antiquarian and Oriental Journal* 16 (1894): 259–65.

10. Gideon Lincecum, tr. and comp., "Traditional History of the Chahta Nation," as told by Chahtaimmataha (Austin: University of Texas Library, n.d.), unpublished ms., typescript version, pp. 227, 371–72; T. N. Campbell, "The Choctaw Afterworld," *Journal of American Folklore* 72 (1959): 150; William Bartram, *Travels of William Bartram* (New York: Dover, 1928), pp. 404–6; George Catlin, *Letters and Notes on the Manners, Customs, and the Conditions of the North American Indians*, 2 (New York: Dover, 1973), pp. 127–28; Wright, "Choctaws: Religious Opinions, Traditions, Etc.," p. 182; IPH 106: 21; IPH 100: 85–87.

11. IPH 106: 21; IPH 100: 85; Bartram, *Travels*, pp. 404–6.

12. Thomas Nairne, *Nairne's Muskhogean Journals: The 1708 Expedition to the Mississippi River*, ed. Alexander Moore (Jackson: University Press of Missis-

sippi, 1988), pp. 40–42; Scholarly Resources, *Chickasaws and Choctaws* (Wilmington, Del.: Scholarly Resources, Inc., 1975), p. 21; Jesse Jennings, ed., "Nutt's Trip to the Chickasaw Country," *Journal of Mississippi History* 9 (1947): 46–47; James Malone, *The Chickasaw Nation: A Short Sketch of a Noble People* (Louisville, Ky.: John P. Morton, 1922), pp. 212–13.

13. Arrell M. Gibson, "Chickasaw Ethnography: An Ethnohistorical Reconstruction," *Ethnohistory* 18 (1971): 102–4.

14. IPH 87: 467; IPH 109: 82; IPH 31: 121; Jennings, "Nutt's Trip," p. 49; Malone, *Chickasaw Nation*, p. 213.

15. John Payne Papers, 9: 93; IPH 47: 112–13; IPH 43: 472; C. L. Grant, ed., *Letters, Journals, and Writings of Benjamin Hawkins*, vol. 1, *1796–1801* (Savannah, Ga.: Bellevue Press, 1980), p. 324; Bartram, *Travels*, p. 384; Adair, *History*, pp. 86, 392; John R. Swanton, "Religious Beliefs and Medical Practices of the Creek Indians," *Forty-Second Report of the Bureau of American Ethnology* (Washington, D.C.: U.S. Government Printing Office, 1928), pp. 547, 569–71.

16. T. N. Campbell, "Choctaw Afterworld," p. 152; Swanton, "Religious Beliefs," p. 513; Bartram, *Travels*, p. 391; Grant, *Benjamin Hawkins*, 1: 325.

17. McLoughlin, *Cherokee Renascence*, p. 14; Hudson, *Southeastern Indians*, pp. 127–28, 136–48; Charles Hudson, *Elements of Southeastern Indian Religion* (Lieden: E. J. Brill, 1984), p. 12.

18. Hudson, *Southeastern Indians*, pp. 159, 340; McLoughlin, *Cherokee Renascence*, p. 14.

19. Raymond Fogelson, "An Analysis of Cherokee Sorcery and Witchcraft," in *Four Centuries of Southern Indians*, ed. Charles M. Hudson (Athens: University of Georgia Press, 1975), pp. 126–27; McLoughlin, *Cherokee Renascence*, p. 14.

20. IPH 100: 85–89; IPH 20: 237; C. Bremer, *The Chata Indians of Pearl River* (New Orleans, La.: Picayune Job Print, 1907), p. 3; Patricia Dillon Woods, *French-Indian Relations on the Southern Frontier, 1699–1762* (Ann Arbor: University of Michigan Press, 1980), pp. 5–6; Grayson Noley, "1540: The First European Contact," in *The Choctaw Before Removal*, ed. Carolyn Keller Reeves (Jackson: University Press of Mississippi, 1985), p. 63.

21. Adair, *History*, pp. 34–46, 99–101; Scholarly Resources, *Chickasaws and Choctaws*, p. 21.

22. J. Leitch Wright, Jr., *Creeks and Seminoles: Destruction and Regeneration of the Muscogulge People* (Lincoln: University of Nebraska Press, 1986), p. 25; Hudson, *Southeastern Indians*, p. 224; Michael D. Green, *The Politics of Indian Removal: Creek Government and Society in Crisis* (Lincoln: University of Nebraska Press, 1982), pp. 15–16; Swanton, "Religious Beliefs," pp. 477–83.

23. Hudson, *Southeastern Indians*, pp. 237–39.

24. William McDowell, Jr., ed., *The Colonial Records of South Carolina: Documents Relating to Indian Affairs, 1754–1765* (Columbia: University of South Carolina Press, 1970), p. 125; Alexander Cuming, "Journal of Sir Alexander Cuming," in *Early Travels in the Tennessee Country, 1540–1800*, ed. Samuel Williams (Johnson City, Tenn.: Watauga Press, 1928), pp. 122, 125, 135; David H. Corkran, *The Carolina Indian Frontier* (Columbia: University of South Carolina Press, 1970), p. 14; David H. Corkran "Cherokee Prehistory," *North Carolina Historical Review* 34 (1957): 363–64, 459–64; Gearing, "Priests and Warriors," pp. 79–82.

25. Swanton, *Source Material*, 91, 95–7; Richard White, *The Roots of Dependency: Subsistence, Environment, and Social Change Among the Choctaws, Pawnees, and Navajos* (Lincoln: University of Nebraska Press, 1983), p. 38; J. R.

Swanton, "Indians of the Southeastern United States," *Bureau of American Ethnology Bulletin* 137 (Washington, D.C.: U.S. Government Printing Office, 1946): 121; Dunbar Rowland, ed. *The Mississippi Provincial Archives, 1763–1766* 1 (Nashville: Brandon Printing, 1911): 38, 90, 100, 108, 116, 145, 155–56; *Missionary Herald* 19 (1823): 10; Jean Bernard Bossu, *Travels in the Interior of North America, 1751–1762,* ed. Seymour Leiler (Norman: University of Oklahoma Press, 1962), pp. 164–65, Bernard Romans, *A Concise Natural History* [1775] (New Orleans, La.: Pelican, 1961), p. 51; *Missionary Herald* 25 (1829): 121.

26. IPH 109: 419–21; Gibson, *The Chickasaws,* pp. 6, 21; Gibson, "Chickasaw Ethnography," pp. 100, 111–16; J. R. Swanton, "Early History of the Creek Indians and Their Neighbors," *U.S. Bureau of Ethnology Bulletin* 73 (Washington, D.C.: U.S. Government Printing Office, 1922): 417.

27. M234, roll 229, frames 536–39; J. Leitch Wright, *Creeks and Seminoles,* pp. 2–4, 30; Green, *Politics of Indian Removal,* pp. 11–13.

28. John Payne Papers, 9: 75; John R. Swanton, "The Social Significance of the Creek Confederacy," *Proceedings of the International Congress of Americanists* 19 (1917): 333; James H. Howard, *Oklahoma Seminoles: Medicines, Magic, and Religion* (Norman: University of Oklahoma Press, 1984), p. 5; John R. Swanton, "Social Organization and Social Usages of the Indians of the Creek Confederacy," *Forty-Second Report of the Bureau of Ethnology* (Washington, D.C.: U.S. Government Printing Office, 1928), pp. 185, 242–46, 276.

29. M234, roll 229, frames 537–38; J. Leitch Wright, *Creeks and Seminoles,* pp. 1–4, 30.

30. John Phillip Reid, *A Better Kind of Hatchet: Law, Trade, and Diplomacy in the Cherokee Nation During the Early Years of European Contact* (University Park: Pennsylvania State University Press, 1976), pp. 5–7; Gearing, "Priests and Warriors," pp. 3–5, 39; William Sturtevant, "The Cherokee Frontier, the French Revolution, and William Augustus Bowles" in King, ed., *The Cherokee Indian Nation,* pp. 93–95.

31. McDowell, *Colonial Records of South Carolina, 1754–1765,* pp. 392–93.

32. John Dickason, "The Judicial History of the Cherokee Nation from 1721 to 1835" (Ph.D. diss., University of Oklahoma, 1964), p. 85; Gearing, "Priests and Warriors," pp. 31–32; Reid, *A Better Kind of Hatchet,* p. 29; Raymond Fogelson, "Cherokee Notions of Power," *The Anthropology of Power,* ed. Raymond Fogelson and Richard Adams (New York: Academic Press, 1977), p. 186.

33. Lincecum, "History of the Chahta Nation," pp. 230, 275, 311.

34. Swanton, "An Early Account of the Choctaw Indians," p. 54; Swanton, *Source Material,* pp. 91, 126.

35. Dunbar Rowland and A. G. Sanders, ed. *Mississippi Provincial Archives, 1729–1740,* 1 (Press of the Mississippi Department of Archives and History, 1927): 156; quote from Romans, *Concise Natural History,* p. 51.

36. Nairne, *Muskhogean Journals,* pp. 38–39, 41, 63; Adair, *History,* pp. 428; Jennings, "Nutt's Trip," p. 53; B. S. Cotterill, *The Southern Indians: The Story of the Civilized Tribes Before Removal* (Norman: University of Oklahoma Press, 1954), pp. 12–21; Scholarly Resources, *Chickasaws and Choctaws,* p. 21; Gibson, *The Chickasaws,* p. 22; Malone, *Chickasaw Nation,* p. 190; Stephen Steacy, "The Chickasaw Nation on the Eve of the Civil War," *Chronicles of Oklahoma* 49 (1971): 52; Gibson, "Chickasaw Ethnography," p. 111.

37. Grant, *Benjamin Hawkins,* 1: xxii, 352; David H. Corkran, *The Creek Frontier, 1540–1783* (Norman: University of Oklahoma Press, 1967), pp. 12–13; Swan-

ton, "Social Organization and Social Usages," p. 279; J. N. B. Hewitt, "Notes on the Creek Indians," *Anthropological Papers*, Bureau of American Ethnology Bulletin 123, ed. J. R. Swanton (Washington, D.C.: U.S. Government Printing Office, 1939): 134; Daniel Jacobson, "The Alabama-Coushatta Indians of Texas and the Coushatta Indians of Louisiana," *(Creek) Indians Alabama-Coushatta*, ed. David Agee Harr (New York: Garland, 1974), p. 45; Bartram, *Travels*, pp. 388–90; Hudson, *Southeastern Indians*, pp. 223–24; Green, *Politics of Indian Removal*, p. 7.

38. William Gilbert, "The Eastern Cherokee," *Bureau of American Ethnology Bulletin* 133 (Washington, D.C.: U.S. Government Printing Office, 1943): 323; Adair, *History*, p. 50; John Payne Papers, 4: 60.

39. IPH 7: 60–62; *Missionary Herald* 25 (1829): 132; Hudson, *Southeastern Indians*, p. 172.

40. IPH 7: 60–61; Adair, *History*, p. 159; John Payne Papers, 4: 15, 64; V. Richard Persico, "Early Nineteenth-Century Cherokee Political Organization," in King, ed., *Cherokee Indian Nation*, pp. 92–93.

41. Lincecum, "History of the Chahta Nation," pp. 283, 336, 497–98.

42. A. Wright, "Choctaws: Religious Opinions, Traditions, Etc.," p. 215.

43. Lincecum, "History of the Chahta Nation," p. 284; Gideon Lincecum, "History of the Chahta Nation: Addenda," pp. 9–14; Rowland and Sanders, *Mississippi Provincial Archives, 1729–1740*, 1: 245; Michael Coleman, *Presbyterian Missionary Attitudes Toward American Indians, 1837–1893* (Jackson: University Press of Mississippi, 1985), p. 130.

44. IPH 72: 431; Adair, *History*, pp. 397, 429–30; Gibson, *The Chickasaws*, pp. 23–24; Malone, *Chickasaw Nation*, p. 207; Steacy, "Chickasaw Nation on the Eve of the Civil War," p. 52; Jennings, "Nutt's Trip," p. 53.

45. Adair, *History*, p. 159; Hewitt, "Notes on the Creek Indians," pp. 137, 147–49; T. N. Campbell, "The Choctaw Afterworld," p. 152; Grant, *Benjamin Hawkins*, 1: 321–22; Swanton, "Social Organization and Social Usages," pp. 342–43; Hudson, *The Southeastern Indians*, p. 229; Bartram, *Travels*, p. 384; Swanton, "Religious Beliefs," p. 512.

46. James Adair, *Adair's History of the American Indians*, ed. Samuel Williams (Johnson City, Tenn.: Watauga Press, 1930), pp. 436–38; Gary Goodwin, *Cherokees in Transition: A Study of Changing Culture and Environment Prior to 1775* (Chicago: University of Chicago Research Paper no. 181, 1977), p. 41.

47. Henry Timberlake, *The Memoirs of Lieut. Henry Timberlake, 1756–1765* (Marietta, Ga.: Continental Book, 1948), p. 91; John Payne Papers, 2: 17; Theda Perdue, *Slavery and the Evolution of Cherokee Society, 1540–1866* (Knoxville: University of Tennessee Press, 1979), p. 13; Reid, *A Better Kind of Hatchet*, p. 8; Grayson Noley, "The Early 1700s: Education, Economics, and Politics," in Reeves, ed., *Choctaw Before Removal*, pp. 98–103; Coleman, *Presbyterian Missionary Attitudes*, p. 55; Lincecum, "History of the Chahta Nation," pp. 268, 286, 311, 477–80; IPH 6:141–42; Adair, *History*, pp. 430–31; Gibson, *The Chickasaws*, pp. 22–24.

48. Charles Hicks and John Ross to John Payne, March 1826, letter no. 2, John Payne Papers, 6: 5–6; Corkran "Cherokee Prehistory," 34: 363–64; Longe, "A Small Postscript," pp. 10–16.

49. Longe, "A Small Postscript," pp. 10, 14, 16, 24–26; Gearing, "Priests and Warriors," p. 23; Gilbert, "The Eastern Cherokee," p. 341; Cuming, "Journal," p. 123; John Brown, *Old Frontiers* (Kingsport, Tenn.: Southern Publishers, 1938),

p. 30; Dickason, "Judicial History," p. 73; McDowell, *Colonial Records of South Carolina, 1754–1765,* pp. 470–72.

50. Lincecum, "History of the Chahta Nation," pp. 20, 22, 28, 48, 79, 145, 185–96, 276–83, 289–91, 307, 321, 333–37, 404, 408–9, 457–59, 472. Other, less detailed, accounts of the migration do not present the story of the struggle between the priests and civil leadership. In Alfred Wright's version, the migration was led by a great leader and prophet who had control over the sacred leadership pole that each day pointed in the direction in which the Great Spirit directed his people to travel toward a good land in the east. In this version, as also in the Lincecum version, the Creek, the Choctaw, and the Chickasaw migrate together from a distant land in the west. See Wright, "Choctaws: Religious Opinions, Traditions, Etc.," pp. 180, 215–16. Henry. S. Halbert's version (1894) also does not mention a struggle between the priesthood and civil authorities but tells of a great prophet who led the people and carried the sacred pole that each morning gave direction to the march. Many of the Mississippi Choctaw lost the story of the migration myth, and believe that the Choctaw originated from a hole on the side of a hill near Nanih Waiya. See Henry S. Halbert, "A Choctaw Migration Legend," *American Antiquarian and Oriental Journal* 16 (1894): 215–16. An earlier version, told to missionaries in the 1820's, suggests that the migration was relatively recent, supposedly a result of invasion by Cortez and company. The national council was called together to decide to emigrate away from the conquest, and the civil chiefs were empowered to select priests to lead the nation in the migration. The leadership pole was under the direction of a prophet and a medicine man, two men who had great wisdom in supernatural things. The leadership pole led the Choctaw to Nanih Waiya. In this version the civil leaders appear powerful, but defer leadership of the migration to priests, who can interpret the signs of the Great Spirit. See IPH 33: 70–74. Everett Pitchlynn, son of the prominent Choctaw personality Peter Pitchlynn, relates the view that the migration started on the shores of the Gulf of Mexico and was led by a prophet. The sacred pole led the Choctaw to Nanih Waiya, where they established a government. See IPH 40: 94–98. Another version (IPH 50: 420) told by Annie Woodward does not give details on the leadership. See also William Brescia, Jr., "Choctaw Oral Tradition Relating to Tribal Origin," in Reeves, ed., *Choctaw Before Removal,* pp. 3–16.

Although the Lincecum version is the most detailed, the story and sequence of events seem distorted. Archaeological evidence indicates that Nanih Waiya was occupied for 2,000 years before early European contact, which makes the story of the destruction of the City of the Sun by Europeans and the subsequent finding and establishment of Nanih Waiya 47 years after the migration implausible. It might be theorized that in the Lincecum story the City of the Sun was a mythical city that was transposed with historical Nanih Waiya—which might have been attacked by Europeans, causing the population to scatter—but this theory is not borne out by the Soto manuscripts which do not mention either Nanih Waiya or the Choctaw by name (*Narratives of the Career of Hernando de Soto,* 2 vols., ed. Edward Bourne [New York: Allerton, 1922]). Also, in the Lincecum version migration occurs after the destruction of the City of the Sun, whereas other versions say the migration must have occurred long ago, perhaps as early as 500 B.C. This suggests that the story of the struggle between the priests and the civil leadership may be of postmigration origin. The Lincecum version portrays the conflict between the priests and civil authorities starting with their differing interpretations of and attitudes toward the arrival of Europeans. In the other versions, the migration may have been an ancient event, before contact with Europeans, and the struggle between the priests and civil leadership an event that occurred largely in the post-European contact era. However this may be, it appears that the struggle between priests and civil authorities in the oral tradition given by the Lincecum manuscript presents a concern and central theme in Choctaw political relations.

51. IPH 7: 2; A. Wright, "Choctaws: Religious Opinions, Traditions, Etc.," p. 216; Scholarly Resources, *Chickasaws and Choctaws*, p. 20; Gibson, "Chickasaw Ethnography," p. 103.

52. Adair, *History*, pp. 31–33, Gibson, *The Chickasaws*, pp. 12–18; Malone, *Chickasaw Nation*, pp. 211–13; W. David Baird, *The Chickasaw People* (Phoenix, Ariz.: Indian Tribal Series, 1974), p. 9.

53. In contrast to the Choctaw and Chickasaw legends, to which it is in many ways analogous, the Creek migration tradition tells of the origins and hierarchical order of Creek villages or tribal towns, and thus legitimated rank and order of Creek towns in the historical period. Along the way on their eastern path, the three leading towns encounter Abihka, which was adopted as a fourth leading town after a few years of fighting. According to this version, the major towns were ranked, with Cussetah the first town in the nation, then Coweta, Chickasaw, and Abihka. (John Payne Papers, 9: 93–98; IPH 19: 432; Grant, *Benjamin Hawkins*, 1:326). In other versions Abihka is given as the oldest town in the nation and the place where the laws of marriage originated. The Chickasaw are only mythically a part of the Creek nation, although during the historical period the people of Cussetah claimed that they were kindred to the Chickasaw and would not go to war against them. Other versions give different central towns, although in most versions both Coweta and Cussetah are mentioned; other major towns include Abihka, Coosa, and Tuckabatchee. Since Abihka and Coosa were closely related during the historical period, any mention of Coosa or Abihka probably refers to the same leading town or towns. Tuckabatchee became an important town in the early 1800's but seems not to have been a central town before then, so the mention of Tuckabatchee as one of the four central towns in a migration myth may be a revisionist mythical tale designed to legitimate Tuckabatchee's rise to political prominence in the early nineteenth century. The significant feature in comparison with the migration myths of the other southeastern nations is that the primary actors in the Creek myths are not people but villages, and the myths seek to establish rank among four leading or principal towns. The myths reflect the cultural and political organization of Creek society, since towns are the major political, economic, and cultural units in society.

54. Bartram, *Travels*, p. 246; Swanton, "Social Significance of the Creek Confederacy," pp. 329–32; Hudson, *Southeastern Indians*, pp. 234–35; Hewitt, "Notes on the Creek Indians," pp. 124–27. There is some disagreement over the interpretation of Creek social and political order during the eighteenth century. J. Leitch Wright in *Creeks and Seminoles* argues that the Creek confederacy was not a single cultural group but an amalgam of tribes, which differed linguistically and culturally, that were adopted and occasionally conquered by the Muskogee; this local particularism, he argues, and the varying ethnic identities of the incorporated and conquered villages within the Creek confederacy, help to explain much of the political action and conflict that is evident in Creek history and society. In my view, Wright's ethnic particularism thesis is only partly correct, because he rejects the argument that the Creek confederacy was symbolically integrated and politically organized by red and white villages and red and white clans. During

the 1700's, Wright argues (p. 14): "The traditional dualism that included war (red) and peace (white) towns had become moribund"; it persisted only in form and not in substance, and organization by local ethnic identity now took its place.

A society organized largely by ethnic particularism would break apart: what institutions would hold such a society together in any coherent way? Wright does not discuss this point. Aside from the theoretical difficulties with Wright's argument, empirical evidence for rejecting Wright's argument comes from a set of interviews made in the early 1880's by J. N. B. Hewitt ("Notes on the Creek Indians") in which two Creek, Pleasant Porter and Legus Perryman, both men who later became principal chiefs, gave a summary history of the Creek nation and specifically interpreted the history of the nation in terms of the struggle between leading red and white towns. "For instance [the Creek informants say, p. 125], the white towns had civil control of the Creeks from time immemorial up to the Revolution of 1776 and then the red towns obtained power and kept it until 1861. Since the Civil War, 1861–1865, the white towns have again been in control." Taking this lead, I interpreted the historical evidence on the Creek (this is the Creek narrative given in the text), and although I found a more varied interpretation of events than the two Creek informants gave, the argument was generally upheld and supported by a variety of data that were uncovered about the political relations between the red and white towns.

Both Wright and I agree that Creek social and political structure was local and particularistic, but Creek villages with ceremonial squares, as I argue, were religiously particularistic, and in some cases the incorporated groups were ethnically particularistic, but most incorporated or conquered groups adopted the red or white symbolism of the confederacy and participated in this capacity within the Creek confederacy. To a large extent Wright's ethnic particularism argument can be covered by the symbolic integration and local religious particularism argument that I present in the text. Although I have cited Wright's work throughout for historical data, I do not cite Wright's interpretations, for I believe that they are only partly correct.

55. IPH 103: 319–21; Adair, *History*, pp. 185, 503; Bartram, *Travels*, p. 360; J. Leitch Wright, *Creeks and Seminoles*, p. 30; Swanton, "Social Significance of the Creek Confederacy," pp. 327–28; Swanton, "Early History of the Creek Indians," p. 277; Angie Debo, *The Road to Disappearance: A History of the Creek Indians* (Norman: University of Oklahoma Press, 1979), pp. 24, 160; Hudson, *Southeastern Indians*, pp. 218, 369; Theodore Stern, "The Creek," in *The Native Americans*, ed. Robert F. Spencer and Jesse D. Jennings (New York: Harper & Row, 1977), p. 441.

56. Hewitt, "Notes on the Creek Indians," p. 133.

57. Bartram, *Travels*, pp. 384–90.

58. Adair, *Adair's History*, p. 19; Gearing, "Priests and Warriors," pp. 20–21; Reid, *Law of Blood*, pp. 36, 48; Goodwin, *Cherokees in Transition*, p. 113; McLoughlin, *Cherokee Renascence*, p. 12. Early sources generally portray seven clans in each village, though it is possible to find references to villages that do not have seven clans. Some villages are daughter villages to larger villages, and the members of the daughter village attend the ceremonial square of its "mother" village. For example, in the spring of 1797, Louis Philippe, the Duke of Orleans and future king of the French (1830–48), visited the small village of Takona, near the old site of Chota, and observed that in the town house "there were three escutcheons of the three [Cherokee] tribes: the snake, the tortoise and the lizard are

their emblems . . . When the Indians gather in their town house, they usually place themselves in the cubicle of their tribe." (I interpret the latter term to mean clan.) See William Sturtevant, "Louis-Philippe on Cherokee Architecture and Clothing in 1797"; *Journal of Cherokee Studies* 3 (Fall 1979): 200. Louis Philippe's statement implies that there were only three clans present in the small village of Takona in 1799, but his observations were made after the turbulent war years of 1777–95 and much dislocation in Cherokee society. After 1795, small Cherokee villages may not have had the cultural ideal of all seven clans present in the village; how they handled this situation is not clear.

59. John Payne Papers, 1: 24, 70–75, 80, 101, 112; John Payne Papers, 4: 305, 315, 504.

60. IPH 6: 504; John Payne Papers, 1: 150–69; *Panopolist and Missionary Herald* 14 (1818): 415–16. The creation myth as described in the text is the Redbird Smith or Nighthawk Keetoowah version; see IPH 9: 492; and Hudson, *Southeastern Indians*, p. 136.

61. John Payne Papers, 1: 24, 28; John Payne Papers, 4: 57, 60, 69, 225.

62. Lincecum, "History of the Chahta Nation," pp. 189–94, 213, 256, 272, 325–28; A. Wright, "Choctaws: Religious Opinions, Traditions, Etc.," pp. 214–15; John R. Swanton, "Choctaw Moieties," *American Anthropologist* 34 (1934): 357; Swanton, *Source Material*, pp. 76–81.

63. Adair, *History*, pp. 101–12; Gibson, *The Chickasaws*, pp. 12–18; Harry Warren, "Chickasaw Traditions, Customs, Etc." *Publications of the Mississippi Historical Society* 8 (1904): 549; Albert S. Gatschet, *A Migration Legend of the Creek Indians* (Philadelphia: D. G. Brinton, 1884), pp. 96–97; Hudson, *Southeastern Indians*, pp. 366–71; Woods, *French-Indian Relations*, p. 15; Gibson, "Chickasaw Ethnography," pp. 104–10.

64. Nairne, *Muskhogean Journals*, p. 48.

65. Hewitt, "Notes on the Creek Indians," pp. 127–29; Hudson, *Southeastern Indians*, pp. 195–202; Swanton, "Social Significance of the Creek Confederacy," pp. 329–30; Swanton, "Social Organization and Social Usages," pp. 114, 120–23, 154, 170, 196–97; Theron Nunez Jr., "Creek Nativism and the Creek War of 1813–1814," *Ethnohistory* 5 (1958): 132; Green, *Politics of Indian Removal*, pp. 4–7.

66. IPH 2: 23–24; Hewitt, "Notes on the Creek Indians," pp. 149–55; J. Leitch Wright, *Creeks and Seminoles*, p. 27; John Payne Papers, 9: 93; Debo, *Road to Disappearance*, pp. 21–24; Green, *Politics of Indian Removal*, pp. 15–16; Bartram, *Travels*, pp. 396–400; Swanton, "Religious Beliefs," pp. 548–49.

67. Gearing, "Priests and Warriors," pp. 5, 22; Persico, "Cherokee Political Organization," p. 5; Reid, *Law of Blood*, pp. 47, 148–51: Reid says (p. 51): "It must be concluded that there is no evidence proving a system of political or legal privilege in the nation, giving either individuals or members of favored clans a status above their fellow Cherokees." This comment refers to the discussion in the entire paragraph and preceding pages, which summarizes a discussion of whether certain clans, specifically referring to Chota where most of the leaders were members of the wolf clan, had special political rights that ensured that only members of the wolf clan would have access to political leadership at Chota, then the central Cherokee village. Reid concludes that there is no reason to believe that the wolf clan at Chota had special political privileges, and therefore affirms the argument of the differentiation of political and clan relations in Cherokee society.

There is a major source that apparently contradicts the argument of differentiation of political and clan roles in Cherokee society: Charles R. Hicks, the

Cherokee Second Chief, testified in 1818, "The national council is composed of persons from each clan; some clans sending more, some less, according to their population, though the number is not very definitely fixed" (*Panopolist and Missionary Herald* 14 [1818]: 415–416). The confusing issue in Hicks's description is that he talks about the seven "clans" earlier in the article and now uses the same term to describe the composition of the national council. When I first saw this reference some years ago, in the early 1980's, I took it at face value and assumed that Hicks was arguing that each of the seven clans sent its leaders to form the national council. But as I continued my research the other evidence contradicted what Hicks appeared to be saying. For example, see the above-cited material, and also see the comment by Major Ridge, the Speaker of the Cherokee Council in 1817: "I am now going to address the council of the Cherokee nation; and each representative will inform his town respectively the result of our deliberations" (*Panopolist and Missionary Herald United*, 13 [1817]: 566). In addition, Reid, *Law of Blood*, says (p. 47): "There was apparently no national clan government, no clan chiefs who spoke for the clans in the councils of the nation. When the clan members sat together in council, it was usually in the town councils."

Hicks was, of course, living in the early 1800's, and was not using the term "clan" in a trained social scientist's way; in this passage, "clan" probably does not refer to the seven clans but rather to clans as local communities, that is, to the old Cherokee villages. In other words, Hicks is merely saying that each local community or village sent a delegation to the national council. This interpretation reconciles Hicks's article with the other interpretations of Cherokee political and kinship relations; otherwise Hicks's statement that the seven clans were the organizing units of the Cherokee national council stands alone.

68. Swanton, *Source Material*, p. 95; White, *Roots of Dependency*, p. 38; Swanton, "Indians of the Southeastern United States," p. 121; Rowland, *Mississippi Provincial Archives, 1729–1740*, I: 38.

69. Rowland and Sanders, *Mississippi Provincial Archives, 1729–1740*, I: 145, 155–56; *Missionary Herald* 19 (1823): 10; Swanton, *Source Material*, p. 91; Bossu, *Travels*, pp. 164–65, Romans, *Concise History*, p. 51.

70. *Missionary Herald* 25 (1829): 121; Swanton, *Source Material*, p. 96.

71. *Missionary Herald* 19 (1823): 9–10; 26 (1830): 251.

72. Gideon Lincecum, "Life of Apushimataha," *Publications of the Mississippi Historical Society* 9 (1906): 415.

73. Bushnell, "The Choctaw of Bayou Lacomb," pp. 16, 26. There is, however, a major source which cannot be immediately reconciled with the argument of local exogamous kinship groups among the Choctaw. Alfred Wright, in "Choctaws: Religious Opinions, Traditions, Etc.," *Missionary Herald* 24 (1828): 215, says that the Choctaw "were divided into two great families, or clans, embracing the whole tribe, or nation. Intermarriages between those of the same clan were forbidden." He goes on to say that children belonged to the family of the mother, and the father belonged to his own division; at funerals and public meetings the father sat with his division and the mother and children sat with the mother's division. So far Wright has said that the society was divided into two exogamous divisions, which regulated marriage and descent and ordered relations at public events and funerals. This part of Wright's description is not contended, although some sources like Bushnell and Lincecum's "Traditional History of the Chahta Nation," which was gathered from an elderly Choctaw informant, do not mention that the Choctaw were divided into two major exogamous divisions.

The difficulties with Wright's description emerge in the next lines (p. 215):

"Each of these great clans is again divided into three subdivisions, or smaller clans, making six in all." Wright would have saved future scholars a great deal of trouble if he had provided the names and other information about the six subdivisions. As it is, lacking details, it is difficult to reconcile his remarks with those of other reports. Wright does go on to say (p. 215), "All these clans intermix and live together in the same town and neighborhood, yet they preserve a knowledge of the clan, and of the particular subdivision to which they belong," and in the next paragraph he describes a judicial procedure based on the six subdivisions and the two major divisions, though again without specific detail. Many other reports—for example, Bushnell's study—cannot be directly reconciled with that statement either. Wright appears to imply that the six subdivisions were located throughout the nation in all the towns and local settlements. If this was indeed the case, then it might not be possible to uphold the argument that polity was not differentiated from kinship in Choctaw society.

J. R. R. Swanton, *Source Material* (pp. 80–81), says: "My own experience has been that of Mr. Bushnell. The Choctaw whom I have interviewed have drawn no distinction between the sorts of divisions (moiety, clans and local groups)"— that is, Swanton's informants viewed local family iksa as exogamous and each had its own leader. Swanton further says (p. 81), "[Horatio] Cushman mentions two original moieties [exogamous divisions], 'subsequently divided into six clans,' thus confirming Wright, but the names which he gives to the latter are wholly different, including those of the three great geographical divisions, and three of the smaller local groups—they are the Okla falaya, Hayip Atokola, Okla hannali, Konshak, Chickasawhay and Apela." Note here that Cushman describes the six subdivisions as geographical or local divisions, which is counterposed to Wright's view. In addition, Swanton quotes (p. 81) Gideon Lincecum, who stated in the 1820's, "Each district was subdivided, with but little system, into Iksa, or kindred clans, and each of these Iksa had its leader." Thus Lincecum describes the three districts of the 1820's as subdivided into local kinship groups, "kindred iksa," who had a single leader—hence in my interpretation political leadership and identity were determined by kinship affiliation, and therefore political and kinship relations were not differentiated in Choctaw society. Swanton further remarks that Lincecum's observations and those of his informant Simpson Tubby "said much the same thing." Tubby (p. 81) "attributed exogamy to the iksas instead of the moieties, of which he remembered nothing." Swanton goes on to say (p. 82) that the term iksa "sometimes seems identical with a town, sometimes it embraced several towns, but more often I believe each town was composed of several iksa." In Swanton's interpretation, even if several iksa lived in the same town, each local iksa was exogamous and had its own leader, since his data conformed to that of Lincecum and Bushnell.

Further evidence is given by H. S. Halbert, "Nanih Waiya, the Sacred Mound of the Choctaws," in *A Choctaw Source Book*, ed. John H. Peterson, Jr. (New York: Garland, 1985), p. 230. Here Halbert follows a Choctaw informant named Folsom: "Soon after the creation, the Great Spirit divided the Choctaws into two 'iksa,' the 'Kashapa Okla,' and the 'Okla in Holahta,' or 'Hattak in Holahta.' Stationing one iksa on the north and the other on the west side of the sacred mound, the Great Spirit gave them the law of marriage." Halbert goes on to describe the rules of exogamous marriage between the two major iksa and then in an apparently contradictory manner says: "The iksa lived promiscuously throughout the nation, but as every one knew to which iksa he belonged, no matrimonial mistake could possibly occur." This apparent contradiction may be resolved by considering that both major divisions, called "iksa" here, and the subdivisions, which are also called iksas, refer to two different levels of organization—the dual exogamous iksa division and geographically scattered local iksa, which kept an identification as part of one of the major exogamous divisions. Furthermore, the first reference is to the mythical origin or early period when the major iksa were probably geographically located, whereas the second reference is to the nineteenth century, after many dislocations had taken place in the Choctaw social order. In the early 1830's there were 99 members on the Choctaw national council, each of whom represented iksa of one level or another. It should be noted that Wright's observations were also made in 1828, after the dislocations of the previous two centuries; that may help to account for his views of scattered iksa about the nation.

Halbert's statement could be interpreted to imply that the two major divisions were exogamous but that numerous subdivisions were located at will throughout the nation, each keeping its particular identity and exogamous relations with the iksas of the opposite division; each local iksa was exogamous and its members married only into an iksa that belonged to the opposite major division. This interpretation reconciles Halbert's data with Swanton's and Bushnell's data, since Bushnell's informants also identify a "Kashapa ogla" and a "Inhulata ogla," which correspond to the "Kashapa Okla," and the "Okla in Holahta," or "Hattak in Holahta" given by Halbert; Wright did not identify the divisions by name. Bushnell's informants in "The Choctaw of Bayou Lacomb" gave the following information (p.16): "*Kashapa ogla*, or the Half people.—They lived at Bayou Lacomb and the remnant of the tribe now dwelling there belong to this division. The name of the village was Butchu'wa . . . *Inhulata ogla*, or the Prairie people.—This was considered the largest and probably the most important division of the Choctaw living in the region. The principal settlement, Hatcha, was located on Pearl river." And to repeat the point, the Choctaw of Bayou Lacomb informed Bushnell that one could not marry within one's own *ogla*, which is according to the above data consistent with Halbert and Wright, but Bushnell's informants indicate that the ogla occupied individual villages or "principal settlements."

I offer my interpretation of Wright's article within the context of the data cited above. Wright says, "All these clans intermix and live together in the same town and neighborhood," and Swanton gives partial agreement. If Lincecum, Cushman, Bushnell, and Halbert can be reconciled as arguing that the family iksa, and iksa containing one or more villages, were exogamous and geographically specific, then Wright's observations are not necessarily wrong. Assuming that each iksa must obtain marriage partners from the iksas of the opposite major division, then the husbands in any given iksa will be members of subdivisions from the opposite major division, since the Choctaw had a matrilocal society where the husbands went to live in the iksa of their wives. With this interpretation, members of the two major subdivisions would be scattered about in the various iksa of the nation, and these would be men who married and went to live in the iksa of their spouse. Furthermore, the various iksa (exogamous villages or exogamous village groups) were also scattered in various localities about the nation, although keeping their identity as one of the dual exogamous major divisions. In Swanton's view and interpreting Wright's view, some villages could contain several family or local iksa, but these iksa would retain their exogamy and also their separate social and political identity.

To combine this discussion with Wright's observation that the "clan" members "preserve a knowledge of the clan and of the particular subdivision to which they belong," and that furthermore "at their funeral solemnities and other public meetings . . . they were arranged according to this order, the father sitting at one fire, and the mother and children at another" (Wright, p. 215), we can say that it was the custom for Choctaw to identify socially, ceremonially, and politically with their native iksa. Husbands, not being members of the iksa of their wives would not be eligible for political leadership in their wives' iksa. This interpretation can support the argument made in the text that social and political identity among the Choctaw was not differentiated from kinship organization. In contrast to the Cherokee, where all seven clans were included in village governments, Choctaw husbands, though they lived in the iksas of their wives, retained their primary political identification within their native iksa. The Cherokee were also matrilocal, but among the Cherokee a man could take part in the political affairs of his wife's village because his clan, and all the other six clans, were included in the village government. Among the Choctaw, the iksas were the primary political groupings, and husbands belonged to a different kinship group. Cherokee were political members of villages. Hence in Choctaw society, political organization and political identity depended on kinship affiliation, whereas among the Cherokee one was socially a member of a clan but politically a member of a village.

74. Nairne, *Muskhogean Journals*, pp. 39, 63; Jennings, "Nutt's Trip," p. 46.

75. Adair, *History*, pp. 15, 31; Gibson, *The Chickasaws*, pp. 18−22, 24; Malone, *Chickasaw Nation*, pp. 185−90; Warren, "Chickasaw Traditions, Customs, Etc.," pp. 549−50; Gatschet, *Migration Legend of the Creek*, pp. 96−97; Steacy, "Chickasaw Nation on the Eve of the Civil War," pp. 52, 64; Baird, *The Chickasaw People*, pp. 7−9; Gibson, "Chickasaw Ethnography," pp. 109−11.

76. Hewitt, "Notes on the Creek Indians," pp. 132−39; Swanton, "Social Organization and Social Usages," pp. 165−71; Hudson, *Southeastern Indians*, p. 220.

77. Swanton, "Social Significance of the Creek Confederacy," p. 333; Hudson, *Southeastern Indians*, pp. 190−202; Debo, *Road to Disappearance*, p. 6.

CHAPTER 3

1. George Quimby, *Indian Culture and European Trade Goods* (Madison: University of Wisconsin Press, 1966), pp. 8−11; William O. Steele, *The Cherokee Crown of Tannassy* (Winston-Salem, N. C.: John Blair, 1977), p. xii; Rachel Caroline Eaton, *John Ross and the Cherokee Indians* (Chicago: University of Chicago Press, 1921), p. 9.

2. Adair, *Adair's History*, p. 456; Edmond Atkins, *Indians of the Southeastern Colonial Frontier*, ed. Wilbur Jacobs (Columbia: University of South Carolina Press, 1954), pp. 10−11; Schoolcraft, *Indian Tribes of the United States*, 6: 178; Werner Crane, *The Southern Frontier, 1670−1732* (Philadelphia: University of Pennsylvania, 1929), p. 177; Rennard Strickland, "Christian Gotelieb Priber: Utopian Precursor of the Cherokee Government," *Chronicles of Oklahoma* 48 (1970): 270.

3. William McDowell, Jr., ed., *The Colonial Records of South Carolina, 1750−1754* (Columbia: University of South Carolina Press, 1958), p. 442; McDowell, *Colonial Records of South Carolina, 1754−1765*, (Columbia: University of South Carolina Press, 1970), pp. 42−45; Rena Vasser, ed., "Some Short Remarks on the Indian Trade in the Charikkees and the Management Therof Since the Year 1717," *Ethnohistory* 8 (1961): 405; David Corkran, *The Cherokee Frontier: Con-*

flict and Survival, 1740-1762 (Norman: University of Oklahoma Press, 1962), p. 11; Atkins, *Indians of the Southeastern Colonial Frontier*, pp. 19-23; Hudson, *Southeastern Indians*, pp. 436-39; Crane, *Southern Frontier*, pp. 95, 124-25; Reid, *A Better Kind of Hatchet*, pp. 45-52, 141.

4. Crane, *Southern Frontier*, p. 123; Paul Phillips, *The Fur Trade*, 1 (Norman: University of Oklahoma Press, 1961), pp. 105-8, 546-47.

5. Woods, *French-Indian Relations*, p. 167.

6. Adair, *History*, pp. 230, 359-63; Adair, *Adair's History*, pp. 390-96, 444; McDowell, *Colonial Records of South Carolina, 1754-1765*, p. 233; White, *Roots of Dependency*, pp. 58-59; Noley, "The Early 1700s: Education, Economics, and Politics," pp. 101-3; E. E. Rich, "Trade Habits and Economic Motivation Among the Indians of North America," *Canadian Journal of Economics and Political Science* 26: 1(1960): 53; Corkran, *Creek Frontier*, p. 53; Arthur J. Ray, *Indians and the Fur Trade* (Toronto: University of Toronto Press, 1974), p. 68; J. Leitch Wright, *Creeks and Seminoles*, pp. 42-46, 56-61.

7. Wright, *Creeks and Seminoles*, pp. 61-62, 67-69, 84, 99; Mary E. Young, *Redskins, Ruffleshirts, and Rednecks: Indian Allotments in Alabama and Mississippi, 1830-1860* (Norman: University of Oklahoma Press, 1961), p. 35; H. B. Cushman, *History of the Choctaw, Chickasaw, and Natchez Indians*, ed. Angie Debo (Stillwater, Okla.: Redlands Press, 1962), pp. 326-34; Daniel F. Littlefield, Jr., *Africans and Creeks* (Westport, Conn.: Greenwood, 1979), pp. 20-37; McLoughlin, *Cherokee Renascence*, pp. 30-32; Brown, *Old Frontiers*, p. 23.

8. Wilbur Jacobs, "Diplomacy and Indian Gifts: Anglo-French Rivalry Along the Ohio and Northwest Frontiers, 1748-1763," *History, Economics, and Political Science* 6 (1950): 44-45; William S. Willis, "The Nation of Bread," *Ethnohistory* 4 (1957): 133-34.

9. Gearing, "Priests and Warriors," pp. 81-82; William Steele, *The Cherokee Crown of Tannassy*, p. 43, says: "Since the early 1700s, South Carolina had steadily tried to make the Cherokee select one of their number as principal head man of the nation and proclaim him 'king.'" Steele goes on to comment that since the middle 1720's the Cherokee had refused to select one headman, and Carolina was forced to deal officially with the several leaders scattered throughout the nation.

10. George Chicken, "Colonel George Chicken's Journal (1725)," in *Early Travels in the Tennessee Country, 1540-1800*, ed. Samuel Cole Williams (Johnson City, Tenn.: Watauga Press, 1928), pp. 98-100. Carolina's recognition of Moytoy was a response to the plans of Christian Priber, who while living among the Cherokee for about seven years (1736-43) persuaded Moytoy to create a centralized state modeled on a utopian plan then current in European thought. Brown, *Old Frontiers* (p. 51), describes it thus: "Priber planned a communistic republic among the Cherokees. All were to be equal; goods were to be held in common; there was to be no marriage contract; men and women were to be equal and to enjoy the same privileges; children were to be the property of the state; each individual was to work for the common good according to his talents, and to have as his only property, books, pen, paper and ink." There was to be a republic with Moytoy as emperor, and Priber as secretary of state. Priber advised the Cherokee to hold on to their territory, and to trade with both the French and English so that they would hold a balance of power between the rival Europeans. In addition he introduced the manufacture of ammunition, and he advocated the formation of a state founded on the merger of the four major southeastern nations. Carolina officials, alarmed by Priber's influence on the Cherokee, had him kidnapped and

sent to prison, where he died. Priber had no lasting influence on Cherokee political institutions, although he did force Carolina to recognize Moytoy as Cherokee emperor. Without such recognition, Carolina officials feared Cherokee defection to French interests under Priber's influence. See Corkran, *Cherokee Frontier*, p. 16; Adair, *Adair's History*, pp. 254–57; James Mooney, "Myths of the Cherokee," *Nineteenth Annual Report of the Bureau of American Ethnology, 1897–1898* (Washington, D.C.: U.S. Government Printing Office, 1900), pp. 35–37; Strickland, "Christian Gotelieb Priber," pp. 271–73, 275, 278.

11. McDowell, *Colonial Records of South Carolina, 1750–1754*, p. 223.

12. Ibid., pp. 253, 263; Corkran, *Cherokee Frontier*, pp. 38, 41; where it is stated that in April 1753 Chota claimed national Cherokee leadership, while the British continued to look to Tellico-Hiwassee. On page 41, Corkran continues: "[Governor] Glen finally realized that Hiwassee-Tellico had failed him, that he must, however, reluctantly look to Chota for control over the Cherokee. Chota, eager for recognition, was ready to respond heartily." Part of Chota's influence was traditional and depended on its symbolic rank as "Mother Town of the Nation," a title it was given even in colonial records, as for instance when a trader, Anthony Dean, in August 1751 wrote from Chota, "This is the Mother Town of the Nation and the Emperor living at Telliquo here now, a great many of the Telliquo people, as well as from the other 6 towns" (McDowell, *Colonial Records of South Carolina, 1750–1754*, p. 116). Other, earlier, references to Chota as "Mother Town of the Nation" are in Corkran, "Cherokee Prehistory," pp. 455–66; Corkran, *Cherokee Frontier*, pp. 3–4; Gearing, *Priests and Warriors*; and Reid, *Law of Blood*, pp. 17–18. The colonial records (McDowell, *Colonial Records of South Carolina, 1750–1754*, p. 253) indicate Chota's growing influence in April 1752, when Old Hop, the headman of "their Mother Town of Chotee," in association with other chiefs and warriors, sent messages to the other towns not to hurt Englishmen. Then again on page 263, "The Tallasee People would certainly, as is said, have killed them [English traders who refused to sell shot and powder] had they not been afraid of Chota."

Whether Chota was the ancient "mother town of the nation" and had revived this rank or reinterpreted the meaning of the title "mother town of the nation" is not entirely clear, but by the early 1750's, Chota was acknowledged to have this rank. Reid, *Law of Blood* (p. 18), misinterprets the rank when he says that Chota "was the capital of the Cherokees and its headman was the headman of the nation, exercising absolute power one would expect to be exercised by a monarch in a savage society." He seems to be assuming that any traditional leadership exercised by the headmen of Chota must be that of "absolute power," which, according to Reid, is usually exercised by the monarch of a savage society. This characterization of political authority, as the descriptions in Chapter 2 of the text show, did not hold for the southeastern societies, and surely did not hold for many, if any, indigenous North American societies. On the contrary, Old Hop and the other leaders at Chota manipulated its largely symbolic and not necessarily political status as "mother town of the nation" as a way of commanding the respect and deference of the Cherokee villages; calling Chota the "mother town of the nation" gave it an advantage over Tellico-Hiwassee within the traditional Cherokee cultural order. For a more detailed argument, see Duane Champagne, "Symbolic Structure and Political Change in Cherokee Society," *Journal of Cherokee Studies* 8 (Fall 1983): 88–94.

13. McDowell, *Colonial Records of South Carolina, 1750–1754*, pp. 434–35,

488; Corkran, *Cherokee Frontier*, pp. 79–84, 89. Corkran says (p. 79): "[Little Carpenter] asserted that he and Old Hop were the 'rulers' and commander-in-chief of all the towns in the Cherokee nation. Ammonscossittie [the former emperor from the Hiwassee-Tellico alliance], he said, lacked authority; nor should any Lower Towns be allowed to go to Charlestown without specific authority from Chota." Corkran (p. 89) further says that in 1756 "[Chota] ordered the Tellicos to break off their talks and come to Tomatly with Demere (a British officer) where they would hear the Little Carpenter and Old Hop [Second and Principal headmen of Chota, respectively] speak for them."

14. Timberlake, *Memoirs*, pp. 89–90; Persico, " Cherokee Political Organization," p. 97. Gearing, "Priests and Warriors," says that during the 1750's and 1760's the Cherokee formed a "tribal state." According to my definition, the Cherokee had not made any significant or permanent changes in political organization toward a more differentiated or politically integrated polity, nor did the Cherokee permanently centralize control over the law of blood revenge during the eighteenth century.

15. McDowell, *Colonial Records of South Carolina, 1750–1754*, pp. 101–18, 494; Corkran, *Cherokee Frontier*, pp. 16–17.

16. Dunbar Rowland and A. G. Sanders, eds., *Mississippi Provincial Archives, 1704–1743*, 1 (Jackson: Mississippi Department of Archives and History, 1927): 20, 162, 173.

17. Ibid., 3 (1932): 50, 277, 338, 700–703, 712, 718.

18. Edmond Atkins, *The Revolt of the Choctaw Indians*, Landowne Manuscript 809, London Museum, early 1750's; Woods, *French-Indian Relations*, pp. 148–153; Charles William Paape, "The Choctaw Revolt: A Chapter in the Intercolonial Rivalry in the Old Southwest" (Ph.D. diss., University of Illinois-Urbana, 1946), pp. 95–96.

19. Paape, *Choctaw Revolt*, pp. 119, 159–61.

20. McDowell, *Colonial Records of South Carolina 1754–1765*, pp. 420–23; Phillips, *The Fur Trade*, 1: 538; Rowland, *Mississippi Provincial Archives, 1763–1766*, 1: 227.

21. Adair, *History*, p. 31; Dunbar Rowland and Albert Godfrey Sanders, eds., *Mississippi Provincial Archives, 1701–1729: French Dominion* (Jackson: Mississippi Department of Archives and History, 1929), p. 23; Malone, *Chickasaw Nation*, p. 223; Woods, *French-Indian Relations*, pp. 13–15.

22. Malone, *Chickasaw Nation*, p. 216.

23. Adair, *History*, p. 290; Gibson, *The Chickasaws*, p. 80; Paape, "Choctaw Revolt," pp. 52–54.

24. McDowell, *Colonial Records of South Carolina, 1754–1765*, pp. 17–23, 109–16, 292, 413, 444–46, 460–61; Paape," Choctaw Revolt," pp. 52–57, 162, 168–69.

25. Adair, *Adair's History*, p. 274.

26. Adair, *History*, pp. 257–58; Swanton, "Social Significance of the Creek Confederacy," p. 333; IPH 108: 292–95; Swanton, "Early History of the Creek Indians," pp. 130–32; Green, *Politics of Indian Removal*, pp. 12–16; J. Leitch Wright, *Creeks and Seminoles*, pp. 3–12, 103–4. For the color of the Creek towns, see Hewitt, "Notes on the Creek Indians," pp. 124–27.

27. Rowland and Sanders, *Mississippi Provincial Archives, 1704–1743*, 3: 735; Adair, *History*, p. 260; Crane, *Southern Frontier*, p. 254; Corkran, *Creek Frontier*, pp. 57–65.

28. McDowell, *Colonial Records of South Carolina, 1754–1765*, pp. xviii-xxi; M234, roll 220, frames 1893–94; Corkran, *Creek Frontier*, pp. 3–5; 78–108, 187–93, 239; Swanton, "Social Organization and Social Usages," pp. 306–8.

29. Nairne, *Muskhogean Journals*, p. 35; McDowell, *Colonial Records of South Carolina 1754–1765*, pp. xviii-xxi, 57–62, 153–54, 234; Corkran, *Creek Frontier*, pp. 65–211.

30. Francis Prucha, *American Indian Policy in the Formative Years* (Cambridge, Mass.: Harvard University Press, 1962), pp. 13–29; Phillips, *The Fur Trade* 1: 553–54.

31. Timberlake, *Memoirs*, p. 60; E. Raymond Evans, "Notable Persons in Cherokee History: Ostenaco," *Journal of Cherokee Studies* 1 (1976): 52; Gearing, "Priests and Warriors," pp. 99–103; Persico, "Cherokee Political Organization," p. 97; Corkran, "Cherokee Prehistory," pp. 463–64; Goodwin, *Cherokees in Transition*, p. 111; Dickason, "Judicial History of the Cherokee Nation," pp. 71–74, 272–75. Dickason says (p. 71), "In the early 1760s the title 'High Priest of War' was given to the Great War Chief in an attempt to bolster nationalism among the Cherokee towns by capitalizing on the influence of magic and religion." The Head Warrior could now sit in judgment of the warriors since he was endowed with religiously legitimatized judicial powers and therefore could help control the young warriors whose actions might involve the Cherokee in war with the colonists.

Gearing, in "Priests and Warriors," talks about priest-chiefs and says that the civil "priest" chiefs had no more religious training than "virtually all Cherokee males." This characterization of civil "priest" chief leads to an apparent contradiction with my argument. Gearing says that the "priest" chiefs gained political prominence before the time of the Revolutionary War, but I am referring to religious specialists. I do agree that the village headmen (civil "priest" chiefs in Gearing's language) had gained considerable influence over the national council during the 1760's and early 1770's. The roles of priestly specialists, not those of the civil village headmen, devolved toward nonpolitical, local activities, like conjuring and doctoring among the people. Gearing's implication that the Cherokee did not have a hereditary priestly group is not supported by other sources: see, for instance, Gilbert, "The Eastern Cherokee"; and Longe, "A Small Postscript on the Ways and Manners of the Indians Called Cherokee," pp. 10–16; and the Payne Papers.

32. Gilbert, "Eastern Cherokee," pp. 321–23; Dickason, "Judicial History of the Cherokee Nation," pp. 48, 83–85.

33. Rowland, *Mississippi Provincial Archives, 1763–1766*, 1: 186–87, 215, 227; White, *Roots of Dependency*, pp. 74–82.

34. White, *Roots of Dependency*, p. 74; Margaret Zehmer Searcy, "Choctaw Subsistence, 1540–1830," in Reeves, ed., *Choctaw Before Removal*, pp. 45–47.

35. Adair, *History*, pp. 133–34, 164, 304.

36. Ibid., pp. 15, 31, 290, 368–70.

37. Ibid., pp. 91–99, 102, 118–20; Gibson, "Chickasaw Ethnography," p. 99.

38. Rowland, *Mississippi Provincial Archives, 1763–1766*, 1: 204–5; Swanton, "Early History of the Creek Indians," pp. 130–32; Corkran, *Creek Frontier*, pp. 239–44, 249–52.

39. Corkran, *Creek Frontier*, pp. 258–86.

40. Adair, *History*, pp. 16–17, 126, 133–34, 259, 430; Bartram, *Travels*, pp. 200, 301, 361, 384–85, 388–401.

41. Phillips, *Fur Trade*, 2: 69, 197–208; D. L. Jack Holmes, "Spanish Policy

Toward the Southern Indians in the 1790s," in Hudson, ed., *Four Centuries of Southern Indians*; Brown, *Old Frontiers*, pp. 220–21, 301–2.

42. Phillips, *The Fur Trade*, 2: 20–26; Joyce Williams and Jill Farrelly, *Diplomacy on the Indiana-Ohio Frontier, 1783–1791* (Bloomington: Indiana University Bicentennial Committee, 1976), pp. 50–52, 60–62; Brown, *Old Frontiers*, pp. 268, 300.

43. Mooney, "Myths of the Cherokee," pp. 68, 80–81; Brown, *Old Frontiers*, pp. 397–433.

44. James Kelly, "Oconostota," *Journal of Cherokee Studies* 3 (Fall 1979): 229; Mooney, "Myths of the Cherokee," pp. 45–50.

45. Dickason, "Judicial History of the Cherokee Nation," pp. 259–60, 275–82; Brown, *Old Frontiers*, pp. 251–53; Gearing, "Priests and Warriors," p. 103.

46. Brown, *Old Frontiers*, pp. 348–50, 444; David Knapp, "The Chickamaugas," *Georgia Historical Quarterly* 51 (1967): 195; Duane King, "Lessons in Cherokee Ethnology from the Captivity of Joseph Brown, 1788–1789," *Journal of Cherokee Studies* 1 (1976): 226–28.

47. John Payne Papers, 4: 314; Gearing, "Priests and Warriors," p. 103; Dickason, "Judicial History of the Cherokee Nation," pp. 259–60; Gilbert, "Eastern Cherokee," p. 366; McLoughlin, *Cherokee Renascence*, p. xvii.

48. Helen Shaw, *British Administration of the Southern Indians, 1756–1783* (Lancaster, Pa.: Lancaster Press, 1931), pp. 123–32, 150–64.

49. W. David Baird, *The Choctaw People* (Phoenix, Ariz.: Tribal Series, 1973), p. 4; Lincecum, "Life of Apushimataha," pp. 415–17; H.S. Halbert, "District Divisions of the Choctaw Nation," *Alabama Historical Society Publications: Miscellaneous Collections* 1 (1900): 375; Swanton, "Source Material," pp. 95–96. The date 1777 is taken from the observations of William Adair, *History*, pp. 133, 164, 401, who makes several remarks about secularization in Choctaw society in the period immediately before the American Revolutionary War.

50. Dr. Nutt ("Nutt's Trip to the Chickasaw Country," p. 46) says that in 1805 "They [the Chickasaw Council] meet at some house appointed (having no town houses or public square) and deliberate on such things as are laid before them . . . This people use no religious ceremonies."

51. Cotterill, *Southern Indians*, pp. 49–60;

52. Gibson, *The Chickasaws*, pp. 80–90; Cotterill, *Southern Indians*, pp. 60, 68–70, 90–121; Arrell Gibson, "The Colberts: Chickasaw Nation Elitism," in *Indian Leaders: Oklahoma's First Statesmen*, ed. H. Glenn Jordan and Thomas M. Holm (Oklahoma City: Oklahoma Historical Society, 1979), pp. 79–81; Baird, *The Chickasaw People*, pp. 25–33.

53. Corkran, *Creek Frontier*, pp. 292–317; Cotterill, *Southern Indians*, pp. 41–46, 55–58.

54. Corkran, *Creek Frontier*, pp. 317–24; Cotterill, *Southern Indians*, pp. 55–57.

55. Florette Henri, *The Southern Indians and Benjamin Hawkins, 1796–1816* (Norman: University of Oklahoma Press, 1986), pp. 73–74.

56. J. Leitch Wright, *Creeks and Seminoles*, p. 140; Cotterill, *Southern Indians*, pp. 75–98.

57. Jacobson, "The Alabama-Coushatta Indians of Texas and the Coushatta Indians of Louisiana," pp. 46–47; Cotterill, *Southern Indians*, pp. 61–62; Green, *Politics of Indian Removal*, pp. xi, 12, 32–36; Swanton, "Social Organization and Social Usages," pp. 324–27.

58. Swanton, "Early History of the Creek Indians," pp. 242–44; Cotterill, *Southern Indians*, pp. 101–4, 106, 124.

CHAPTER 4

1. Benjamin Hawkins, *Letters of Benjamin Hawkins, 1796–1806* (Savannah, Ga.: Collections of the Georgia Historical Society, 1916), pp. 338–39, 360–66; Jedidiah Morse, *A Report to the Secretary of War on Indian Affairs* (New Haven, Conn.: S. Converse, 1822), p. 290; Baird, *The Choctaw People*, p. 24; Young, *Redskins, Ruffleshirts, and Rednecks*, p. 8; Arthur DeRosier, "Thomas Jefferson and the Removal of the Choctaw Indians," *Southern Quarterly* 1 (1962): 55–56.

2. Ronald Satz, *American Indian Policy in the Jacksonian Era* (Lincoln: University of Nebraska Press, 1975), p. 1; DeRosier, "Thomas Jefferson and the Removal," p. 57; Mooney, "Myths of the Cherokee," p. 100; Samuel Carter, *Cherokee Sunset* (Garden City, N.Y.: Doubleday, 1976), pp. 25–29.

3. M208, roll 4, Return Jonathan Meigs, Letter, Nov. 2, 1809; Abraham Steiner and Frederick C. De Schweintz, "Report of the Journey of the Brethren Abraham Steiner and Frederick C. De Schweintz to the Cherokees and the Cumberland Settlements," in Williams, ed., *Early Travels in the Tennessee Country, 1540–1800*, pp. 445, 463, 484–85, 488–93; Wilkins, *Cherokee Tragedy*, p. 194; Merritt B. Pound, *Benjamin Hawkins: Indian Agent* (Athens: University of Georgia Press, 1951), pp. 103–6; Ralph Henry Gabriel, *Elias Boudinot, Cherokee, and His America* (Norman: University of Oklahoma Press, 1941), pp. 21–27, 101–7; McLoughlin, Cherokee Renascence, pp. 3, 43.

4. John Norton, *Journal of Major John Norton*, ed. Carl Klinck and James Talman (Toronto: Champlain Society, 1970), pp. 124, 131–32; McLoughlin, *Cherokee Renascence*, pp. 42–43, 61–69.

5. Hawkins, *Letters*, pp. 57, 412–22; Grant, *Benjamin Hawkins*, 1: 63; C. L. Grant, ed., *Letters, Journals, and Writings of Benjamin Hawkins*, vol. 2, *1802–1816*, (Savannah, Ga.: Belleview Press, 1980), pp. 526–27; Henri, *Southern Indians and Benjamin Hawkins*, pp. 110, 119–20, 130, 137.

6. Thomas C. Cochran, ed., *The New American State Papers, 1789–1860*, 12 (Wilmington, Del.: Scholarly Resources, 1972); 325; Hawkins, *Letters*, p. 411; Jennings, "Nutt's Trip," pp. 80–83; Daniel F. Littlefield, Jr., *The Chickasaw Freedmen: A People Without a Country* (Westport, Conn.: Greenwood, 1980), p. 4; White, *Roots of Dependency*, pp. 92–104; 122.

7. Hawkins, *Letters*, pp. 24–30, 359–66, 392–93; *Panopolist and Missionary Herald* 14 (1818): 339; M208, roll 5, R. J. Meigs, Letter, July 20, 1810; M271, roll 1, frames 1135, 1182, 1187; M271, roll 2, frame 742; Chapman J. Milling, *Red Carolinians* (Chapel Hill: University of North Carolina Press, 1940), p. 334; McLoughlin, *Cherokee Renascence*, pp. xviii–xix, 31–32, 64; J. Leitch Wright, *Creeks and Seminoles*, pp. 75–76, 79, 84, 99; Schoolcraft, *Indian Tribes of the United States*, 6: 417; Pound, *Benjamin Hawkins*, p. 110; Littlefield, *Africans and Creeks*, p. 51; Gibson, *The Chickasaws*, pp. 80, 99–100, 146–50; Jennings, "Nutt's Trip," p. 41; Guy B. Barden, "The Colberts and the Chickasaw Nation," *Tennessee Historical Quarterly* 17 (1953): 236; Gibson, "The Colberts," pp. 81–82; Baird, *The Chickasaw People*, p. 35; White, *Roots of Dependency*, p. 110.

8. M234, roll 223, frames 460–61; M208, roll 4, R. J. Meigs, Letter, June 3, 1808; M208, roll 4, R. J. Meigs, Letter, Nov. 2, 1809; M208, R. J. Meigs, roll 5, Letter, Feb. 4, 1810; M208, roll 5, R. J. Meigs, Letter, Apr. 5, 1811; M208, roll 7,

R. J. Meigs, Letter, Jan. 17, 1817; Lincecum, "Life of Apushimataha," p. 482; John Payne Papers, 8, letter no. 1 by John Ridge, Feb. 26, 1826; Grant, *Benjamin Hawkins*, 1: 284; Jennings, "Nutt's Trip," pp. 46–47; Coleman, *Presbyterian Missionary Attitudes*, pp. 56–57, 61, 81–82; Henri, *Southern Indians and Benjamin Hawkins*, p. 21; Gabriel, *Elias Boudinot*, p. 136; Theda Perdue, "Rising from the Ashes: The *Cherokee Phoenix* as an Ethnohistorical Source," *Ethnohistory* 24 (Summer 1977): 211; McLoughlin, *Cherokee Renascence*, pp. 64–65, 172–73.

9. M208, Cherokee National Council at Ustanali, address, Apr. 25, 1806; Carter, *Cherokee Sunset*, pp. 21–22; *Missionary Herald* 18 (1822): 301; Cotterill, *Southern Indians*, pp. 131–32.

10. Grant, *Benjamin Hawkins*, 1: 364, 368, 379–80; McLoughlin, *Cherokee Renascence*, pp. 32–33, 53–60.

11. Hawkins, *Letters*, pp. 136, 139, 156; Mary Young, "Indian Removal and the Attack on Tribal Autonomy: The Cherokee Case," in *Indians of the Lower South: Past and Present*, ed. John K. Mahon (Proceedings of the Gulf History and Humanities Conference, vol. 5, 1975), p. 128; McLoughlin, *Cherokee Renascence*, pp. 52–53.

12. Theda Perdue, *Slavery and the Evolution of Cherokee Society, 1540–1866* (Knoxville: University of Tennessee Press, 1979), p. 56; McLoughlin, *Cherokee Renascence*, p. 94; Milling, *Red Carolinians*, pp. 340–34.

13. Michelle Daniel, "From Blood Feud to Jury System: The Metamorphosis of Cherokee Law from 1750 to 1840," *American Indian Quarterly* 11 (Spring 1987): 108.

14. M208, roll 4, Path Killer et al., Letter, May 27, 1809; M208, roll 4, Ridge et al., Letter, May 1809; Cherokee National Committee and Council, *Laws of the Cherokee Nation Passed by the National Committee and Council* (Knoxville, Tenn.: Herskill & Brown, 1821), pp. 21–22; Wilkins, *Cherokee Tragedy*, pp. 29–32; McLoughlin, *Cherokee Renascence*, pp. 43–47; Dickason, "Judicial History of the Cherokee Nation," pp. 287–90.

15. Gabriel, *Elias Boudinot*, pp. 121–22; Carter, *Cherokee Sunset*, pp. 22–29; Gibson, *The Chickasaws*, p. 90.

16. M208, roll 1, Ustanali Council, Mar. 20, 1801; M208, roll 3, R. J. Meigs, Letter, August 1805; Hawkins, *Letters*, pp. 21–24, 379–80, 385; Mooney, "Myths of the Cherokee," pp. 81–83; Gary E. Moulton, *John Ross, Cherokee Chief* (Athens: University of Georgia Press, 1978), pp. 7–10.

17. M208, roll 1, R. J. Meigs, Letter, Apr. 12, 1802; M208, roll 2, Ustanali Council, Apr. 29, 1803; M208, roll 2, R. J. Meigs, Letter, Feb. 19, 1804; M271, roll 1, frame 105; Cotterill, *Southern Indians*, pp. 143–44.

18. John Payne Papers, 2: 41–42, 46–47; John Payne Papers, 6: 43–45; M208, roll 3, Jos. Phillips to R. J. Meigs, Letter, Aug. 15, 1807; M208, roll 3, Black Fox et al., Letter, September 1807, Wills Town; Norton, *Journal*, p. 73; Mooney, "Myths of the Cherokee," pp. 84–86; Cotterill, *Southern Indians*, pp. 152–60; Carter, *Cherokee Sunset*, pp. 25–29; McLoughlin, *Cherokee Renascence*, pp. 110–11.

19. John Payne Papers, 2: 43–45; M208, roll 4, Stone Carrier, Letter, May 5, 1808; M208, roll 4, R. J. Meigs, Letter, July 11, 1808; Cotterill, *Southern Indians*, pp. 153–60.

20. John Payne Papers, 6: 9–11; McLoughlin, *Cherokee Renascence*, pp. 144–48.

21. John Payne Papers, 2: 37; IPH 11: 279–80; McLoughlin, *Cherokee Renascence*, pp. 149–54.

22. Norton, *Journal*, pp. 73, 75–76, 111–17, 124–25; M208, roll 4, Path Killer et al., Letter, Sept. 27, 1809, Willstown.

23. Norton, *Journal*, pp. 60–71; M208, roll 4, R. J. Meigs, Letter, Dec. 1, 1809; McLoughlin, *Cherokee Renascence*, p. 109, 163–67.

24. Gary E. Moulton, ed., *The Papers of Chief John Ross*, vol. 1 *1807–1839* (Norman: University of Oklahoma Press, 1984), p. 240; John Payne Papers, 2: 16; Norton, *Journal*, pp. 73, 111–17; Cotterill, *Southern Indians*, p. 160.

25. M208, roll 4, Path Killer et al., Letter, Sept. 27, 1809, Willstown; Cotterill, *Southern Indians*, p. 160.

26. Cherokee National Committee and Council, *Laws of the Cherokee Nation*, p. 23; Carter, *Cherokee Sunset*, p. 31; William G. McLoughlin, *The Cherokee Ghost Dance* (Mercer, Ga.: Mercer University Press, 1984), p. 108.

27. Young, "Indian Removal," p. 128; McLoughlin, *Cherokee Renascence*, pp. 44–46.

28. IPH 19: 60–62; Reid, *Law of Blood*, pp. 235, 243, 263, 271–72; Perdue, "Rising from the Ashes," p. 211.

29. Mooney, "Myths of the Cherokee," pp. 88–89; Carter, *Cherokee Sunset*, pp. 33–36; Wilkins, *Cherokee Tragedy*, pp. 58–61; McLoughlin, *Cherokee Ghost Dance*, pp. 111–51.

30. M208, roll 5, R. J. Meigs, Letter, May 8, 1812; M208, roll 6, R. J. Meigs, Letter, Dec. 21, 1815; McLoughlin, *Cherokee Renascence*, pp. 180–84; McLoughlin, *Cherokee Ghost Dance*, p. 147.

31. McLoughlin, *Cherokee Renascence*, pp. 176–78; Fogelson, "Cherokee Notions of Power," p. 188.

32. Eaton, *John Ross*, p. 17; *Missionary Herald* 25 (1929): 375; Gerard Alexander Reed, "The Ross-Watie Conflict: Factionalism in the Cherokee Nation, 1839–1865" (Ph.D. diss., University of Oklahoma, 1967), p. 25.

33. John Payne Papers, 2: 41, 43–45; John Payne Papers, 6: 9, 43–45; M208, roll 3, J. Phillips, Letter, Aug. 15, 1807; M208, roll 3, R. J. Meigs, Letter, May 21, 1805; Norton, *Journal*, pp. 82, 133–34.

34. M208, roll 7, R. J. Meigs to William Crawford, Letter, Nov. 8, 1816; M208, roll 4, R. J. Meigs, Letter, Sept. 20, 1808; M208, roll 5, R. J. Meigs, Letter, Oct. 15, 1810; "The Chiefs do not cede land; but in the presence of the populace who will attend to all treaties . . . It is extremely unpopular to talk of selling land"; M208, roll 5, R. J. Meigs, Letter, May 8, 1812; McLoughlin, *Cherokee Renascence*, p. 71.

35. M271, roll 1, frames 162–65.

36. Cotterill, *Southern Indians*, p. 134; White, *Roots of Dependency*, pp. 111–12.

37. M234, roll 181, frames 135–36; John D. Guire, "Face to Face in Mississippi Territory, 1798–1817," in Reeves, ed., *Choctaw Before Removal*, pp. 165–68; Alan V. Briceland, "Ephraim Kirby: Mr. Jefferson's Emissary on the Tombigbee-Mobile Frontier in 1804," *Alabama Review* 24 (1971): 100–102; Thelma Bounds, *Children of Nanih Waiya* (San Antonio, Tex.: Naylor, 1964), pp. 20–24; Angie Debo, *The Rise and Fall of the Choctaw Republic* (Norman: University of Oklahoma Press, 1972), p. 35.

38. M271, roll 1, frames 1201, 1207, 1210; Cushman, *History*, pp. 191, 248–55; Lincecum, "Life of Apushimataha," pp. 415, 423–24; Lincecum, "History of the Chahta Nation: Addenda," p. 103. According to Cushman (pp. 211–65), the Choctaw consulted a seer in 1811 to decide whether to follow Tecumseh in a war against the United States or to follow Chief Pushmataha in alliance with the U.S.

Consulting a seer is not necessarily a contradiction of the argument of a Choctaw tradition for excluding religious specialists from political positions and decision making. The seer was not one of the political leaders but an old man who was not present at the Choctaw councils that were discussing the question of whether to join Tecumseh or ally with the Americans, and the fact that the Choctaw council debated this difficult matter without reaching a compromise solution implies that seers were not routinely consulted in political matters. The Choctaw consulted a seer only after failing to reach an agreement—as a last resort on an important decision that could not be resolved by "secular" political institutions. The general Choctaw world view still contained belief in magic and belief in the efficacy of ceremonies to effect causal events, and consulting a seer on an important issue that threatened to tear the Choctaw nation into a civil war—as Cushman says— would not be inconsistent with the beliefs of many Choctaw. Though the seer's decision went against Tecumseh, Cushman notes (pp. 260–65) that Pushmataha threatened to execute any Choctaw warrior who joined Tecumseh. By the 1800's, so far as I know, the Choctaw did not routinely consult seers in political matters, and Cushman's account of the events of 1811 is unusual.

39. M271, roll 1, frames 1201, 1207, 1210; M234, Choctaw Agency 1824–31, frames 153–55; Debo, *Choctaw Republic*, pp. 39–40; Lincecum, "Life of Apushimataha," p. 424.

40. Dawson A. Phelps, "The Chickasaw Council House," *Journal of Mississippi History* 14 (1952): 173–74; Jennings, "Nutt's Trip," pp. 46–47, 53.

41. M234, roll 136, frames 282–83; M208, roll 3, R. J. Meigs, Letter, Mar. 7, 1805; M208, roll 3, Chickasaw Chiefs, Letter, July 1805; Henri, *Southern Indians and Benjamin Hawkins*, pp. 255–56; Harry Warren, "Some Chickasaw Chiefs and Prominent Men," *Publications of the Mississippi Historical Society* 8 (1904): 555–60.

42. M271, roll 1, frames 992–994, 1016; M208, roll 4, R. J. Meigs, Letter, Mar. 1, 1809; Gibson, *The Chickasaw*, pp. 143, 150; Jennings, "Nutt's Trip," p. 53; Scholarly Resources, *Chickasaws and Choctaws*, p. 22; Henri, *Southern Indians and Benjamin Hawkins*, p. 224.

43. M208, roll 5, G. W. Lever, Letter, Apr. 15, 1812; M208, roll 6, George Colbert, Letter, May 4, 1813; M208, roll 6, M. McGee, Letter, Mar. 2, 1815; Cushman, *History*, pp. 385–86, 391; Baird, *The Chickasaw People*, pp. 33–35.

44. M 234, roll 135, frame 259; M208, roll 5, La Robert, Letter, Aug. 14, 1812; Jennings, "Nutt's Trip," p. 46; John E. Parsons, "Letters on the Chickasaw Removal of 1837," *New York Historical Society Quarterly* 37 (1953): 282.

45. Jennings, "Nutt's Trip," p. 48; Cushman, *History*, pp. 385–86, 391.

46. M234, roll 135, frame 259; Gibson, *The Chickasaw*, pp. 80, 99–101, 150; Baird, *The Chickasaw People*, pp. 35–36; Barden, "The Colberts and the Chickasaw Nation," pp. 222–29, 236–45; Gibson, "The Colberts," pp. 81–89. There are obvious difficulties in an argument for political change and stability that is made primarily on the basis of class groups or mixed-blood elites, while the social and political organization of the majority of the society remains underanalyzed and is given secondary accounting. Gibson seems particularly impressed by the mixed bloods, especially the Colberts, and gives little weight to the social and political organization and action of the full-bloods who made up the majority of the Chickasaw population. For example, in *The Chickasaws* (p. 80) he refers to the period ending in 1818 as the twilight of traditional leadership and the beginning of mixed-blood control over tribal affairs; he also says (p. 99) that by 1800 the Col-

berts as leaders of the mixed bloods "dominated the nation." In "The Colberts" (p. 85) Gibson says that three-fourths of the nation was composed of full-bloods who in the 1820's "increasingly withdrew [from politics] or transported themselves out of their confusion with rum and brandy"; furthermore (p. 85), he describes Piomingo, who died in 1795, as the last assertive full-blood leader. Gibson laments the death of Levi Colbert in 1834 (pp. 92–93), who according to Gibson ruled through the ancient apparatus of Chickasaw chief and council. Gibson also says (p. 95) that the passing of the traditional Chickasaw government after 1837 merely led to greater tribal confusion and divisiveness. Baird and Barden are less harsh than Gibson in their treatment of the conservative majority, but they, too, characterize the Chickasaw government as class dominated and do not give a balanced account of the political action and organization of the conservative majority.

I should say that none of these authors actually makes the argument of class domination, but by focusing on the mixed-blood elite, they underplay the political action, culture, and social order of most members of the society.

47. M234, roll 135, frames 151, 155, 194, 259, 693–95; Barden, "The Colberts and the Chickasaw Nation," pp. 222–29. The argument for the planters not being in a position to advocate institutional change refers to the nondifferentiated national Chickasaw polity, where kinship and political organization are fused together. This institutional configuration should create considerable resistance to political change among the kinship groups, who will not want to lose their political prerogatives. The data indicate that indeed there was considerable normative resistance to change. For example, in the documents of M234, Letters Received by the Office of Indian Affairs, 1824–1881, roll 135, frame 259, the Chickasaw agent in 1826 speaks of "a few educated Indians and half breeds who are accumulating wealth and lording it over their ignorant countrymen . . . Although a majority are now opposed to the introduction of laws amongst them." In the same year, when the Chickasaw leaders were pressed by American officials to remove west, they replied: "We cannot act contrary to the will of the nation . . . They are determined on staying in this native country (p. 194)." It was this sort of characterization of normative resistance to change (I could cite more examples) that convinced me that the nondifferentiated Chickasaw social order created strong barriers to increased political differentiation.

48. Grant, *Benjamin Hawkins*, 1: xv–xviii, 135–36, 268, 290; Pound, *Benjamin Hawkins*, pp. 85–92.

49. Hawkins, *Letters*, pp. 90, 288, 297–98, 355, 435–36, 464, 478; Grant, *Benjamin Hawkins*, 1: xviii–xxii, 63–66, 189, 268, 275, 277; Henri, *Southern Indians and Benjamin Hawkins*, pp. 59–60, 92, 103; J. Leitch Wright, *Creeks and Seminoles*, pp. 143–45.

50. Hawkins, *Letters*, pp. 301, 304; Grant, *Benjamin Hawkins*, 2: 417, 422–24, 535; Henri, *Southern Indians and Benjamin Hawkins*, pp. 98–99, 103–4; Cotterill, *Southern Indians*, pp. 125, 145–52.

51. Cotterill, *Southern Indians*, pp. 125–29, 145.

52. Grant, *Benjamin Hawkins*, 2: 433; J. Leitch Wright, *Creeks and Seminoles*, p. 150.

53. Grant, *Benjamin Hawkins*, 2: 450, 473–78; J. Leitch Wright, *Creeks and Seminoles*, p. 149; Henri, *Southern Indians and Benjamin Hawkins*, p. 236.

54. M208, roll 4, Talk by Big Warrior, May 1809; Grant, *Benjamin Hawkins*, 2: 478–80, 546; J. Leitch Wright, *Creeks and Seminoles*, p. 152; Henri, *Southern*

Indians and Benjamin Hawkins, pp. 246–47; Green, *Politics of Indian Removal*, pp. 37–40.

55. Grant, *Benjamin Hawkins*, 2: 505–6, 508, 522, 526–27, 562–65, 576.

56. Ibid., pp. 543, 564, 576, 579–83.

57. Ibid., pp. 522, 526, 535, 539, 588–90; Nunez, Jr., "Creek Nativism and the Creek War of 1813–1814," pp. 3–8; J. Leitch Wright, *Creeks and Seminoles*, pp. 153–60; Hudson, *Elements of Southeastern Indian Religion*, pp. 22–23; Debo, *Road to Disappearance*, pp. 76–78; Green, *Politics of Indian Removal*, pp. 39–40.

58. IPH 35: 438; McLoughlin, *Cherokee Renascence*, pp. 186–88.

59. Grant, *Benjamin Hawkins*, 2: 588–90, 598–604, 609–15, 618, 620, 626, 628, 631–33, 638–39, 642, 647–48, 757.

60. Ibid., p. 733; Green, *Politics of Indian Removal*, pp. 41–42.

61. Grant, *Benjamin Hawkins*, 2: 692, 731–33; Green, *Politics of Indian Removal*, pp. 42–43.

62. M234, roll 219, frame 1487; Grant, *Benjamin Hawkins*, 2: 733.

63. Debo, *The Road to Disappearance*, p. 85; Swanton, "Social Organization and Social Usages," pp. 315–16.

64. Debo, *Road to Disappearance*, pp. 84–85.

CHAPTER 5

1. Francis Prucha, *American Indian Policy in the Formative Years: The Indian Trade and Intercourse Acts of 1790–1834* (Cambridge, Mass.: Harvard University Press, 1962), pp. 3, 141–86; *Missionary Herald* 18 (1822): 183; George Harmon, *Sixty Years of Indian Affairs: Political, Economic, and Diplomatic, 1789–1850* (Chapel Hill: University of North Carolina Press, 1971), pp. 189–228; Young, *Redskins, Ruffleshirts, and Rednecks*, p. 74; Debo, *Rise and Fall of the Choctaw Republic*, p. 49.

2. Prucha, *American Indian Policy*, p. 225; Young, *Redskins, Ruffleshirts, and Rednecks*, pp. 5–6; Mooney, "Myths of the Cherokee," p. 105; Brown, *Old Frontiers*, pp. 447–48; Carter, *Cherokee Sunset*, p. 59; Satz, *Indian Policy in the Jacksonian Era*, pp. 3–9.

3. Satz, *Indian Policy in the Jacksonian Era*, p. 9.

4. *Panopolist and Missionary Magazine United* 4 (1811–12): 339; *Missionary Herald* 25 (1829): 59–60; Reed, "Ross-Watie Conflict," p. 267; Gabriel, *Elias Boudinot*, p. 136. All the southeastern nations had been engaged in horticulture (farming with hand implements) for hundreds of years before Columbus landed in the New World; the Cherokee, the Choctaw, and the Chickasaw began working with plows and domesticated animals under the supervision of U.S. agents early in the nineteenth century. Agriculture, involving more sustained husbanding of new draft animals, previously unknown to Indians, was a significant change over horticultural farming, not a continuation of traditional farming methods.

5. IPH 34: 161–62; M234, roll 220 (1825), frame 2014; M234, roll 220, (1826), frames 20–21, 691–96; M234, roll 222, frame 562; J. Leitch Wright, *Creeks and Seminoles*, pp. 75–76, 79, 84, 99; Morse, *Report on Indian Affairs*, pp. 169, 178–80, 182; Cushman, *History*, p. 104; *Missionary Herald* 26 (1830): 83; *Missionary Herald* 25 (1829): 57–59; *Missionary Herald* 26 (1830): 155; Baird, *The Chickasaw People*, p. 35; Norton, *Journal*, pp. 57–64, 77–82, 117; William McLoughlin and Walter Conser, Jr., "The Cherokee in Transition: A Statistical Analysis of the Fed-

eral Cherokee Census of 1835," *Journal of American History* 64 (1977): 690–92; Perdue, *Slavery and the Evolution of Cherokee Society*, pp. 57–61; Gibson, *The Chickasaws*, pp. 80, 138–43, 145–46, 158–60, 179; Jennings, "Nutt's Trip," pp. 47–48; Barden, "The Colberts and the Chickasaw Nation," pp. 236–38; Gibson, "The Colberts," pp. 80–86; Littlefield, *Chickasaw Freedmen*, pp. 6–10; Littlefield, *Africans and Creeks*, p. 51; M. Thomas Bailey, *Reconstruction in Indian Territory* (Port Washington, NY: Kennikot, 1972), pp. 4–10, 22; Schoolcraft, *Indian Tribes of the United States*, 6: 526; Lincecum, "Life of Apushimataha," pp. 416, 423–24; Debo, *Rise and Fall of the Choctaw Republic*, pp. 60, 111–14.

Not cited are extensive readings of interviews from and about subsistence farmers in the Indian-Pioneer Papers of Oklahoma (about 60,000 pages), where by their own account subsistence farmers explain their lifestyle and how much they often cultivated. Other reports in the Indian-Pioneer papers come from observers who lived in the societies and gave estimates about the acreage use by various classes of people. The farm size of five to seven acres should be considered an estimate, but it seems to hold throughout the data, and is similar to Richard White's estimates of four to five acres from the Choctaw removal census of 1830. White estimates that only 20 percent of the Choctaw in 1831 were "even marginally in market agriculture," that is, farming ten or more acres of land (*Roots of Dependency*, p. 135). The concept of subsistence farmer that I have used regards nearly all farmers as being at least marginally engaged in the market. In the 1800's, the southeastern Indians were still dependent on manufactured goods, which meant that even subsistence farmers had to sell cattle or farm produce in order to trade or buy goods such as farming equipment, guns, ammunition, cloth, and sugar that they now required. The position that even subsistence-oriented farmers are located in a network of market relations is one of the fundamental insights of world-system theory. White's estimate of 20 percent of the Choctaw in 1831 as being marginally in the commercial market has to include the members of the planter class who were actively engaged in profit making and extensive accumulation of wealth. Ronald Satz, in "The Mississippi Choctaw: From the Removal Treaty to the Federal Agency," in *After Removal: The Choctaw in Mississippi*, ed. Samuel J. Wells and Roseanna Tubby (1986), states (p. 6) that among the Choctaw in 1830 there were about 200 "highly acculturated mixed bloods with extensive property holdings, including black slaves." The Choctaw population is generally estimated at about 30,000 in 1830, and the estimated percentage for the planter class is then one percent, which is certainly within my range estimate of over 90 percent subsistence farmers. If we consider that each of the 200 planters has a family of four to five, the proportion of individuals in the planter class would be less than 4–5 percent of the total Choctaw population. Similarly in 1835, some 8 percent of the Cherokee were slaveholders, but not all slaveholders were engaged in the for-profit export market (McLoughlin and Conser, "Cherokee in Transition," pp. 690–92). I am willing to allow for error of several percentage points, but an estimate that "more than 90 percent" of the Cherokee, Choctaw, and Creek were not planters or merchants who obtained most of their livelihood in market exchange is, I believe, a reasonable estimate. My purpose in explaining this at length is to show that those who were actively engaged in entrepreneurial market enterprise and accumulating significant personal wealth, as a class, were only a small minority of the respective nation and therefore could not dominate their government or induce change merely by force of numbers; they had to mobilize the subsistence farmers in support of their political leadership, and, more importantly, in support of any innovations they wanted to introduce into their government.

6. M208, roll 7, R. J. Meigs to A. Jackson, Letter, June 17, 1816; M208, roll 7, Hicks to R. J. Meigs, Letter, Aug. 10, 1816; M208, roll 7, C. Hicks to R. J. Meigs, Letter, Sept. 9, 1816; M208, roll 7, Cherokee Chiefs to R. J. Meigs, Letter, Dec. 9, 1816; McLoughlin, *Cherokee Renascence*, pp. 201–4.

7. M208, roll 7, Cherokee National Council, Sept. 19, 1817; Moulton, *John Ross*, pp. 15–19; McLoughlin, *Cherokee Renascence*, pp. 214–17.

8. John Payne Papers, 6: 295–97; M208, roll 7, R. J. Meigs, Letter, Oct. 30, 1817; Cochran, *The New American State Papers*, 12: 179–81; Perdue, *Slavery and the Evolution of Cherokee Society*, pp. 59–61; McLoughlin, *Cherokee Renascence*, pp. 222–24; Gabriel, *Elias Boudinot*, pp. 136–38; Young, "Indian Removal," pp. 128–29.

9. John Payne Papers, 6: 295–96; Gabriel, *Elias Boudinot*, pp. 136–37; Carolyn Thomas Foreman, *Indian Women Chiefs* (Norman: University of Oklahoma Press, 1966), pp. 7, 72–73, 79–81; Norma Tucker, "Nancy Ward, Ghighau of the Cherokees," *Georgia Historical Quarterly* 53 (June 1969): 192–93, 197–98.

10. IPH 100: 432–34; John Payne Papers, 6: 295–96; Emmett Starr, *Starr's History of the Cherokee*, ed. Jack Gregory and Rennard Strickland (Fayetteville, Ark.: Indian Heritage Association, 1967), pp. 42–43; McLoughlin, *Cherokee Renascence*, pp. 224–27.

11. John Payne Papers, 6: 20–26; M208, roll 7, R. J. Meigs to Crawford, Letter, Nov. 8, 1816; Carter, *Cherokee Sunset*, p. 38; Moulton, *John Ross*, pp. 19–23.

12. M208, roll 7, R. J. Meigs to Path Killer et al., July 4, 1818; M208, roll 7, Big Half Breed et al. to R. J. Meigs, Apr. 29, 1817; M208, roll 7, R. J. Meigs to Graham, May 6, 1817; M208, roll 7, Path Killer et al, Letter, Sept. 19, 1817; M208, roll 7, Toochelar to R. J. Meigs, Jan. 9, 1817; M208, roll 7, R. J. Meigs to McMinn, Jan. 17, 1817; Cochran, *New American State Papers*, 12: 181; McLoughlin, *Cherokee Renascence*, pp. 229–31, 420.

13. John Payne Papers, 6: 24–26; M208, roll 7, Path Killer et al, Letter, Sept. 19, 1817; M208, roll 7, Cherokee Chiefs, Letter, Aug. 7, 1818; M208, roll 7, Path Killer et al., Letter, Nov. 25, 1818; Cochran, *New American State Papers*, 12: 257–58.

14. "These people consider the offer of taking reserves, and becoming citizens of the United States as of no service to them. They know they are not to be admitted to the rights of freemen, or the privileges of their oath, and say, no Cherokee, or white man with a Cherokee family, can possibly live among such white people, as will first settle their country," *Panoplist, and Missionary Herald* 5 (1819): 46; M208, roll 14, Calhoun to McMinn, July 29, 1818; John Payne Papers, 9: 56–59; Eaton, *John Ross and the Cherokee Indians*, pp. 21–29.

15. John Payne Papers, 6: 30–31; John Payne Papers, 8: John Ridge, Letter, Feb. 27, 1826; M234, roll 71, frame 295; Foreman, *Indian Women Chiefs*, pp. 72–73.

16. M208, roll 9, Cherokee Chiefs, Letter, March 21, 1821; McLoughlin, *Cherokee Renascence*, pp. 276–78; Carter, *Cherokee Sunset*, p. 38; Moulton, *John Ross*, pp. 24–29; Mooney, "Myths of the Cherokee," p. 114.

17. M208, roll 8, Path Killer to R. J. Meigs, July 7, 1819; M208, roll 14, Calhoun to McMinn, July 29, 1818; M234, roll 71, frames 5–13, 295–300, 520; M234, roll 72, frames 42–51, 86, 188–89; M271, roll 3, frames 473–76; Eaton, *John Ross and the Cherokee Indians*, pp. 29–43; Carter, *Cherokee Sunset*, pp. 53–59.

18. M208, roll 14, Calhoun to McMinn, July 29, 1818; M234, roll 72, Hicks et al. to Montgomery, Dec. 11, 1826; Cochran, *New American State Papers*, 11: 645; M208, roll 9, Cherokee National Council, Oct. 23, 1822; M208, roll 9, Path Killer et al. to R. J. Meigs, Oct. 26, 1822; M271, roll 4, frames 58—59.

19. IPH 83: 404; John Payne Papers 8: John Ridge, Letter, Feb. 27, 1826; McLoughlin, *Cherokee Renascence*, p. 284.

20. *Panopolist and Missionary Herald* 16 (1820): 122.

21. Persico, "Cherokee Political Organization," pp. 99—103.

22. John Payne Papers, 8: John Ridge, Letter, Feb. 27, 1826; Eaton, *John Ross and the Cherokee Indians*, p. 29; Morse, *Report on Indian Affairs, 1820*, pp. 169, 172—80; Mooney, "Myths of the Cherokee," pp. 105—7; Cherokee National Committee and Council, *Laws of the Cherokee Nation*, pp. 1—14.

23. John Payne Papers, 8: John Ridge, Letter, Feb. 27, 1826; M271, roll 4, frames 54—55; *Missionary Herald* 18 (1822): 234—35.

24. John Payne Papers, 2: 16—18; Persico, "Cherokee Political Organization," pp. 99—103; Carter, *Cherokee Sunset*, pp. 54—55; Milling, *Red Carolinians*, p. 341; Reed, "Ross-Watie Conflict," p. 12; *Missionary Herald* 18 (1822): 234—35.

25. IPH 39: 368—75; M234, roll 72, frames 217—19; Cochran, *New American State Papers*, 11: 645; Carter, *Cherokee Sunset*, pp. 53—54.

26. *Missionary Herald*, 23 (1827): 213, 328, 381; IPH 39: 373—74; Moulton, *John Ross*, pp. 32—33; John Payne Papers, 2: 16—18; M234, roll 72, Hicks and Ross to Montgomery, Dec. 11, 1826; IPH 11: 279—82; IPH 39: 374; Wilkins, *Cherokee Tragedy*, pp. 201—3.

27. Wilkins, *Cherokee Tragedy*, pp. 201—2.

28. Persico, "Cherokee Political Organization," p. 107; William McLoughlin, "Cherokee Anti-Mission Sentiment, 1824—1828," *Ethnohistory* 21 (Fall 1974): 362, 363, 367; Wilkins, *Cherokee Tragedy*, p. 203; McLoughlin, *Cherokee Renascence*, pp. 388, 392—94.

29. ABCFM Papers, 18.3.1.IV:185, I. Proctor to J. Evarts, May 10, 1827; ABCFM Papers 18.3.1. V:235—38, S. Worcester to J. Evarts, March 1827; ABCFM Papers 18.3.1. V:388, S. Worcester to J. Evarts, May 11, 1827; John Payne Papers, 6: 49—58, 304—5; *Missionary Herald* 24 (1828): 9; McLoughlin, "Cherokee Anti-Mission Sentiment," pp. 362—65, 367; McLoughlin, *Cherokee Renascence*, pp. 405—8.

30. M234, roll 72, frames 264—66.

31. M234, roll 72, frames 497—517; John Payne Papers, 2: 162—64; IPH 100: 432; Perdue, "Rising from the Ashes," p. 214; Persico, "Cherokee Political Organization," pp. 99—103.

32. John Payne Papers, 2: 141—56; John Payne Papers, 6: 68; *Missionary Herald* 25 (1829): 20, 185, 318, 345—46.

33. See: John Payne Papers, 6: 303—5; M234, roll 72, frame 260; Perdue, *Slavery and the Evolution of Cherokee Society*, pp. 56—59, Theda Perdue, "Cherokee Planters: The Development of Plantation Slavery Before Removal," in King, ed., *Cherokee Indian Nation*, pp. 112—13; Perdue, "Rising from the Ashes," p. 214; Gabriel, *Elias Boudinot*, pp. 137—38.

34. Supporters of the class domination argument err in focusing their analysis on personalities, on the mixed-blood and economic-elite Cherokee groups, and not paying enough attention to Cherokee social structure, culture, and the organization and activities of the majority of Cherokee conservatives. They tend to underplay the role of culture, differences in institutional order, and group activities

and organization of the conservative majority in each of the southeastern nations. I am not alone in believing that it is not possible to explain institutional change without consideration of the culture, institutions, and group activities of both the elites and the action of the conservatives. For example, in a review of McLough- lin's book *Cherokee Renascence*, James McClurken remarks that in McLoughlin's portrayal of the Cherokee, "The educated, English-speaking Metis (mixed-bloods) coopted a few traditional leaders but in the end the power and authority remained in the hands of a privileged aristocracy . . . McLoughlin fails to balance the per- spectives of the traditionalist majority who opposed or gave only tacit approval to a nationalist program promoted by the Metis minority. He pays lip service to the importance of indigenous cultural religious leaders like the Adonisgi and clan structures in political decisions made by the traditionalist Cherokee . . . we are told these structures were secondary." (James McClurken, "Review of *Chero- kee Renascence in the New Republic*," *American Culture and Research Journal* 11: 3 [1987]: 197–208.) Theda Perdue's work shows a sensitivity to the social and political conditions of the Cherokee conservatives, but in more than one publi- cation she gives a class-based argument that the Cherokee Constitution of 1827 was created to further the economic interests of the Cherokee slaveholders. For example, in "Rising from the Ashes" (p. 214) she says, "The 12 founding fathers owned 22 percent of all the black slaves in the Cherokee nation," and she em- phasizes that 40 percent of the laws passed in the Cherokee legislative sessions of 1827 and 1828 were associated with the economic activities of the planters, and that a considerable body of additional legislation was passed to enforce the new economic laws.

In my view, a position that emphasizes class domination or the role of leading personalities cannot explain how the Cherokee formed a constitutional govern- ment, since during the same period and under similar economic and geopolitical conditions, the small planter classes and charismatic personalities in the other major southeastern societies did not mobilize their societal members to adopt political change as did the Cherokee. We need to look at the social and political organization of the conservatives as well as that of the political and economic action of the planter class and charismatic personalities in order to understand why some societies adopted more centralized and differentiated polities while others did not. The point here is methodological and conceptual; the elite, individual- ist, or class-focused arguments need to be supplemented with a more systematic analysis of institutional order and the contributions of the conservatives toward accepting change (as in the Cherokee case in the 1820's) or their role in blocking change, as among the Choctaw, Chickasaw, and Creek during the same period.

35. This point is made by Albert Wahrhaftig and Jane Lukins-Wahrhaftig, "The Thrice Powerless: The Cherokee Indians in Oklahoma," in Fogelson and Adams, eds., *Anthropology of Power*, p. 229; see also Albert Wahrhaftig, "Institution Building Among Oklahoma's Traditional Cherokees," in Hudson, ed., *Four Cen- turies of Southern Indians*, pp. 133–34;

36. J. H. Eaton, "The Progress Made in Civilizing the Indians for the Last Eight Years, and Their Present Conditions," *Report From the Secretary of War*, 21st Congress, First Session, 2 (1830): 22. "Particularly is there overwhelming evidence that no man, whatever degree of talent he might possess, could possibly [win] his way into office at the present time; whose views were known to counter over those of the masses of people on the grand subject of national interest—a removal west." John Payne Papers, 6: 9–11, 17, 26, 114; see also John Payne Papers, 2: 41–

46, 141–56; M208, roll 9, R. J. Meigs to Floyd, Oct. 24, 1822; M271, roll 1, frame 629; M271, roll 2, frame 135; *Missionary Herald* 27 (1831): 83; *Missionary Herald* 26 (1830): 382; Moulton, *John Ross*, p. 47; Duane King and E. Raymond Evans, "The Death of John Walker, Jr.: Political Assassination or Personal Vengeance," *Journal of Cherokee Studies* 1 (Summer 1976): 6–13.

37. IPH 39: 368–69, 374; IPH 43: 44, 85–86; McLoughlin, *Cherokee Renascence*, p. 330; John Payne Papers, 6; J. P. Evans, "Observations on Conservative Cherokee Communities," pp. 1–36; Persico, "Cherokee Political Organization," p. 92; Carter, *Cherokee Sunset*, p. 183; *Panoplist and Missionary Herald* 15 (1819): 313; *Missionary Herald* 24 (1828): 339; Wilkins, *Cherokee Tragedy*, pp. 274–76, 279, 291; McLoughlin, "Cherokee Anti-Mission Sentiment," pp. 363–65; Perdue, "Rising From the Ashes," p. 213; Champagne, "Symbolic Structure and Political Change in Cherokee Society," pp. 87–96.

I do not contend that my emphasis on negotiation within the Cherokee polity is original. I do not make this claim, and I have cited Wahrhaftig's work (n. 35) in this regard and use his work to argue for the position that the actions of the Cherokee conservatives were more important in understanding Cherokee political change than they are usually given credit for. Mary Young, "The Cherokee Nation: Mirror of the Republic," in *The American Indian: Past and Present*, ed. Roger L. Nichols (New York: Knopf, 1986), pp. 150–65, does a good job in describing the negotiations and compromises among the Cherokee, but although the paper is historically interesting, it does not give a satisfactory analysis of the rise of the Cherokee constitutional government, because during the same period one can find negotiated political decision making among the Chickasaw, the Choctaw, and the Creek. Merely having negotiated decision making in social and political relations is not enough to explain the differences in political change among the southeastern nations. In my view, one needs to develop a more specific and systematic analysis of institutional order—cultural differentiation, political differentiation, institutions of social and political solidarity—in order to explain the variations in political change among the southeastern nations. It is in this systematic comparison of institutional order with respect to social change in the four nations that I believe my analysis goes beyond the existing literature: I am not describing the power of the conservatives but rather analyzing their role within a comparative study of institutional order and political change.

38. IPH 39: 375–77; IPH 66: 24–25; IPH 83: 405–9, 415–22; John Payne Papers, 2: 163–65, 184, 188; *Missionary Herald* 27 (1831): 184, 247; *Missionary Herald* 28 (1832): 7, 158, 191.

39. Cochran, *New American State Papers*, 12: 641–57; McLoughlin, *Cherokee Renascence*, p. 446.

40. John Payne Papers, 2:141–56; John Payne Papers, 6: 305; Gerard Reed, "Postremoval Factionalism in the Cherokee Nation" in King, ed., *Cherokee Indian Nation*, p. 150; William R. Snell, "The Councils at Red Clay Council Ground, Bradley County, Tennessee, 1832–1837," *Journal of Cherokee Studies* 2 (Fall 1977): 345–48; Wilkins, *Cherokee Tragedy*, pp. 235–41, 337–39.

41. IPH 11: 527; IPH 15: 279, 283–84; IPH 17: 329; IPH 19: 55, 64; IPH 20: 314–16; IPH 26: 199; IPH 29: 260–65; IPH 32: 377; IPH 33: 326–27; IPH 43: 269, 278–79, 486; IPH 78: 265–66.

42. IPH 20: 314–16; IPH 29: 260–65; IPH 33: 326–27; IPH 43: 278–79; IPH 78: 265–66. The statements and information on the Keetoowah Society were taken from the Indian-Pioneer papers and constitute new data. The Keetoowah Society

may have already been politically active during the elections of the 1820's and, as is documented in the text, it was politically active during the 1840's and again after 1858.

43. M271, roll 2, frames 1186, 1192, 1220, 1270; M271, roll 3, frame 271; M234, roll 173, frames 35–39.

44. M234, roll 173, frames 35–39; Lincecum, "Adenda," pp. 79–97; White, *Roots of Dependency*, p. 114.

45. *Panopolist and Missionary Herald* 16 (1820): 379; White, *Roots of Dependency*, pp. 114, 118–21.

46. M234, Choctaw Agency 1824–31, frames 153, 157–58; M271, roll 1, frame 1187; Lincecum, "Life of Apushimataha," p. 482; William A. Love, "Mingo Moshulatubee's Prairie Village," *Publications of the Mississippi Historical Society* 7 (1903): 373–75; Coleman, *Presbyterian Missionary Attitudes*, pp. 61, 81–82; Satz, "The Mississippi Choctaw," pp. 6–7; Samuel J. Wells, "The Role of Mixed Bloods in Mississippi Choctaw History," in Wells and Tubby, eds., *After Removal: The Choctaw in Mississippi*, pp. 49–51; White, *Roots of Dependency*, pp. 116–17, 130–37.

47. Clara Sue Kidwell, "Choctaws and Missionaries in Mississippi Before 1830," *American Indian Culture and Research Journal* 11:2 (1987): 51–70.

48. M234, Choctaw Agency 1824–31, frame 148; M271, roll 4, frames 688–89, 708, 711, 713; *Missionary Herald* 19 (1823): 8–11, 46, 115; Cushman, *History*, pp. 78–105; Edward Davis, "Early Advancement Among the Five Civilized Tribes," *Chronicles of Oklahoma* 14 (1936): 170–71; White, *Roots of Dependency*, pp. 118–21.

49. M234, Choctaw Agency 1824–31, frames 247–48, 277–79; White, *Roots of Dependency*, pp. 124–26.

50. M234, Choctaw Agency 1824–31, frames 345, 390–91, 627–29; *Missionary Herald* 26 (1830): 251–54; John Edwards, "The Choctaw Nation in the Middle of the Nineteenth Century," *Chronicles of Oklahoma* 10:3 (1932): 396.

51. M234, Choctaw Agency 1824–31, frame 277.

52. Ibid., frames 421–28; *Missionary Herald* 15 (1829): 348–49; W. David Baird, *Peter Pitchlynn: Chief of the Choctaws* (Norman: University of Oklahoma Press, 1972), p. 27; Young, *Redskins, Ruffleshirts, and Rednecks*, pp. 23–29; White, *Roots of Dependency*, pp. 120–28, 130–33.

53. Young, *Redskins, Ruffleshirts, and Rednecks*, pp. 25–29; Robert F. Berkhofer, *Salvation and the Savage: An Analysis of Protestant Missions and American Indian Response, 1787–1862* (Westport, Conn.: Greenwood, 1977), p. 140; Debo, *Rise and Fall of the Choctaw Republic*, pp. 45–49.

54. *Missionary Herald* 25 (1829): 121, 187–89, 282–84, 348; M234, Choctaw Agency 1824–1831, frame 617; H. S. Halbert, "Nanih Waiya, the Sacred Mound of the Choctaws," *Mississippi Historical Society Publications* 2 (1899): 234; Young, *Redskins, Ruffleshirts, and Rednecks*, pp. 24–29; Lincecum, "Addenda," pp. 110–13.

55. M234, Choctaw Agency 1824–31, frames 647, 659, 670–73, 675, 690–97, 703.

56. Ibid., frames 759–64; *Missionary Herald* 26 (1830): 252–54; Young, *Redskins, Ruffleshirts, and Rednecks*, pp. 29–30; James D. Morrison, "Social History of the Choctaw, 1865–1907," (Ph.D. diss., University of Oklahoma, Norman, 1951), pp. 27–30; White, *Roots of Dependency*, pp. 139–40.

57. *Missionary Herald* 26 (1830): 253.

58. Young, *Redskins, Ruffleshirts, and Rednecks*, p. 30.

59. M234, Choctaw Agency 1824–31, frames 759, 769; *Missionary Herald* 26 (1830): 253–54; Baird, *Peter Pitchlynn*, pp. 36–37; White, *Roots of Dependency*, pp. 139–42.

60. M234, Choctaw Agency 1824–31, frames 704–5; *Missionary Herald* 26 (1830): 348; Debo, *Rise and Fall of the Choctaw Republic*, p. 53.

61. M234, roll 173, frames 42–45; Cochran, *New American State Papers*, 12: 336; Robert B. Ferguson, "Treaties Between the United States and the Choctaw Nation," in Reeves, ed., *Choctaw Before Removal*, pp. 220–25; White, *Roots of Dependency*, pp. 142–43.

62. M234, Choctaw Agency 1824–31, frames 789–97, 804–13, 841, 867, 871, 875–76; *Missionary Herald* 26 (1830): 384–85; IPH 5: 398; IPH 25: 141–42; W. David Baird, "Peter Pitchlynn and the Reconstruction of the Choctaw Republic," in Jordan and Holm, eds., *Indian Leaders*, pp. 13–15.

63. Lincecum, "Addenda," pp. 12–14; *Missionary Herald* 24 (1828): 380; *Missionary Herald* 25 (1829): 121, 187–88; *Missionary Herald* 26 (1830): 251; M234, Choctaw Agency 1824–31, frames 148, 155–56, 320–25, 435, 456, 670–72; Lincecum, "Life of Apushimataha," pp. 420–21, 424; F. D. Young, "Notices of the Choctaw or Choktah Tribe of North America," *Edinburgh Journal* 2 (1830): 13–14; CTN 1. Mississippi Choctaw Census and Citizenship, documents 24324–26; IPH 85: 360, 364; Coleman, *Presbyterian Missionary Attitudes*, p. 56.

64. M271, roll 4, frames 779–81; M234, roll 136, frames 16–21; J. H. Eaton, "Progress Made in Civilizing the Indians," pp. 7–8, 15; Gibson, *The Chickasaws*, pp. 138–51; Littlefield, *Chickasaw Freedmen*, pp. 4–6, 9–10; Baird, *The Chickasaw People*, pp. 33–36.

65. M271, roll 2, frame 666; Samuel Cole Williams, *Beginnings of West Tennessee* (Johnson City, Tenn.: Watauga Press, 1930), pp. 284–86; Gibson, *The Chickasaws*, pp. 101–6.

66. M234, roll 135, frames 693–94, 718; J. H. Eaton, "Progress Made Civilizing the Indians," p. 7; Gibson, *The Chickasaws*, pp. 106–36; Barden, "The Colberts and the Chickasaw Nation," p. 249.

67. M234, roll 135, frames 136–40, 171–76; Williams, *Beginnings of West Tennessee*, pp. 298–305; Muriel H. Wright, "Brief Outline of the Choctaw and the Chickasaw Nations in the Indian Territory, 1820–1860," *Chronicles of Oklahoma* 7 (1929): 397–99; Gibson, *The Chickasaws*, pp. 153–54.

68. M234, roll 135, frame 171; Barden, "The Colberts and the Chickasaw Nation," p. 319.

69. M234, roll 135, frame 259; Gibson, *The Chickasaws*, pp. 154–55; Warren, "Chickasaw Traditions, Customs, Etc.," p. 552. American agents and missionaries observed that most Chickasaw were strongly and consciously resistant to American influence of any sort. An American agent in 1825 observed that after 50 years of contact with the Americans the Chickasaw showed little perceptible change: "So far from endeavoring to adopt the manner of the whites, if one of them insofar shows a disposition to conform to them, say in dress, he is forced to abandon them or subject himself to frequent insult and his influence amongst them completely destroyed . . . They still maintain their old customs, and no argument, however cogent, can induce them to depart from them." M234, roll 135, frames 154–55.

70. Gibson, *The Chickasaws*, pp. 154–57; Cecil L. Summers, *Chief Tishomingo: A History of the Chickasaw Indians and Some Historical Events of Their Era* (Amory, Miss.: Amory Advertiser, 1974), pp. 116–17, 120–25.

71. M234, roll 136, frames 21–22; W. A. Evans, "The Trial of Tishomingo," *Journal of Mississippi History* 2 (1940): 154; Gaston L. Litton, ed., "The Negotiations Leading to the Chickasaw-Choctaw Agreement, January 17, 1837," *Chronicles of Oklahoma* 17 (1939): pp. 417–18; Barden, "The Colberts and the Chickasaw Nation," p. 323; Gibson, "The Colberts," pp. 91–92; J. H. Eaton, "The Progress Made in Civilizing the Indians," pp. 8–11; Baird, *The Chickasaw People*, pp. 37–40; Gibson, *The Chickasaws*, pp. 157–58, 162–63.

72. M234, roll 135, frames 281–82.

73. Summers, *Chief Tishomingo*, pp. 116–20; Baird, *The Chickasaw People*, pp. 38–40.

74. Summers, *Chief Tishomingo*, pp. 4, 13–14; Gibson, *The Chickasaws*, p. 240; Litton, "The Negotiations Leading to the Chickasaw-Choctaw Agreement," p. 427.

75. Cochran, *The New American State Papers*, 13:320, 330; Litton, "Negotiations Leading to the Chickasaw-Choctaw Agreement," pp. 418–27; Barden, "The Colberts and the Chickasaw Nation," pp. 327–30.

76. M234, roll 219, frames 911, 934, 968–69; M234, roll 220, frames 210–11; Swanton, "Social Organization and Social Usage," pp. 329–30.

77. M234, roll 219, frames 1301, 1305, 1328, 1436–37, 1444; M234, roll 223, frame 460; M. Young, *Redskins, Ruffleshirts, and Rednecks*, pp. 35–36; J. H. Eaton, "The Progress Made in Civilizing the Indians," pp. 15–17; Debo, *Road to Disappearance*, p. 84.

78. IPH 58: 250; IPH 89: 394–97; M234, roll 219, frames 38–62, 195, 207–8; M234, roll 223, frames 467–69; M234, roll 225, frames 39–40; M271, roll 2, frame 742; Cushman, *History*, p. 357; *Missionary Herald*, 17 (1821): 21; J. Leitch Wright, *Creeks and Seminoles*, pp. 79, 224–27; Green, *Politics of Indian Removal*, pp. 63–65; Littlefield, *Africans and Creeks*, p. 87.

79. IPH 29: 147–58; IPH 30: 483–87; IPH 68: 109–11; IPH 86: 31; M234, roll 219, frames 248–49, 264, 269, 354–55, 371, 502, 521–22, 547, 596, 634, 637, 806, 949, 968, 969–70, 1635; M234, roll 220, frames 1745–46 (1825), 349–50, 382–86, 389 (1826).

80. IPH 29: 155, 157; M234, roll 219, frames 547, 802, 806; J. Leitch Wright, *Creeks and Seminoles*, pp. 239–40.

81. Debo, *Road to Disappearance*, pp. 95–97.

82. Ibid. p. 128; Green, *Politics of Indian Removal*, pp. 91–130, 150.

83. M234, roll 222, frames 286; 303–4, 450; Green, *Politics of Indian Removal*, p. 165.

84. M234, roll 222, frames 272–74, 283, 413–14, 429, 434–35, 441–43, 447, 464–65, 562, 564–65, 573; M234, roll 223, frames 55–56, 73, 77–80, 82, 88–91, 95–96, 544–45; Green, *Politics of Indian Removal*, pp. 137–58; J. Leitch Wright, *Creeks and Seminoles*, pp. 222–24.

85. M234, roll 222, frames 520–22; Green, *Politics of Indian Removal*, pp. 150–51, 171–72.

86. M234, roll 225, frames 602–3, 627–30; M234, roll 226, frames 495–98; M234, roll 224, frames 16, 231–32, 248, 274–80, 310–13; IPH 5: 104–6; IPH 9: 346–48; Cochran, *New American State Papers*, 10: 42, 87, 109–10; Hudson, *Southeastern Indians*, pp. 455–63; J. Leitch Wright, *Creeks and Seminoles*, pp. 248–68; Carter Blue Clark, " 'Drove Off Like Dogs'—Creek Removal," in Mahon, ed., *Indians of the Lower South*, pp. 119–21; Green, *Politics of Indian Removal*, pp. 171–85.

CHAPTER 6

1. For the continuity of the slaveholder class, see: IPH 4: 404–5; IPH 6: 214–15; IPH 7: 73, 167; IPH 9: 350; IPH 43: 406–8; IPH 61: 23; IPH 78: 217–19; IPH 81: 390; IPH 107: 469; M234, roll 226, frames 357, 643; M234, roll 227, frames 119, 125; M234, roll 231, frame 103; *Missionary Herald* 44 (1848): 346–50; Norman A. Graebner, "Provincial Indian Society in Eastern Oklahoma," *Chronicles of Oklahoma* 23 (1945): 323–29; Carter Blue Clark, "Opothleyoholo and the Creeks During the Civil War," in Jordan and Holm, eds., *Indian Leaders*, pp. 49–51; Steacy, "Chickasaw Nation on the Eve of the Civil War," p. 72; Norman A. Graebner, "Pioneer Indian Agriculture in Oklahoma," *Chronicles of Oklahoma*, 23 (1945): 241; Gibson, "The Colberts," pp. 95–97; Littlefield, *Africans and Creeks*, pp. 138–39, 256–58; Bailey, *Reconstruction in Indian Territory*, pp. 10, 22–23; Lincecum, "Addenda," p. 122; Debo, *Road to Disappearance*, pp. 111–13, 120; Gibson, *The Chickasaws*, pp. 221–30; Littlefield, *Chickasaw Freedmen*, pp. 7–11; Baird, *Chickasaw People*, p. 46; Schoolcraft, *Indian Tribes of the United States*, 6: 526–33; Henry Benson, *Life Among the Choctaw and Sketches of the Southwest* (Cincinnati, Ohio: Swormstedt and Poe, 1860), pp. 33, 228; Morrison, "Social History of the Choctaw, 1865–1907," p. 32.

For the world view and labor ethic of the subsistence farmers, see: IPH 1: 238, 445–50; IPH 3: 171–75; IPH 7: 243; IPH 9: 351, 431–33; IPH 14: 148, 155; IPH 22: 370; IPH 26: 244, 256, 322; IPH 65: 238–40; IPH 81: 401; IPH 95: 60–64; IPH 107: 464; IPH 121 (bound vol. 40), Elizabeth Sipes, interview no. 7477, Sept. 13, 1937; M234, roll 99, J. P. Evens to George Butler, July 29, 1859; M234, roll 138, frames 851–52, 859, 1244; M234, roll 170, frames 399–402; M234, roll 171, frame 811; M234, roll 231, frame 101; M234, roll 225, frames 380–82; M234, roll 228, frames 556–59; Graebner, "Provincial Indian Society," 327–28; Steacy, "Chickasaw Nation on the Eve of the Civil War," p. 73; Graebner, "Pioneer Indian Agriculture," pp. 232–33, 240; Gibson, "The Colberts," pp. 95–97; Lincecum, "Addenda," pp. 123–28; Debo, *Road to Disappearance*, pp. 111–14; Littlefield, *Chickasaw Freedmen*, pp. 9–11, 16–18; Gibson, *The Chickasaws*, p. 233; Baird, *The Chickasaw People*, p. 46; Schoolcraft, *Indian Tribes of the United States*, 6: 526–33; Benson, *Life Among the Choctaw*, pp. 32–33; Scholarly Resources, *Chickasaws and Choctaws*, p. 23; John Edwards, "The Choctaw Nation in the Middle of the Nineteenth Century," *Chronicles of Oklahoma* 10: 3 (1832): 411, 423; Coleman, *Presbyterian Missionary Attitudes*, pp. 83–85, 99–101, 130; Reed, "Ross-Watie Conflict," pp. 158–60.

2. IPH 7: 243; IPH 9: 495–96; IPH 11: 283–84; IPH 20: 312–16; IPH 29: 260–65; IPH 32: 377–80; IPH 43: 269, 278, 297.

3. IPH 39: 379; Wilkins, *Cherokee Tragedy*, pp. 334–41.

4. IPH 1: 36; IPH 14: 152–54; IPH 15: 279, 283–84; IPH 20: 312–16; IPH 23: 45–47; IPH 26: 199; IPH 29: 264–65; IPH 32: 377–80; IPH 43: 103; IPH 95: 443–46.

5. IPH 3: 80; IPH 19: 64; IPH 34: 76–77; IPH 95: 456–57; IPH 121 (bound vol. 40), Clarence Starr, interview no. 12216, Nov. 3, 1937; Reed, "Ross-Watie Conflict," 103, 112–13, 143–47, 151, 180, 188, 190, 193, 195, 198, 207; Wilkins, *Cherokee Tragedy*, pp. 341–42; Edward Dale and Gaston Litton, *Cherokee Cavaliers* (Norman: University of Oklahoma Press, 1939), pp. 32–56; Morris L. Wardell, *A Political History of the Cherokee Nation, 1838–1907* (Norman: University of Oklahoma Press, 1938), pp. 63–69.

6. IPH 95: 457–62; IPH 121 (bound vol. 40), Clarence Starr, interview no. 12216, Nov. 3, 1937; Reed, "The Ross-Watie Conflict," pp. 230–38; Gary E. Moulton, "Chief John Ross and the Internal Crises of the Cherokee Nation," in Jordan and Holm, eds., pp. 120–24.

7. IPH 100: 434–36; Hugh T. Cunningham, "A History of the Cherokee Indians," *Chronicles of Oklahoma* 8 (1930): 415–16.

8. IPH 9: 497, 506; IPH 11: 284–85, 331; IPH 39: 391–93; IPH 54: 38–39; IPH 98: 367; M234, roll 97, frames 76–77, 81, 111; M234, roll 98, William Aanin, Letter, Aug. 21, 1858; M234, roll 98, Evan Jones to George Butler, Sept. 3, 1858; Wardell, *Political History of the Cherokee Nation*, pp. 117–21; Bailey, *Reconstruction in Indian Territory*, p. 24; Perdue, *Slavery and the Evolution of Cherokee Society*, pp. 120–36; R. Halliburton, *Red Over Black: Black Slaves Among the Cherokee Indians* (Westport, Conn.: Greenwood, 1977), pp. 100, 117–30; Moulton, *John Ross*, pp. 163–64; Annie Heloise Abel, *The American Indian as Slaveholder and Secessionist* (Cleveland, Ohio: Arthur H. Clark, 1915), pp. 46–48.

9. IPH 2: 124–26; IPH 19: 65; IPH 92: 375; Dale and Litton, *Cherokee Cavaliers*, pp. 119–210; R. Eaton, *John Ross and the Cherokee Indians*, pp. 123–24, 128; Wardell, *Political History of the Cherokee Nation*, pp. 129–37; Halliburton, *Red Over Black*, p. 168; Moulton, *John Ross*, pp. 171–83; Reed, "Postremoval Factionalism in the Cherokee Nation," p. 160; Abel, *American Indian as Slaveholder*, pp. 67–68, 153, 216, 256, 291–93.

10. M234, roll 184, frames 89, 92, 116–17, 179; M234, roll 236, frame 698; M. H. Wright, "Brief Outline." p. 395; Baird, "Pitchlynn and the Reconstruction," p. 15.

11. M234, roll 170, frames 414–20, 880; IPH 25: 330; Baird, "Pitchlynn and the Reconstruction," p. 15. My argument about coercion is that through the prodding of the American agent and Article 15 of the 1830 Treaty, the Americans and those Choctaw in favor of change were in a position to demand that a constitution be adopted. Choctaw reluctance can be seen in the rejection of a central chief, despite the inducement of a $500 annual salary, and also by the need to make numerous revisions in the constitution of 1834 in subsequent decades.

12. Baird, *Pitchlynn*, ch. 3; Fred Eggan, "Historical Changes in the Choctaw Kinship System," *American Anthropologist* 39: 1 (1937): 42; *Missionary Herald* 38 (1842): 413; Coleman, *Presbyterian Missionary Attitudes*, 92; M234, roll 171, frames 452–53.

13. John William Wade, "The Removal of the Mississippi Choctaws," *Mississippi Historical Society Publications* 8 (1904): 424–25; IPH 34: 63–66, 288–90; IPH 40: 130, 179–80; IPH 54: 247–390; IPH 60: 213–14; IPH 81: 510–11; IPH 100: 94–97; CTN 53, Records of the Principal Chiefs, frame 36; M234, roll 171, frame 238; Benson, *Life Among the Choctaw*, pp. 28–29.

14. M234, roll 170, pp. 414–18, 880; M234, roll 184, frame 315; Arminto Spalding, "From the Natchez Trace to Oklahoma: Development of Christian Civilization Among the Choctaws, 1800–1860," *Chronicles of Oklahoma* 45: 1 (1967): 17–18; Baird, "Pitchlynn and the Reconstruction," pp. 15–16.

15. M234, roll 172, pp. 278–80; Benson, *Life Among the Choctaw*, pp. 102–5; *Missionary Herald* 37 (1841): 211; Debo, *Rise and Fall of the Choctaw Republic*, pp. 64–65, 76–77; Gibson, *The Chickasaws*, pp. 240–42; M. H. Wright, "Brief Outline," pp. 399–400; Searcy, "Choctaw Subsistence," p. 35.

16. Baird, "Pitchlynn and the Reconstruction," p. 16; M. H. Wright, "Brief Outline," pp. 399–400; Coleman, *Presbyterian Missionary Attitudes*, p. 60.

17. Muriel H. Wright, "Organization of the Counties in the Choctaw and Chickasaw Nations," *Chronicles of Oklahoma* 8 (1930): 317–18, 321; M. H. Wright, "Brief Outline," pp. 403–6; Baird, "Pitchlynn and the Reconstruction," pp. 16–18; Oliver Knight, "Fifty Years of Choctaw Law, 1834–1884," *Chronicles of Oklahoma* 31 (Spring 1953): 77–78.

18. CTN 16, Letters and Documents Concerning the General Council, frame 61; M234, roll 172, frames 211; 249–57, 261–83; M234, roll 173, frame 296; M234, roll 174, frames 74–75, 86–87, 330–31; M234, roll 175, frames 52, 65; CTN 16, Letters and Documents Concerning the General Council, frames 40–41; Debo, *Rise and Fall of the Choctaw Republic*, pp. 74–75; M. H. Wright, "Brief Outline," pp. 406–9.

19. M234, roll 172, frame 309; M234, roll 173, frame 147; M234, roll 142, frames 266–67, 308.

20. M234, roll 98, A. G. Moffet to Peter Folsom, Oct. 10, 1857; M234, roll 98, Peter Folsom, Letter, Nov. 19, 1857; M234, roll 175, frame 52; CTN 16, Letters and Documents Concerning the General Council, document 18299; Debo, *Rise and Fall of the Choctaw Republic*, pp. 74–75; *Missionary Herald* 55 (1859): 11; Paul Bonnifield, "The Choctaw Nation on the Eve of the Civil War," *Journal of the West* 12 (July 1973): 400–1; Berkhofer, *Salvation and the Savage*, pp. 141–42; Baird, "Pitchlynn and the Reconstruction," p. 18; M. H. Wright, "Brief Outline," pp. 411–12.

21. M234, roll 175, frames 293–301, 310, 315–17; Peter James Hudson, "A Story of Choctaw Chiefs," *Chronicles of Oklahoma* 17: 2 (1939): 192–94; IPH 78: 442–44; CTN 8, Senate Records, frames 7–9.

22. CTN 8, House Records, frames 42–43, 55–56, 59, 61; CTN 8, Senate Records, frames 36–41; CTN 16, Acts and Resolutions of the General Council, frames 121–32; IPH 15: 317–18.

23. M234, roll 175, frames 208, 223, 229–34, 297–301, 315–17, 337–52.

24. M234, roll 175, frames 342–52; M. H. Wright, "Brief Outline," pp. 411–12.

25. M234, roll 175, frames 332–37; CTN 8, Senate Records, frames 86, 109, 120, 125; CTN 16, Acts and Resolutions of the General Council of the Choctaw Nation for the Year 1859, frame 43; M. H. Wright, "Brief Outline," p. 412.

26. CTN 8, Senate Records 1860, frames 78–80; CTN 8, Duties of the Principal Chief, frames 12, 42, 153, 157; CTN 16, Acts and Resolutions of the General Council of the Choctaw Nation for the Year 1859, frames 335, 340; M. H. Wright, "Brief Outline," p. 412; Cushman, *History*, p. 356; Debo, *Rise and Fall of the Choctaw Republic*, pp. 150–52; Hudson, "Story of Choctaw Chiefs," pp. 194–95.

27. M234, roll 176, frames 82–85; Morrison, "Social History of the Choctaw," p. 38; Bonnifield, "Choctaw Nation on the Eve of the Civil War," pp. 400–401; Lewis Anthony Kensell, "Phases of Reconstruction in the Choctaw Nation, 1865–1870," *Chronicles of Oklahoma* 47 (Summer 1969): 145; Knight, "Fifty Years of Choctaw Law," pp. 77–78.

28. IPH 4: 183; IPH 34: 407–8; IPH 64: 108; IPH 65: 105–111; IPH 79: 390; M234, roll 142, frames 599–602; M234, roll 180, frame 594.

29. M234, roll 137, frame 472; Gibson, *The Chickasaws*, pp. 217–19; Baird, *The Chickasaw People*, pp. 40–48; Scholarly Resources, *Chickasaws and Choctaws*, p. 23.

30. M234, roll 138, frame 144, 296–98, 313, 343; Gibson, *The Chickasaws*, pp. 223, 242; Baird, *The Chickasaw People*, pp. 50–52.

31. M234, roll 138, frames 851, 859; Scholarly Resources, *Chickasaws and Choctaws*, p. 22; Gibson, *The Chickasaws*, p. 216.

32. Baird, *The Chickasaw People*, pp. 52–55.

33. M234, roll 139, frames 142, 148–49, 153–54, 219, 227, 232, 236–39; Gibson, *The Chickasaws*, pp. 246–48; Baird, *The Chickasaw People*, pp. 52–55; M. H. Wright, "Brief Outline," pp. 401–2.

34. M234, roll 139, frames 253–54, 456; M234, roll 140, frames 174–75; Gibson, *The Chickasaws*, p. 248; M. H. Wright, "Brief Outline," pp. 401–2.

35. M234, roll 139, frame 522.

36. M234, roll 140, frames 171–77.

37. CKN 4, Constitution and Laws 1848–1856, "A Constitution of the Chickasaw Nation," frames 33, 45.

38. CKN 4, Chickasaw Councils 1851, "A Convention to Amend the Chickasaw Constitution"; M234, roll 140, frames 502–5.

39. CKN 4, Chickasaw Councils 1855, Called Session December 12, 1855, frame 210; CKN 4, Chickasaw Councils 1852, Memorial of the Chickasaws; CKN 4, Chickasaw Councils 1855, Called Session January 8, 1855; M234, roll 140, frames 296–97, 340–42; M234, roll 141, frame 193; M234, roll 142, frames 139, 300–2, 304, 308; CTN 16, Letters and Documents Concerning the General Council (Choctaw), document 18295; IPH 120 (bound vol. 40): 4; IPH 72: 428; M234, roll 172, frames 263–83; Gibson, *The Chickasaws*, pp. 225–28, 231, 249–57; Littlefield, *Chickasaw Freedmen*, p. 11; M. H. Wright, "Brief Outline," pp. 400–3.

40. M234, roll 142, frames 139–69; CKN 4, Chickasaw Council Sessions 1856, Called Session January 5, 1856; CKN 8, Constitution and Laws of the Chickasaw Nation; Gibson, *The Chickasaws*, pp. 249–57; Littlefield, *Chickasaw Freedmen*, pp. 11–16; Baird, *The Chickasaw People*, pp. 52–57; M. H. Wright, "Organization of the Counties," pp. 318–27; M. H. Wright, "Brief Outline," pp. 409–10.

41. CKN 7, Senate Journals 1860–1865, frames 2–3, 15–16, 128; CKN 9, Officials Acts of Governor Cyrus Harris; IPH 4: 395; IPH 78: 219–20; IPH 93: 420; Gibson, *The Chickasaws*, pp. 257–58; John Bartlett Meserve, "Governor Cyrus Harris," *Chronicles of Oklahoma* 15 (1937): 374–77.

42. IPH 72: 208–9; IPH 89: 355–56; IPH 103: 319; M234, roll 228, frames 123, 126, 162, 169; Swanton, "Social Organization and Social Usages," pp. 321–23; Littlefield, *Africans and Creeks*, p. 136; Debo, *Road to Disappearance*, p. 109, 123; Clark, " 'Drove Off Like Dogs,' " p. 122.

43. IPH 103: 319–21; M234, roll 227, frame 555; M234, roll 236, frames 681–84, 697–700, 709.

44. IPH 108: 200; M234, roll 225, frames 479, 486, 492; M234, roll 226, frames 399, 419; M234, roll 228, frames 123, 162, 168, 173, 178; Swanton, "Social Organization and Social Usages," pp. 319–21, 330; Bailey, *Reconstruction in Indian Territory*, pp. 10–14; Schoolcraft, *Indian Tribes of the United States*, 6: 532–33; Debo, *Road to Disappearance*, p. 124; Littlefield, *Africans and Creeks*, pp. 135–36; Morton Ohland, "The Government of the Creek Indians," *Chronicles of Oklahoma* 8 (1930): 45–46; Andre Paul Ouchateau, "The Creek Nation on the Eve of the Civil War," *Chronicles of Oklahoma* 52 (Fall 1974): 282, 294–95.

45. CRN 9, Samuel Checote's Book of Records, frames 24–26; Swanton, "Social Organization and Social Usages," pp. 334–44; Littlefield, *Africans and Creeks*, pp. 142, 150; Debo, *Road to Disappearance*, pp. 125–28.

46. CRN 9, Samuel Checote's Book of Records, frames 24–26; Debo, *Road to Disappearance*, pp. 125–26, 128; Swanton, "Social Organization and Social Usages," pp. 332–33; Ouchateau, "Creek Nation on the Eve of the Civil War," p. 296.

47. CRN 9, Samuel Checote's Book of Records, frames 6–26; Ohland, "Gov-

ernment of the Creek Indians," p. 46; Bailey, *Reconstruction in Indian Territory*, p. 14; Ouchateau, "Creek Nation on the Eve of the Civil War," p. 295.

48. CRN 9, Samuel Checote's Book of Records, frames 3–6; Debo, *Road to Disappearance*, pp. 124–26; Ohland, "Government of the Creek Indians," pp. 47–48; Ouchateau, "Creek Nation on the Eve of the Civil War," p. 296.

49. CRN 9, Creek National Council, July 1861–December 1862; IPH 9: 352; IPH 81: 236; Clark, "Opothleyoholo and the Creeks," pp. 49–54; Debo, *Road to Disappearance*, pp. 141–69.

50. M234, roll 228, frame 174. Also see an oral report that Checote's ancestors were from the daughter town of Apatoni, which was an incorporated town associated with Cussetah, the major white town: IPH 108: 97–99; Debo, *Road to Disappearance*, p. 191.

51. M234, roll 231, frames 235, 245, 263, 272, 301, 307–10, 324, 326–27, 341–42, 454.

52. M234, roll 231, frames 101–6, 129, 145, 149–50, 161, 215, 341–42; M234, roll 232, frames 342–44; IPH 62: 8–9; IPH 63: 206; IPH 92: 336; Bailey, *Reconstruction in Indian Territory*, p. 108; George Washington Grayson, *A Creek Warrior for the Confederacy: The Autobiography of Chief G. W. Grayson*, ed. W. David Baird (Norman: University Press of Oklahoma, 1988), p. 124; Ohland, "Government of the Creek Indians," p. 48; Debo, *Road to Disappearance*, p. 179.

53. M234, roll 233, frame 435; Ohland, "Government of the Creek Indians," p. 49.

CHAPTER 7

1. IPH 29: 176–78; Milling, *Red Carolinians*, p. 361; Littlefield, *Cherokee Freedmen*, pp. 37–43, 75; Debo, *Rise and Fall of the Choctaw Republic*, pp. 194–95, 212–13, 217–18; Baird, *Peter Pitchlynn*, p. 184; Wardell, *Political History of the Cherokee Nation*, pp. 260–66, 289, 297–306; H. Craig Miner, *The Corporation and the Indian* (Columbia: University of Missouri Press, 1976), p. 214; Knight, "Fifty Years of Choctaw Law," p. 85.

2. IPH 53: 23–34, 47; Baird, *Peter Pitchlynn*, p. 184; D. S. Otis, *The Dawes Act and the Allotment of Indian Lands*, ed. Francis Paul Prucha (Norman: University of Oklahoma Press, 1973), pp. i-20, 42–43, 55, 84, 105, 135; Littlefield, *Chickasaw Freedmen*, pp. 158, 179, 203.

3. For descriptions of the export economy in Indian Territory, see: IPH 2: 247–50; IPH 4: 343–44, 375, 415–16, IPH 9: 352–75, 378; IPH 10: 96–97; IPH 17: 489; IPH 40: 193; IPH 42: 261; IPH 60: 109; IPH 68: 115; IPH 70: 13, 193; IPH 72: 445; IPH 77: 111, 237–49; IPH 86: 13–14; IPH 95: 67–68; IPH 101: 408; Debo, *Road to Disappearance*, pp. 285–91; Miner, *The Corporation and the Indian*, pp. 51–75; Bailey, *Reconstruction in Indian Territory*, pp. 122–28, 131, 139; Debo, *Rise and Fall of the Choctaw Republic*, pp. 129–30; Scholarly Resources, *Chickasaws and Choctaws*, p. 31.

4. IPH 2: 145; IPH 4: 340; IPH 7: 35–37, 209; IPH 10: 66–67, 154–56; IPH 11: 575; IPH 13: 385; IPH 14: 210, 348; IPH 15: 277–79; IPH 25: 171; IPH 27: 255; IPH 28: 286; IPH 33: 576; IPH 46: 162–63; IPH 49: 470; IPH 64: 178; IPH 72: 442–44; IPH 86: 375; IPH 90: 46–51; IPH 101: 476–77; Miner, *The Corporation and the Indian*, pp. 9–14; Wardell, *Political History of the Cherokee Nation*, pp. 274–75; Scholarly Resources, *Chickasaws and Choctaws*, pp. 27–31, 54–59; Graebner, "Provincial Indian Society," pp. 328–29; Debo, *Rise and Fall of the Choctaw Republic*, pp. 109–15; Morrison, "Social History of the Choctaw,"

pp. 142–49, 162, 234; Joe T. Roff, "Reminiscences of Early Days in the Chickasaw Nation," *Chronicles of Oklahoma* 13 (1935): 177–79; Baird, *The Chickasaw People*, pp. 61–68.

5. IPH 26: 450–51; IPH 40: 314; IPH 90: 48–51; IPH 93: 228; IPH 101: 476–77; IPH 112: 78–83; Scholarly Resources, *Chickasaws and Choctaws*, pp. 29–31, 54–55, 58; Wardell, *Political History of the Cherokee Nation*, pp. 274–81; Roff, "Reminiscences," pp. 177–79.

6. For descriptions of the subsistence labor ethic and lifestyle, see: IPH 1: 27–35, 225, 238, 480; IPH 2: 57, 122, 176–80, 186, 195, 250, 289–90, 292, 374, 432, 442, 587–90; IPH 3: 62–63, 174–80, 282–87, 352, 414–18, 471, 483; IPH 4: 340–41; IPH 5: 182, 299–302, 325–26, 396–97, 446, 501, 509–12; IPH 6: 16–18, 91–98, 366–72, 393, 510–13; IPH 7: 74–79, 209–11, 243–48, 344; IPH 9: 47, 155–56, 237, 416, 422–24; IPH 10: 9, 27–30, 150, 240, 251, 261–64, 512; IPH 11: 523, 527, 541, 544, 575; IPH 12: 354, 358, 459; IPH 13: 157–58, 330, 335; IPH 14: 330, 422, 438; IPH 15: 170–71, 177, 310; IPH 17: 24, 26, 80, 420, 473; IPH 18: 191; IPH 20: 228–37; IPH 21: 80, 291–92; IPH 24: 66–67; IPH 25: 353–55, 462; IPH 26: 41, 252, 256, 361; IPH 28: 318–19, 503–6; IPH 31: 444–46; IPH 37: 254, 520–23; IPH 38: 163; IPH 39: 3, 122–28, 153; IPH 40: 37; IPH 41: 200, 302; IPH 42: 212; IPH 43: 273, 443; IPH 44: 74; IPH 46: 163, 448; IPH 48: 165; IPH 49: 362–64; IPH 52: 14, 263–64; IPH 59: 139; IPH 60: 82; IPH 64: 175–77; IPH 67: 299, 373–75, 402–3; IPH 78: 482, 490; IPH 79: 158–62; IPH 81: 401; IPH 82: 360; IPH 90: 17, 46–51, 189; IPH 93: 162; IPH 94: 147; IPH 101: 486–88; IPH 103: 147, 151; IPH 104: 467; IPH 106: 75; IPH 112: 81; IPH vol. 121, bound vol. 40, interview no. 7477, Elizabeth Sipes; IPH 121: 304, interview no. 7142, Winey Lewis, interview with Maholey Lowe, interview with Shelby Simpson; Scholarly Resources, *Chickasaws and Choctaws*, pp. 30, 53–54, 57, 59; Roff, "Reminiscences," p. 177; Debo, *Rise and Fall of the Choctaw Republic*, pp. 109–115; Morrison, "Social History of the Choctaw," pp. 125–29, 143, 146, 232–34; U.S. Department of the Interior, *Extra-Census Bulletin: The Five Civilized Tribes in Indian Territory* (Washington, D.C.: U.S. Government Printing Office, 1894), pp. 58–61; Wardell, *Political History of the Cherokee Nation*, pp. 274–75.

7. For the world view and community organization of the conservatives, see: IPH 1: 29, 186, 445–50; IPH 2: 344; IPH 3: 446; IPH 4: 290, 340; IPH 5: 60–64, 89–92, 135–36; IPH 6: 17, 141–42, 292–97; IPH 7: 31, 148, 246; IPH 9: 40, 490; IPH 10: 383; IPH 11: 423–25, 438; IPH 13: 242; IPH 14: 14, 69, 78, 156–57, 325–26, 330; IPH 15: 253, 257; IPH 16: 484–85; IPH 18: 246; IPH 20: 40, 43, 193–200; IPH 23: 132–33; IPH 24: 236–39, 248–56; IPH 25: 186, 254–56, 258–60; IPH 26: 62, 244–45, 454; IPH 28: 12; IPH 29: 111–15, 364, 411; IPH 30: 162, 167–68; IPH 31: 119–21; IPH 35: 205; IPH 36: 313, 316; 351–53; IPH 37: 299, 432, 436–39; IPH 38: 163, 444; IPH 39: 3, 21–22; IPH 43: 472; IPH 44: 55–56; IPH 52: 411–12, 444; IPH 62: 55; IPH 63: 399–405; IPH 64: 164–67; IPH 66: 458–61; IPH 70: 193–94; IPH 72: 44, 214; IPH 81: 510–11; IPH 90: 136, 189; IPH 95: 78–80; IPH 98: 251–52, 270–71; IPH 99: 129, 140; IPH 100: 42–43, 56–58; IPH 101: 486–88; IPH 105: 454–56; IPH 109: 82–98, 418–21; Miner, *The Corporation and the Indian*, pp. 1–7, 12–14; Kensell, "Phases of Reconstruction in the Choctaw Nation," p. 146; Coleman, *Presbyterian Missionary Attitudes*, pp. 83–88.

8. IPH 26: 199–200; Bailey, *Reconstruction in Indian Territory*, pp. 48–64; Dale and Litton, *Cherokee Cavaliers*, pp. 246, 249–50; R. Eaton, *John Ross and the Cherokee Indians*, pp. 145–49; Perdue, *Slavery and the Evolution of Cherokee Society*, pp. 139–44; Moulton, *John Ross*, pp. 183–91.

9. CHN 115, Letters Sent and Letters Received, "Downing's Address to the

Cherokee Senate (1869)"; Cherokee National Council, *Constitution and Laws of the Cherokee Nation* (Parsons, Kans.: Foley, 1893), pp. 36–37; IPH 42: 475–76; IPH 43: 269; IPH 49: 122–23; IPH 52: 505–7; IPH 54: 33–34; IPH 69: 117–18; IPH 71: 21–23; IPH 98: 339; M234, roll 100, frames 43–44; Dale and Litton, *Cherokee Cavaliers*, pp. 249–50; Wardell, *Political History of the Cherokee Nation*, pp. 205, 335; Bailey, *Reconstruction in Indian Territory*, pp. 172–78, 186–89; Littlefield, *Cherokee Freedmen*, pp. 35–38; Reed, "Ross-Watie Conflict," pp. 296, 309–11; Wilkins, *Cherokee Tragedy*, p. 344.

10. Littlefield, *Cherokee Freedmen*, pp. 35–37, 75–79; Miner, *The Corporation and the Indian*, pp. 23–43.

11. IPH 54: 35; IPH 67: 452–58; IPH 69:117–18; IPH 75: 396–98; IPH 78: 57–58; IPH 98: 367; Bailey, *Reconstruction in Indian Territory*, pp. 172–82; Littlefield, *Cherokee Freedmen*, pp. 56–111; Wardell, *Political History of the Cherokee Nation*, pp. 336–38.

12. IPH 66: 9; Littlefield, *Cherokee Freedmen*, pp. 102–38; Miner, *The Corporation and the Indian*, pp. 103–15; 125–49; CHN 89, *Cherokee Advocate*, Address of Chief Bushyhead, 1883.

13. IPH 2: 70; IPH 23: 440; IPH 48: 165–67; IPH 103: 154–55; Littlefield, *Cherokee Freedmen*, p. 138.

14. IPH 2: 203–4; IPH 6: 521; IPH 7: 257; IPH 49: 470–77; IPH 59: 196–97; IPH 65: 137; Littlefield, *Cherokee Freedmen*, pp. 138, 170–72.

15. IPH 59: 196–97; IPH 65: 17; IPH 105: 41; Cunningham, "History of the Cherokee Indians," pp. 433–36; Wardell, *Political History of the Cherokee Nation*, pp. 306–23.

16. IPH 9: 492–538; IPH 19: 55–59, 130–34; IPH 78: 265–70; Wardell, *Political History of the Cherokee Nation*, p. 323,

17. IPH 1: 402–10; IPH 22: 379–81; IPH 29: 178, 196, 264–65; IPH 32: 380; IPH 39: 14; IPH 43: 269–79; IPH 53: 23–34; IPH 59: 197–99; IPH 62: 123–25; IPH 65: 17–20; IPH 66: 44; IPH 79: 116–31; IPH 98: 120; CHN 115, Fourth Annual Message of Chief T. M. Buffington, Nov. 16, 1902; Littlefield, *Cherokee Freedmen*, pp. 218–24.

18. IPH 7: 298; IPH 10: 384; IPH 86: 13–14; IPH 102: 86–87; M234, roll 180, frame 391; M234, roll 183, frames 160, 164, 166; CTN 53, Records of the Principal Chiefs 1866–1880, frames 12, 18, 28–29, 132–36, 161, 172, 190, 214–15; Debo, *Rise and Fall of the Choctaw Republic*, pp. 109–11, 114–15, 130–31, 150; Baird, *The Choctaw People*, p. 63; Scholarly Resources, *Chickasaws and Choctaws*, pp. 30–31; Kensell, "Phases of Reconstruction," pp. 145–46; Knight, "Fifty Years of Choctaw Law," pp. 76, 79, 86–93.

19. M234, roll 179, frame 201; M234, roll 180, frame 348, 772; M234, roll 181, frames 401–3, 415–16, 439, 352; CTN 53, frames 128, 132–36, 186–91; 224–27, 233–35; Bailey, *Reconstruction in Indian Territory*, pp. 122–28; Debo, *Rise and Fall of the Choctaw Republic*, pp. 109–11, 212–18; Miner, *The Corporation and the Indian*, pp. 23–26, 51–63; Cheryl H. Morris, "Choctaw and Chickasaw Indian Agents, 1831–1874," *Chronicles of Oklahoma* 50: 4 (1972): 432, 434; Morrison, "Social History of the Choctaw," pp. 142–43.

20. IPH 24: 393–96, 412; IPH 39: 31–34; IPH 40: 36–37; IPH 67: 179–80; IPH 73: 286; IPH 93: 261–62; IPH 102: 86–87; IPH 105: 125–28; IPH 109: 189–90, 329–35; Wade, "The Removal of the Mississippi Choctaws," pp. 424–26.

21. IPH 12: 334–43; IPH 35: 321; IPH 37: 503; IPH 39: 31–34; IPH 47: 90; IPH 52: 120; IPH 54: 392; IPH 60: 441; IPH 63: 303; IPH 65: 328–32; IPH 78: 488–

90; IPH 79: 149, 238; IPH 81: 257; IPH 85: 52; IPH 94: 417–18; IPH 109: 329–41; IPH 112: 83. For a description of Choctaw judiciary procedures and norms in the case of the insurgent national party leaders of 1893, see IPH 47: 96–99; also see: IPH 54: 246–48; IPH 91: 162–64; IPH 93: 540; IPH 102: 87. For descriptions of the Choctaw legal and normative order in the post–Civil War period, see: IPH 5: 157; IPH 7: 301; IPH 9: 199, 431; IPH 21: 396, 450; IPH 25: 28, 186; IPH 34: 63–66, 289–90; IPH 40: 130, 179–80; IPH 42: 50–51; IPH 54: 246–48; IPH 60: 213; IPH 81: 236; IPH 87: 456; IPH 100: 94–99; IPH 102: 181; Wade, "Removal of the Mississippi Choctaws," pp. 424–25.

22. Debo, *Rise and Fall of the Choctaw Republic*, pp. 247–49, 258–63; IPH 80: 287–88.

23. IPH 6: 11–14; IPH 24: 412; IPH 34: 340; IPH 37: 480–81, 501–3; IPH 42: 50–51; IPH 43: 497; IPH 46: 447; IPH 54: 390–92; IPH 78: 225–27, 482–90; IPH 80: 287–88; IPH 101: 115–16; IPH 103: 183–84; Morrison, "Social History of the Choctaw," pp. 279–84.

24. CKN 4, frame 144; M234, roll 179, frames 201–2; John Bartlett Meserve, "Governor Dougherty (Winchester) Colbert," *Chronicles of Oklahoma* 18 (Dec. 1940): 352–54; Meserve, "Governor Cyrus Harris," p. 382.

25. M234, roll 181, frames 348, 384, 391, 400–3; John Bartlett Meserve, "Governor Benjamin Franklin Overton and Governor Benjamin Crooks Burney," *Chronicles of Oklahoma* 16 (June 1938): 221.

26. CKN 8, frames 283–301; CTN 53, frames 172–73; IPH 105: 69; Scholarly Resources, *Chickasaws and Choctaws*, pp. 31–35; Baird, *The Chickasaw People*, pp. 62–66; Roff, "Reminiscences," pp. 177–79.

27. IPH 5: 499–501; IPH 21: 299, 349; IPH 66: 484, 470–71; Scholarly Resources, *Chickasaws and Choctaws*, pp. 24, 30–31; Meserve, "Governor Overton and Governor Burney," pp. 224–26, 232.

28. Scholarly Resources, *Chickasaws and Choctaws*, p. 38; John Bartlett Meserve, "Governor William Leander Byrd," *Chronicles of Oklahoma* 12 (1934): 438–40; John Bartlett Meserve, "Governor Jonas Wolf and Governor Palmer Simeon Mosely," *Chronicles of Oklahoma* 18 (Sept. 1940): 245; Gibson, *The Chickasaws*, p. 298.

29. CKN 7, frames 311–12, 324–26; IPH 78: 206–7; IPH 109: 79–84; Scholarly Resources, *Chickasaws and Choctaws*, pp. 24, 38–40; Littlefield, *Chickasaw Freedmen*, pp. 143–44, 149, 158.

30. IPH 15: 183; IPH 19: 71–82; Scholarly Resources, *Chickasaws and Choctaws*, pp. 24–26, 30–35, 57; Meserve, "Governor Byrd," pp. 438–41.

31. Baird, *The Chickasaw People*, pp. 68–72; Meserve, "Governor Wolf and Governor Mosely," pp. 245–49; John Bartlett Meserve, "Governor Robert Maxwell Harris," *Chronicles of Oklahoma* 17 (1939): 361–63; IPH 4: 396; IPH 90: 433.

32. Meserve, "Governor Byrd," pp. 440–41; Meserve, "Governor Wolf and Governor Mosely," p. 250; Baird, *The Chickasaw People*, pp. 72–83; IPH 5: 499–501.

33. CRN 23, documents 34471, 35573, 35577, 35582, 35586; IPH 107: 369–71; Hewitt, "Notes on the Creek Indians," pp. 125–32; Debo, *Road to Disappearance*, pp. 191, 292–301.

34. IPH 5: 89–92; IPH 13: 429–34; IPH 26: 45; IPH 31: 224, 299–301; IPH 59: 351; IPH 63: 207, 376; IPH 72: 207–14; IPH 107: 369–71; IPH 119 (bound vol. 40): interview no. 7142; CRN 9, frames 12–18; Debo, *Road to Disappearance*, pp. 291–94.

35. IPH 2: 127; IPH 3: 466–67; IPH 4: 424; IPH 35: 414; IPH 62: 71; IPH 68: 121; IPH 92: 339–41; CRN 9, Creek vol. 11, frames 30, 43, 88, 114, 135, 150–51, 165, 184, 185, 186, 188; CRN 9, Creek vol. 28, frames 72, 112, 118, 130; CRN 21, frames 580, 654; CRN 23, documents 35589–90, 35667.

36. IPH 3: 310; IPH 26: 364; IPH 36: 476–79; IPH 92: 336–39; M234, roll 231, frames 19, 100–4, 496, 538–39, 704–6; M234, roll 232, frames 142–49, 173–74, 178, 278, 341; M234, roll 233, frame 501; Debo, *Road to Disappearance*, pp. 182–85, 191; Ohland, "Government of the Creek Indians," pp. 58–59.

37. CRN 7, frames 49–50; M234, roll 232, frames 25–34, 37, 44, 93, 143–46, 173–78, 278, 342–44, 795–97; M234, roll 233, frames 234–38, 435, 445–47; Debo, *Road to Disappearance*, pp. 182–93; Ohland, "Government of the Creek Indians," pp. 55–58.

38. CRN 7, frames 42–50; M234, roll 232, frames 178, 278; Bailey, *Reconstruction in Indian Territory*, pp. 109–18; Debo, *Road to Disappearance*, pp. 191–93; Ohland, "Government of the Creek Indians," p. 56.

39. M234, roll 233, frames 126–27, 215–22, 234–38, 258–59, 433–37, 448, 455, 460–89, 500–1, 525–26, 540–42, 577, 701; M234, roll 234, frames 57–62, 354–57; M234, roll 235, frames 22–25; CRN 7, frames 87, 96; Debo, *Road to Disappearance*, pp. 192–99.

40. M234, roll 234, frames 60–62, 354–57; CRN 7, frames 138–39, 242–43, 354–56, 373, 386–88; CRN 9, Creek vol. 11, frame 48; CRN 23, documents 35570N-P; Debo, *Road to Disappearance*, pp. 199, 213–15.

41. M234, roll 235, frames 414, 538–42; CRN 9, Creek vol. 9, frames 51, 56, 98, 102, 119, 121–26; CRN 9, Creek vol. 22, frames 91, 96, 128; Debo, *Road to Disappearance*, pp. 213–44.

42. IPH 72: 207–14; CRN 9, Creek vol. 11, frame 33; CRN 9, Creek vol. 22, frames 96, 128; CRN 23, documents 35584a-b; Debo, *Road to Disappearance*, pp. 240–44.

43. IPH 36: 351–53; IPH 38: 458; CRN 21, Creek vol. 63, frame 86; CRN 23, document 35576; CRN 40, document 34168; M234, roll 233, frames 448, 455, 460–62; Debo, *Road to Disappearance*, pp. 238–48.

44. CRN 9, Creek vol. 22, frames 132–34, 172, 178, 189, 220–23; CRN 9, Creek vol. 11, frame 223; CRN 23, documents 35586, 35590; Debo, *Road to Disappearance*, pp. 264–68.

45. CRN 41, documents 34288–89; IPH 40: 487; IPH 62: 8–13; IPH 82: 196–201; Ohland, "Government of the Creek Indians," p. 59.

46. CRN 7, Journal of the House of Warriors 1886–1887, frame 59; CRN 9, Creek vol. 22, frame 239–40; CRN 23, documents 32409, 35591; CRN 40, documents 34170–71, 34176, 34178, 34182, 34185; CRN 41, Creek Outbreaks, documents 34263, 34266, 34267–69, 34274, 34278, 34282–83, 34285, 34288, 34292, 34298–99, 34301, 34304, 34553; IPH 2: 231, 385–78; IPH 3: 303–4; IPH 5: 8; IPH 8: 533; IPH 16: 227; IPH 32: 106–10; IPH 36: 351–53; IPH 38: 458; IPH 40: 522, 531; IPH 52: 38; IPH 59: 496–97; IPH 62: 10–13, 334; IPH 63: 206; IPH 68: 10–11; IPH 69: 459; IPH 82: 196–201; IPH 100: 26; IPH 103: 321–22; IPH 110: 182, 290–93; IPH 119 (bound vol. 40): interview no. 12012; Ohland, "Government of the Creek Indians," p. 59.

47. CRN 7, Journal of the House of Warriors 1883–1885, frames 31, 112, 121; CRN 7, Journal of the House of Warriors, 1886–1887, frames 59, 70, 79; CRN 8, Journal of the House of Kings, 1882, frames 6, 38–39, 50; CRN 9, Creek vol. 11, frames 114, 124–25, 135–38, 150; CRN 9, Creek vol. 28, frames 28–29, 72, 112,

119; CRN 23, documents 35591, 35593, 35595, Letter from Secretary H. M. Teller, Feb. 27, 1884; IPH 76: 313.

48. CRN 7, Creek vol. 6, frames 132–33; CRN 7, Journal of the House of Warriors 1892–1894, frames 18, 24, 29, 45, 65; Debo, *Road to Disappearance*, pp. 321–26.

49. IPH 78: 447–52; Debo, *Road to Disappearance*, pp. 356–68; Ohland, "Government of the Creek Indians," pp. 189, 215–18.

50. IPH 31: 74–75, 100–3; IPH 52: 41; IPH 58: 353–54; IPH 63: 208; IPH 70: 477–78; IPH 75: 427; IPH 104: 93; Ohland, "Government of the Creek Indians," pp. 189–90.

51. CRN 40: 696; CRN 41, Creek Outbreaks, documents 34545–47; CHN 89, Cherokee National Papers, *Cherokee Advocate*, Mar. 3, 1906, vol. 30 (no. 3); IPH 2: 197; IPH 4: 60–61, 289, 427; IPH 6: 34–43; IPH 9: 404; IPH 11: 274; IPH 13: 460–61; IPH 14: 398–400; IPH 16: 230–31; IPH 18: 92–95; IPH 19: 433; IPH 22: 49–50; IPH 29: 47–49; IPH 31: 74, 100–3; IPH 48: 453–54; IPH 51: 173; IPH 52: 41; IPH 58: 353–54; IPH 63: 208; IPH 66: 425, 458; IPH 79: 372; IPH 81: 195; IPH 89: 140–44; IPH 104: 93–96; IPH 112: 305; Ohland, "Government of the Creek Indians," pp. 189–93.

INDEX

INDEX

In this index an "f" after a number indicates a separate reference on the next page, and an "ff" indicates separate references on the next two pages. A continuous discussion over two or more pages is indicated by a span of page numbers, e.g., "57–59." *Passim* is used for a cluster of references in close but not consecutive sequence.

marriage, 40, 42, 54, 91f, 152, 271f. *See also*
    Intermarriage
Marx, Karl, 5f
matrilineal, 26, 38–42 *passim*, 200
Mayes, Joel, 216f
McClurken, James, 287
McCurtain, Green, 222
McGillivary, William, 80–83, 172
McIntosh, Roley, 202, 205, 235
McIntosh, William, 119f, 137, 150f, 160,
    164–68, 172, 201f
McIntosh faction, 168f
McLoughlin, William, 104, 287
medicine men, 17, 19, 36. *See also* Doctors
Meigs, Return Jonathan, 94, 98f, 104, 106,
    134
membership, 38–45 *passim*, 54, 82ff, 145,
    229, 272
mercenaries, 55, 60, 71
merchants, 54–57 *passim*, 106, 119, 135,
    222–25 *passim*; Indian, 10, 54, 85, 91,
    122, 127f, 135ff, 179, 216; Cherokee, 93,
    98–106 *passim*, 284; Chickasaw, 109–
    12, 128, 158–63, 194, 225, 284. *See also*
    Class; Market orientation; Trade
Methodists, 203, 230
Mexico, 181, 222
Micco Hutke (White King), 230
miccos, 83
middle towns, 25, 57, 75
Mikusuki, 82, 115
military, 46, 50f, 57, 63, 110
Mingo Chitto, 60
Mingo Homa, 79
minko, 35f, 45
missionaries, 133, 138–42 *passim*, 146–54
    passim, 159, 166, 171, 176–82 *passim*,
    188f, 243
Mississippi, 14, 110, 146f, 153–62 *passim*,
    185
Mississippi River, 1, 54f, 60ff, 67, 71, 89,
    97, 124–29 *passim*, 146f, 153, 160
Mississippi Valley, 54, 62, 74, 78f, 126
model, 1, 5, 11, 240, 273; American politi-
    cal, 82, 91, 125, 131, 135ff, 141, 175–78
    passim, 205–7, 243–50 *passim*. *See also*
    Change; Class; Differentiation; Planters
Moore, Barrington, 5
moral codes, 14–20, 145
Mortar, 66–68
Mosely, Palmer, 226f
Moshulatubee, 147–56 *passim*, 186, 220
mother towns, 25–27, 37, 56–59 *passim*,
    76f. *See also* Chota
Mother Town of the Nation, 274

Moytoy, 56, 273f
Muccolossus, 66f
murder, 18–21 *passim*, 31ff, 43, 58, 69–73
    passim, 94–99 *passim*, 111–18 *passim*,
    181. *See also* Blood revenge
Muskogee, 14, 64f, 205, 210, 266
Muskogee party, 233–35
myths, 35–39 *passim*, 265

Nail, Joe, 156
Nanih Waiya, 44, 265
Napoleon, 75
Natchez, 60–65 *passim*
national party, 178–83 *passim*, 214–22 *pas-
    sim*. *See also* Keetoowah Society; Ross
    party
nationalism, 134, 137, 148, 193–99 *passim*,
    206, 216, 219, 223f, 228, 238ff, 253, 276,
    287
nationality, 99, 106f, 133, 143, 161–64 *pas-
    sim*, 194, 206, 224–27 *passim*, 247–51
    passim; political, 38, 65, 72, 84, 156, 173,
    221, 247, 251ff. *See also* Integration;
    Solidarity; Unification
national survival, 213f, 239, 247
Naucee town, 63
Neahmathla, 171
Nehathie Hopia (Little Doctor), 169f
neutrality, 55, 66f, 75ff, 80f, 93, 104, 192,
    203. *See also* Geopolitics
New Echota, 139
New England, 168, 189
New Orleans, 51f
New York, 82
next world, *see* Afterlife
Nighthawk Keetoowah, 145, 180, 217f. *See
    also* Keetoowah Society
Nitakechi, 154, 156
nondifferentiation, 7, 14, 16, 33, 38–48 *pas-
    sim*, 71, 84ff, 156ff, 164–67, 199ff, 212,
    237–53 *passim*, 270, 282; kinship and
    polity, 45ff, 78f, 87, 200; polity, 64, 164,
    175, 229, 240, 244, 251ff; cultural world
    views and, 19, 35, 92, 105, 122, 141, 157f,
    177, 233. *See also* Differentiation
norms, 3f, 24, 28f, 35, 47, 71ff, 92, 103, 118
North, *see* Union
North America, 50–54, 61, 67f, 74–78
    passim
North Carolina, 138, 143
North Fork Town, 210
Noyohee, 25
Nuyuka, 229–37 *passim*

Oakfuskie, 66f, 80–83, 118f, 167, 231, 237

Wright, Alfred, 265, 269ff
Wright, J. Leitch, 266f

Yamasee War, 51, 53, 65f

Yazoo Fraud, 97
Yazoo River, 97
Yuchi, 65, 80, 119, 171

Library of Congress Cataloging-in-Publication Data

Champagne, Duane.
    Social order and political change : constitutional governments
    among the Cherokee, the Choctaw, the Chickasaw, and the
    Creek / Duane Champagne.
        p.   cm.
    Includes bibliographical references (p.   ) and index.
    ISBN 0-8047-1995-0 (cloth : alk. paper)
    1. Cherokee Indians—Politics and government.   2. Creek
    Indians—Politics and government.   3. Chickasaw Indians—
    Politics and government.   4. Choctaw Indians—Politics and
    government.   5. Constitutional history.   I. Title.
    E99.C5C34   1992   91-27600
    323.1'197—dc20   CIP

    ⊗   This book is printed on acid-free paper.